Legisprudence Library

Studies on the Theory and Practice of Legislation

Volume 8

The objective of the *Legisprudence Library* is to publish excellent research on legislation and related areas (such as regulation and policy-making) from the standpoint of legal theory. This series' title points to an emerging, comprehensive conception of lawmaking which focuses on the justification of laws and the overarching principles which should guide legislation and norm-giving altogether, with the rationality, the reasonableness and the quality of legislation being its major concerns. Taking on legal theory as its pivotal perspective, the series attempts to fill a significant gap in the field of legislative studies, where political science and sociological approaches remain dominant through date. Inasmuch as it fosters legal-theoretical research in lawmaking, it also contributes to widen the scope of standard jurisprudence, which has been up to recent times overwhelmingly centred on the judicial application and the interpretation of law, thereby underestimating the central role of lawmakers within the legal system.

Contributions preferably address topics connected to legislation theory, including (but not limited to) legislative rationality, legislative technique, legistics, legislative effectiveness and social compliance of laws, legislative efficiency and lawmaking economics, evaluation, legislative and regulative impact assessment, regulation management, legislative implementation, public access to legislation, democratic legitimacy of legislation, codification, legislative reasoning and argumentation, science and expertise within lawmaking, legislative language, symbolic legislation, legal policy analysis, lawmaking and adjudication, or judicial review of legislation and legislative process. Comparative and system transcending approaches are encouraged. Purely dogmatic descriptions of positive law or legislative proceedings are not taken into consideration though connections with legislative and legal practice are welcomed. The series welcomes monographs and edited volumes.

More information about this series at http://www.springer.com/series/11058

Ittai Bar-Siman-Tov

Editor

Comparative Multidisciplinary Perspectives on Omnibus Legislation

 Springer

Editor
Ittai Bar-Siman-Tov
Faculty of Law
Bar-Ilan University
Ramat-Gan, Israel

ISSN 2213-2813 ISSN 2213-2856 (electronic)
Legisprudence Library
ISBN 978-3-030-72750-5 ISBN 978-3-030-72748-2 (eBook)
https://doi.org/10.1007/978-3-030-72748-2

This Springer imprint is published by the registered company Springer Nature Switzerland AG.
The registered company address is: Gewerbestrasse 11, 6330 Cham, Switzerland

For Reut

Acknowledgments

My interest in omnibus legislation was sparked some 16 years ago while working on a constitutional case on this matter for Justice Dorit Beinisch at the Supreme Court of Israel. I am deeply indebted to Justice Beinisch for introducing me to this subject. Since entering academia, I have been working on other projects in the broader field of legislation, but continuously touching on the subject of omnibus legislation, and have long pondered the idea of a comparative and multidisciplinary book on the subject. Fortunately, in 2019, under the auspices of Bar-Ilan University and the Israeli Association of Legislation, we were able to group together a superb and diverse group of international experts together in a conference on "Rearranging the Arrangements Law: Comparative, Multidisciplinary, Empirical and Normative Perspectives on Omnibus Legislation." This conference was the springboard for this book. It was kindly supported by two grants from the Israel Science Foundation (research grant #1436/15 and conference grant #2207/18).

I am deeply indebted to all the contributing authors for their excellent contributions. It was a real privilege and pleasure to work with such a fine group of scholars. I am also very grateful to A. Daniel Oliver-Lalana, to Abdus Salam Mazumder, and to everyone at Springer Nature for their endless support and patience and to the two anonymous reviewers for their helpful and gracious feedback on the manuscript. I also thank Itay Cohen, Yehonatan Dayan, Tal Eyal Lipschutz, and Chani Koth for excellent research assistance. Finally yet most importantly, I am deeply thankful to my senior research assistant and deputy editor, Tair Ben Zeev for her excellent and dedicated work. She was instrumental in helping me turn this book project from an aspiration to completion.

2020

Ramat Gan, Israel   Ittai Bar-Siman-Tov

Contents

Part II   Regulating the Use of Omnibus Legislation

Editor and Contributors

About the Editor

Ittai Bar-Siman-Tov is a Senior Lecturer (Associate Professor), Co-Director of the dual degree program in law and political science, and Head of the BIU LawData Lab, at Bar Ilan University Faculty of Law. He is also General Editor of the international journal *The Theory and Practice of Legislation* and founding Co-Chair of the Israeli Association of Legislation. He obtained his J.S.D. and LL.M. from Columbia Law School, where he was an Associate-in-Law, James Kent Scholar, Fulbright Scholar, Fischman Scholar, and Morris Fellow. He received his LL.B., magna cum laude, from the Hebrew University of Jerusalem.

His scholarship has been published, inter alia, in the *Georgetown Law Journal*; *Boston University Law Review*; *American Journal of Comparative Law*; and *Regulation and Governance*. His scholarship received multiple awards (including, among others, the Giandomenico Majone Prize, awarded by the European Consortium for Political Research's Standing Group on Regulatory Governance; the Gorney Prize for Outstanding Research in Public Law, awarded by the Israeli Association of Public Law; and the Cheshin Prize for Academic Excellence in Law) and research grants (including, inter alia, from the German-Israeli Foundation for Scientific Research and Development; the Volkswagen Foundation; the Israel Science Foundation; the Ministry of Science and Technology; and the Israel National Institute for Health Policy Research).

Contributors

Richard Briffault Columbia University School of Law, New York, NY, USA

Abbe R. Gluck Yale Law School, New Haven, CT, USA

Susan Hattis Rolef The Knesset Research and Information Center, Jerusalem, Israel

Nir Kosti Department of Political Science, Hebrew University of Jerusalem, Jerusalem, Israel

Glen S. Krutz Department of Political Science, College of Arts and Sciences, Oklahoma State University, Stillwater, OK, USA

Nicola Lupo Center for Parliamentary Studies at LUISS Guido Carli, University of Rome, Rome, Italy

Louis Massicotte Department of Political Science, Université Laval, Québec, QC, Canada

Klaus Meßerschmidt Department of Tax Law and Public Law, University of Erlangen-Nürnberg, Nürnberg, Germany

A. Daniel Oliver-Lalana Facultad de Derecho, Universidad de Zaragoza, Ciudad Universitaria, Zaragoza, Spain

Giovanni Piccirilli Center for Parliamentary Studies at LUISS Guido Carli, University of Rome, Rome, Italy

Patricia Popelier Faculty of Law, University of Antwerp, Antwerpen, Belgium

Olivier Rozenberg Center for European Studies & Comparative Politics, Sciences Po, Paris, France

Mauro Zamboni Faculty of Law, Stockholm University, Stockholm, Sweden

An Introduction to the Comparative and Multidisciplinary Study of Omnibus Legislation

Ittai Bar-Siman-Tov

Abstract Omnibus legislation is the legislative practice of packaging together numerous unrelated measures in one long bill, which is often passed via an expedited process. In many jurisdictions around the world, this practice has become one of the major developments in the legislative process, a powerful policy tool, and a governance device with important implications for democratic governance. Omnibus legislation is known by many names (e.g., "Christmas tree bills"; "portmanteau bills"; "mosaic laws"; "arrangements laws"), and there is no one agreed-upon definition or conceptualization of this legislative practice. It is also one of the most controversial and hotly contested legislative practices. This chapter introduces the book and its rich array of contributions. The chapter presents and analyzes these contributions around four main themes: (1) conceptualizing and defining omnibus legislation; (2) multiple perspectives on omnibus legislation, including extent of its use, reasons for its use, and governance implications of its use, in various countries; (3) cross-national experiences with various means to regulate the use omnibus legislation; (4) normative evaluation of omnibus legislation.

Keywords Omnibus · Christmas tree bills · Portmanteau bills · Mosaic laws · Monster bills · Arrangements laws · Single subject rule · Lawmaking · Legislation · Legislative process · Legislatures · Courts · Comparative law · Comparative politics

1 Introduction

A major and controversial reform is enacted via a hundreds-of-pages long omnibus bill, which includes many unrelated provisions. It is rammed through the legislative process in a highly accelerated pace. The legislators receive the final version of the bill in the very last minute, and protest that they have no opportunity to read the

I. Bar-Siman-Tov (✉)
Faculty of Law, Bar-Ilan University, Ramat-Gan, Israel
e-mail: Ittai.Bar-Siman-Tov@biu.ac.il

© The Author(s), under exclusive license to Springer Nature Switzerland AG 2021
I. Bar-Siman-Tov (ed.), *Comparative Multidisciplinary Perspectives on Omnibus Legislation*, Legisprudence Library 8, https://doi.org/10.1007/978-3-030-72748-2_1

massive and complex bill and know what they are voting upon. The majority's legislative leaders, however, are unimpressed, and the law is eventually passed on strict party discipline. For American readers, this description may sound like the legislative process of Donald Trump's tax reform bill in the U.S. Congress.[1] Israeli readers might recognize the very same description as depicting the enactment of third apartment tax in the Israeli Parliament.[2] I suspect that such a description may sound familiar to observers of legislatures in multiple countries.

The legislative practice of packaging together numerous unrelated measures in one long bill (which is often passed via a highly expedited process), has become a familiar sight in many legislatures around the world.[3] This practice, known as "omnibus legislation," is one of the major mechanisms for facilitating and accelerating the passage of legislation. It is one of the major developments in the legislative process,[4] and an important phenomenon in the rise of unorthodox lawmaking.[5] Omnibus legislation has become one of the most powerful policy tools (and in some countries, particularly fiscal policy tool), and a governance device with important implications for democratic governance and the separation of powers.[6] It is a phenomenon at the intersection of law, politics, public policy, governance and economics.

Omnibus legislation is also one of the most controversial and hotly contested legislative practices. Some see this legislative practice, which departs from the time-honored maxim that each bill should have one subject,[7] as violating principles of proper lawmaking and a threat to democratic values, as undermining the quality of the legislative output, or even as an epitome a broken legislative process. Others see it as a necessary, effective and useful legislative device, and as legitimate and successful institutional adaptation of legislative procedure to the demands and constraints of modern governance. Others still, see it as a necessary evil or an inevitability.[8]

The purpose of this book is to contribute to the global debate about omnibus legislation, and to provide a novel cross-national and multidisciplinary exploration of this legislative practice. The goal is to offer a comparative, comprehensive, thorough and multifaceted debate, which will contribute to the academic fields of legislation and legisprudence, comparative law and comparative politics, political

---

[1]Individual Tax Reform and Alternative Minimum Tax, Pub. L. No. 115-97 (2017); Bar-Siman-Tov (2018).

[2]Bar-Siman-Tov (2019).

[3]Bar-Siman-Tov (2015); Popelier (2006); Mousmouti (2019), p. 74; Hattis Rolef (this volume).

[4]See Krutz (this volume).

[5]Gluck et al. (2015) and Sinclair (2016).

[6]See Krutz (this volume) and Kosti (this volume).

[7]As Hattis Rolef in this book notes, the origin of this principle goes back to a Roman law of 98 B.C., known as *Lex Caecilia Didia*, which prohibited the practice of *lex satura*—i.e. the proposal of laws that include provisions unrelated to each other.

[8]See Sect. 5 below.

science and legislative studies, public policy and economics. The goal, moreover, is to contribute not only to the academic debates, but also to benefit practitioners in parliaments, governments and courts, thereby making potential impact on the actual use of omnibus legislation.

To achieve these goals, this volume brings together leading experts from political science, public policy and law, who provide a broad range of comparative, empirical and normative perspectives on omnibus legislation. This first-rate and diverse group of expert scholars represent multiple countries, with some of the most germane experiences in dealing with omnibus legislation, as well as jurisdictions representing the possibility (or attempts) of life without omnibus legislation. In addition to providing diverse perspectives and observations about omnibus legislation in various countries, these contributions also represent various solutions and means to regulate the use of omnibus legislation. These range from constitutional single-subject rules to changes in parliamentary rules of procedure, to official, yet unenforceable legistic guidelines, to the role of courts through judicial review or statutory interpretation, to the role of legal counsels and legislative drafters.

The contributions to this book are therefore divided into two parts. The first part of the book presents chapters that provide multiple perspectives, from various countries, on omnibus legislation and its use (including extent of its use, reasons for its use, governance implications of its use, and normative evaluations). The second part of the book presents chapters that deal with various solutions and ways to regulate the use of omnibus legislation. It should be clarified, however, that this is a rough division, as many chapters do several things, such as providing a theoretical, descriptive, empirical, historical or comparative account on omnibus legislation and its usage in their country; offering a normative evaluation of this legislative practice; and discussing various solutions. Hence, the chapters were divided into the two parts of the book based on whether they are primarily focused on discussing omnibus legislation and its usage or on regulating its use.

As way of introduction to the book and its rich array of contributions, this chapter presents these contributions by focusing on four main themes. It begins with exploring the question of conceptualizing and defining omnibus legislation, by presenting and analyzing the multiple views on this question by the authors in this volume (Sect. 2). Next, Sect. 3 presents the multiple perspectives on omnibus legislation and its usage, providing an overview of the chapters in Part I of the book. Then, Sect. 4 turns to discussing multiple experiences with efforts to regulate the use omnibus legislation, providing an overview of the chapters in Part II of the book. Finally, Sect. 5 draws on the contributions to this volume to offer some meta-observations and thoughts on normative evaluations of omnibus legislation.

2   Conceptualizing and Defining Omnibus Legislation

Omnibus legislation (and its various forms around the world) has come to be known by many additional names. These include, inter alia, "Christmas tree bills"; "portmanteau bills"; "mosaic bills"; "patchwork laws"; "monster bills"; "mammoth bills"; "salad laws"; "arrangements laws"; "program laws", "omnibudget bills" or "money bills" (when they deal with fiscal legislation); or even "garbage bills".[9] In other countries and other languages, we can find additional names for various forms of omnibus legislation, such as *"chorizo"*, *"cajón de sastre"* or *"ley de acompañamiento"* (in Spanish speaking countries); *"loi fourre-tout"* or *"loi programme"* (in French speaking countries); *"Artikelgesetz"*, *"Mantelgesetz"* and *"Budgetbegleitgesetz"* (in German speaking countries); *"leggi finanziarie"*, *"leggi di stabilità"*, and *"milleproroghe"* (in Italian); and *"hok hahesderim"* (in Hebrew).[10]

The diversity of names for omnibus legislation is coupled with a diversity in definitions and conceptualizations of omnibus legislation. In one of the classic and oft-cited contributions to the field, Sinclair offered the following definition: "Legislation that addresses numerous and not necessarily related subjects, issues, and programs – and therefore is usually highly complex and long – is referred to as omnibus legislation."[11] This definition captures two typical features of omnibus legislation: the packaging of various (unrelated) measures in one bill and the length of the bill. I believe that most definitions of omnibus legislation could be understood in relation to one or both of these two features.

Indeed, many of the contributors to this book offer various formulations that could be analyzed based on the two features I mentioned: packaging of various measures and length. The definitions differ on the question of whether the packaging is the sole criterion, the length is the sole criterion, or whether the definition requires some combination of the two. Additionally, most definitions focus on packaging of unrelated measures as the main (or sole) criterion, and differ somewhat on questions such as the extent of the heterogeneous nature or scope of the bill (i.e., how unrelated are the measures and how many unrelated measures or policy areas are required to be considered an omnibus bill).

For example, Gluck observes that there is no single definition of omnibus legislation in the U.S., but that there is general agreement that "legislation that packages together several measures into one or combines diverse subjects into a single bill fits the label" of omnibus legislation.[12] Note that in this definition, the packaging is the sole criterion, while not requiring the bill to be of a particular length. Gluck also recognizes, however, the existence of other definitions that focus solely (or at least mostly) on the length, while being more lax about the heterogeneous nature of the measures. She notes that under such definitions, a highly complex and

---

[9]Popelier (2006); Mousmouti (2019), p. 74; Szabó (2020).

[10]Hattis Rolef (2006).

[11]Sinclair (2016) (originally published in the first edition in 1997, p. 64).

[12]Gluck (this volume).

long bill that takes on numerous issues, even within a single subject area (such as the 800-page Clean Air Act or the 2700-page Affordable Care Act) would be considered omnibus legislation.[13] Interestingly, when Gluck herself conceptualizes omnibus legislation, she seems to combine the features of length, complexity and the packaging of heterogeneous subjects: "Omnibus vehicles are marked by their length, complexity, and the way in which they often bring together multiple congressional and administrative stakeholders to cover various unrelated subject areas and thus garner broader support."

Meßerschmidt observes that any packaging together of different laws meets the German definition of "*Artikelgesetz*", while length is irrelevant. Under this approach, any bill that encompasses more than one new bill or alteration to a bill (even a law consisting of only three Articles) meets the formal definition of "*Artikelgesetz*".[14] He notes that within this definition, there could be various extents of heterogeneity. Meßerschmidt offers a critical analysis of this board definition, but adopts it as his working definition for his chapter, since this is the well-established German definition. Interestingly, however, it appears that length and extent of heterogeneity do figure in Meßerschmidt's analysis as supplementary indications for distinguishing between various cases of omnibus legislation, as he notes that "focusing on massive bills with component measures from disparate substantive policy areas helps identify hard cases."

Massicotte observes that until 2017 there was no agreed upon definition of an omnibus bill in Canada, but that in 2017 the Standing Orders were amended to provide an authoritative definition. He observes that in the authoritative Canadian definition, the packaging of heterogeneous measures is the only requirement, while the length of the bill is immaterial (even if in common parlance there is often focus on length). Under this approach, any bill, of any length, that seeks to repeal, amend or enact "more than one" act would be considered an "omnibus bill," provided that "there is not a common element connecting the various provisions *or* where unrelated matters are linked."[15]

The heterogeneous nature of the bill, rather than its length, is also the essential element in Zamboni's definition. Zamboni defines omnibus legislation as bills that cover a number of diverse topics. Yet he also offers an approach to distinguish between degrees of heterogeneity. He distinguishes between "*superficial*" omnibus legislation, "which covers very different topics, but where there is a functional link unifying the various parts which are regulated" (such as a budget bill in which the unifying function behind all its measures is the regulation of the state budget for the upcoming financial year); and "*deep*" omnibus legislation, "which regulates different topics... where their regulation lacks a unifying underlying function" (such as a

---

[13]Ibid. See also Gluck et al. (2015), p. 1804.

[14]Meßerschmidt (this volume).

[15]Massicotte (this volume), discussing Standing Order (69.1) of the House as adopted in 2017.

bill that increases the budget for the police force and also authorizes Sunday opening of food stores).[16]

The packaging of heterogeneous subjects in one bill is also the key to Oliver-Lalana's discussion of omnibus legislation in Spain. He defines omnibus legislation as "multiple subject bills containing unrelated measures" or "heterogeneous content" legislation. Oliver-Lalana acknowledges the conceptual challenges of determining the extent that a law includes a single or multiple subjects or the "homogenous" or "heterogeneous" nature of the law. He argues, however, that the difficulty should not be overstated, suggesting that "'Single subject' is just one of the many concepts that can hardly be grasped positively, and are better dealt with in the negative: in our case, by arguing on what (and why) is *not* covered by, or *not* related to, a given subject." He adds that "there are quite obvious instances of omnibus laws which are easily recognizable as such, for they are often deliberately designed to deal with plural matters or to modify a miscellany of pre-existing legislation. . ."[17]

Identifying what should be considered as packaging of heterogeneous subjects in one bill is also central to Briffault's discussion of single-subject rules and their enforcement in the American states. Briffault canvases a variety of formulas developed by state courts for defining when bills should be considered multi-subject bills, thereby violating the single-subject rule. The heterogeneous nature of the bill is key in many state courts' approaches, for as Briffault observes, "the question in many single subject cases is not the definition of 'subject' *per se*, but whether the different topics, sections, or parts of a bill are sufficiently closely connected that they can be treated as dealing with a single subject." Hence, he presents a range of judicial tests for determining whether the multiple parts of a bill are sufficiently related, including whether they are "germane" or "reasonably germane" to each other or to some general subject; whether they are "rationally related;" whether there is "natural and logical connection;" a "unifying principle;" or a "common purpose or relationship . . . between the topics;" "whether they have a nexus to a common purpose;" and many other variations. Interestingly, Briffault observes that length and scope may also play a role, noting that courts "struggled over the significance of the length or number of sections of a bill or the number of articles or titles of the state code that the measure amends." He concludes, however, that while length could be a factor, it is not a decisive factor. Another approach Briffault observes is trying to determine whether the provisions were a product of "logrolling" (defined as "when two or more separate proposals, none of which is able to command majority support, are combined so that the minorities behind each measure aggregate to a majority capable of passing the resulting bill") or a "rider" (defined as "a provision which could not pass on its own but is then attached to a bill considered likely to pass and so "rides" on that more popular measure to enactment") or taking a legislative-process-focused approach. In the end, he reaches a much more skeptical conclusion than Oliver-Lalana, arguing that courts have generally been unable to come up with a

---

[16]Zamboni (this volume).

[17]Oliver-Lalana (this volume).

consistent definition, resulting in unpredictable "I know it when I see it" decisions.[18]

The heterogeneous nature of the bill is also evident in Lupo and Piccirilli's discussion of omnibus legislation in Italy. In discussing the two main forms of omnibus legislation in Italy (omnibudget bills and omnibus decree-laws), they mention their heterogeneous nature and refer to omnibus legislation as a "bill containing unrelated measures." However, the length of the bill also features in their discussion. This is particularly evident when they refer to the related legislative practice of "maxi-amendments," which they define as "long and heterogeneous proposals for amendment, aimed at substituting the whole text of a bill, by virtue of which the Executive poses a question of confidence..." While Oliver-Lalana and Briffault conceptualize omnibus bills as the opposite of the single-subject rule, Lupo and Piccirilli present "maxi-amendments" as contrasting the Italian constitutional provision requiring that every bill should be examined and approved "article by article," prior to the vote on its final text.[19]

Popelier begins with a general definition that focuses solely on the packaging feature, stating that "omnibus laws" are laws that "assemble a bulk of unrelated rules in one law to modify a whole range of existing statutes."[20] To identify omnibus laws in Belgium, she searched for laws that contain the words "diverse provisions" or "arrangement law" in their title, and selected those laws that hold amendments of at least three other laws. Yet, when Popelier develops measures to categorize and assess omnibus laws, it becomes apparent that she also focuses on the extent of the heterogeneous nature of the bill (which she calls coherency), and its length (in her measure of complexity). Popelier distinguishes between omnibus laws that contain amendments to a variety of unrelated laws within several policy fields, which is the type of omnibus laws she sees as problematic, and other types of omnibus laws (such as omnibus laws within the domain of one specific policy field; omnibus laws with the purpose of transposing EU Directives within one policy field; and "arrangement laws," which only consist of budget related provisions). In measuring complexity, she suggests a formula on the relation between the number of articles and the number of amended laws in the omnibus law. Popelier additionally develops measures to evaluate the characteristics of the legislative procedures and parliamentary debate in enacting omnibus bills.[21]

Israel's version of omnibus legislation is also called "arrangements law" (*hok hahesderim*), which are omnibus bills passed in conjunction with the Budget Law. Yet, while for Belgium, Popelier defines "arrangement laws" as omnibus laws that only consist of budget related provisions, as Hattis Rolef point outs, in their Israeli version, over the years, the arrangements laws started to contain a growing number of chapters that were not directly connected either to the budget or to economic reforms. Consequently, arrangements laws (and their various parts) can be

---

[18]Briffault (this volume).

[19]Lupo and Piccirilli (this volume).

[20]Popelier (this volume).

[21]Ibid.

categorized into provisions directly connected to the current budget proposal; provisions that are relevant to the implementation of the budget but are not directly linked to it; and provisions that are not connected to the budget at all.[22] Hence, the heterogeneous nature of the bill is key to categorizing omnibus laws in Israel as well.

It is interesting to note, however, that the two Israeli contributors to this book provide somewhat different definitions. Kosti's definition emphasizes the packaging feature. He notes that "[a]s an omnibus legislation, every arrangements law consists of various bills, amendments, and cancellations to existing legislation within a single law." While it is generally easy to recognize arrangements laws in Israel according to their title, Kosti suggests two criteria for their identification: their legislation along the Budget law, and "having a feature of omnibus legislation (the inclusion of various bills and amendments)."[23] Hattis Rolef offers a definition that combines the features of length and the packaging, as well as features of the expedited enactment process. According to her definition, the arrangements law "is a law of vast dimensions, that is formally supposed to amend existing legislation, or enact new laws on a variety of usually unrelated subjects, allegedly in order to enable the implementation of the budget and the Government's economic reform program, which is passed in parallel with the Budget Law, in an expedited timetable."[24]

Kurz presents an approach that combines both the feature of packaging unrelated issues and the length of the bill. He also provides precise measures for the scope of packaging and for the length of the bill (which he calls "size"). Krutz argues that "Omnibus bills differ from typical major bills in their *scope* (number of substantive policy areas spanned), in their *size*, and following from scope and size, in their *complexity*." He therefore offers a definition that combines the key attributes of the scope of packaging and the length. Employing the established topic coding scheme for policy areas by Baumgartner and Jones and the Comparative Agendas project, Kurz defines an omnibus bill as any piece of major legislation that: (1) spans three or more major-topic policy areas OR ten or more sub-topic policy areas, AND (2) is one standard deviation above the mean length of major bills.[25]

Rozenberg's approach also deals with the key attributes of length and of packaging heterogeneous measures, and he also offers measures for these two criteria. Rozenberg suggests distinguishing between three types of laws that could all be considered a close phenomenon to omnibus bills: "*big bills*" relates to length (the top 5% of bills in terms of their length); "*heterogeneous bills*" relates to the scope of packaging unrelated subjects (the top 5% of bills that make reference to the highest numbers of legal codes, which in France is a proxy for policy fields), while "*monster bills*" are bills that meet the definitions of both big bills and heterogeneous bills.[26]

---

[22]Hattis Rolef (this volume).

[23]Kosti (this volume).

[24]Hattis Rolef (this volume).

[25]Krutz (this volume).

[26]Rozenberg (this volume).

My own view is that the mere fact that a bill contains more than one subject, or the mere fact that a bill is relatively long, do not fully capture the phenomenon of omnibus legislation. I believe that the packaging of various unrelated measures in one bill is the minimal and necessary criterion in defining omnibus legislation, but that it is insufficient in itself for understanding omnibus legislation. The extent of the heterogeneous nature of the bill, as well as the length of the bill, are also relevant and important criteria. I also believe that these features should be considered together with the typical procedural feature that omnibus bills tend to be enacted through an expedited legislative process that diverts from regular procedure. I do not claim that this is a necessary part of the definition of omnibus legislation in all jurisdictions, but it is a very common feature, and an important exacerbating factor. Hence, my own working definition for omnibus legislation is the legislative practice of packaging together numerous unrelated measures in one long bill, which is often passed via an expedited process. Conceptually, I believe that to fully capture the multiple facets of omnibus legislation, and to understand why it stirs so much interest and controversy, it is important to consider the multitude of its typical features: the packaging of heterogeneous measures, the scope and length of omnibus bills (and therefore their complexity), and the process in which they are enacted. It is the combination of these features that make them particularly problematic and interesting to me. Omnibus legislation that combines these features, like the example I gave at the beginning of this introduction, is what I have in mind when I say that omnibus legislation is a controversial and hotly contested legislative practice.

Yet, I emphasize that this is my personal view, because, in this book, we have taken a decidedly pluralistic approach to the definition and conceptualization of omnibus legislation. This is because, as this section clearly demonstrates, there is no one correct conceptualization of omnibus legislation, and definitions vary across jurisdictions and among scholars. In fact, the one thing that most contributors to this book seem to agree upon is that there is no single agreed-upon universal definition. As we shall see in the next sections, plurality of perspectives is a continuing theme throughout this book, whether in discussing the use of omnibus legislation, the regulation of its use, or its normative evaluation.

3   Perspectives on Omnibus Legislation

Part I of the book begins with one of the jurisdictions with the longest and most extensive experience in using omnibus legislation, presented by one of the researchers with the longest and most extensive experience in studying them.[27] Glen Krutz's chapter on "*Omnibus Legislating in the U.S. Congress*" explores omnibus usage in the American national legislature from 1948 to 2018. His

---

[27]As Glen notes in his now classic book on omnibus legislation from 20 years ago, he has been studying omnibus legislation since his graduate studies. Krutz (2001).

empirical study shows, inter alia, an explosion of omnibus use beginning in 1979 and lasting until the mid-1990s. While Krutz reveals a contraction in omnibus use since then, he observes that usage certainly continues and is especially robust around the annual budget reconciliation bill, and that the motivations for packaging appropriations bills remains persistent. In addition to examining trends in usage of omnibus legislation, Krutz contributes to the theorization and understanding of omnibus legislation, including the questions of how to define omnibus legislation, why is omnibus legislation used, and what are the governance implications of this use.

Krutz argues that omnibus legislation is seen by legislatures as "a way to get things done in an otherwise impossible legislative process." Hence, he argues that omnibus usage is likely to increase in circumstances that challenge the capabilities of Congress (such as deficit politics, divided party control, ripe conditions for minority obstructionism, issue complexity and committee fragmentation, and burgeoning congressional workloads). Yet, Krutz particularly highlights omnibus usage vis-à-vis two types of dynamics: the relationship between congressional leaders and members-at-large, and presidential-congressional relations. He theorizes about the motivations of each of these actors in using (or accepting) omnibus legislation, and on the effect of omnibus usage on these two types of dynamics. Within Congress, Krutz argues that congressional leaders benefit from omnibus legislation, and gain more power with omnibus bills. He also argues that majority party members benefit more from the use of omnibus legislation than do minority party members. This is not surprising, and I suspect that this is probably true about omnibus legislation in most (if not all) legislatures. Yet, Krutz's finding on the presidential-congressional dynamic might surprise readers from non-Presidential systems. He empirically shows that omnibus bills by and large benefit Congress more than the President, and therefore concludes that they "appear to strengthen, rather than weaken, the legislature vis-à-vis the executive." This of course makes sense, given that omnibus bills (and even more so, omnibus appropriations bills) are a tool for Congress to undermine the capacity or will of the President to wield his veto power.[28] Still, as we shall see, this conclusion is in stark contrast to the conventional wisdom in many parliamentary systems, in which omnibus legislation is usually seen as a powerful tool of the executive to dominate the legislature. It should be noted that Krutz's study is complemented and buttressed by Abbe Gluck's empirical study on the rise of unorthodox lawmaking and changes in lawmaking in the U.S. Congress more generally. Yet, as a major part of her contribution focuses on the role of courts vis-à-vis omnibus legislation, her chapter appears in Part II of the book and would be discussed in the next section.

Another country in which the use of omnibus legislation is quite frequent is Italy, albeit the spike in its use occurred later than in the US. As Nicola Lupo and Giovanni Piccirilli explain in their chapter, *"Omnibus Legislation and Maxi-Amendments in Italy: How to Circumvent the Constitutional Provision Requiring Approval of Bills*

---

[28]Bar-Siman-Tov (2010), pp. 855–857.

'Article by Article'," omnibus legislation in its two main forms (omnibudget legislation and omnibus decree-laws) started to increase in the early 1990s. Maxi-amendments, as well, have spread over the last 25 years (although they have first emerged in the 1950s). Yet, the more important difference between the US and Italy is not the chronology, but the fact that in Italy, these legislative instruments (and the maxi-amendments probably above all) are measures for enhancing the government's dominant role in the legislative process.

Lupo and Piccirilli analyze the reasons for the rise of these legislative instruments in Italy in light of the features of its political and institutional system, and particularly its fragmented party system. Their main explanation for the usage of these legislative mechanisms is the heterogeneous and conflictual charter of parliamentary coalitions in Italy (coupled with the weak rationalization of the parliamentary government in the Constitution). They argue that this feature of the Italian political system explains the growing popularity of these legislative "mechanisms aimed. . . at ensuring a fast-track path to varied provisions, each of which was promoted and supported by different parts of the majority (and some even by the opposition), and which aimed to keep the parliamentary majority united in the subsequent phases of its parliamentary path." Hence, as they explain later, these mechanisms help the government "to unite, although artificially, its own heterogeneous parliamentary majority." Indeed, as it is universally recognized that omnibus legislation is a means to facilitate the passage of legislation and overcome political opposition and procedural hurdles, the assumption that more fragmented coalitions make greater use of this legislative mechanism has been acknowledged in other jurisdictions as well.[29] Finally, in addition to analyzing developments in these parliamentary practices, their political explanations, and their normative evaluation, Lupo and Piccirilli analyze the role of the Constitutional Court in trying to establish some limits on the abuses of these instruments. This is a separate important theme that will be discussed in Sect. 4.

The type of omnibus legislation used in Israel, the arrangements law, is quite similar to the Italian omnibus finance legislation that accompanied the budget bill. And like Italy, and in contrast to the US, it is a mechanism that empowers the position of the government vis-à-vis the legislature in the policymaking process. In this respect, Nir Kosti's chapter "*Centralization via Delegation: The Long-term Implications of the Israeli Arrangements Laws*" could be seen as the mirror image of Krutz's chapter. Like Krutz, Kosti conducted an empirical study to investigate the governance implications of the use of omnibus legislation. Yet, while Krutz ends with the conclusion that omnibus legislation strengthens the legislature vis-à-vis the government, Kosti begins with the claim that "[t]he Israeli arrangements law (*Hok Hahesderim*) has become one of the most powerful policy tools used by the Israeli government in recent decades." This statement has already been supported by previous studies, but Kosti adds a novel contribution by focusing on the impacts of the arrangements laws on the "everyday process of government." In particular, he

---

[29]E.g., Meydani (2008) and Nahmias and Klein (1999).

investigates how the Ministry of Finance (MoF), who initiates and drafts the arrangement laws, uses this mechanism to gain more regulatory power, not only at the expense of the legislature, but also at the expense of other ministries.

Kosti analyzed almost 900 delegation provisions included in 38 arrangements laws between 1985 and 2018, to examine the extent to which the Arrangements laws authorized ministers to issue regulations. His study reveals the mechanisms used by MoF in Arrangements laws to extend the Minister of Finance's power in the everyday regulatory processes. In particular, the MoF was involved in nearly 60% of all delegations in Arrangement laws through four mechanisms of centralization: (1) granting itself an authority to create regulation; (2) granting itself and another ministry an authority to create regulation; and holding veto power over the regulations of other ministries either by requiring (3) its consent or (4) consultation prior publication. Hence, the study shows that the process of delegation of authority from parliament to the executive, against common wisdom, is a process that centralizes, rather decentralizes, regulatory powers.

France also has Finance bills, which appear to be the closest legal instruments to the Israeli Arrangements laws or Italian finance laws. As Olivier Rozenberg explains in *"When Rationalization of Bureaucracy De-Rationalizes Laws and Legislatures: 'Monster Bills' in France,"* these bills do exhibit some heterogeneity in their content, in the sense that any type of provisions holding financial consequences can be included in them. Yet, unlike the Israeli case, all provisions in the French Finance bills must deal with financial issues. Hence, Rozenberg opines that, strictly speaking, these bills cannot be considered as "genuine omnibus laws." Instead, he focuses on a type of laws he calls "monster laws," which (as elaborated in the previous section) package together many heterogeneous elements and are also remarkably long. Rozenberg's contribution offers an in-depth investigation of these legal instruments, and like Kurz and Lupo and Piccirilli, he also explores the reasons for their use.

Rozenberg first provides an empirical overview of monster bills (as well as big bills and heterogeneous bills) over the decade between 2008 and 2018, and then provides an in-depth exploration of two main monster bills. He finds, inter alia, that these legislative mechanisms are almost entirely used by the government,[30] therefore concluding that "the rationale for [their use] has to be found on the executive side." Rozenberg offers two main rationales. First, he argues that monster bills are an effective signaling device: "the very fact of proposing long and heterogeneous bills is assumed and staged by the executive power as a communication strategy." He explains that "the monstrosity" of these bills helps draw attention to them and to turn them into a proof of the government capability and willingness to act. Moreover, given the diversity of issues in these bills, they enable the government to target a diversity of audiences in one bill: public opinion in general, voters from a specific

---

[30]Finding that 96% (all but one) of monster bills are governmental bills. And that the vast majority of the other bills with "family resemblance" to omnibus bills (88% of heterogeneous bills, 92% of big bills, and 100% of Finance bills) are also governmental bills. This is in contrast to all laws, in which 57% are governmental bills.

social group or region, stakeholders, etc. The second rationale is that long and/or heterogeneous bills give ministers procedural advantages and help facilitate passage, which is particularly important in France given the scarcity of floor time in the French parliament. Rozenberg concludes with a normative assessment of these legislative devices, according to three criteria: the legitimacy brought by the parliamentary procedure, the capacity of elected representatives to influence the bill content, and the quality of the final product.

Germany is another jurisdiction in which omnibus legislation is widespread; yet, interestingly, appears to have attracted much less attention. Klaus Meßerschmidt's *"Omnibus Legislation in Germany: A Widespread yet Understudied Lawmaking Practice"* fills this gap. Meßerschmidt analyzes the motives and reasons for the widespread use of omnibus legislation, noting that "[s]ome are universal and some reflect the specific conditions of legislation in Germany." Among the universal reasons for the use of omnibus legislation, Meßerschmidt notes that "[b]undling multiple legal measures into a single legal package, in general, facilitates the law-making process in Germany as it probably does everywhere....Efficiency of lawmaking... thus is a strong reason for legislative packaging in most countries, Germany included." Yet, he notes, that unlike the U.S., omnibus legislation is influenced by the idea of executive law-making and the dominance of the government in the legislative process. Hence, he argues that "the idea that the omnibus method generally improves the productivity of law-making by giving coalition leaders a tool to get around gridlock, is of far less importance in Germany than in the United States, and nor does an explanation of the use of omnibus legislation in the context of the Congress-President relationship have any bearing on Germany."

Hence, Meßerschmidt offers explanations that are more specific to Germany. He argues that a major reason for omnibus legislation is the need for implementation of EU Directives, which often affect a multitude of national laws. Another interesting reason Meßerschmidt offers is the sophistication of the statutory system and its degree of connectivity. He argues that the "network character of legislation and the systematic approach of continental jurisprudence" means that "any new legislation almost inevitably results in the need to change various other bills." He therefore argues that "the rise of omnibus bills results from the high degree of 'connectivity' typical of a mature Continental European legal system," and that the "amount and importance of omnibus legislation increase depending on the sophistication of the statutory system." A third explanation offered by Meßerschmidt for the proliferation of omnibus legislation is that German law places very few restrictions on the use of omnibus legislation (with the exception of some limits regarding budgetary legislation). He therefore concludes by discussing other legal instruments to regulate omnibus legislation, as well as a normative evaluation of this legislative practice.

I believe Meßerschmidt's German-specific explanations could be generalizable to other jurisdictions as well. The first explanation may be true for several EU member states, and indeed, the use of omnibus bills as a tool for implementing EU Directives is also cited by other European authors in this book, such as Popelier. As for the second explanation, Meßerschmidt himself indicates that it may be true for any "mature Continental European legal system." I wonder, however, if the observation that any new legislation almost inevitably results in the need to change various other bills is not applicable to any mature legal system, which already has an extensive body of legislation in place. If this is true, than this may demonstrate that the German definition of omnibus legislation (which covers any bill that amends more than one law) is too broad. The third explanation of lack of constitutional and other formal legal restrictions on omnibus legislation is also common to many jurisdictions.

The first part of the book ends with Susan Hattis Rolef's chapter, *"Israel's Economic Arrangements Law and Similar Omnibudget Laws in Other Countries."* Like Kosti, Hattis Rolef deals with omnibus legislation in Israel, but she takes a different methodological approach. While Kosti investigated the subject from an empirical perspective, Hattis Rolef offers a historic and comparative perspective. She first describes the history of arrangements laws in Israel, as well as efforts to deal with this legislative practice and limit its abuses. She details how this legislative mechanism was first introduced in Israel in 1985 as an emergency economic measure, with the expectation that it would be a one-time exception to regular legislative procedure only to deal with an economic crisis; but how the Ministry of Finance discovered its advantages, and started using it on an annual basis. She also details how arrangements laws turned from a fiscal instrument into a governance tool used by the government to pass policies it was having difficulty enacting as ordinary governmental bills, and to put off the implementation of legislation enacted by the Knesset, which the government disapproved of. Hence, she observes that the arrangements laws kept growing in length and scope, with a growing number of chapters that were not related to the budget or even to economic issues. Hattis Rolef also observes how this legislative practice prompted growing criticisms, and provides an historical overview of the various measures that were considered over the years for dealing with this practice and curbing its abuse. She also analyzes the various actors in such reform efforts, from legislative initiatives and efforts by Knesset Speakers, to Attorney Generals and Knesset Legal Advisors, to the Supreme Court of Israel.

Indeed, I believe Israel is interesting, because it represents a novel approach, with a unique judicial role in regulating parliament's use of omnibus legislation. The Israeli Supreme Court developed a new model of judicial review, which enables judicial review of this legislative mechanism, even in the absence of formal legislative rules limiting the legislature's power to use omnibus legislation.[31] This makes Israel particularly interesting from a comparative perspective,[32] and as we shall see in the next section, also quite unique.

Israel is also interesting from a comparative perspective because its form of omnibus legislation (the arrangements laws) has many similarities to omnibudget bills or omnibus finance bills accompanying the budget law in many other countries. And indeed, the second part of Hattis Rolef's chapter takes a comparative approach,

---

[31] HCJ 4885/03 *Israel Poultry Farmers Association v. Government of Israel* (2004); HCJ 10042/16 *Quantinsky v. the Israeli Knesset* (2017).

[32] Bar-Siman-Tov (2018), Gardbaum (2020) and Zipper and Dahan (2020).

providing a comparative survey of omnibus and omnibudget laws in other countries, including additional countries not covered by the other chapters in this book. Her chapter therefore serves as a fitting conclusion for the first part of the book and its cross-country exploration of omnibus legislation and its uses. The third part of Hattis Rolef's chapter deals with the various measures that can be taken to deal with omnibus legislation, based on the experience of other countries. Her main conclusion is that countries where such legislation exists, find it impossible to get rid of it altogether and permanently, but that if there is political will some of its worst abuses can be modified. Her chapter therefore lends itself as a perfect bridge to the second part of the book.

4   Regulating the Use of Omnibus Legislation

The strongest legal attempt to limit or even prohibit the use of omnibus legislation is through a constitutional single-subject rule. This rule typically holds that "No bill shall contain more than one subject, which shall be clearly expressed in its title."[33] Hence, Part II of the book begins with Richard Briffault's *"The Single-Subject Rule: Uncertain Solution for Omnibus Legislation."* While the single-subject rule has ancient origins, and it exists in several places around the world, the American states serve as a particularly salient case for examining the experience with this rule.[34] As Briffault points out, forty-three states in the U.S. contain some version of the single-subject rule in their constitution, and in many states the rule dates back to the mid-nineteenth century. Moreover, he observes that this rule is probably the most litigated procedural requirement in state constitutions. Hence, the American states provide a fertile ground for examining the experience with the single-subject rule, and with judicial enforcement of this rule. Briffault begins with reviewing the history and purposes behind the single-subject rule, and then most of his chapter is dedicated to an in-depth and extensive examination of the experience of state courts in enforcing this rule.

Briffault shows that courts have had difficulty defining and applying the concept of "subject," as well as determining whether the different sections or parts of a bill are sufficiently closely connected that they can be treated as dealing with a single subject. He also demonstrates the limits of more purposivist approaches that sought to resolve the problem by turning to the purposes behind the single-subject rule: prevention of logrolling and riders, and more generally protection of the legislative process from improper manipulation. He argues that courts have had difficulty in determining whether a provision is a logroll or rider or simply the product of legitimate legislative compromise. Given these difficulties, courts have generally adopted a deferential approach to the legislature's determination that a bill addresses

---

[33]Briffault (this volume) citing Ohio Const. Art II, § 15(D) as a typical formulation of the rule.
[34]Hattis Rolef (this volume).

only a single subject; while limiting their intervention to egregious violations of the rule. Briffault argues, however, that the case law is not clear enough on what counts as egregious violations of the rule. Hence, while there are cases that are relatively clear violations and there are certainly cases where courts "got it right," Briffault opines that overall, judicial enforcement has been intermittent, and sometimes inconsistent. He concludes, therefore, that the American states' experience has been that the single-subject rule does not provide an effective, judicially-enforceable tool against omnibus legislation.

Unlike the states in the U.S., at the American federal level there is no single subject rule. Against this backdrop, Abbe Gluck's "*Unorthodox Lawmaking and Legislative Complexity in American Statutory Interpretation*" asks what is the role of federal courts in dealing with omnibus legislation, either through judicial review or statutory interpretation. Her contribution begins by documenting the rise of unorthodox modern lawmaking, including omnibus lawmaking, in the U.S. Congress and discussion of its causes. Gluck argues that the traditional "textbook" legislative process "is dead in the U.S." She argues that "departures from... 'regular order' have become the norm, not the exception," and that astonishingly, only about 1% of enacted laws go through "the standard legislative process set out by Congress's own rules." She therefore places the rise of omnibus legislation in the broader context of the rise of unorthodox lawmaking and the increasing complexity of the U.S. Code. Gluck observes that omnibus legislation has comprised approximately 11% of major legislation in recent Congresses, and provides a detailed empirical account demonstrating the increasing complexity of the US statute book. She shows, inter alia, that the length of statues has grown steadily and exponentially in in the U.S., and that the number of absolute cross references as well as the number of cross references per public law have also exponentially increased in amount and in variance. She finds that the major shift appears to have happened in 1975—a few years after the Legislative Reorganization Act of 1970, which invigorated the committee system. She also argues that major drivers of these trends are a hostile partisan political climate; gridlock; the rise in the use of filibusters, as well as the advent of a more individualistic, as opposed to communitarian, Senate; the increasingly overlapping jurisdictions of congressional committees (and possibly also the creation of professional drafting offices). These findings nicely complement the findings by Krutz described in the previous section.

After detailing the changes in Congressional lawmaking, the balance of Gluck's chapter focuses on the role of courts. Gluck criticizes American federal courts for being oblivious to these dramatic changes in Congressional lawmaking. She observes that federal courts have never been willing to adopt a "due process of lawmaking" approach and to strike down federal statutes for lack of deliberation or process. She likewise argues that the "judicial approach to statutory interpretation has been generally uninterested in the realities of our legislative process, even as many judges claim either that their interpretive approach approximates how Congress drafts, reflects a set of conventions shared by the judiciary and the legislature, or captures Congress's purposes." To remedy this oversight, her contribution is aimed at bringing understanding of the legislative process, and how it has changed, into theories and doctrines of statutory interpretation and judicial review. She therefore discusses the implications of omnibus lawmaking, as well as some other kinds of unorthodox lawmaking, for both statutory interpretation and judicial review.

The role of courts in regulating the use of omnibus legislation is also at the center of A. Daniel Oliver-Lalana's contribution, *"Omnibus Legislation in Spain: Between Political Expediency, Doctrinal Condemnation, and Judicial Indulgence."* Similarly to the situation in the US, in Spain, some regional legislatures have established limits on the subject of bills, but on the federal level, neither the Constitution nor the parliamentary standing orders of the Congress and the Senate set any specific constraint on the processing or enactment of multiple subject bills. And like the US federal courts, the Spanish Constitutional Court has been reluctant to set limits on omnibus laws, holding that the Spanish Constitution poses "no obstacle precluding or limiting the inclusion of a host of heterogeneous normative measures into a single legislative text." This is particularly interesting, because while American federal courts are known for their general resistance to judicial review of the legislative process,[35] the Spanish Constitutional Court has generally been much more active in reviewing the legislative process and parliamentary procedures in other areas.[36] The Spanish case is therefore illustrative of the situation in other countries as well (including the US federal system and Canada), where the general judicial assumption has been that in the absence of explicit constitutional restrictions, there is not much courts can do in limiting omnibus legislation.[37] Oliver-Lalana's contribution is dedicated to reviewing the background, justification and implications of this judicial approach, and discussing to what extent it is actually defensible.

After discussing the single subject dogma, Oliver-Lalana offers a survey of the Spanish experience in this area (starting from the abuse of budget laws as a multipurpose regulatory tool in the 1980s). He then concentrates on the latest constitutional case law dealing with the problem of disparate legislative contents. He considers two distinct, albeit interwoven issues: on one hand, the legal feasibility of multiple subject statutes, which the Constitutional Court has repeatedly affirmed when reviewing budget accompanying laws and government's urgency legislation; on the other, the somewhat loose ban the Court has established on "unconnected amendments" or riders. Overall, Oliver-Lalana argues that the "Spanish experience with omnibus and omnibudget legislation is a cat and mouse story about constitutional judges – the cats – who have no claws but on certain occasions use their fangs to bite, and cabinets and their supporting parliamentary majorities – the mice – which always find how to get their way." Oliver-Lalana concludes with offering lessons from the Spanish experience, and suggesting an approach that deviates from the usual scholarly plea for adding constraints on multiple subject bills to

---

[35] See Bar-Siman-Tov (2009, 2011).
[36] Oliver-Lalana (2016) and Navot (2006).
[37] Dodek (2017) and Dunn (2003).

constitutions or parliamentary standing orders. Instead, he advocates semi-substantive constitutional review standards that focus on the process of legislative justification.

It is worth mentioning that the contribution by Lupo and Piccirilli, discussed in the previous section, also explores the role of the Italian Constitutional Court in regulating the forms of omnibus legislation and maxi-amendments in Italy. Indeed, there are fascinating parallels between their analysis and Oliver-Lalana's. Like its Spanish counterpart, the Italian Constitutional Court similarly refused to hold these legislative practices unconstitutional, but did engage in some judicial review meant to curb some of their abuses. Moreover, like Oliver-Lalana, Lupo and Piccirilli also call for a greater judicial role, and discuss recent developments that may signal greater willingness to exercise more significant judicial oversight in the future.[38]

While this has not been the central focus of Oliver-Lalana's chapter, the Spanish case also provides interesting lessons on the limited promise of non-enforceable political commitments to curb omnibus legislation. In 2003, after two sessions in the opposition, the Socialist Party promised that that if elected, they would end the use of budget accompanying laws, which were the main form of omnibus legislation used at the time. Upon winning the elections, the new Socialist cabinet seemed to live up to its promise. As Oliver-Lalana notes, "[t]he preamble of the Act 2/2004 approving the State budget for 2005 proudly stated that [accompanying] laws, from then on, would be replaced with normal legislative reforms adopted through regular parliamentary procedures." Additionally, in 2005, the Spanish Government adopted legistic guidelines stating that "as far as possible, legislative acts shall regulate one single subject, all aspects of the subject and, if necessary, those aspects which are directly related to it,"[39] Yet, as Oliver-Lalana observes, "the guidelines are widely assumed to be non-enforceable, aspirational recommendations"; and as to the "nominal abandonment of accompanying laws," he observed that the government soon began to employ alternative vehicle's to pass omnibus legislation. In practice, Oliver-Lalana observes that "multiple subject legislation plagues the current landscape of Spanish law" and concludes that "[u]nfortunately, good purposes alone cannot tame certain legislative interties."

This Spanish experience with campaign promises and political commitments to curb omnibus legislation calls for a comparison to the somewhat similar experience in Canada, which is discussed in Louis Massicotte's chapter, *"Canada: If Controversial, Omnibus Legislation is Here to Stay."* Massicotte describes how all major opposition parties promised to curb omnibus legislation during the 2015 election campaign. The Liberal Party's platform promised to "bring an end to this undemocratic practice," as did two additional opposition parties that castigated omnibus legislation and inserted in their electoral platforms commitments to curb or abolish this practice. And indeed, after Justin Trudeau's Liberal Party won the elections, the newly-elected government's first Throne speech included a promise that "it will not

---

[38]Particularly order no. 17/2019 of the Constitutional Court.

[39]Ministerio de la Presidencia 2011, § I.3 cited in Oliver-Lalana (this volume).

resort to devices like... omnibus bills to avoid scrutiny." Massicotte's contribution is dedicated to investigating what happed with this promise, studying omnibus legislation in the Canadian federal arena since Justin Trudeau's Liberals came to office in 2015.

Massicotte finds that the new Liberal government did not abandon the practice of omnibus legislation. He concludes that budget implementation bills are here to stay, and that many other omnibus bills are still being introduced and passed. He also notes that during the 2019 campaign, no major party's platform had a word to say about omnibus bills. He therefore concludes that "omnibus bills are seemingly bound to be vilified by one side of the House, but gleefully used once those members find themselves on the other side. Some healthy dose of cynicism, hopefully blended with a touch of humour, may be helpful for those whose duty it is to observe closely the antics of politicians."

At the same time, Massicotte emphasizes that it would be unfair to conclude that "*Plus ça change, plus c'est pareil.*" Instead, he finds that rather than abandoning the practice of omnibus legislation, the Liberal government adopted a milder solution of adopting new procedural parliamentary rules meant to curb its abuse. The government initiated a reform to the House Standing Orders that granted the Speaker of the House the power to divide an omnibus bill into distinct parts for the purposes of voting, and to do the same for the portions of budget implementation bills that had not been announced in the budget speech. While this solution falls short of meeting the campaign promises, Massicotte does give the government credit that "for the first time in Canadian parliamentary history, the Speaker has been empowered to throw a pinch of sand in the carefully oiled government legislative machine that ensures the passing of omnibus legislation." In examining the operation of this new rule in practice, he finds that it has "been successfully invoked against the government too many times so far for being dismissed as a mere decorative ornament, a fig leaf covering a broken promise." He concludes that this mechanism allowed the opposition to win numerous points of order, and arguably obliged the government to curb the worst abuses associated with omnibus bills.

Hence, in addition to providing lessons on the (limited) promise of political promises to end omnibus legislation, the Canadian experience provides important comparative lessons on the potential of using procedural parliamentary rules as a means to regulate the use of omnibus legislation. This calls for a comparison to Belgium, and its experience with procedural mechanisms to regulate omnibus legislation. As Patricia Popelier mentions in her chapter, "*The Practice of Omnibus Laws in Belgium: An Empirical Test,*" Belgium serves as a particularly illuminating case on this issue: It was one of the first countries to adopt omnibus legislation and arrangements laws, and more importantly, it introduced several procedural requirements to regulate the use of omnibus laws. Popelier's contribution is dedicated to investigating these procedural measures and evaluating their success.

Popelier begins with an overview of the procedural requirements, mostly flowing from the House's Rules of Procedures and the Council of State's guidelines on legislative drafting, that regulate omnibus legislation and arrangement laws. She enumerates the advantages and disadvantages of omnibus legislations, and analyzes how these procedural requirements are meant to address the disadvantages and risks of abuse of omnibus legislation and to optimize its use. She then develops an empirical framework for investigating whether these procedural safeguards proved effective safeguards for the democratic and legal quality of the law, both in fact and in the perception of advisors to and members of Parliament. To this end, Popelier subdivides omnibus laws in different categories and develops indicators to find whether the use of omnibus laws in each category is still problematic. Subsequently, she examines whether possible problematic use is also identified by the advisors to and members of Parliament.

Popelier finds that some procedural requirements (such as the requirement to lift provisions that are unrelated to the budget from the arrangement laws; the practice to use omnibus laws by preference for amendments within one policy field; and the inclusion of a coordination table) have led to some improvement, particularly in reducing complexity. Yet, she finds that that omnibus laws in Belgium are still used with a high frequency and remain vulnerable for abuse, and that arrangement laws are the most problematic of all. She further finds that the actors in the parliamentary process are aware of the problems, but "even if they have objections, rarely stand in the way." The Council of State "vents very occasionally," whereas "MPs from the opposition raise objections on all aspects, but the majority very easily close the ranks." She therefore concludes that "once introduced, omnibus laws are there to stay," and that it would require "a serious shift in political culture to make safeguards effective."

This last conclusion by Popelier and the more general lessons from the previous chapters about the difficulties of doing away with omnibus legislation or even limiting its use, may lead to the conclusion that omnibus legislation is inevitable. In fact, however, there are many countries that do without omnibus legislation, and actually do quite well. Hence, the final chapter of the book is dedicated to a county representing such an example. Mauro Zamboni's contribution *"(Absence of) Omnibus Legislation in Sweden: When Legislative Drafting Affects the Political Discourse"* begins with the striking observation that "Sweden has had an astoundingly low rate of omnibus legislation in its legislative history." He observes that since World War II, there was not even a single case of a deep omnibus legislation,[40] either as an act or simply as a bill. He states that "the reality is rather simple and uncontroversial: this type of omnibus legislation (where a bill or statute regulates different and unrelated topics) is practically absent on both the legal practitioners' and legal scholars' horizon." Zamboni's contribution is dedicated to investigating the reasons for this reality, as well as attempting to draw some general conclusions, particularly on the role of legal actors and legislative drafters in the political arena.

Zamboni begins his investigation by noting that the lack of omnibus legislation in Sweden is surprising, as several of the factors and conditions that are theoretically supposed to promote the usage of omnibus legislation are also present in Sweden. He notes that Swedish political actors are no different than political actors elsewhere in

---

[40]For Zamboni's definition of "deep" omnibus legislation see Sect. 2 above.

their motivations and incentives to use tools to facilitate the passage of legislation, and that these motivations may in fact be enhanced by Sweden's social-democratic model, as the welfare state agenda is dependent on enacting statutory instruments for its implementation. He further notes that "statutes are considered by [Swedish] politicians as simple vessels capable of transporting their different and most hetero-geneous political merchandise." Zamboni also notes that Swedish political culture has been described as involving a pragmatic approach to decision-making and as emphasizing utilitarian considerations and compromise. Pressures for tools promot-ing compromise are also expected to be high due to the fact that the vast majority of the Swedish governments after World War II have been minority governments. Finally, he argues, Swedish constitutional culture gives elected political actors a predominate position over unelected actors, and is marked by "the dominance of the logics of the political discourse over the legal ones, with a flexible idea and use of the law [to] help to fulfill the goals set by the political actors." Hence, in theory, Swedish legislators could have been expected to embrace the use of omnibus legislation, as an effective tool to promote compromises and facilitate the passage of legislation; and in theory, legal constraints or legal actors were not expected to stand in the way of this political motivation.

Against this backdrop, Zamboni investigates the factors that have nevertheless stopped omnibus legislation from appearing in the Swedish legislative landscape. He highlights the central role of legislative drafters, and identifies several main factors. These include the position of legislative drafters as apolitical public servants in the Swedish system, which makes them more loyal to the dogmas of the legal discourse than the ones of the political world. Another factor is the high status of the preparatory works in the Swedish legal system, which makes it difficult for the political actors to insert "ad hoc" provisions, which are unrelated and do not logically fit into the contents of the bill. He also mentions the well-established praxis to aim, already in the drafting stage, at reaching the largest consensus possible, which is often coupled with a rather strict cross-party discipline in the later stages, preventing the jeopardizing of the text of the bill so precariously drawn up during the drafting. Together, they create a legislative process that tends to reject deep omnibus legislation. These factors may be attributed to the specific Swedish system. How-ever, Zamboni argues that many Western legal systems with a rule of law tradition contain the factors that contribute to the legalization of legislative lawmaking and therefore the marginalization of forms of legislation which, like omnibus legislation, tend to disrupt the legal logics in favor of the political ones. More broadly, Zamboni argues that the Swedish example highlights how the legal discourse, its culture, and its institutions (in particular the legislative ones) can impact the political discourse, and block problematic legislative behaviors.

5 Normative Views of Omnibus Legislation

In Sect. 2, I have highlighted the plurality of opinions on how to define and conceptualize omnibus legislation. In Sects. 3 and 4 we have seen multiple perspectives and comparative experiences regarding the usage of omnibus legislation and its regulation. I conclude this introduction by observing that this book also reveals a plurality of normative views about omnibus legislation. One observation that I found particularly fascinating is that the contributions in this book nicely demonstrate that normative views of omnibus legislation vary not only across scholars, but also across countries and legal systems. In this section, I present two illustrative sets of comparisons, one from North America and one from Europe, and try to offer some broader thoughts on what can influence such differences in normative views about omnibus legislation.

First, it is illuminating to compare the different normative discussions about omnibus legislation in the two North American constitutional democracies in this volume. Massicotte describes the normative views about omnibus legislation in Canada in the last decade as follows: "Omnibus bills became vilified by the opposition parties, in the media, by parliamentary scholars... [and] former bureaucrats... as authoritarian devices purporting to avoid proper scrutiny of government measures, that exemplified the ruling [party's] contempt of Parliament..." As we have seen, "bring[ing] an end to this undemocratic practice" even became a camping promise of several parties at a certain point (albeit, Massicotte is critical of the extent that this promise has been fulfilled). In describing the general view about omnibus legislation in Canada, Massicotte concludes that he "found ample evidence of discomfort with that legislative technique, within Parliament and outside of it, though not necessarily among the wider public." Overall, it appears that omnibus legislation is highly controversial in Canada, and that the general view in the academic discourse is quite critical of this legislative practice.[41]

In contrast, the three American contributors from the US present a more positive normative evaluation. This is not to say that omnibus legislation is not controversial in the US, and it certainly has its critics there as well.[42] Briffault, Gluck, and Krutz are also certainly mindful of both drawbacks and benefits of omnibus legislation. Yet, it is fascinating to observe that all three seem to share the view that this legislative device is necessary, perhaps even desirable, and see it as an overall justified institutional adaptation to challenging circumstances.[43]

---

[41] See also Albert (2017), Dodek (2017) and Massicotte (2013).

[42] See, e.g., Mann and Ornstein (2008), pp. 170–175; Dunn (2003).

[43] In their respective chapters in this book, Briffault writes: "Comprehensive, multi-topic legislation will often be necessary, if not desirable, in order for the legislature to act at all, and a proliferation of small, piecemeal single-subject measures would not improve legislative efficiency or, given the time limits many legislatures are under, legislative deliberation." Gluck writes: "Unorthodox lawmaking, including omnibus lawmaking, is not an unmitigated negative; rather, it is an adaptation to the changing complexities of the American political system and the expectations facing today's Congress. And it enables Congress to get the work of government done under these circumstances."

In theory, one possible explanation for this difference in normative views of omnibus legislation between Canada and the US may be that this practice is employed in more abusive or objectionable ways in Canada. And it is true that Massicotte attributes part of the growing discontent of this legislative practice to perceived abuses of this legislative technique under Conservative Prime Minister Harper (in addition to mentioning a more recent scandalous case of abuse by Trudeau's Liberal government). We can also note that Massicotte observes that omnibus legislation has been on the rise in recent decades in Canada, while Krutz observes a contraction in omnibus use since the mid-1990s. Generally, I am sure that part of the factors that influence normative views of omnibus legislation in various countries is the extent that this practice is used and abused, and that high profile scandalous cases surely also have an effect. Yet, I do not think that this is the sole or even main reason for the difference in the case of these two countries. The use of omnibus legislation in US Congress is still quite extensive, probably more than in many other countries, and the US has certainly had its share of egregious abuses of this legislative device.[44] Hence, I want to offer two other explanations.

The main explanation relates to the feasibility of passing bills through regular legislation. There are various discussions about the pros and cons of omnibus legislation (and many of the chapters in this book provide excellent and more detailed discussions of the arguments on both sides, as well as develop criteria for its evaluation).[45] Yet, there seems to be general agreement that the main advantage of omnibus legislation is that it facilitates the passage of legislation. At the same time, there is also general agreement that this facilitating legislative device may come with heavy costs to democratic procedural principles, such as transparency, accountability, deliberation, participation, etc., and can also have significant costs to the quality of legislation. To be sure, choosing between these tradeoffs is contingent on one's normative theory of the optimal legislative process, and the proper balance between the competing goals of parliamentary procedure.[46] Yet, beyond differences in personal normative preferences, I think the decision in this tradeoff is also determined by the feasibility of enacting policies in each country.[47] In some

---

Krutz opines: "There are clearly drawbacks of omnibus legislation. . . in terms of democratic theory. On the other hand, there are many benefits of omnibus legislation. . . . .In this regard, at least in the US case, omnibus bills tell a collective story of successful strategic-level and institutional adaptation to challenging circumstances."

[44]For a discussion of several of the most egregious examples see Bar-Siman-Tov (2010), pp. 820–827, as well as the more recent example discussed in Bar-Siman-Tov (2018).

[45]See for example the criteria for evaluation developed by Popelier and by Rozenberg (this volume).

[46]For more detailed explnations see Bar-Siman-Tov (2015, 2016) and Voermans et al. (2015).

[47]The feasibility of passing bills through regular legislation in a certain legislature can be measured in various ways, from an analysis of its veto gates (e.g., Tsebelis 1995; Wiberg 2009; Eskridge 2012), to measures of the pace of the legislative process and the time its takes to pass a bill through parliament (e.g., Voermans et al. 2012) to various measures of gridlock (e.g., Binder 2003, 2015; Chiou and Rothenberg 2007; Chafetz 2013).

legislatures, the coalition or majority party can almost always get its way and pass its policy initiatives relatively easily. In other countries, passing legislation through regular lawmaking can be much more difficult. And I believe that this is the crucial factor in normative debates about omnibus legislation in the US. As Gluck argues, "the U.S. Congress is in a period of historic gridlock. Without... omnibus legislation, Congress would get little done." Briffault similarly argues that "Comprehensive, multi-topic legislation will often be necessary... in order for the legislature to act at all." And Krutz expresses a similar position.[48] In sum, in some countries omnibus legislation may be perceived as helpful and effective (but not indispensable) for passing controversial policies; whereas in other countries (such as the US, and to a lesser extent, Italy),[49] it may be perceived as necessary for passing legislation at all. Obviously, this difference influences the overall evaluation of whether this legislative device is worth its costs.

A final explanation in the Canadian-US comparison relates to the impact of omnibus legislation on the separation of powers and the status of the legislature vis-à-vis the executive. As we have seen in the quote above from Massicotte's description of the Canadian views about omnibus legislation, this practice has become "vilified" to a large extent because it is seen as a tool used by the government to "avoid proper scrutiny of government measures," and even as exemplifying the government's "contempt of Parliament." I believe this is a major source of criticisms against omnibus legislation in other parliamentary democracies as well.[50] Indeed, as we have seen in Sects. 2–3, in many parliamentary systems, omnibus legislation is seen as an instrument used by the executive to dominate the legislature. In contrast, Krutz concludes that in the US, omnibus bills "appear to strengthen, rather than weaken, the legislature vis-à-vis the executive," and this adds to his reasons for concluding that "at least in the US case, omnibus bills tell a collective story of successful strategic-level and institutional adaptation to challenging circumstances."

And yet, as the next set of comparison demonstrates, the division of countries with negative vs. positive views of omnibus legislation is not necessarily limited to parliamentary vs. presidential systems. Indeed, it is particularly fascinating to see the stark contrast between the normative discussions about omnibus legislation in two European parliamentary democracies: Spain and Germany. Oliver-Lalana begins his

---

[48]In discussing the benefits of omnibus legislation Krutz writes: "First among these is the potential to get things done in the legislative process... Omnibus bills provide a way to enact policies that might not make it alone. They provide a way to circumvent the pressures of deficit politics and issue complexity, the gridlock of divided government, and the gridlock of committee jurisdiction fragmentation."

[49]See Lupo and Piccirilli (this volume).

[50]The Israeli Supreme Court, for example, has said on the usage of the Arrangements law mechanism that it is used to force the will of the government on parliament and that "this legislative mechanism, which is used by the government as a device for 'overcoming parliamentary obstacles' (in other words, preventing effective parliamentary scrutiny of the government's legislative initiatives), may harm the proper balance, according to the principle of the separation of powers, between the executive and the legislature in the legislative process." HCJ 4885/03 *Israel Poultry Association v Government of Israel* 14(2) PD 36 (2004) (Isr.).

chapter with the observation that omnibus legislation "has always been condemned as a legislative perversion." In discussing the normative academic views about omnibus legislation in Spain, he observes that this practice has been subject to "[p]ervasive doctrinal attacks," and provides the following overview of the Spanish debate:

> I am not aware of any study in the Spanish literature which vindicates the virtues or the social import of omnibus legislation *as such*. All we can find are objections: criticism has been levelled at every kind of miscellaneous laws, with reproaches coming from all sides, including the Council of State, the MPs themselves (when speaking from the opposition benches), and the legal scholarship *en bloc* – even transversal superstatutes on e.g. gender equality, whose spirit is yet applauded, have also been criticized for regulating too wide a number of issues.

In contrast, Meßerschmidt observes that omnibus legislation is not considered controversial in Germany, and that this practice garners little attention or debate. In reviewing the views in the extant German debate, he observes that the "spectrum of opinions range from diffuse scepticism to full endorsement." He further observes that "the prevailing opinion" in Germany views omnibus legislation as "a practical and necessary means of ensuring up-to-date legislation," and as "constitutionally unobjectionable." He adds that "[f]rom the German point of view, omnibus legislation is rather a matter of drafting than a political vehicle, yielding minimal legal problems and never stirring political debate." Meßerschmidt argues that in contrast to other countries, in Germany, "nobody would call omnibus bills a 'crying evil' [...or] 'fundamentally undemocratic'" or consider banning their use. "On the contrary, omnibus legislation is often regarded as contributing to the production of high-quality laws and, thus, as a convenient tool for the management of legislation. It is, in general, institutionally and technically efficient."[51]

Of the countries surveyed in this book, Germany is by far the country with the most positive normative view of omnibus legislation. It is worth noting, however, that Germany is also the country with the most expansive definition of omnibus legislation. As noted in Sect. 1, in Germany, any bill that encompasses more than one new bill or alteration to a bill, regardless of length or the heterogonous nature of its subjects, is considered an omnibus bill. As Meßerschmidt explains, given this broad definition, German "omnibus legislation" may include "monstrous compilations of dozens or hundreds of Articles," but also "a law consisting of only three Articles (the third one deals with the entry into force), which Americans or Canadians will hardly view as 'omnibus'." I would add that Americans or Canadians would also hardly view it as normatively problematic. Indeed, as Meßerschmidt himself seems to acknowledge later in his chapter, "[t]he main drawback of the

---

[51]Meßerschmidt himself seems to be more cognizant of the possibilities of controversial uses (and abuses) of omnibus legislation. Nevertheless, his own view of is still relatively positive. He argues "that omnibus legislation, irrespective of the problems, is not intrinsically wrong and its contribution to efficient law-making should be acknowledged. Codes of conduct, however, are necessary to avoid abuses."

[German] understanding of omnibus legislation is that it runs the risk of ignoring the political controversies and fundamental legal problems of this type of legislation."

Now, I am not arguing that omnibus legislation is necessarily viewed more positively in Germany only due to their definition of omnibus legislation. There certainly could be other reasons as well. Yet, the German example illustrates my broader argument: that one's normative evaluation of omnibus legislation may be influenced by one's definition of this legislative practice. Naturally, a very broad definition of omnibus legislation would capture much more cases of legislation that many would not consider too objectionable.

Consider, for example, the Israeli Insolvency and Rehabilitation Law, 2018. This law codified and consolidated insolvency and rehabilitation rules from multiple sources, as well as reformed and modernized this legal area. Naturally, it amended a host of existing laws: 15 different laws to be exact. It was also quite long: the enacted law contained 381 articles and three appendices, spanning a total of 113 pages. It additionally covered many subjects within this legal field, containing, for example, a part about insolvency law for individuals and a separate part on insolvency law for corporations, and within each of these parts, covering various aspects relating to a comprehensive regulation of insolvency. It should also be mentioned that this law was a product of a very long, detailed and careful legislative process.[52] This law would certainly be considered as a clear case of omnibus legislation by the German definition (and by some other definitions, such as, Zamboni's definition for "*superficial*" omnibus legislation, and definitions that focus only on length or only on the number of subjects regardless of how homogenous they are). Yet, it is not omnibus legislation according to my definition of omnibus legislation and to several of the other definitions discussed in Sect. 1 above.

More importantly, this law is not normatively undesirable in my view. In my view, the fact that a bill amends more than one law is hardly objectionable, in and of itself. Similarly, I believe that the fact that a bill is longer than average is not necessarily problematic, in and of itself. Even a bill with many dozens of articles is not necessarily wrong, if all articles are relevant and justified by the nature of the regulation in question, do not create unnecessary complexity, and legislators have sufficient time to scrutinize the bill. Furthermore, the mere fact that a bill covers several (related) subjects is not necessarily objectionable in my eyes. If the bill adopts a comprehensive reform or regulation of a specific policy area and covers serval related subjects within this same area, there is nothing inherently wrong with it. I believe that many readers would not see this law as a case of bad lawmaking. Quite the contrary. Indeed, comprehensive codification efforts of a certain legal area would generally be seen as appropriate lawmaking, certainly if they are a product of an extensive and meticulous legislative process. This is quite different from a bill packaging together various unrelated subjects. It is certainly different from the

---

[52]For its full legislative history, see the Israeli National Legislative Database, at https://main. knesset.gov.il/Activity/Legislation/Laws/Pages/LawBill.aspx?t=LawReshumot& lawitemid=577400.

practice of enacting long, heterogeneous complex bills through an expedited process that subverts participation, deliberation, transparency and accountability.

In short, broad definitions of omnibus legislation are likely to capture many more cases of appropriate lawmaking, whereas definitions that combine several of the features of omnibus legislation (the packaging of heterogeneous subjects, the scope, length and complexity of omnibus bills, and the process in which they are enacted) are likely to target the more problematic and objectionable cases of omnibus legislation. It is therefore only natural that people (and countries) that have in mind the broader conception of omnibus legislation would tend to view it more favorably.

In this section, I focused on two comparisons between two sets of countries to offer general thoughts on some of the factors that can influence normative evaluations of omnibus bills in various countries. Obviously, I have not exhausted all the considerations in the normative debates about omnibus legislation. I also did not do justice to all possible comparisons between the countries represented in this book. Yet, I believe the comparisons between Canada and the US, Spain and Germany is illustrative, given the clear contrasts and given that the discourses particularly in Spain and Germany represent the two poles of normative views. I believe that normative discourses about omnibus legislation in other countries can be placed somewhere on this spectrum, ranging from overwhelming universal condemnation; to viewing omnibus legislation as generally negative but a necessary evil; to viewing it as an overall positive practice whose advantages outweigh its disadvantages; to full endorsement.[53] Of course, views about omnibus legislation may vary across scholars even within the same country, and I suspect that within some countries, there is greater divergence of opinions than others. I should note, however, that at least based on the contributions to this volume, the differences among scholars do not necessarily fall across disciplinary lines. That is, contrary to what might be expected, it is not necessarily the case that legal scholars are the critics of omnibus legislation while political scientists are the supporters. In this book, there has been a plurality of views within the group of legal scholars as well as within the group of non-lawyers.[54]

---

[53]My impression about the normative discourse on omnibus legislation in Israel is that it is closer to the Spanish and Canadian side of the spectrum. With the exception of the Ministry of Finance and the Prime Minister Office (and their legal services), the normative view about arrangements laws is almost universally negative (and this includes views by MPs, the Knesset Legal Advisor, the Supreme Court, the State Comptroller, virtually all legal scholarship, and most, if not all, political science and public policy scholarship).

[54]For example, in this volume, the group of scholars that can be seen as generally on the more positive side of the spectrum of views about omnibus legislation included several legal scholars (particularly Briffault, Gluck, Meßerschmidt, and Popiler). Meanwhile, the group of scholars that can be seen as generally on the more negative side of the spectrum included several non-lawyers (particularly Hattis Rolef, Massicotte, and Rozenberg) or scholars who are both legal scholars and political scientists (such as Lupo).

Admittedly, I came to this book project with relatively established views on omnibus legislation,[55] which have certainly been shaped by the jurisdictions I was most familiar with from my previous studies (namely, the US and Israel). In editing this book, I have learned a great deal from the insightful and diverse perspectives offered by the superb group of authors in this volume. Even if I have not been converted from a skeptic to a fan, my thinking about omnibus legislation and its regulation has certainly become much richer and more nuanced. I am sure that readers of this book would be similarly rewarded.

Acknowledgements I thank the two anonymous reviewers and the participants of the conferences "Rearranging the Arrangements Law: Comparative, Multidisciplinary, Empirical and Normative Perspectives on Omnibus Legislation" at Bar-Ilan University and "Parliaments in Change – Changes in Parliaments" organized by Brill & Ludovika – University of Public Service. I also thank Tair Ben Zeev, Itay Cohen, Yehonatan Dayan, Tal Eyal Lipschutz, and Chani Koth for excellent research assistance. This research was supported by grants #1436/15 and #2207/18 from the Israel Science Foundation.

Constitutions Cited

Ohio Const.

Statutes Cited

Individual Tax Reform and Alternative Minimum Tax, Pub. L. No. 115-97 (2017) (USA)
Insolvency and Rehabilitation Law, 2018 (Israel)

Cases Cited

HCJ 4885/03 Israel Poultry Farmers Association v. Government of Israel (2004) (Israel)
HCJ 10042/16 Quantinsky v. the Israeli Knesset (2017) (Israel)
Order no. 17/2019 of the Constitutional Court (Italy)

---

[55]See, e.g., Bar-Siman-Tov (2009), pp. 338–339; Bar-Siman-Tov (2010), pp. 821–227, 867; Bar-Siman-Tov (2016), pp. 681, 683, 692–696; Bar-Siman-Tov (2018, 2019).

Websites Cited

Israeli National Legislative Database, at https://main.knesset.gov.il/Activity/Legislation/Laws/Pages/LawBill.aspx?t=LawReshumot&lawitemid=577400

References

Albert R (2017) Single-subject constitutional amendments. SSRN Electron J. https://doi.org/10.2139/ssrn.3054051

Bar-Siman-Tov I (2009) Legislative supremacy in the United States: rethinking the enrolled bill doctrine. Georgetown Law J 97:323

Bar-Siman-Tov I (2010) Lawmakers as lawbreakers. William Mary Law Rev 52:805

Bar-Siman-Tov I (2011) The puzzling resistance to judicial review of the legislative process. Bost Univ Law Rev 91:1915–1974

Bar-Siman-Tov I (2015) Mending the legislative process – the preliminaries. Theory Pract Legis 3:245

Bar-Siman-Tov I (2016) The law of lawmaking. Tel Aviv Univ Law Rev 37:645

Bar-Siman-Tov I (2018) In wake of controversial enactment process of Trump's tax bill, Israeli SC offers a novel approach to regulating omnibus legislation. I-CONnect Int J Const Law Blog

Bar-Siman-Tov I (2019) Quantinsky v. the Knesset in the matter of the third apartment tax: a necessary decision or an unjustified "major deviation" from the case law? Bar-Ilan Univ Law Rev 32:877–906

Binder SA (2003) Stalemate: causes and consequences of legislative gridlock. Brookings Institution Press

Binder SA (2015) The dysfunctional Congress. Annu Rev Polit Sci 18:85–101

Briffault R (this volume) The single-subject rule: uncertain solution for omnibus legislation. In: Bar-Siman-Tov I (ed) Comparative multidisciplinary perspectives on omnibus legislation. Springer, Cham

Chafetz J (2013) The phenomenology of gridlock. Notre Dame Law Rev 88:2065–2088

Chiou F-Y, Rothenberg LS (2007) Comparing legislators and legislatures: the dynamics of legislative gridlock reconsidered. Polit Anal 16:197–212

Dodek AM (2017) Omnibus bills: constitutional constraints and legislative liberations. Ottawa Law Rev 48:1–42

Dunn CW (2003) Playing by the rules: the need for constitutions to define the boundaries of the legislative game with a one-subject rule. UWLA Law Rev 35:129

Eskridge WN (2012) Vetogates and American public law. J Law Econ Organ 31:756–781

Gardbaum S (2020) Comparative political process theory. Int J Const Law 18

Gluck A (this volume) Unorthodox lawmaking and legislative complexity in American statutory interpretation. In: Bar-Siman-Tov I (ed) Comparative multidisciplinary perspectives on omnibus legislation. Springer, Cham

Gluck AR, O'Connell AJ, Po R (2015) Unorthodox lawmaking, unorthodox rulemaking. Columbia Law Rev 115:1789–1866

Hattis Rolef S (2006) The arrangements law: issues and international comparisons

Hattis Rolef S (this volume) Israel's economic arrangements law and similar omnibudget laws in other countries. In: Bar-Siman-Tov I (ed) Comparative multidisciplinary perspectives on omnibus legislation. Springer, Cham

Kosti N (this volume) Centralization via delegation: the long-term implications of the Israeli arrangements laws. In: Bar-Siman-Tov I (ed) Comparative multidisciplinary perspectives on omnibus legislation. Springer, Cham

Krutz GS (2001) Hitching a ride: omnibus legislating in the U.S. Congress. Ohio State University Press, Columbus

Krutz GS (this volume) Omnibus legislating in the U.S. Congress. In: Bar-Siman-Tov I (ed) Comparative multidisciplinary perspectives on omnibus legislation. Springer, Cham

Lupo N, Piccirilli G (this volume) Omnibus legislation and maxi-amendments in Italy: how to circumvent the constitutional provision requiring approval of bills 'Article by Article'. In: Bar-Siman-Tov I (ed) Comparative multidisciplinary perspectives on omnibus legislation. Springer, Cham

Mann TE, Ornstein NJ (2008) The Broken Branch: how Congress is failing America and how to get it back on track. Oxford University Press

Massicotte L (2013) Omnibus bills in theory and practice. Can Parliam Rev 36:13–17

Massicotte L (this volume) Canada: if controversial, omnibus legislation is here to stay. In: Bar-Siman-Tov I (ed) Comparative multidisciplinary perspectives on omnibus legislation. Springer, Cham

Meßerschmidt K (this volume) Omnibus legislation in Germany: a widespread yet understudied lawmaking practice. In: Bar-Siman-Tov I (ed) Comparative multidisciplinary perspectives on omnibus legislation. Springer, Cham

Meydani A (2008) Political entrepreneurs and electoral capital: the case of the Israeli state economy arrangement law. Const Polit Econ 19:301–312

Mousmouti M (2019) Designing effective legislation. Edward Elgar

Nahmias D, Klein E (1999) The economic arrangements bill: between economics and politics. Israel Democracy Institute

Navot S (2006) Judicial review of the legislative process. Isr Law Rev 39:182

Oliver-Lalana D (2016) On the (judicial) method to review the (legislative) method. Theory Pract Legis 4:135

Oliver-Lalana AD (this volume) Omnibus legislation in Spain: between political expediency, doctrinal condemnation, and judicial indulgence. In: Bar-Siman-Tov I (ed) Comparative multidisciplinary perspectives on omnibus legislation. Springer, Cham

Popelier P (2006) Mosaics of legal provisions. Eur J Law Reform 7:47–57

Popelier P (this volume) The practice of omnibus laws in Belgium: an empirical test. In: Bar-Siman-Tov I (ed) Comparative multidisciplinary perspectives on omnibus legislation. Springer, Cham

Rozenberg O (this volume) When rationalization of bureaucracy de-rationalizes laws and legislatures: 'Monster Bills' in France. In: Bar-Siman-Tov I (ed) Comparative multidisciplinary perspectives on omnibus legislation. Springer, Cham

Sinclair B (2016) Unorthodox lawmaking: new legislative processes in the U.S. Congress, 5th edn. CQ Press

Szabó Z (2020) Hungary. In: The cradle of laws: drafting and negotiating bills within the executives in Central Europe. Nomos, Baden-Baden, pp 85–105

Tsebelis G (1995) Decision making in political systems: Veto players in presidentialism, parliamentarism, multicameralism and multipartyism. Br J Polit Sci 25:289

Voermans W, ten Napel H-M, Diamant M et al (2012) Legislative processes in transition. Comparative study of the legislative processes in Finland, Slovenia and the United Kingdom as a source of inspiration for enhancing the efficiency of the Dutch legislative process. WODC/Ministry of Security and Justice, Leiden

Voermans W, ten Napel H-M, Passchier R (2015) Combining efficiency and transparency in legislative processes. Theory Pract Legis 3:279–294

Wiberg M (2009) Veto players in legislative games: fake and real. In: Ganghof S, Hönnige C, Stecker C (eds) Parlamente, Agendasetzung und Vetospieler. VS Verlag für Sozialwissenschaften, Wiesbaden, pp 41–51

Zamboni M (this volume) (Absence of) omnibus legislation in Sweden: when legislative drafting affects the political discourse. In: Bar-Siman-Tov I (ed) Comparative multidisciplinary perspectives on omnibus legislation. Springer, Cham

Zipper T, Dahan R (2020) To review, or not to review? A comparative perspective of judicial review over the legislative process. Indones J Int Comp Law 7:329–384

Ittai Bar-Siman-Tov, JSD, LLM (Columbia University), LLB (Hebrew University), is a Senior Lecturer (Associate Professor), Co-Director of the dual degree program in law and political science, and Head of the BIU LawData Lab, at Bar Ilan University Faculty of Law. He is also General Editor of the international journal *The Theory and Practice of Legislation*, and founding Co-Chair of the Israeli Association of Legislation.

Part I
Perspectives on Omnibus Legislation

Omnibus Legislating in the U.S. Congress

Glen S. Krutz

Abstract Scholars regard the proliferation of omnibus legislative packages as an important institutional change with various implications for democratic governance. After first considering the reasons why omnibus packages are employed in the U.S. Congress and the best way to measure omnibus legislating, this paper examines the aggregate trends in omnibus usage from 1948–2018 and the effect of omnibus usage on presidential-congressional relations. The trend data show an explosion of omnibus use in the U.S. national legislature from 1979–1996, followed by a contraction in omnibus use since that time. However, large bill usage continues and is especially robust around the annual budget reconciliation bill in Congress and there is a persistent incentive to use the technique to package many of the 12–14 U.S. appropriations bills together in larger measures. Unlike the apparent trend in other democratic systems, wherein the executive benefits disproportionately from omnibus usage to the detriment of the legislature, omnibus bills by and large benefit Congress more than the president. Within Congress, majority party members benefit more from their use than do minority party members. The discussion section explores the good and bad of the omnibus technique for American governance.

Keywords Omnibus legislation · Presidential-congressional relations · Party leaders · Divided government

G. S. Krutz (✉)
Department of Political Science, College of Arts and Sciences, Oklahoma State University, Stillwater, OK, USA
e-mail: gkrutz@okstate.edu

1 Introduction: Why Study Omnibus Bills?

Several scholars conclude that a major recent change in the legislative process is the development of omnibus legislation.[1] Omnibus bills are large measures with components from disparate policy areas. By focusing on one part of an omnibus bill that enjoys widespread support, party leaders (who assemble the bills) take attention away from more controversial items that face uncertainty either: (1) within Congress, or (2) at the president's desk. While generally considered a way to manage legislative uncertainty in an era of increasing fragmentation, omnibus legislating sacrifices member participation (these bills are typically fast-tracked and come up under a closed rule in the House) and increases party leader power at the expense of the standing committees. Members-at-large are seldom aware of the details contained in omnibus bills. When asked about the contents of the 1998 omnibus budget bill, Senator Robert Byrd (D-WV) replied: "Do I know what's in this bill? Are you kidding? No. Only God knows what's in this monstrosity."[2]

Others see omnibus bills in a positive light. Proponents argue that omnibus bills are a way to get things done in an otherwise impossible legislative process. "The only way you can get things through is to package them," said Rep. Barber B. Conable Jr., R-NY.[3] Legislative scholar Walter Oleszek argues that packaged bills are one way Congress "can develop coherent responses to public problems."[4] Through this lens, omnibus bills are indicative of the adaptive nature of congressional institutions to tough governing circumstances.

Despite intense and differing views on their value, omnibus bills have proliferated. Figures 1 and 2 demonstrate the move to omnibus legislating across the post-World War II period. Figure 1 shows the number of public laws per 2-year Congress from 1949–1994. Figure 2 displays the number of omnibus bills per Congress from 1949–1994. As these data bear out, there has been a decrease in raw numbers of statutory output beginning after the Great Society juxtaposed with an increased propensity to pass larger, bundled bills into law. The first modern use of the omnibus procedure was in 1950 and the omnibus technique was employed on a regular, increasing basis until the 1980s, when use increased dramatically. There was a slight decline and leveling-off in raw numbers of omnibus bills after the 99th Congress (1985–1986), but the omnibus technique is still employed much more in recent times than earlier in the post-World War II period.[5] In sum, the congressional currency has changed from large numbers of small statutes to fewer, but much larger public laws.

---

[1]Browne (1995), p. 45; Krutz (2001), p. 3; Mayhew (1991), p. 43; Oleszek (1996), p. 276; Sinclair (1997), p. 64.

[2]Hager (1998), A1.

[3]Tate (1982), p. 2383.

[4]Oleszek (1989), p. 285.

[5]This slight decline and leveling-off in raw numbers is somewhat misleading. Omnibus bills are indeed even larger after the mid-1980s than before.

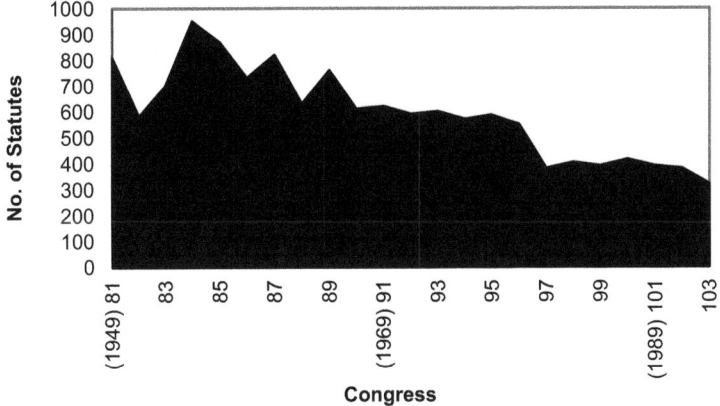

Fig. 1 Number of statutes per Congress, 1949–1994

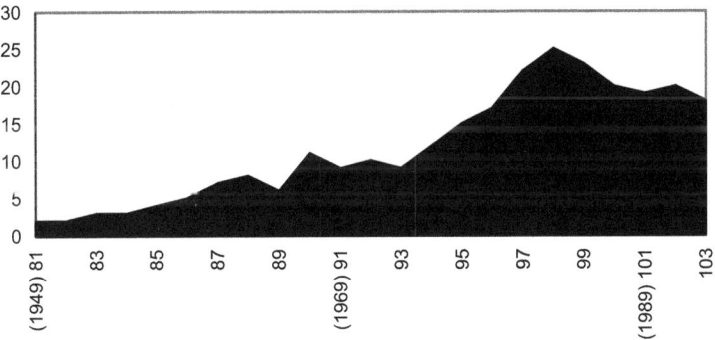

Fig. 2 Number of omnibus bills per Congress, 1949–1994

The move to omnibus legislating is particularly important because these packages present a viable alternative route for policy entrepreneurs pushing legislation. Omnibus packages invariably succeed. Hence, measures that become attached to them almost always become law. In contrast, the overwhelming majority of standard bills fail at some point in the legislative process. Of 3190 "seriously-considered" measures from 1979–1994, 16% (511) "hitched a ride on the omnibus," while 84% of legislative initiatives had to "go it alone" through the legislative gauntlet.[6] Of those hitching a ride, 98% became law.

In this chapter on the use of omnibus bills in the U.S. Congress, I will next discuss the theory of omnibus use, that is reasons or explanations for the use of bundled legislation. Then, I will consider how to measure their use over-time and discuss a method for assessing how their use affects presidential-congressional relations. I will

---

[6]Seriously considered measures are legislative initiatives (most of which are bills) receiving coverage in *Congressional Quarterly Almanac*.

follow with findings of a longitudinal analysis of omnibus use as well as a cross-sectional analysis of presidential-congressional relations. Finally, conclusions and implications will be considered.

2   Theory: Explaining Omnibus Use

Omnibus bills may take several forms, such as program reauthorizations, budget reconciliation bills, continuing appropriations legislation, or original bills. Omnibus bills are often fast-tracked through committees with less consideration than typical bills and once assembled by leaders in the pre-floor process, they are treated as one piece of legislation, thus seriously restricting the choices available to members on the floor. Rather than opting to accept or reject individual parts of the legislation, they must take or leave the entire package. "Large, complex bills, with many provisions. . . .also put rank-and-file members on the floor at a severe informational disadvantage."[7] Leaders, on the other hand, possess the critical and complex information on these measures and are strengthened by omnibus bills. "These are must-pass bills and only the party leadership possess the coordination capacity required to put together and pass such legislation."[8]

Comprehensive bills unifying diverse topics are not entirely new, and have always been subject to agenda manipulation. The use of riders by leaders has traditionally been an opportunity to move unpopular or ignored proposals through the legislative process while avoiding the need to construct coalitions in favor of the particular measure. By combining measures, the legislative leadership can force members to accept a measure than might not survive alone because they want the entire bill (or another part of it) to pass.

In recent times, however, rolling many measures into one bill has become more common, the resulting bills have spanned a greater number of diverse policy areas, and significant policy change has occurred through omnibus bills. Further, while riders are often attempted by members to kill legislative initiatives, omnibus bills are pursued in order to get something passed. The bigger bill has its own locus (or multiple loci) of attention and is more likely to have the broad support needed for passage. Omnibus bills are powerful in terms of focusing attention away from controversial items to other main items that enjoy widespread support and/or are seen as necessary.

There is another critical difference between traditional agenda control methods and omnibus bills. That is, while the ordering of alternatives and closed rules are strategies aimed at building a coalition within the Congress and feature a game played between leaders and members, omnibus bills introduce a second legislative game that is played between Congress and the president. Omnibus packages

---

[7]Smith (1989), p. 56.

[8]Sinclair (1992), p. 668.

typically attract the president's interest because of their prominence. Omnibus legislation may potentially be a congressional tool used to discourage presidential vetoes.[9] Presidents who favor one part of an omnibus bill are forced to sign a larger bill that includes provisions they find distasteful. These two games (between members and leaders and between Congress and the president) reflect the two major steps that bills must clear to be enacted as designed in the Constitution. Keith Krehbiel's pivotal politics theory of lawmaking[10] and David Brady and Craig Volden's revolving gridlock conception[11] similarly envision that two critical pivots exist in lawmaking: one within Congress (particularly the filibuster) and the other the presidential veto.

Omnibus bills provide one way to enact policies whose outcome in one or both of these two steps is doubtful or unclear. The following examples illustrate these dual purposes.

In 1982, several members and leaders sought to revive a dormant airport development program that had failed to be reauthorized in the previous Congress. The previous act expired in 1980. Lawmakers had failed in numerous prior attempts to bring the airport improvement act to the floor for two reasons. First, there was "...controversy over the program's direction."[12] Second, if considered alone, the bill was required to take a circuitous route because five House and four Senate committees had to be coordinated to secure such an airport development program.

To get the bill through the legislative process, Senate Majority Leader Robert Dole (R-Kan.) together with Commerce Committee Chairman Bob Packwood (R-Ore.) attached the measure to an omnibus tax bill with widespread support making its way through Congress. House leaders reciprocated by also later approving the attachment. Norman Mineta (D-CA), chairman of the House Public Works Aviation Subcommittee, said the procedure helped insulate the controversial airport measure: "Frankly, it was a good way to do it. We would otherwise have had contentious amendments offered." Several senators vehemently complained about the tactic.

Also in the 97th Congress, House leaders, Banking Committee leaders and members, and the president all favored approval of U.S. contributions to four international development banks. Realizing that this funding was controversial and that previous attempts had failed, the leaders attached this funding to the omnibus reconciliation bill. "Banking Committee members argued that bank funding—always an unpopular item on Capitol Hill—might not pass as separate legislation. Committee members argued, successfully, that the only way to get the bank measure through Congress was to attach it to legislation that was certain to be passed."[13] The

---

[9]Oleszek (1989), Sinclair (1997), and Smith (1989).

[10]Krehbiel (1991), ch. 1.

[11]Brady and Volden (1998), ch. 1.

[12]Sarasohn (1982), p. 2382.

[13]Congressional Quarterly (1982 [1980–1988]), p. 142.

Fig. 3 Theoretical
framework

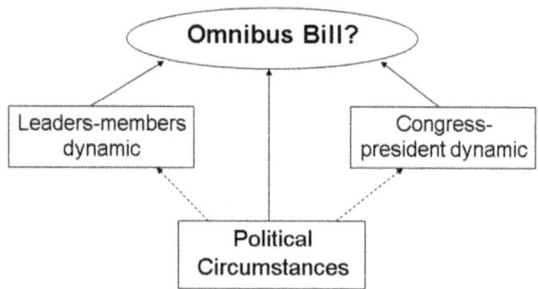

reconciliation bill subsequently passed overwhelmingly in both chambers and the
president signed it into law.

In 1985–1986, both chambers favored several items that President Reagan
publicly opposed.[14] These included reauthorization of the Small Business Administration, which Reagan had long sought to abolish, and several health care bills. In
the 99th Congress, leaders pursued another reauthorization of the Small Business
Administration. Reagan almost immediately promised to veto the bill. To get around
the specter of the presidential veto, congressional leaders in both chambers included
a multi-year reauthorization of the Small Business Administration in the omnibus
budget reconciliation bill. Reagan favored other major components of the omnibus
bill and, therefore, signed the bill into law even though it contained the Small
Business Administration measure.

In that same Congress (1985–1986), health care policy featured a strong disagreement between congressional leaders and the president. Reagan promised vetoes
of several individual bills related to child vaccinations and the Medicare program,
while favoring other established programs in the health care policy domain that were
being considered in the legislative process. To get the opposed programs by the
president, leaders packaged numerous bills into a large and complex omnibus health
measure. Expressing publicly major reservations about provisions in the bill, the
president nevertheless signed it.

I theorize that omnibus bills involve two dynamics that reflect the two-step flow
that bills must traverse to become law. One dynamic exists between congressional
leaders and members-at-large. A second dynamic involves the Congress and president. How does omnibus lawmaking help these strategic actors in achieving their
goals? Further, and particularly pertinent to our examination of the rise of omnibus
legislation, these two dynamics play out within unique governing contexts that may
change across time. Certain contexts place strain on congressional institutions and
make it more likely for actors to rely on non-traditional means of policymaking such
as omnibus legislating. Figure 3 presents a graphical outline of the basic framework.

---

[14]Congressional Quarterly (1987 [1980–1988]).

2.1   Leaders-Members

I focus first on the relationship between those with the resources to package bills (party leaders) and members-at-large. What do leaders and members have to gain from omnibus legislation? How are their goals advanced? Leaders gain more power with omnibus bills, and because they assemble omnibus bills, are afforded the opportunity to advance party agenda items. Both of these (more power and pushing an agenda) are principal goals of party leaders.

Why do members allow leaders to package bills? Members surrender the right to consider items one at a time so leaders can get legislative items passed that face uncertainty in the regular legislative process. In allowing packaging to occur, members are disadvantaged in three ways. First, they are giving the leaders a potent source of power to enact items. Second, in allowing leaders to package bills, members are giving up traditional channels of deliberation. On omnibus items, rank-and-file members seldom are included in the minutiae of lawmaking and have a severe informational disadvantage on the floor.[15] Third, omnibus bills are so vast, election opponents may potentially pick whatever part of an omnibus bill they want to hammer the incumbent in a campaign.

What do members gain while they are disadvantaged? After all, a bargain suggests that both sides benefit; what incentives do members have to allow omnibus packaging by leaders? Members are driven by many goals, but primarily by re-election and the desire to enact their policy preferences. In exchange for allowing packaged bills by leaders, members get in omnibus bills two major benefits that aid in achieving these over-arching goals of re-election and making public policy. These benefits help us to see why members accept the costs associated with omnibus use.

First, omnibus bills potentially aid the members' re-election chances. The omnibus mechanism in part serves the needs of incumbents through the use of distributive or pork-barrel politics. Members may put up with omnibus bills if the mechanism provides some distributive benefit that will aid re-election. Because omnibus bills nearly always succeed, members get a surefire way to get distributive items incorporated into omnibus bills that might be opposed if pursued sequentially.

Second, through the omnibus bill attachment process, members also get a potential vehicle for enacting policies they care about. Among other things (position-taking and credit claiming[16]), members want to get their bills passed. In institutions with large continuing agendas and therefore a scarcity of attention, members find it difficult to get their bills noticed and moved forward. The overwhelming majority of bills fail before getting a hearing.[17] One way to get around the traditional and extremely challenging typical legislative channels is to get your provision included in an omnibus bill. Leaders help in this regard because if members are re-elected, then their party retains majority status, a principal goal of leaders.

---

[15]Smith (1989) and Sinclair (1997).

[16]Mayhew (1974), ch. 1.

[17]Krutz (2005), p. 316.

2.2 Congress-President

A second omnibus bargain occurs between Congress and the president (really between congressional leaders and the president). What does the president gain? After all, one expectation above is that omnibus bills will include measures that the president opposes in order to avert a veto. Why does the president even participate in omnibus bargains? Why hold his nose and sign these measures into law? Why not just veto everything?

Presidents, too, want to enact their policy preferences. Beyond that assumption, the motivations of presidents in policymaking are less focused upon than the much-discussed motivations of members of Congress. First-term presidents surely want to get re-elected. Getting something done in policymaking may aid a president's re-election prospects (in the case of first-term presidents). There is also some indication that presidents care about their historical legacy. Enacting policies they prefer and promises they make may lead to a favorable historical rating of their presidency.

Presidents understand that our legislative institutions were designed to block items rather than enact policy. One important thing presidents can gain from omnibus bills is the possibility of having their own agenda items folded in as attachments to omnibus bills. This alternate route gets the president around having his bills go it alone in the legislative process and perhaps getting blocked. The president, like members of Congress, faces a presumption of failure for bills introduced in Congress. While more likely to succeed in the legislative process than a typical member of Congress, only one-fourth of presidential proposals are enacted into law in a form still recognizable to the president. In congressional committees, presidential drafts are less likely to move forward than legislation pushed by the given committee and sub-committee leaders.[18] Presidents, therefore, have something potentially very helpful to gain in omnibus bargains. Congress (in the form of the leaders and their members), on the other hand, is willing on occasion to incorporate the president's legislative items in order to avert a veto of items the Congress wants that are contained in omnibus bills.

2.3 Governing Circumstances

Party leaders, members-at-large, and the president operate under political circumstances, some of which complicate the legislative process. In such scenarios, it becomes particularly necessary to find a way to bring certainty and omnibus use is more likely. Circumstances that challenge the capabilities of our legislative institutions include deficit politics, divided party control, ripe conditions for minority obstructionism, issue complexity and committee fragmentation, and burgeoning

---

[18]Larocca (1995).

congressional workloads. These five factors break-up nicely into political explanations (divided government, ripe conditions for minority obstructionism), efficiency explanations (issue complexity and workload), and a hybrid of the two (deficit politics).

3   Measures and Findings: How Many Omnibus Bills?

Studying omnibus legislation in a systematic fashion requires first providing an operational definition and measure of omnibus legislation. No such definition currently exists. On a conceptual level, scholars offer similar sentiments of what constitutes "omnibus legislation." Sinclair summarizes the general thoughts of scholars well: "Legislation that addresses numerous and not necessarily related subjects, issues, and programs, and therefore is usually highly complex and long, is referred to as omnibus legislation."[19]

Omnibus bills are typically assembled in order to get something passed. The big bill has its own locus of attention and is more likely to have support from the important players in the legislative process. Omnibus bills are powerful in terms of focusing attention away from controversial items of certain substantive policy areas to other main items than enjoy widespread support and/or are necessary. The controversial items if considered alone are thought to face opposition within Congress or at the president's desk. Omnibus bills provide a way to get by the Congress and the president in enacting such policies; they provide greater certainty.[20] While many scholars have discussed omnibus bills conceptually, no agreed upon operational definition exists.

What are the options for defining omnibus bill? One option is to use the name of the bill. However, this is problematic. The term "omnibus" may potentially be used arbitrarily. At the introduction stage of the process, members of Congress may call a bill whatever they choose. They may simply label a bill "omnibus" to make it sound more important. Moreover, several omnibus bills do not have the word omnibus in their title, like certain budget reconciliation bills and continuing appropriations measures.

This state of affairs poses a challenge. Relying on political observers to identify omnibus legislation could lead to substantial error, since they report what the bill was called rather than relying on a precise definition. It also points to the need for the development of a reliable measure of omnibus legislation.

I choose to take an alternative route to simply using the name of the bill. I seek to provide a behavioral definition of omnibus that follows from the concept. Omnibus bills differ from typical major bills in their *scope* (number of substantive policy areas

---

[19]Sinclair (1997), p. 64.
[20]Bach and Smith (1988), ch. 1.

spanned), in their *size*, and following from scope and size, in their *complexity*. My definition captures the key attributes of scope and size.

Omnibus Bill: *any piece of major legislation that: (1) spans three or more major-topic policy areas OR ten or more sub-topic policy areas, AND (2) is greater than the mean plus one standard deviation of major bills in size.*

This definition requires further explanation of major legislation, major-topic policy area, sub-topic policy area, and size. Defining *major legislation* provides a group of bills from which to isolate the omnibus bills. Defining *major topic and sub-topic policy area* provides one of the tools to distinguish omnibus bills from other major bills by ascertaining how many policy areas they span. The other tool for distinguishing omnibus bills from other major bills is the *size* of the bill.

Major Legislation Omnibus bills are quite prominent. Hence, we expect to find them in the list of important bills compiled regularly in *Congressional Quarterly Weekly Report* and to receive prominent coverage in annual editions of *CQ Almanac*. Several scholars have utilized these sources to identify samples of important bills for analysis.[21] The *CQ Almanac* has featured consistent coverage since 1948. *CQ Weekly Report*, on the other hand, has varied in title and length.

I use a two-pronged approach to get a list of major bills from which to classify omnibus bills. First, I utilize the top ten percent of covered bills in *CQ Almanac* from the Baumgartner and Jones dataset.[22] Second, I check that list of bills against the same list from *CQ Weekly Report* that Sinclair used to identify major bills in her study of unorthodox lawmaking (about 50 per Congress).[23] If *CQ Weekly* contains bills not in the top ten percent of *CQ Almanac* bills, I also include those bills (only a few such cases). This procedure yields 1180 major bills from 1949–1994 (an average of 51 per Congress).

Major-Topic and Sub-topic Policy Area I utilize a recent topic coding scheme of major policy areas and sub-topics that gets us to a consistent level of analysis in which important political actors discuss matters of public policy. This coding system is the 19 area major topic and 228 sub-topic coding scheme of Baumgartner and Jones used in their studies of all congressional hearings and statutes since World War II.[24] This topic coding scheme proceeds by substance, rather than by typology of policy "types". In discussing the omnibus change conceptually, scholars have been consistent in arguing that a major difference of these bills from typical bills is that

---

[21]Edwards et al. (1997), pp. 545–563; Sinclair (1997), p. 8; Taylor (1998), pp. 373–398.

[22]As part of their Policy Agendas Project, Baumgartner and Jones coded information on every story in annual editions of *CQ Almanac* from 1948–1994 (Baumgartner et al. 1997). These data are available at: http://weber.u.washington.edu/~ampol/agendasproject.html.

[23]Sinclair (1997), p. 8.

[24]Baumgartner et al. (1998), p. 3.

they span numerous substantive policy areas. Therefore, the substantive policy scheme of Baumgartner and Jones provides a good fit.[25]

This topic coding scheme has face validity because it covers the major areas of policy considered in American politics. Further, in coding all congressional hearings and statutes in the period since the second World War, these areas lead to homogenous groupings at the major topic level and particularly at the sub-topic level, an argument for empirical validity.

In studying the major bills to identify those that are omnibus measures (which consisted of reading legislative summaries and histories of each), I looked for the number of different substantive major policy areas and sub-topic areas they spanned. Those spanning three or more major policy areas OR ten or more sub-topic policy areas met one of the necessary conditions to be included in my population of omnibus bills.

Size The second condition to be met for omnibus classification is size. I measured size as the number of words in each of the bills from LEGI-SLATE (when it was solvent), publications of Congressional Quarterly, or the relevant sections of the *United States Code* for those major bills becoming law. Major bills clearing one standard deviation above the mean length of major bills met the size requirement. This procedure yielded 242 omnibus bills of the 1180 major bills from 1949–1994. The trends in omnibus bill employment are displayed in Fig. 2.

To bring this analysis into the twenty-first century, I utilized data from the Comparative Agendas project. I worked on this research project and helped determine the original methodology to code omnibus bills from the pages of Congressional Quarterly. Thus, while the measures are slightly different from those above, they are quite similar and an efficient way to follow omnibus trends into the twenty-first century.

This updated time series of omnibus usage, while somewhat variant from my original project, shows similar trends early in the series. Moreover, utilizing these freely-accessible data allows us to see trends into the twenty-first century. Figure 4 shows the trends in omnibus usage with this particular measure.

The trend data show an explosion of omnibus use in the U.S. national legislature from 1979–1996, followed by a contraction in omnibus use since that time.

---

[25]The major areas of the Baumgartner and Jones topic coding scheme are:

Macroeconomics   Civil Rights and Liberties, Minority Issues
Health   Agriculture
Labor, Employment, and Immigration   Education
Environment   Energy
Transportation   Law, Crime, and Family Issues
Social Welfare   Community Development and Housing
Banking, Finance, and Commerce   Defense
Foreign Trade   Space/Science, Technology, Communication
International Affairs and Foreign Aid   Government Operations
Public Lands and Water Management
Underneath each of these major-topic areas are numerous sub-topic areas.

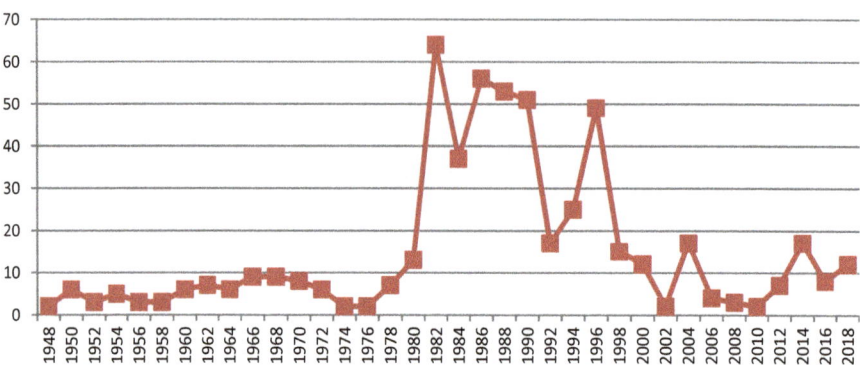

Fig. 4 Number of omnibus bills per Congress

However, large bill usage continues and is especially robust around the annual budget reconciliation bill in Congress and there is a persistent incentive to use the technique to package many of the 12–14 U.S. appropriations bills together in larger measures.

Another interesting way to study the impact of omnibus bills is to examine their effect on presidential power vis-à-vis the Congress. Should we expect omnibus bills to be more a presidential tool or a congressional tool compared to typical major bills? The Congress-president omnibus dynamic is a bargain in which both sides potentially benefit. Congressional leaders incorporate items that might be vetoed by the president if considered sequentially. In exchange, the president benefits by gaining an opportunity to have his agenda items incorporated. Such a conceptualization suggests some balance or shared power in omnibus lawmaking; the branches need one another. This is not entirely unexpected in a system of separated branches sharing power.[26]

But, which of the branches gets more out of omnibus bills than the other? Working from theory, rather than from conventional wisdom, let us ponder this. If you were the president, in what manner would you prefer for ten bills to arrive at the White House from Capitol Hill? Assume that eight of the bills the president favors and two bills the president opposes. You would rather see the ten bills in turn (sequentially) so that you could sign the eight you like and veto the two you dislike. On traditional bills, therefore, it is easy to understand why vetoes and veto threats are such powerful weapons for a president.

However, if you received a massive omnibus bill with all ten measures incorporated, you have to think about accepting provisions you dislike in order to get something you really want. It is important to note that decisions on the final form that legislation will take ultimately reside with the Congress. In bundled bills, the president—even if he obtains some of the items he desires—may have to sign measures he dislikes to get what he wants. Therefore, a veto comes at a high cost

---

[26]Jones (1994), p. 17; Neustadt (1960), ch. 1; Peterson (1990), ch. 1.

because the president would be vetoing some items he really favors. In sum, contrary to the conventional wisdom, theory predicts omnibus bills to be more a congressional tool than a presidential tool, and shared lawmaking to be the most likely state of affairs.

To test the question of whether omnibus bills are more a congressional tool or a presidential tool, I used *CQ Almanac* to build a legislative history for each omnibus budget bill and each typical major budget bill from 1979–2002. There were 115 omnibus bills in this period and 136 typical major budget bills (which includes successes and failures like Chamberlain).

In studying these bills, I paid careful attention to the presidential-congressional interaction. Jones, in particular, shared in some detail how he went about studying the bills in his sample and how he determined in which category they belonged. I followed his lead wherever possible in hopes of making replication of my work a possibility. Specifically, Jones mentioned several telltale signs of presidential-preponderance, congressional preponderance, and shared lawmaking. I followed these tips quite closely; hence, I share them here.

Presidential preponderant bills include instances "when an issue is accepted as sufficiently vital to require bipartisan support for an administration plan. When that occurs, congressional support follows. Neither Congress nor the opposition party forgoes it prerogatives, but all sides have reason to work with the administration."[27] Other regular instances of presidential preponderance include instances "when presidents are entrusted with a mandate and therefore normal presidential-congressional politics is suspended."[28]

The initiative for congressional preponderant legislation often comes primarily from Capitol Hill, not the White House. "The president was essentially an observer for much of this legislation--an active monitor, to be sure, but hardly serving as leader or manager of the lawmaking process."[29] And, while presidential-preponderant bills often followed a more or less standard sequence, Congress-preponderant acts show considerable variation in sequence.

The shared lawmaking category includes "enactments that reflect more balanced participation in lawmaking by the White House and Congress."[30] Given that our lawmaking system by design requires laws to have the blessing of both branches, it is not surprising that this was the modal category in Jones' study.

Table 1 displays branch preponderance by type of bill (omnibus or typical major bill). This table demonstrates that lawmaking on both types of bills features much joint action. Shared lawmaking describes 63% of major bills and about 70% of omnibus bills. For the remaining bills, there is a distinct difference between typical major bills and omnibus bills. On typical bills, presidential preponderance occurs 29% of the time and congressional preponderance only 7%. For omnibus bills, the

---

[27]Jones (1994), p. 212.

[28]Ibid, p. 212.

[29]Ibid, p. 222.

[30]Ibid, p. 226.

Table 1 Preponderance by type of budgetary bill, 1979–2002

Institutional preponderance	Bill type			
	Typical major		Omnibus	
	%	(N)	%	(N)
Congress	7.4	(10)	20.0	(23)
Shared	63.2	(86)	69.6	(80)
President	29.4	(40)	10.4	(12)
Totals	100.0	(136)	100.0	(115)
$\chi^2 = 18.79$*** (2 d.f.)				

Source: Compiled by author
***p < 0.001

results are quite different. Presidential preponderance occurs only on 10% of cases, while congressional preponderance occurs 20% of the time. The relationship between type of bill and branch preponderance is statistically significant in a two-way chi-square test ($\chi^2 = 18.70$, p < 0.001).

It appears that Congress gets its way on omnibus bills more than the president, at least in comparison to the control group of typical major bills. It is also interesting to note that I find more presidential preponderant bills relative to congressional preponderant bills in the typical major bills category than Jones. This discrepancy is largely due to the fact that Jones analyzed only successes, while I consider both successes and failures. Some of the bills exhibiting presidential preponderance were failures in which the president exercised the veto or a veto threat to block major legislation he disliked (this finding is consistent with results in Edwards, Barrett, and Peake[31]). By excluding failures, Jones missed cases of presidential preponderance. Chamberlain examined both passed and failed major bills, and for the 1931–1940 time frame found a similar breakdown of preponderance to that observed here (more presidential preponderance relative to congressional preponderance than Jones).

The results were also analyzed by presidential administration. The overall finding from Table 1 that lawmaking is mostly shared with more presidential preponderance on typical bills and more congressional preponderance on omnibus bills holds across most administrations. One notable exception is the first Reagan administration (1981–1984), only the first 2 years of which featured Reagan leading on omnibus bills (and prompted the conventional wisdom that presidents dominate on omnibus bills). Suffice to say that the overall finding for the first Reagan Administration is that there is no difference in the two distributions.

Table 2 divides the first Reagan Administration (1981–1984) into two Congresses for separate analysis. In so doing, the table demonstrates that the 1983–1984 Reagan omnibus experience is quite similar to the general finding in Table 1. Budget-making is mostly shared with more congressional preponderance on omnibus bills. The 1981–1982 Reagan scenario is different in that Reagan led more on omnibus bills than did the Congress. It was in this Congress that Reagan successfully moved his

---

[31]Edwards et al. (1997), p. 557.

Table 2 Preponderance on omnibus budget bills, 1st Reagan Administration

Institutional preponderance	1981–1982		1983–1984	
	%	(N)	%	(N)
Congress	16.7	(2)	27.3	(3)
Shared	58.3	(7)	63.6	(7)
President	25.0	(3)	9.1	(1)
Totals	100.0	(12)	100.0	(11)

Source: Compiled by author

economic agenda in omnibus bills. That experience started the conventional wisdom.

In successive sessions of Congress, however, President Reagan learned to dislike the omnibus technique. Congressional leaders used the packages to push through measures the president opposed, such as several health care changes and reauthorizations for the Small Business Administration and the Department of Education.[32] In his final State of the Union address in 1988, Reagan declared: "Congress shouldn't send another one of these (omnibus budgetary acts). No, and if you do, I will not sign it."[33] Reagan signed five omnibus bills into law that year.

4 Conclusion and Discussion

What are the normative implications of the findings of this paper? What are the costs and benefits of doing business aboard an omnibus? What is the value of omnibus legislation?

There are clearly drawbacks of omnibus legislation. This technique alters law-making in important ways. Omnibus use potentially changes many critical concepts and relationships in American politics, including the member-constituent relationship and the proper level of deliberation on legislation.

Omnibus bills cloud the pathways of representation and affect democratic accountability. Because of their size and complexity, these packages make it less clear to constituents where members of Congress stand on the important issues of the day. They potentially dissolve what Doug Arnold calls the "causal chain" between members and constituents. Members can choose which of many parts of an omnibus bill with which to call attention to explain their vote. Challengers, too, can pick particular parts of omnibus bills with which to hammer their election opponent.

This technique changes the deliberative process. Omnibus bills are often fast-tracked through committees with fewer hearings and less mark-up consideration than would be expected from several important standard bills. Once assembled in the pre-floor process, they are treated as one piece of legislation, thus seriously

---

[32]Congressional Quarterly, Inc. (1980–1988).

[33]U.S. Government Printing Office (1989), p. 86.

restricting the choices available to members on the floor. In sum, there are drawbacks to omnibus lawmaking in terms of democratic theory.

On the other hand, there are many benefits of omnibus legislation. First among these is the potential to get things done in the legislative process by managing uncertainty. Omnibus bills provide a way to enact policies that might not make it alone. They provide a way to circumvent the pressures of deficit politics and issue complexity, the gridlock of divided government, and the gridlock of committee jurisdiction fragmentation. They appear to strengthen, rather than weaken, the legislature vis-à-vis the executive. In this regard, at least in the US case, omnibus bills tell a collective story of successful strategic-level and institutional adaptation to challenging circumstances.

References

Bach S, Smith SS (1988) Managing uncertainty in the house of representatives: adaptation and innovation in special rules, Ch. 1. The Brookings Institution, Washington

Baumgartner FR, Jones BD, Krutz GS, Rosenstiehl MC (1997) Trends in the production of legislation, 1949–1994. Paper presented at the American Political Science Association meetings, Washington

Baumgartner FR, Jones BD, MacLeod MC (1998) New issues and old committees: jurisdictional change in Congress, 1947–1993. Paper presented at the Midwest Political Science Association meetings, Chicago, April 1998

Brady DW, Volden C (1998) Revolving gridlock: politics and policy from Carter to Clinton. Westview, Boulder

Browne WP (1995) Cultivating Congress: constituents, issues, and interests in agricultural policymaking. University Press of Kansas, Lawrence

Congressional Quarterly, Inc., Congressional Quarterly Almanac, 1980–1988. Congressional Quarterly, 1981–1989 annually, Washington

Edwards GC, Barrett A, Peake JS (1997) The legislative impact of divided government. Am J Polit Sci 41:545–563

Hager G (1998) House passes spending bill. The Washington Post, 21 October 1998, sec. A, p 1

Jones CO (1994) The presidency in a separated system. Brookings, Washington

Krehbiel KK (1991) Information and legislative organization. University of Michigan Press, Ann Arbor

Krutz GS (2001) Hitching a ride: omnibus legislating in the U.S. Congress. Ohio State University Press, Columbus

Krutz GS (2005) Issues and institutions: 'Winnowing' in the U.S. Congress. Am J Polit Sci 49:313–326

Larocca R (1995) Measuring presidential influence on the congressional agenda. Paper presented at the Midwest Political Science Association meetings, Chicago

Mayhew DR (1974) Congress: the electoral connection. Yale University Press, New Haven

Mayhew DR (1991) Divided we govern. Yale University Press, New Haven

Neustadt R (1960) Presidential power. Wiley, New York

Oleszek WJ (1989) Congressional procedures and the policy process, 3rd edn. Congressional Quarterly Press, Washington, DC

Oleszek WJ (1996) Congressional procedures and the policy process, 4th edn. Congressional Quarterly, Washington

Peterson MA (1990) Legislating together. Harvard University Press, Cambridge

Sarasohn J (1982) Airport program slipped into tax bill. Congressional Q Weekly Rep 40(39, Sept. 25):2382–2383

Sinclair B (1992) The emergence of strong leadership in the 1980s house of representatives. J Polit 54:657–684

Sinclair B (1997) Unorthodox lawmaking: new legislative processes in the U.S. Congress. Congressional Quarterly, Washington, p 64

Smith SS (1989) Call to order: floor politics in the house and senate. The Brookings Institution, Washington

Tate D (1982) Use of omnibus bills burgeons despite members' misgivings. Congressional Quarterly Weekly Report 25:2379–2383

Taylor A (1998) Domestic agenda-setting, 1947–1994. Legis Stud Q 22:373–398

U.S. Government Printing Office, Public Papers of the Presidents of the United States, 1988 (1989) United States Government Printing Office, Washington, DC

Glen S. Krutz   is the Dean of the College of Arts and Sciences at Oklahoma State University. He is also a Professor of Political Science and the holder of the Puterbaugh Foundation Endowed Chair. He previously served on the faculty at the University of Oklahoma and Arizona State University. Dr. Krutz is the author of Hitching a Ride: Omnibus Legislating in the U.S. Congress (2001, Ohio State University Press). He holds a Ph.D. from Texas A&M University and B.A. and MPA degree from the University of Nevada, Reno.

Omnibus Legislation and Maxi-Amendments in Italy: How to Circumvent the Constitutional Provision Requiring Approval of Bills 'Article by Article'

Nicola Lupo and Giovanni Piccirilli

Abstract The chapter analyzes, with reference to the Italian legal order, the main forms of omnibus legislation (budget legislation and decree-laws) and the practice of maxi-amendments, namely long and heterogeneous amendments approved by a unique parliamentary vote tied to a question of confidence posed by the Government. It highlights the reasons for their success, due to the features of the political and institutional system, as well as their downsides, in terms of the quality of both the parliamentary process and the legislation so approved. It also addresses the latest developments in the parliamentary practices and in the case law of the Constitutional Court, which is seeking to establish some limits on the abuses of these instruments and to revamp the potential of the constitutional provision pursuant to which legislative bills need to be approved "article by article" (Art. 72 Const.).

Keywords Decree-Law · Maxi-amendments · Question of confidence · Article · Budget bill

1 Introduction

Omnibus legislation has been rather frequent in the Italian legal order and took several different shapes: from "omnibudget bills" (called "leggi finanziarie", "leggi di stabilità", and "leggi di bilancio", depending on the legislative framework in force) to "omnibus decree-laws", adopted by the Government and becoming even more heterogeneous when converted into law by the Parliament in the following 60 days. The advantages of a unique bill containing unrelated measures are indeed particularly evident within a political and institutional system in which legislative

N. Lupo (✉) · G. Piccirilli
Center for Parliamentary Studies at LUISS Guido Carli, University of Rome, Rome, Italy
e-mail: nlupo@luiss.it; gpiccirilli@luiss.it

© The Author(s), under exclusive license to Springer Nature Switzerland AG 2021   53
I. Bar-Siman-Tov (ed.), *Comparative Multidisciplinary Perspectives on Omnibus Legislation*, Legisprudence Library 8, https://doi.org/10.1007/978-3-030-72748-2_3

processes are traditionally long and tiresome, and Executives are supported by heterogeneous parliamentary majorities.

During the first 40 years of the Italian Republic, the phenomenon was markedly less significant. At that time, most of the legislation comprised micro and homogeneous bills, entirely drafted and approved by parliamentary standing committees, where the consensual dynamics of the party system and the absence of strict budgetary constraints broadly allowed practices of "logrolling". Consequently, the scope of each bill remained predominantly within the jurisdiction of a single committee, with the effect of giving rise to an extremely high number of laws, which were very sectoral and internally homogeneous. Once this form of legislation reduced rather abruptly from 1993, following the renovation of the party system and the severe restriction of budgetary constraints,[1] omnibus legislation—both as "omnibus decree-laws" and "omnibudget bills"—has increased, independently from the features of the governing Executive and its parliamentary majority.

Additionally, the practice of maxi-amendments is very revealing with respect to the functioning of the Italian democracy in recent decades. Maxi-amendments are long and heterogeneous proposals for amendment, aimed at substituting the whole text of a bill, by virtue of which the Executive poses a question of confidence (i.e. linking its own destiny to Parliament's vote, which in effect becomes a vote of confidence), thereby resulting in "take-it-or-leave-it" roll-call votes on such bills. It is a practice that, despite having emerged in the 1950s, has spread over the last 25 years, clearly circumventing the constitutional provision pursuant to which every bill should be examined and approved "article by article", prior to the vote on its final text (Art. 72 Const.). The outcome is a legislative text comprising only one maxi-article, divided into hundreds of sub-sections (the record is 1364), whose proponents and supporters are often unknown, as they are only voted for as a whole. This practice, which ends up being convenient for most of the political actors, has been allowed by the Speakers of the two Houses and, initially, even by the Constitutional Court (judgment no. 391/1995).

In the last few years, however, there have been some reactions to the use of this practice by both the Presidents of the Republic and the Constitutional Court. Moreover, some more limited rethinking of the parliamentary practice has taken place.

To limit the omnibus decree-laws and their conversion laws, the Constitutional Court, over the course of the last decade, has highlighted the restrictions on the amendments that can be inserted by the Parliament into a bill converting a decree-law, and has declared unconstitutional some of the clearest examples of this bad practice. The principles underpinning this new trend in the case law were outlined in judgment no. 22/2012, and concrete developments have been evident in subsequent decisions nos. 32/2014 and 247/2019. For their part, the Speakers of the two Houses,

---

[1]On the concentration of the various factors, endogenous and exogenous to the political system, that led to a complete renovation of the Italian political and institutional dynamics in 1993, see Manzella (2003), pp. 7 ff.

and especially of the Senate, mostly continue to declare admissible amendments to the conversion bills that have a limited connection with the contents of the decree-law to which they refer. However, a more restrictive approach has been adopted in some cases, although without completely overturning the previous practice.

Furthermore, the Constitutional Court, in an important decision (order no. 17/2019)—while declaring inadmissible the action against the procedure followed in the Senate to approve, by a maxi-amendment, the 2019 budget bill—stated that the procedural steps set out by Art. 72 Const., including the approval of bills "article by article", must always be respected. In the same judgment, the Court explicitly recognized, for the first time, the possibility for single members of Parliament to raise a conflict of attribution before the Constitutional Court, although only in cases of "manifest violations of the constitutional prerogatives of the members of Parliament".

In order to analyze these two phenomena, this chapter is organized as follows. After a brief reminder of the main features of the Italian party system and legislative activity (par. 2), the subsequent two paragraphs are devoted to omnibus bills, separately considering their procedural origins, as well as their application to decree-laws (par. 3) and financial legislation (par. 4): examining, in both cases, the evolution of legislative practice and, especially for the decree-laws, the case-law of the Constitutional Court. Then, a paragraph (par. 5) is devoted to maxi-amendments and the question of confidence, illustrating the peculiar procedural features that have led to majorities making intensive use of these instruments over the last thirty years. A further paragraph (par. 6) is specifically dedicated to the already mentioned, and much discussed, order no. 17/2019 of the Constitutional Court and to possible future developments of the its oversight of the way in which constitutional provisions regarding the legislative process are respected. Finally, a concluding paragraph (par. 7) summarizes the reasons for the success of these procedural mechanisms within the Italian legal order.

2 The Features of the Party Systems and the Main Trends in Italian Legislation

The high level of instability of Italian governments is renowned. The fragmented party system, characterised as a "polarized pluralism",[2] combined with the deliberate choice of the Constituent Assembly to avoid any possibility of repeating the undemocratic drift of the fascist regime (also having regard to the extreme uncertainty of the outcome of the 1948 elections),[3] has led to the establishment of a parliamentary form of government with only marginal elements of rationalization.

---

[2]Sartori (1976).

[3]On the so-called "complesso del tiranno", see Pasquino (2015), pp. 23 ff.

This constitutional context, which has necessitated and encouraged the formation of multi-party coalition Governments, was further boosted by the impossibility of overturning the majority and the opposition. Due to its international connections, the Italian Communist party was considered unfit to be part of the Government, at least until the 1980s (*"conventio ad excludendum"*).[4] However, the Communist party fully took part in the Constituent phase, actively participating in the agreement and compromise of the drafting and approval of the Republican 1947 Constitution.[5] Moreover, during the first few decades of the Republic, constitutional choices were viewed as a continuation of that phase, and major reforms to the implementing steps of the new Constitution were subject to the same wide agreement.

Furthermore, the legislation and parliamentary activity at that time were generally largely consensual or even consociational. The practice of logrolling became the rule, via the exploitation of a minor tool foreseen by the Constitution: art. 72 allows parliamentary committees to pass laws in almost any policy area, without the need for a further vote by the plenary, upon the condition of almost unanimous political support.[6] This has provided the means by which the majority of legislation was enacted during the 1950–1970s, with micro-private members' bills being reciprocally supported by almost the entire political spectrum. According to this logic, the scope of each bill remained predominantly within the jurisdiction of a single parliamentary committee, with the effect of giving rise to an extremely high number of laws, which were very sectoral and internally homogeneous (at least most of them, called "leggine").[7]

A significant transformation took place at the beginning of the 1990s, not coincidentally soon after the fall of the Berlin wall, which signposted the end of the *"conventio ad excludendum"*, and after the signature of the Maastricht Treaty, on February 1992, which established quantitative limits on the expansion of public debt and budget deficits. In the face of the so-called 'Bribesville' ('Tangentopoli') scandal, the political system revealed itself to be unsustainable and had to undergo

---

[4]Elia (1970).

[5]Significantly, the signatures on the Italian Constitution are by a Christian Democrat (De Gasperi, President of the Council of Ministers), a Communist (Terracini, Speaker of the Constituent Assembly), a Liberal (Grassi, Minister of Justice), and a Monarchist (De Nicola, provisional Head of State).

[6]According to Art. 72.3 Const., parliamentary rules of procedure may "establish when and how the consideration and approval of bills may be referred to Committees, including Standing Committees, composed so as to reflect the proportion of the Parliamentary Groups. Even in such cases, until the moment of its final approval, a bill may be referred back to the whole House, if the Government or one-tenth of the members of the House or one-fifth of the Committee request that it be debated and voted on by the House itself or that it be submitted to the House for final approval, following explanations of the vote. The Rules shall establish the ways in which the proceedings of Committees are made public". According to Art. 72.4, however, "The ordinary procedure for consideration and direct approval by the House is always followed in the case of bills on constitutional and electoral matters, delegating legislation, ratification of international treaties and the approval of budgets and accounts": see Fasone (2012).

[7]Predieri (1963).

widescale change, via two abrogative referendums (in 1991 and 1993, respectively), of the electoral law: moving from a proportional system to a mainly majoritarian one. One of the primary consequences of the shift in the electoral legislation was to anticipate the formation of political coalitions during the pre-electoral phase, in order to enhance the prospects of winning the single-member constituencies. This led to political coalitions which were even more heterogeneous, established in order to win the elections but not to run the government.

After the 1994 elections, a sort of earthquake hit the political system: none of the original political parties, on which the Republic had been established, survived. The consociational dynamics were replaced by a deeply divided political spectrum, polarized by the figure of Berlusconi.[8] In the field of legislative activity, this "earthquake" signalled the substantial end of the massive approval of legislation directly by parliamentary committees and, concurrently, the growth of the normative role of the Government, especially through the use of decree-laws and delegated legislation.

In any case, throughout the whole Italian Republican history, the majority supporting the Government has always been heterogenous and conflictual. This element, together with the weak rationalization of the parliamentary government in the Constitution, helps to explain the appeal, and the reasons for the success, of different forms of "omnibus legislation" and "maxi-amendments": mechanisms aimed—respectively—at ensuring a fast-track path to varied provisions, each of which was promoted and supported by different parts of the majority (and some even by the opposition), and which aimed to keep the parliamentary majority united in the subsequent phases of its parliamentary path.

The aforementioned dynamics in party politics fostered a self-restraint within the Constitutional Court, especially during the first four decades following the commencement of its operation, in 1956, from intervening in, and sanctioning, deviations from the parliamentary process. The necessary autonomy of politics from external legal scrutiny has been acknowledged since the very first years of the Court's activity.

In its seminal, and still valid, judgment no. 9/1959, the Constitutional Court limited the scope of its jurisdiction to constitutional provisions regarding the legislative process, thereby affirming its inability to enter into the interpretation of the parliamentary rules of procedure. This position was later refined, in particular in the 1980s, with decisions in which the Court declared the inadmissibility of questions of constitutionality related to parliamentary rules of procedure and, in general, confirming the necessity of preserving parliamentary autonomy as guaranteed by the Constitution itself (see especially judgment no. 154/1985).

With the reshuffle of the political system in 1994 and the renovation of the general principles underpinning it, the Court was asked to play a different and

---

[8]On the role of Berlusconi in determining both majority and opposition coalitions, see Colarizi and Gervasoni (2012). More generally on the impact of Berlusconi, his "premises" and his heritage in Italian politics, see Orsina (2014).

more active role, consisting not only in striking down the pre-republican legislation which was not fully compliant with the Constitution, but also in solving inter-institutional conflicts that the weaker political parties were no longer able to avoid. In this new context, the Court started to tighten its scrutiny of decree-laws (see *infra*, next paragraph) and launched, initially, some warnings regarding the autonomy of parliament. The clearest warning was embedded in judgment no. 379/1996, in which the Court, while confirming the autonomy of each House of Parliament in adopting and interpreting its rules of procedure, as well as in anticipating and applying sanctions for the misconduct of its members (in that case, MPs voting for themselves as well as on behalf of other colleagues), denounced the risk for the Parliament to have a negative effect on the perception of its legitimacy in the face of the public opinion.

3   The Omnibus Decree-Laws and Their Even More Heterogeneous Conversion Laws, in Light of the Constitutional Court's Case Law

The first kind of "omnibus legislation", and possibly the most relevant to be considered, is "omnibus decree-laws" (*decreti-legge "omnibus"*).

Decree-laws are Governmental decrees that, according to Art. 77 Const., the Government may adopt "in extraordinary cases of necessity and urgency", which have the force of law. They are explicitly defined by the Constitution as "provisional", because, after being approved by the Council of Ministers, they are enacted by the President of the Republic and immediately transmitted to one of the two Houses, to be converted into law by the Parliament, within 60 days of enactment. If the conversion does not occur by this deadline, the decree-laws shall lapse and retrospectively lose their effects ("*ex tunc*"). The two Houses have the power to amend the decree-law and, if they want to convert it into law, they must complete the process by approving the conversion law, in the same terms, within 60 days.

Notwithstanding all the precautions inserted into Article 77 Const., the use of decree-laws has been rather extensive since the beginning, and has progressively increased, particularly accelerating during the 1970s and the 1990s. Instead of exceptional measures to be taken in extraordinary circumstances, they were often conceived (by the Government) and perceived (by the Parliament) as a kind of "reinforced legislative initiative",[9] open to amendments and additions. In other words, the "necessity and urgency" mentioned by Article 77 have primarily been considered to be of a merely political nature, especially in light of the reference to the "responsibility" of the Government under which such measures are taken. This also explains why, in several cases, the two Houses did not complete the conversion within 60 days, thereby permitting the decree-law to lapse (with *ex tunc* effects, as already clarified). When this happened, the Government usually decided to

---

[9]Predieri (1975).

systematically re-adopt the same decree-law on the very day the previous one lapsed, normally also taking into account any amendments approved during the parliamentary examination. This practice, called the "reiteration" of decree-laws, became extremely common in the 1990s: it suffices to note that the same decree-law was reiterated more than 20 times, thereby maintaining its effects for around 4 years! And the rhythm of enacting decree-laws—including their reiterations—dramatically increased, reaching an average of more than one per day.

However, the practice of reiteration ceased, as the Constitutional Court declared it to be inconsistent with Article 77 Const. (judgment no. 360/1996). According to the Court, in fact, the reiteration: (a) "alters the provisional nature of decree-laws, *de facto* postponing the peremptory deadline"; (b) reduces the value of the extraordinary character of the pre-requisites of necessity and urgency; and (c) weakens the sanction of the retrospective lapse of the unconverted decree-law. Furthermore, from a more general perspective, the practice, "if diffused and prolonged over time as happened in recent times, affects the institutional equilibrium, altering the same form of government and the ordinary attribution of the legislative power to the Parliament (Article 70 Const.)" and damages "the certainty of law in the relationship among citizens".[10]

Putting an end to this unconstitutional practice did not terminate the misuse of decree-laws. Their frequency reduced—to around 2 to 4 per month[11]—, and almost all were timely converted, with several amendments, within 60 days, but their dimension and the variety of their content increased very significantly, canvassing vastly different subject matters in single—giant—texts.

Indeed, in the context arising after judgment no. 360/1996, heterogeneous decree-laws (called "omnibus") have been more successful, as they have been advanced by a stronger engine, represented by all the supporters—from different political parties and distinct ministries—of their many provisions. They tend to become even richer during the parliamentary examination due to the approval of several amendments and, at the conclusion of the legislative process, their conversion is often achieved thanks to a question of confidence posed by the Government on a maxi-amendment, which, in this way, manages to unify a heterogeneous and often conflicting parliamentary majority (see *infra*, par. 5).

Among the clearest examples are the so-called "thousand-extensions" (*milleproroghe*) decree-laws. Normally enacted either at the end of the year or just before the 30th June, when most of the legislative deadlines tend to elapse, this category of decree-laws—originating in the mid-1990s, but then becoming systematic[12]—are by nature heterogeneous acts: the only element that unites the different

---

[10]See, for the translation of the judgment and for some further steps, Barsotti et al. (2016), pp. 166 ff.

[11]Simoncini (2006).

[12]The first example was the decree-law no. 1/1992, which was repeated twenty times and which, as is natural, was enriched with further extensions introduced on the initiative of the government or parliament). See, also for further references, Lupo (2006).

provisions included in each of them is the nature of the provisions (often accompanied by transitional disciplines or interventions aimed at addressing the substantive, true or presumed, issue which is believed to have prevented compliance with the deadlines in question).

The heterogeneity of the decree-laws violated Article 15 of the Law no. 400/1988,[13] which affirmed the principle of the homogeneity of the decree-law, as an integral part of the extraordinary conditions under which it could be adopted. This limit, however, was generally considered to be relative, in light of the impossibility for parliamentary legislation to effectively constrain the adoption of subsequent measures having the same legal force.

With respect to the admissibility of amendments to decree-laws, the Chamber and the Senate follow different patterns. The rules of procedure of the Chamber provide for a "strict scrutiny" of the admissibility of amendments relating to the conversion bills, establishing that those "which are not closely related to the matter of the decree-law" must be declared inadmissible (Article 96 bis, paragraph 7). By contrast, the Senate's rules of procedure do not differentiate this Speaker's assessment from that which occurs in relation to the amendments referring to ordinary legislative bills, thereby excluding only those "unrelated to the subject of the discussion" (Article 97, paragraph 1).

This disharmony has been accentuated in practice, often giving rise to two kinds of effects. First, that the same amendment might be declared inadmissible by the Speaker of the Chamber, and instead deemed to be admissible by the Speaker of the Senate (and often consequently approved by the plenary of the Senate). Second, that the Government, fully aware of this disharmony, tends to first submit to the Chamber the decree-laws that are more homogeneous and whose contents it wants to retain, with minimal variation. By contrast, the more heterogeneous decree-laws, in relation to which many amendments could be approved, tend to be submitted first to the Senate. In both cases, in fact, given the 60 days deadline, the other House ordinarily confirms the text as already amended by the first one.

This divergence has been further enhanced by other disharmonies in the parliamentary treatment of conversion bills between the two Houses.

From a procedural point of view, conversions bills in the Senate are the only example in which the work undertaken at the committee stage is not decisive, and amendments passed therein must be re-approved in the plenary. This singularity was originally intended to make it more difficult to amend conversion bills (as the same amendment must be passed twice in order to be inserted in the text) but ended up fostering completely different effects. Rather, the plenary recasts the debate held in the committee and the text, although already in force, loses its political sponsors as the political compromises reached in the precedent phase are nullified. This situation leads to the debate being completely reopened, easing the approval of many amendments.

---

[13]Law no. 400/1988 is the seminal piece of legislation that, for the first time in the Republic's history, provided a statutory framework for the organisation of the Presidency of the Council and the normative powers of the executive.

From a structural point of view, with the modification of the rules of procedure in 1997–1998, the Chamber of Deputies established an internal body, the "Committee on Legislation", specifically focused on the quality of legislation. This committee delivers opinions on every conversion bill, evaluating its coherence with both Article 15 of Law 400/1988 and the case law of the Constitutional Court.

The combination of these two factors, as well as the aforementioned different levels of scrutiny regarding the same amendments, renders the procedure in the Senate particularly problematic and, generally speaking, results in a different approach being taken by parliamentary bodies regarding the same critical issue.

The rules of procedure and the practice of the Chamber of Deputies also deserve some close consideration. In particular, there is an inherent ambiguity with regard to the management of time spent debating the conversion bills: they are explicitly excluded from the allocation of limited time for discussion.[14] Consequently, it was argued that the use of the question of confidence would have been the only possible measure for avoiding filibustering, having regard to the 60 day time limit for the conversion.[15] However, more recent practice has demonstrated that the Speaker of the Chamber can stymie the debate in order to allow the final vote before the constitutional deadline.[16]

Turning to the approach of the Constitutional Court on the topic, it also tried to limit most of the abuses by decree-laws and their conversion procedure. On the one hand, the Court affirmed (in judgment no. 29/1995, and then, more decisively, in judgment no. 171/2007) its potential for declaring a decree-law unconstitutional, even once converted into law, in the event of unambiguous absence of the "extraordinary cases of necessity and urgency" required by Article 77 Const. However, the Court has been very reluctant to scrutinise the pre-requisites of decree-laws, because it considers that the decision to adopt a decree-law, and the definition of its—often plural—objects fall within the margin of discretionary power of the political bodies.

On the other hand, the Court clarified (especially in judgments nos. 22/2012 and 32/2014) that the conversion law is not an ordinary law, and therefore it can neither legalize a decree-law which was originally adopted without meeting the prerequisites of necessity and urgency, nor insert amendments devoid of any connection with the content of the decree-law. In other words, "The power of conversion cannot in fact be regarded as a mere manifestation of the ordinary legislative power of the Chambers of Parliament, as the conversion law is 'specialised and intended for a specific function'". The conversion law is "premised on the existence of a decree to be converted, and must reflect the legislative content of that decree". So, the limits set by art. 15 of the Law no. 400/1988 with respect to the decree-laws have been

---

[14]See the allegedly "transitory" provision set forth by art. 154 of the rules of procedure of the Chamber.

[15]Perna (2010).

[16]Polimeni (2014).

deemed to be a "development of the ratio inherent to art. 77 Const."[17] and have therefore also been extended to the powers of the Parliament in approving conversion bills.

Consequently, the Court struck down some provisions inserted by the Parliament while converting the decree-law that were clearly unrelated to the latter, on the basis that they were *ultra vires*, because they did "not respect the typical function of the conversion law", using the special procedure provided for this category of laws.[18]

The potential for this case law related to decree-laws to give rise to a general rethinking of the position of the Constitutional Court with regard to omnibus legislation has already been highlighted in academic literature.[19] The acknowledgment of the limits to parliamentary autonomy in regulating and practicing the legislative process could be developed by returning to the original message conveyed by the judgment no. 9/1959, and by enforcing constitutional provisions regarding diverging parliamentary usages.

4 Omnibudget Legislation: From "Financial Law" to a More Comprehensive Budget Law

The other kind of "omnibus legislation" in Italy is "omnibudget legislation": that is, legislation which forms part of the annual budgetary procedure, to be approved during an "ad hoc" parliamentary session, which is called the "budgetary session" (*sessione di bilancio*).

This type of legislation has existed in various forms since 1978 but its names have varied. Originally (between 1978 and 2009), it was called "financial law" (*legge finanziaria*), then (between 2010 and 2015) "stability law" (*legge di stabilità*), in both cases accompanying the budget law (*legge di bilancio*). Since 2017, this content has been transferred into (the first section of) the budget law itself. Such an evolution is worthy of a brief analysis.

According to the original text of Article 81 of the Constitution, inspired by the traditional theory of budget law as a merely formal law, budget law was not allowed to introduce any new taxes or new expenditures. Law no. 468/1978, circumventing this constitutional prohibition, created a legislative instrument to be approved annually together with the budget law, which was called upon to do what the budget law could not do: that is, "establish new taxes and new expenses".[20] The instrument in question was the financial law, called upon, initially, to "translate into action the

---

[17]See judgment no. 22/2012, §3.3 in Law. *Contra*, judgment no. 391/1995.

[18]See Judgment no. 32/2014, quoting judgment no. 22/2012 and order no. 34/2013. See also judgment no. 247/2019.

[19]Manetti (2012).

[20]Lupo (2007), p. 82; Laze (2019), p. 141.

budget maneuver for the revenue and expenditure that is intended to be pursued".[21] It did so for all the possible objects with some financial effects, and originally without any budgetary cap, so its omnibus nature was indeed very clear and widely criticized. Law no. 362/1988 managed to move the decision about the budgetary objective (to be determined in a programmatic document drafted by the Government and approved by the Parliament) away from the budgetary session, and to transfer some of its contents to other legislative bills (*provvedimenti collegati*). Then, law no. 196/2009 changed its name to "stability law" in the framework of a general reorganization of the budgetary session.

After a constitutional amendment removed the limit on its content outlined by Art. 81 (constitutional law no. 1/2012), the budget law has been able, since 2017, to also bear responsibility (in its first part) for the introduction of new taxes or new expenditures, although always consistently with the equilibrium already agreed in the programmatic phase and re-affirmed by the same budget law (in its second part).

After four years of this approach, the regulatory content of the four new budget laws which have been enacted in the meantime appears varied and still contains, despite the express prohibition in art. 5, paragraph 2, third sentence, of law no. 243/2012, and reaffirmed in Article 21, paragraph 1-quinquies, of law no. 196/2009, certain "organizational norms", as well as norms "of a localistic or micro-sectorial nature".[22]

The presence of these provisions—which are also reported on by the Court of Auditors in its quarterly reports[23]—confirms the strength of the "bad parliamentary precedent", which is capable of prevailing over its discontinuance brought about by the constitutional revision. The malpractice continued, despite the fact that the ban in question is now primarily dictated by law no. 243/2012: a source which is ordinarily characterized as a "reinforced" or "organic" law,[24] clearly interposed between the Constitution and the budget laws themselves, which are ordinary laws.

The habit of tabling a high number of amendments in the budget session is evidently difficult to overcome, also considering the nature of the bill, responsibility for which is assigned by law to the Government. The Speakers of the two Houses, while continuing to exercise their delicate prerogatives in assessing the admissibility of the amendments, seem to have implicitly accepted the presence of a high volume of local and micro-sectorial provisions; and they have consequently, on the whole, lost control of the decision-making process in the budget session.

The direction of the procedure—which is obviously also essential to assuring compliance with the European Semester framework—is now solidly in the hands of the Government, and in particular the Ministry of Economy and Finance. The

---

[21] Article 11 of the original text of law no. 468/1978.

[22] See Bergonzini (2014), pp. 58 ff; Bergonzini (2017), pp. 5 ff.

[23] See, for instance, Corte dei conti, *Relazione quadrimestrale sulla tipologia delle coperture adottate e sulle tecniche di quantificazione degli oneri*, September-December 2017, Rome, 18 April 2018, pp. 43 ff.

[24] Lupo (2013).

position of the question of confidence on the maxi-amendments (see *infra*, the following paragraph) determines the actual timing of the session and the content of the final decision. In turn, the maxi-amendment is substantially drafted by the Government, which is able, in this way, to summon its majority, for the price of limited compromises, and also to convey in the final text part of the proposals tabled by the oppositions.

The prohibition on the introduction into the budget law of legislative delegation norms has been substantially respected. The effect of this prohibition was already made clear following a debate dating back to the 1990s, relating to the financial law and the stability law,[25] and has subsequently been confirmed by the current legislation.[26] However, all the budget laws provide for a very conspicuous series of implementing interventions that occupy, for their preparation and enactment, the first months, if not more, of the following year. This has the clear consequence, among other things, of limiting the quantum of financial effects—in positive or negative terms for public finance–, given that these effects, of course, are produced only if the implementing norms have been issued and from the time they enter into force.[27]

5   Maxi-Amendments and the Question of Confidence: Powerful, Although Unconstitutional, Instruments for the Government to Accelerate the Legislative Process

Apart from budget decisions, most of the legislation approved during the first decades of the Republic were passed, as noted, directly by sectoral committees, having regard to the consociational dynamics of the political system. This pattern could obviously not be followed in the event of divisive pieces of legislation, as, in such cases, minorities had the power to impose the ordinary legislative procedure with the involvement of the plenary.[28]

As for the rest, no formal instruments had been anticipated by the Constitution or by the rules of procedures of the Houses to be put in the hands of the Government to impose its priorities. Moreover, generally speaking, the position of the Government in the legislative process was not assisted by any specific procedural tools.

On the occasion of the passage of some important (and divisive) bills during the Republic's first legislative term (1948–1953), a unique procedure emerged in the parliamentary practice, with some continuity with the pre-Republican period: the

---

[25]Lupo (2002), pp. 42 ff.

[26]See art. 5, paragraph 2, third sentence, of law no. 243/2012 and art. 21, paragraph 1-quinquies, of law no. 196/2009.

[27]Bartolucci (2019).

[28]One fifth of the committee members or one tenth of the members of the plenary (Article 73.2 Const.).

question of confidence.[29] The idea was to solidify something inherent in the parliamentary form of government, namely the possibility for the executive to resign if it becomes evident that it lacks the political support of the Assembly. The specific means of implementing such a prerogative was to allow the Government to transform the discussion of any bill in a single "take-it-or-leave-it" vote, the result of which would determine the destiny of the bill and that of the Government itself. In other terms, this procedure allows the Government to pre-alert the Parliament as to the crucial impact to which a future parliamentary vote could give rise in relation to the existence of the confidence relationship. In substance, this constitutes a sort of blackmail on the part of the Government to the Parliament, and most of all to its majority: "on a certain issue, either you vote following my advice, or else I will resign".

As noted, there was no overt procedure of this nature, either in the constitution, or in the rules of procedure, in force at that time.[30] That is why, during the early years of the Italian republican experience, the procedural effects and the constitutionality of the question of confidence were strongly disputed, even causing a rift between the Speaker of the Chamber of Deputies, Gronchi, and his deputy, Leone (both leaders of the Christian Democratic party and destined to become, in the subsequent years, Presidents of the Republic).

However, a constitutional custom progressively emerged, which was partially codified, first in the Chamber's (in 1971), and then in the Senate's (in 1988), rules of procedure, as well as, eventually, in the law no. 400/1988 (in order to require an authorisation by the Council of Ministers for the question of confidence to be posed in one of the two Houses).[31]

According to this constitutional custom, the question of confidence involves three main procedural effects: first, the application of the roll-call vote, as in all the other confidence procedures; second, the chronological priority of the vote with respect to the object on which the question of confidence has been posed; third, the unamendability and indivisibility of the text on which the Government has posed the question of confidence. As a consequence, the question of confidence makes the parliamentary vote entirely take-it-or-leave-it, without any third option.

These procedural effects are so significant, especially when applied to the legislative process, that often the Government targets them and makes use of the question of confidence only instrumentally, not because it deems the vote in question crucial to its survival, but because it aims to accelerate the process and to avoid the many parliamentary votes otherwise required (with all the accompanying unknowns). If it sounds like a powerful weapon on the side of the Government (and it undoubtedly is), it is also evidence of the Government's weakness, as a confirmation of its narrow and divided parliamentary support.

---

[29]Olivetti (1996) and Rossi (2001).

[30]Art. 128 of the rules of procedure of the Chamber of Deputies (as in force since 27 April 1949).

[31]Manzella (1969), Olivetti (1996), Gianniti and Lupo (2018).

These procedural advantages become particularly evident when the question of confidence is posed on maxi-amendments, that is, on amendments aimed at substituting the entire text of a bill. In fact, in this case, through a unique roll-call vote, the Government is able to determine the text of the bill that is going to be approved by each House, obliging its parliamentary majority to accept it as a whole, avoiding the risk of having different outcomes on each article and amendment, depending on their parliamentary support. In this way, the Government "effectively impedes debate and eliminates all margin for negotiation" within both its majority and the opposition.[32]

The practice of questions of confidence on maxi-amendments consolidated itself in the form of the omnibudget bills at the end of the 1980s,[33] but it became dominant during the following decade, especially for conversion bills and for budget bills. It suffices to remark that, since 2004, not a single budget law has been approved without the question of confidence.[34]

The use of the question of confidence on maxi-amendments has been extremely frequent during the last 30 years, although many scholars doubt its conformity with art. 72 (1) Const., which requires any bill to be voted on "article by article" and then as a whole.[35]

Furthermore, in the case of maxi-amendments to budget laws (see *supra*, par. 4), the practice of maxi-amendments also reveals a contrast in its outcome with Article 15 paragraphs 2 and 4 of the already mentioned "organic" or "reinforced" law no. 243/2012, which requires some public finance balances to be placed "in separate articles" or "with a specific article" of the budget law.[36] Also in this case, the strength of the "bad parliamentary precedent" seems to have prevailed over the novelty represented by an interposed source that clearly requires a structuring of the contents of the budget law "in separate articles", with forecasts that should be imposed on the ordinary legislator and the Parliament itself.

However, both the Speakers of the two Houses and, at least initially, the Constitutional Court (judgment no. 391/1995) have avoided, to date, declaring an end to this practice, which has managed to ensure some kind of functioning of the

---

[32]Vassallo (2015), p. 114.

[33]Pisaneschi (1988).

[34]The precedent from 2004 is interesting. The Government was defeated on an amendment tabled by the opposition, which left out crucial parts of the basic elements for the budget decision. As a solution, on that occasion and in every single subsequent budget bill (when it was called either "legge finanziaria", "di stabilità" or "di bilancio"), at least the final text was passed with maxi-amendments.

[35]Even the Presidency of the Republic repeatedly denounced the problematic nature of this practice. Already in 2001 President Ciampi underlined the impossibility of reconstructing the ratio underlying laws approved via this procedure: see Lupo (2001) and Scagliarini (2005). Similarly, President Napolitano sent a letter in 2009 (and a second one in 2011) to the Speakers of the Chambers and the President of the Council, inviting them to end this practice: see Carnevale and Chinni (2011). In the literature, specifically on the unconstitutionality of the practice, see Piccirilli (2008), Pistorio (2018).

[36]Macciotta (2020), p. 2.

legislative process and to recognize the Government's dominant role within it, to unite, although artificially, its own heterogeneous parliamentary majority. Even the opposition sometimes seems to have become accustomed to this practice, as it is much easier for it to complain about the abuse of this instrument and to generically criticize a certain bill than to examine and challenge it, article by article and amendment by amendment.

6 In Search of a Judicial Review of the Legislative Process: The Innovative, But Contradictory, Order No. 17/2019 of the Constitutional Court

As already noted, the Constitutional Court has never declared the unconstitutionality of maxi-amendments, nor retracted from the foundations offered by the abovementioned judgments nos. 9/1959 and 154/1985.[37] However, the Court has progressively revised the principal findings of decision no. 391/1995 in its most recent case law, thereby offering some important signals of change.

First, the abovementioned judgment no. 32/2014 struck down—although for violating Art. 77 Const., not Art. 72 Const.—a provision inserted in a maxi-amendment "tabled by the government, which replaced the entire text of the draft conversion law", remarking that it was tabled directly in the Senate Assembly and was associated by the government with a vote of confidence.

Second, in the judgment no. 251/2014, the practice of maxi-amendments was not viewed as a custom, but as "a problematic practice" (albeit without leading to the unconstitutionality of transplanting one decree-law into the conversion bill of another).[38]

More recently, a new series of decisions has emerged, in response to the consolidation of a strategy by opposition MPs to bring actions before the Constitutional Court within the framework of disputes between branches of government ("conflitto di attribuzioni"), which is intended to ensure respect for the constitutional attributions of the constitutional bodies, rather than the judicial review of legislation.

The first important step in this new direction was taken with the order no. 17/2019 (anticipated *supra*, par. 1). At the end of the parliamentary debate of the 2019 budget bill (and slightly before its approval), 37 senators of the Democratic party (at that time in opposition) raised a complaint regarding a constitutional dispute in the procedure which had been followed by the Senate in that case, which included the question of confidence on a maxi-amendment rather different from the text that had been previously examined by the Chamber and by the Senate's committees.

---

[37]The inadmissibility of questions of constitutionality related to parliamentary rules of procedure has more recently been re-affirmed by judgment no. 120/2014.

[38]Piccirilli (2014).

The Court ruled the conflict inadmissible, but for rather innovative and controversial reasons. On the one hand, for the first time, the Court explicitly recognized the possibility for single members of Parliament to raise a constitutional dispute, although only in the case of "manifest violations of the constitutional prerogatives of the members of Parliament". On the other hand, in the circumstances that were brought before it, the Court did not identify any violation that could be characterized as "manifest", although it did suggest—almost menacingly, as it has been remarked—that "the outcome could be different in other circumstances involving a similar impairment of the constitutional function of members of Parliament".

However, most of all, the Court highlighted, in contrast with its own arguments in the judgment no. 391/1995, that the procedural stages set out by Article 72 Const. "must always be respected in order to guarantee the role of Parliament as a forum for debate and discussion between the various political forces as well as for approving individual legislative acts, and in order to guarantee the legal order as a whole, which is premised on the prerequisite that all representatives be afforded broad scope to contribute to the formation of the will of Parliament". And, in its final statement, summarizing its decision of inadmissibility, pointed out that "the manner in which parliamentary business was conducted in relation to the bill on the state budget for 2019 aggravated the problematic aspects of the practice of associating block amendments with a confidence motion; nevertheless, it is important not to disregard the fact that the business was conducted under time pressure due to the lengthy engagement with European Union institutions, in accordance with rules provided for under the Senate Regulations and without entirely excluding effective discussion during the previous stages concerning texts that were incorporated, at least in part, into the final version".[39]

In the absence of any changes to the rules of procedure of the two Houses, a similar dispute was raised again—this time by MPs of Forza Italia, Fratelli d'Italia and the League—complaining about the way in which the Chamber of Deputies examined the state budget bill for 2020 in only eight days. The outcome was, indeed, not very different as the Court, in its order no. 60/2020, also ruled this new dispute inadmissible, at a preliminary stage, remarking that the absence of the supporting circumstances referred to by order no. 17/2019 is not decisive and that the objective sequence of facts did not demonstrate an unreasonable imbalance between the demands at stake in the parliamentary procedures and, thus, any manifest violation of the MPs' constitutional powers.[40]

The same outcome of inadmissibility resulted in two MPs individually complaining, each raising a dispute, about the heterogeneity of the provisions inserted by the Senate in the conversion procedure of decree-laws (orders nos.

[39] All the expressions are taken from order no. 17/2019 in the official translation available on https://www.cortecostituzionale.it/documenti/download/doc/recent_judgments/O_17_2019_EN.pdf.   A very broad academic debate has taken place on this order: see Lupo (2019) and, for further references, Morrone (2019), Fabrizzi (2019).

[40] Order no. 60/2020, on which see Dickmann (2020).

274 and 275/2019).[41] However, these developments may be promising, both procedurally and substantially, with respect to the capacity of the Constitutional Court to sanction such critical deviations from the genuine and well-balanced parliamentary process.

7 Conclusion

The analysis of the main kinds of omnibus legislation (decree-laws and omnibudget legislation), on the one hand, and of the procedure of the question of confidence on maxi-amendments, on the other, has shown how all these procedural devices are fully functional to a political system in which majorities are composed of multiple and heterogeneous majority coalitions. Their success over the last 30 years derives from the block of legislation passed by committees, which prevailed during the first 40 years of the Italian Republic, and from the need for the majority to overcome the many veto powers that exist in the Italian system.

However, the legislative measures which have been achieved in this way—for instance, by maxi-amendments approved by a conversion bill, or within an annual budget law examined quickly and almost without any possibility to amend it—reveal themselves to be hardly the best: far from being conceived as proper and organic reforms, they tend to be taken made in a hurry, just for the sake of maintaining overall political agreement and without any clear allocation of the political responsibility for the measure approved. A further confirmation is offered by the fact that, very often, norms so approved do not last long, being frequently modified in the months or weeks following their adoption.[42]

Moreover, from a more theoretical standpoint, it is also noticeable that the Italian experience, as analyzed, seems to confirm that drafting rules are strictly and irreversibly intertwined with the rules of parliamentary procedure and *vice versa*. Legislative drafting rules are not only aimed at setting linguistic guidelines for the composition of a text, but they also constitute the framework in light of which the most effective procedure must be found. In turn, procedural rules are not only followed to reach a specific formulation of the provision, but are also instrumentally exploited by the strategic drafting of amendments, in order to reduce the debate. In sum, it is impossible to view parliamentary lawmaking as a mono-dimensional activity: it is a delicate combination of politics and practice, mirroring the complexity of the political system and the society underpinning it, and all these elements together determine the quality of the legislation approved.

---

[41]In particular, the inclusion, in an amendment to the Senate (which examined the bill at first reading), of an additional article unrelated to the original content of the decree-law (a provision aimed at blocking hydrocarbon research activities in a decree-law dedicated to simplification and support for businesses): see Piccirilli (2020).

[42]Longo (2017).

References

Barsotti V, Carozza P, Cartabia M, Simoncini A (2016) Italian constitutional justice in global context. OUP, Oxford-New York

Bartolucci L (2019) Osservazioni a prima lettura sulla Nota di aggiornamento al Documento di Economia e Finanza 2019. In: Osservatorio AIC, issue 6

Bergonzini C (2014) Parlamento e decisioni di bilancio. Franco Angeli, Milano

Bergonzini C (2017) La riforma della legge di contabilità pubblica (l. n. 163/2016): le principali novità (e alcuni profili critici). In: www.federalismi.it, issue 9

Carnevale P, Chinni D (2011) C'è posta per tre. Prime osservazioni a margine della lettera del Presidente Napolitano inviata ai Presidenti delle Camere ed al Presidente del Consiglio in ordine alla conversione del c.d. decreto milleproroghe. In: Rivista AIC, issue 2

Colarizi S, Gervasoni M (2012) La tela di Penelope. Storia della seconda Repubblica. Laterza, Roma-Bari

Dickmann R (2020) Ancora in tema di legittimazione al conflitto di attribuzione dei singoli membri delle Camere . . . ma non dei gruppi parlamentari. In: www.forumcostituzionale.it

Elia L (1970) Governo (forme di). In: Enciclopedia del diritto, vol IX. Giuffrè, Milano, pp 634–675

Fabrizzi F (2019) Il conflitto tra poteri quale strumento a tutela del procedimento legislativo. In: Osservatorio AIC, issue 5

Fasone C (2012) Sistemi di commissioni parlamentari e forme di governo. Cedam, Padova

Giannitti L, Lupo N (2018) Corso di diritto parlamentare[3]. Il mulino, Bologna

Laze M (2019) La natura giuridica della legge di bilancio: una questione ancora attuale. In: Bergonzini C (ed) Costituzione e bilancio. Franco Angeli, Milano, pp 131–149

Longo E (2017) La legge precaria. Le trasformazioni della funzione legislativa nell'età dell'accelerazione. Giappichelli, Torino

Lupo N (2001) Verso una motivazione delle leggi? A proposito del primo rinvio di Ciampi. In: Quaderni costituzionali, pp 362–364

Lupo N (2002) La formazione parlamentare delle leggi di delega. In: De Siervo U (ed) Osservatorio sulle fonti 2001. Giappichelli, Torino, pp 15–53

Lupo N (2006) Decreto-legge e manutenzione legislativa: i decreti-legge "milleproroghe". In: Simoncini A (ed) L'emergenza infinita. La decretazione d'urgenza in Italia. EUM, Macerata, pp 173–210

Lupo N (2007) Costituzione e bilancio. L'art. 81 della Costituzione tra interpretazione, attuazione e aggiramento, Luiss University Press, Roma

Lupo N (2013) Il nuovo articolo 81 della Costituzione e la legge "rinforzata" o "organica". In: Dalla crisi economica al pareggio di bilancio. Giuffrè, Milano, pp 425–462

Lupo N (2019) Un'ordinanza compromissoria, ma che pone le basi per un procedimento legislativo più rispettoso della Costituzione. In: www.federalismi.it, issue 4

Macciotta G (2020) La disciplina di bilancio. In Astrid-Rassegna, issue 2

Manetti M (2012) La via maestra che dall'inemendabilità dei decreti legge conduce all'illegittimità dei maxi-emendamenti. Giurisprudenza costituzionale 1:292–298

Manzella A (1969) Note sulla questione di fiducia. Ancora sui rapporti fra maggioranza ed opposizione. Studi parlamentari e di politica costituzionale 5–6:39–90

Manzella A (2003) Il Parlamento[3]. Il mulino, Bologna

Morrone A (2019) Lucciole per lanterne. La n. 17/2019 e la terra promessa di quote di potere per il singolo parlamentare. In: www.federalismi.it, issue 4

Olivetti M (1996) La questione di fiducia nel sistema parlamentare italiano. Giuffrè, Milano

Orsina G (2014) Berlusconism and Italy: a historical interpretation. Palgrave, London

Pasquino G (2015) Cittadini senza scettro: Le riforme sbagliate. Egea-Bocconi, Milano

Perna R (2010) Tempi della decisione ed abuso della decretazione d'urgenza. Quaderni costituzionali 1:59–74

Piccirilli G (2008) L'emendamento nel processo di decisione parlamentare. Cedam, Padova

Piccirilli G (2014) Non è incostituzionale l'"accorpamento" tra decreti-legge, se si mantiene l'omogeneità materiale. Giurisprudenza costituzionale:4460–4467

Piccirilli G (2020) Vizi formali della legge e conflitto di attribuzioni sollevato da singoli parlamentari: in un vicolo cieco? Quaderni costituzionali 1:144–147

Pisaneschi A (1988) Fondamento costituzionale del potere di emendamento, limiti di coerenza e questione di fiducia. Diritto e società 2:203–258

Pistorio G (2018) Maxi-emendamento e questione di fiducia: contributo allo studio di una prassi illegittima. Editoriale scientifica, Napoli

Polimeni S (2014) La "geometria" della c.d. ghigliottina parlamentare: un difficile quadrilatero di interessi. www.forumcostituzionale.it

Predieri A (1963) La produzione legislativa. In: Sartori G (ed) Il Parlamento italiano (1946-1963). Edizioni scientifiche italiane, Napoli, pp 205–276

Predieri A (1975) Il governo colegislatore. In: Cazzola F et al. (eds) Il decreto legge fra governo e parlamento. Giuffrè, Milano, pp VII–LI

Rossi F (2001) Saggio sul sistema politico dell'Italia liberale: procedure fiduciarie e sistema dei partiti fra Otto e Novecento. Rubbettino, Soveria Mannelli

Sartori G (1976) Parties and party systems: a framework for analysis. Cambridge University Press, New York

Scagliarini S (2005) Il Presidente e la tecnica legislativa. In: Diritto pubblico, pp 265–290

Simoncini A (2006) L'emergenza infinita. La decretazione d'urgenza in Italia. EUM, Macerata

Vassallo S (2015) Parliament. In: Jones E, Pasquino G (eds) The Oxford handbook of Italian politics, Oxford, pp 107–119

Centralization via Delegation: The Long-Term Implications of the Israeli Arrangements Laws

Nir Kosti

Abstract The "Arrangements Law" has become one of the most powerful policy tools used by the Israeli government since 1985. Under this omnibus legislation, the Budgets Department at the Ministry of Finance (MOF) introduces various bills and amendments in various policy areas almost on an annual basis. While previous studies presented how the MOF reached a powerful position in the policymaking process through this institutional architecture, this chapter examines how the MOF has also sought control in the everyday regulatory processes. More specifically, the chapter examines the extent to which the Arrangements Law authorized ministers to issue regulations (e.g., secondary legislation), based on a content analysis of 38 Arrangements laws legislated between 1985 and 2018. This chapter shows that against the conventional wisdom, the process of delegation of authority from parliament to the executive is a process that centralizes, rather than decentralizes, regulatory powers. In particular, the MOF was involved in nearly 60 percent of all delegations through four mechanisms of centralization: (1) vesting itself with an authority to create regulation; (2) vesting itself and another ministry with a joint authority to create regulation; and holding veto power over the regulations of other ministries either by requiring (3) its consent or (4) consultation prior to publication. Altogether, these mechanisms extended the MOF's power in everyday regulatory processes.

Keywords Omnibus legislation · Legislative delegation · Power centralization · Veto players

I would like to express my special thank David Levi-Faur, Adi Ayal, and Ittai-Bar-Siman-Tov for the helpful comments on this paper. I also thank the participants of the International Conference on "Rearranging the Arrangements Law: Comparative, Multidisciplinary, Empirical and Normative Perspectives on Omnibus Legislation" at Bar-Ilan University (January 1–3, 2019).

N. Kosti (✉)
Department of Political Science, Hebrew University of Jerusalem, Jerusalem, Israel

1 Introduction

The Israeli Arrangements Law (*Hok Hahesderim*) has become one of the most powerful policy tools used by the Israeli government in recent decades. The academic research on the Arrangements Law has focused, so far, on explicating their roles in dismantling the Israeli welfare state;[1] how they undermine the Knesset's ordinary legislative process;[2] their effect on the budgeting process;[3] the extent of their use;[4] and how it has given the Ministry of Finance (MOF) advantaged position in the policymaking process and changed the structure of powers in the bureaucracy.[5]

This chapter joins the latter group of studies, but from a different, often neglected perspective, on the impacts of the Arrangements Laws on the "everyday process of government",[6] that is, the making of regulation. Under the Arrangements Laws, the Budgets Department at the MOF combines various bills and amendments pertaining to various policy areas in one single law. In doing so, the chapter argues that the MOF has used, *inter alia,* the respective Arrangements Laws to gain more powers in the everyday regulatory process of other ministries.

Studies on the MOF often impute its excessive powers vis-à-vis other ministries to its budgetary and policymaking powers. This chapter unpacks the latter, arguing that unlike its budgetary and policymaking powers, the MOF's clout over other ministries' regulations allows it to possess an enormous control on everyday politics. This chapter shows that Arrangements Laws have provided the MOF with new powers to make regulations in other domains. Additionally, it illustrates how the Arrangements Laws have enabled the MOF to take over the power to veto other ministries' authorities to create regulations. These mechanisms ensure that initiatives promoted under the Arrangements Laws are not only set during its legislation phase, but also implemented or circumvented through the regulatory process.

The relationship between legislation and regulation is a relatively unexplored topic in the literature.[7] In fact, the bureaucracy's powers to engender regulation are derived from law and are not inherent. Therefore, laws in democratic countries often delegate authorities to government ministries and agencies to make regulations (i.e., secondary legislation, subordinated legislation, delegated legislation, etc.).[8] These regulations are supposed to 'implement' laws, but in practice, they usually assign

---

[1]Asiskovich (2011), Golan (2008) and Kop (2010).

[2]Maor and Bar Nir (2008).

[3]Ben-Bassat and Dahan (2006).

[4]Nahmias and Klein (1999).

[5]Cohen (2013), Gilad and Cohen (2018) and Sperling and Cohen (2012).

[6]Page (2001), p. 5.

[7]Kosti et al. (2019a).

[8]Epstein and O'Halloran (1999) and Huber and Shipan (2002).

ample discretion to implementors, not only when it comes to trivial or mundane issues, but also regarding controversial and high politics.[9]

In parliamentary democracies, the power to create regulations are vested in cabinet ministers that, at a minimum, ratify them but often devote little attention in the process of making them.[10] In fact, democratic countries issue between hundreds and thousands of regulations every year. Although legislation in democratic states is mostly identified with the legislature, regulation or secondary legislation, in fact, outnumber the volume of laws in any democratic states.[11] Compared to legislation, the regulatory process, is insufficiently transparent or expresses fewer democratic values.[12] While there are several functional arguments in favor of delegation, this paper shows that it is primarily a political process,[13] that is used to centralize, rather than decentralize, regulatory powers.

More specifically, this chapter argues that the Arrangement Laws introduces four broad mechanisms of centralization of such powers: (1) additional authorities to create regulations; (2) shared authorities with other ministers to crate regulations; (3) requiring other ministers to have the consent of the MOF or to (4) consult the MOF prior to publication. Such mechanisms, the chapter suggests, grant the MOF an advantaged position in everyday government, as both a policymaker and a veto player.

This chapter has been divided into six parts. Part two of the paper includes the background to the legislation of the Arrangements Laws. Parts three presents the theoretical framework of the paper. It demonstrates the rationales and arguments in favor of delegation of lawmaking powers and discusses literature on veto players and the mechanisms of centralization that the Arrangements Laws introduce. The Fourth part of the chapter presents the methodology and discusses the processes of data collection and data analysis. The fifth part demonstrate the findings, focusing on the four mechanisms of centralization. The final part broaches the long-term implications of the findings and identifies areas for future research.

2 Background

The Arrangements Law was first enacted in 1985 as part of the Economic Stabilization Program in response to Israel's inflation crisis, and made provisions related to the 1986 budget.[14] The law deliberately addressed budgetary issues, prioritizing the

---

[9]Page (2001).

[10]Ibid.; Page (2012).

[11]Kosti and Levi-Faur (2019).

[12]Rose-Ackerman (2019).

[13]Huber and Shipan (2002).

[14]For more information on the historical grounds of the arrangements laws, see Hetis-Rolf in this book.

achievements of the economic goals set by the Economic Stabilization Program. However, since 1985 and over the years, the law has become one of the most influential policy tools used by Israeli governments, and especially by the MOF, that set it in motion.

As an omnibus legislation, every Arrangements Law consists of various bills, amendments, and cancellations to existing legislation within a single law. The law has enabled the Israeli government to enforce its majority for the promotion of its goals and agendas, overcoming Israel's unstable and fragile coalitions.[15] Put differently, the MOF's ability to combine various policy initiatives within the framework of one long bill allowed it to promote extensive reforms almost annually in various policy domains.[16]

Studies on the Arrangements Laws examined, among others, how they made large changes in various policy areas.[17] Other studies sought to explain the stability and expansion of the laws, based on the number of veto players in the coalition,[18] the combination of bureaucratic politics and veto players,[19] and the judicial impact on legislative behavior (Bar-Siman-Tov 2015).

This chapter is less focused on changes over time, but on the long-term impacts of the Arrangements Laws. More specifically, it seeks to gain a better understanding of the long-term impact of the Arrangements Laws on the regulatory process. As described by Kosti and Levi-Faur (2019), the decline in Israel's annual production of regulation between 1985 and 2004 has been driven by changes in the rate of production of laws as well as their length and type, presenting a "substitutive relationship" between laws and regulation. As this chapter shows, the way the Arrangements Laws shaped the regulatory process throughout the years may play a pivotal role in incentivizing ministries to use means other than regulation to avoid the MOF's impingement on their policymaking.

3 Theoretical Framework

3.1 Delegation of Legislative Power

Following Thatcher and Sweet,[20] delegation is defined here as "an authoritative decision, formalized as a matter of public law, that (a) transfers policy making

---

[15]Nahmias and Klein (1999).

[16]Kosti et al. (2019b).

[17]Asiskovich (2011); Golan (2008); Horev T, Kedar N, *Light and Shadow in the Development and Implementation of the National Health Insurance Law: Reflection of the Reform from Fifteen Years of Legislation*, 2010; Kosti et al. (2019b).

[18]Nahmias and Klein (1999).

[19]Gilad and Cohen (2018).

[20]Thatcher and Sweet (2002), p. 3.

authority away from established, representative organs (those that are directly elected, or are managed directly by elected politicians), to (b) a non-majoritarian institution, whether public or private". This chapter focuses primarily on delegation of legislative powers to ministers who sign secondary legislations on behalf of their ministry.[21] Ministers in parliamentary democracies, compared to presidential systems, have two different hats. Their first role is to take part in the cabinet, that is, the government decision-making body. Their second role is to administer government departments, which is more relevant to the everyday process of creating regulations.

Regarding their second role, ministers in parliamentary democracies serve as the heads of the government ministries, where civil servants formulate public policy.[22] Israel followed the British tradition and the practice of other parliamentary democracies, whereby the power to issue secondary legislation is mostly vested in a minister.[23] As stated in the Attorney General guidelines on secondary legislation, authorities to create secondary legislation should be generally given to ministers.[24] However, while ministers in some case are highly involved in the craft of secondary legislation, their role in designing and shaping regulation is minimal, allowing bureaucrats to dominate the process.[25]

The literature provides several explanations for the delegation of legislative powers from parliaments to bureaucracies, such as the expansion of the state's roles,[26] their shortened procedures to promote regulation;[27] the expertise of civil servants;[28] and blame-shifting strategies of politicians.[29]

In the context of omnibus legislation, delegating powers may grant advantaged players, such as the MOF, more control over the everyday use of other ministries' regulations. This, in turn, may allow the MOF better control on both the content and the constraints of their use of regulations.

3.2 Veto Players

Veto players, according to Tsebelis, refer to "an individual or collective actor whose agreement is necessary for a change of the status quo".[30] But veto actors, in fact,

---

[21]Page (2001, 2012).

[22]Huber (2000).

[23]Page (2001).

[24](2003) Attorney General Guidelines on Secondary Legislation.

[25]Page (2001).

[26]Croley (1998), Miers and Page (1982), Page (2001), Slapper and Kelly (2012) and Taggart (2005).

[27]Baldwin (1995), Miers and Page (1982), ibid., Slapper and Kelly (2012) and Taggart (2005).

[28]Baldwin (1995), Kerwin (2010) and Slapper and Kelly (2012).

[29]Frickey and Farber (1991), pp. 80–83.

[30]Tsebelis (1999, p. 593).

appear to a greater extent in everyday regulatory processes. Delegation of powers, in many cases, requires the cooperation of other players prior to publication. Such players may include second chambers, parliamentary committees, cabinet ministers, citizens, organizations, etc.

In this regard, the fragile and unstable structure of some coalitions is assumed to have incentivized the use of the Arrangements Laws in Israel. The more the coalition is unstable, argued Nachmias and Klein, the greater is the size of the Arrangements Laws.[31] This assumption was tentatively confirmed by the time of their study, but in fact the relative sizes of coalitions has shrunk over the years, while the size of the laws has increased.

A more nuanced explanation for the MOF's domination in the design of the laws was provided by Cohen and Gilad, suggesting a perspective of two-tiered bureaucratic and political struggles, according to which "the policy preferences of institutionally advantaged bureaus prevail only so long as politicians choose to, or are compelled to, remain offstage. Conversely, when powerful politicians choose to intervene on behalf of marginal bureaus, or when weakly positioned politicians successfully coordinate, overcoming their differences, powerful bureaus may find themselves forced to compromise against their will".[32] Cohen and Gilad argued that as long as the Prime Minister or the Finance Minister are from the same party, the MOF can enjoy its advantaged position over other government ministries. However, when weakly positioned politicians coordinate either the Prime Minister or the Finance Minister on behalf of their marginal ministry and the Prime Minister and the Finance Minister are not from the same party, the MOF may be forced to comprise.

This study observed the notion of veto players from a different perspective. Rather than focusing on the conditions whereby the MOF is more likely to gain powers at the expense of other ministries, this chapter shows how the MOF becomes a veto player by itself in the regulatory process and the everyday process of government through the delegation of legislative powers in the Arrangements Laws. In this regard, the emergence of veto actors has several implications to the theory of regulation in general. Above all, the existence of a larger number of veto players has a decisive impact on the ability to regulate in general. In short, the greater the number of veto players, the harder it is to make regulation.[33]

The Israeli Arrangements Law provides a promising case study in this regard. Recent governmental documents suggested that when the consent of ministers was required to implement regulations, the likelihood that the regulation would be published decreased.[34] In 2017, a government decision required the reduction of the number of mandatory regulations that have not yet been implemented.[35] The

---

[31]Nahmias and Klein (1999).

[32]Gilad and Cohen (2018).

[33]Tsebelis (1995, 1999).

[34]Knesset's Website (2014) The Government Violated the Obligation to Implement Regulations in 50 Laws.

[35]*Government Decision No. 2588*, 2017.

Table 1 Four mechanisms of the centralization through delegation in the arrangements laws

	Authority	Co-Authority	Consent	Consultation
Formulation	MOF	MOF and another cabinet minister	Another cabinet minister	Another cabinet minister
MOF's veto powers	–	High	High	Low
Level of cooperation between ministers	–	High	Low	Low

government decision followed the mapping of regulations that were not yet installed. The list of regulations amounted to 150, but the entire amount of potential regulations that have not yet made was probably much larger, as many regulations were not mandatory but rather equipped government ministries with discretionary powers.

3.3 Centralization via Delegation

This section introduces four mechanisms of centralization through delegation that appeared in the Arrangements Laws: new authorities to create regulation, shared authorities to create regulation, consent, and consultation (Table 1). Each of these mechanisms varies in the level of coordination between the MOF and other ministries and the existence of veto powers on regulatory decisions. Together they exemplify how delegations can be used to centralize power rather than decentralize.

The first mechanism, the granting of new authorities, presents delegation of authorities to the MOF on issues that were not necessarily under its implementation responsibility. The exercise of such authority does not require any collaboration with other players. Co-authorization, on the other hand, displays a mechanism of centralization that authorizes the MOF to create regulation along with other players. Under this mechanism, both players can veto the initiatives of each other, and thus high levels of cooperation are required. As early as 1985, under the guidelines of the Attorney General regarding secondary legislation, it was mentioned that: "such an arrangement can cause multiple difficulties and sometimes thwart the proper implementation of the law" (p. 11). For most of the laws, implementation responsibility often lies with one ministry, a case of co-authority that includes the MOF can be seen as its own attempt to gain veto powers on a future decision of another ministry.

In contrast, consent and consultation are additional mechanisms that require one or more players to either approve or consult with the MOF during the regulatory process and before publication.[36] Although these mechanisms differ in the levels of veto powers the latter has (Table 1), both of them require the involvement of the

---

[36]This research focuses mainly on the consent and approvals mechanisms as longs as they were given by governmental actors, such as cabinet ministers, and not by legislative actors, such as parliamentary committees.

MOF in the regulatory process. In the case of consent, other ministries with regulatory powers cannot bring into effect a regulation without prior agreement of the MOF. In contrast to the mechanism of consent, consultation does not require an agreement of the MOF before signing a regulation. The mechanism of consent provides the MOF with excessive veto powers on other ministries' decision. The case of consultation, on the other hand, provides a more complex category of a veto mechanism. It does require a particular ministry to consult the MOF before an action is taken, but regulation can take effect even without the MOF's consent.

4   Methodology

The data for this study was collected from 38 Arrangements Laws legislated between 1985 and 2019 (Appendix 1). While it was not difficult to recognize most of the Arrangements Laws according to their title and date of publication, some laws required a more complex decision.

Overall, the choice of whether to include certain laws was based on their characteristics. Such criteria include their legislation along the Budget Law, as well as having a feature of omnibus legislation (the inclusion of various bills and amendments). In addition, in some years, the Arrangements Laws were separated into several pieces. For example, in 1991, three laws were enacted: on January 31, the Arrangements in the State Economy Law (levies and municipal taxes) passed together with the state budget. On March 27, the Arrangement in the State Economy Law (Legislative Amendments) passed along the Arrangements in the State Economy Law (Creation of Conditions for Growth and Immigrant Absorption). Although the legislative process of the latter two was different from the former, they were all included in the dataset, based on their omnibus character. Furthermore, since 2009, the budget has been converted to a biennial budget plan, thus no such legislation passed some years afterwards. Another change has taken place since 2015, as Arrangements Laws were separated into two bills—one for the legislative reforms and one for the budgetary provisions.[37]

---

[37]Zarhia Z (2018) 'Third Apartment Tax Case Restored Our Deterrence' (Hebrew). In: Calcalist. https://www.calcalist.co.il/local/articles/0,7340,L-3739857,00.html. Accessed 27 December 2018.

Moving from data collection to data analysis,[38] delegation has three elements that are crucial to any strategy of its measurement:[39] authority, content and constrains. First, the agent or agents as holders of policy-making power (authority). Second, a set of constraints or conditions on the granted authority (constrains). Finally, the substantive content of those powers (content). In this paper, the focus was mainly on the first and third elements, examining both delegation of powers to cabinet ministers, and three types of constraints on delegation as appeared in Israeli laws: consent, approval, and consultation.[40]

The analysis of all delegations was done both on corpus-based methods and manual content analysis. First, I converted the PDfs files of the 38 Arrangements Laws to text files, using the Public Knowledge Workshop (*Hasadna*) optical character recognition (OCR). Second, I created a word dictionary comprising the government ministers, which was used to identify every mention of a minister in the law. Third, I extracted all sentences mentioning ministers and classified only those which contained delegation of authorities to create binding regulations.

In contrast to other works on delegation,[41] the unit of analysis here is a sentence providing an authority to a cabinet minister rather than an article of a law. The advantage of this approach is that the division of laws into articles and sub-articles is not uniform. Some articles are, in fact, very long, and may include several granted authorities. Breaking articles into sentences, thus, allows a better comparison between all the authorities granted through the Arrangements Laws.

After collecting all the delegation sentences, I coded each sentence according to a list of enabling verbs for the creation of secondary legislation: to determine (*likboa'a*), to regulate (*lehatkin, lehasdir*), etc. Note that I focused only on delegations to create binding regulations, omitting authorities given to ministers for other activities. Overall, 893 delegations were detected in the Arrangements Laws.

---

[38] Note that for the data analysis, the allocation of laws to years was not clear-cut. While most of the arrangements laws are legislated in the beginning or an end of a calendar year, referring either to the same budgetary year or the subsequent budgetary year correspondingly, there are two caveats. The first are laws that were legislated in the middle of a calendar year with a fragile connection to specific budgetary year. In such cases, if the law was legislated before June 30, I assigned it to its year of legislation, and otherwise, to the subsequent year of legislation. Additionally, as some laws were enacted along a biennial budget, I decided again to allocate them to one of or two years based on the same rule (for the match between years and laws, see Appendix 1).

[39] Anastasopoulos and Bertelli (Forthcoming).

[40] The legal language distinguishes approval (*Eyishur*) and agreement (*Haskama*), but we treat them similarly here.

[41] Anastasopoulos and Bertelli (Forthcoming), Franchino (2007) and Huber and Shipan (2002).

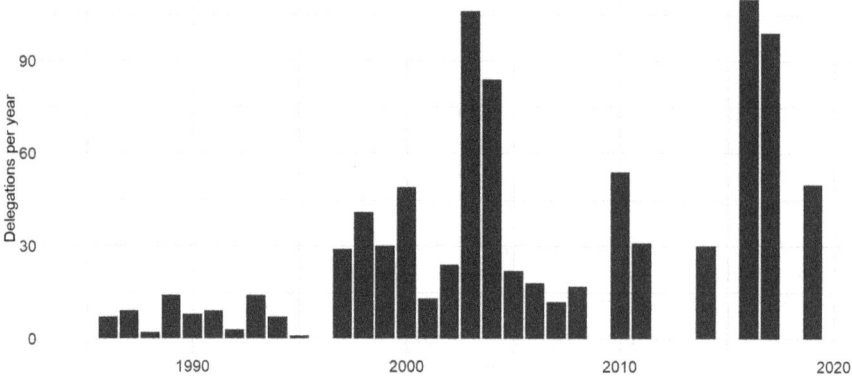

Fig. 1 Number of delegations included in the arrangements laws during 1985–2019

5   Findings

5.1   *Delegations by Minister*

Figure 1 presents the number of delegations included in all Arrangements Laws during 1985–2018. As shown, the number of delegations sharply fluctuated along the years, ranging from zero in 1996 to 110 in 2016. However, there has been a significant increase over the years in the number of delegations.

As noted in a previous work,[42] the number of policy issues covered by the Arrangements Laws had been tremendously extended over the years. More specifically, the turning point of the Arrangements Laws—from relatively limited omnibus legislation pertaining exclusively to economic goals to an extensive omnibus legislation covering various policy domains—was 1997. As the laws have become longer and their policy agendas expanded, they also delegated much more authorities to ministries to create regulations.

In line with these findings, until 1996 the average number of delegations in the laws was 6.7 with a standard deviation of 4.8. Since 1996, it rose to 45.5 with a standard deviation of 32.5 due to considerable fluctuations. As shown, delegations culminated in 2003 and 2016 with 106 and 110 delegations correspondingly, whereas other periods such as 2001–2002 and 2005–2008 introduced relatively fewer delegations, ranging from 13 to 22.

Taken together, Fig. 1 indicates that the impact of the Arrangements Laws on the regulatory process has increased over the years. Unlike previous studies that primarily focused on the effect of the Arrangements Laws on primary legislation, such as the National Insurance Law or the National Health Insurance Law, it is evident that the Arrangements Laws have had, in fact, large impact on the regulatory process too.

---

[42]Kosti et al. (2019b).

In other words, the Arrangements Laws have granted extensive authorities to ministries for the creation of new regulations. But as illustrated in the next sections, these regulatory powers were mainly used by the MOF to gain greater control over other ministries' regulatory activities.

5.2   Four Mechanisms of Centralization

5.2.1   Authority

Delegations in the Arrangements Laws have granted authorities to most of the Israeli ministries over the years.[43] Figure 2 provides a dynamic overview of all delegation sentences by the ministers (and ministries accordingly) they authorize to create regulation. As each delegation authorizes either one or more ministries to create regulations, any such authority, even if it was shared with more than one ministry, was counted one time for each ministry.[44] As shown, the number of delegations varies largely among ministries.[45] The Minister of Foreign Affairs, for example, was never any authorities to create regulations through the Arrangements Laws, whereas other ministers, such as the Minister of Public Security, the Minister of Tourism, the Minister of Religious Issues, the Minister of Culture, and the Prime Minister granted authorities to issue regulations through the laws only rarely.

From the data in Fig. 2, it is apparent that the Minister of Finance was delegated authorities to create regulations 364 times—a number that makes him the leading minister in terms of authorities to create regulation through the Arrangements Laws. This number constitutes 40 percent of all delegations included in the Arrangements Laws. However, almost half of these authorities were shared with other ministers, a mechanism that will be discussed in the next section. As shown in Fig. 2, until 1997, the authorities delegated to the Minister of Finance's share of delegations were relatively high compared to other ministers. Through the years, however, as the number of authorities given to the MOF has increased, as other ministers had also granted powers to make regulations. This happened as the Arrangements Laws have become more considerable. Yet, there is no clear-cut connection between the size of the laws as illustrated by the number of words they contain (for further information, see Appendix 2), and the number of delegations in these laws.[46]

---

[43]The "General" category refers potentially to all ministers.

[44]The overall number of delegations included in the Arrangements laws between 1986 and 2019 was 893. Since some delegations provided authority to more than one minister, and due to the counting scheme, the overall number of authorities given to ministries was 1104.

[45]As mentioned in the introduction, while Ministers are formally authorized to make regulations, the process of such everyday policymaking is dominated by the ministries.

[46]Overall, it seems that the larger the law, the more likelihood it contains more delegations. Yet, the amount of delegation sharply differs.

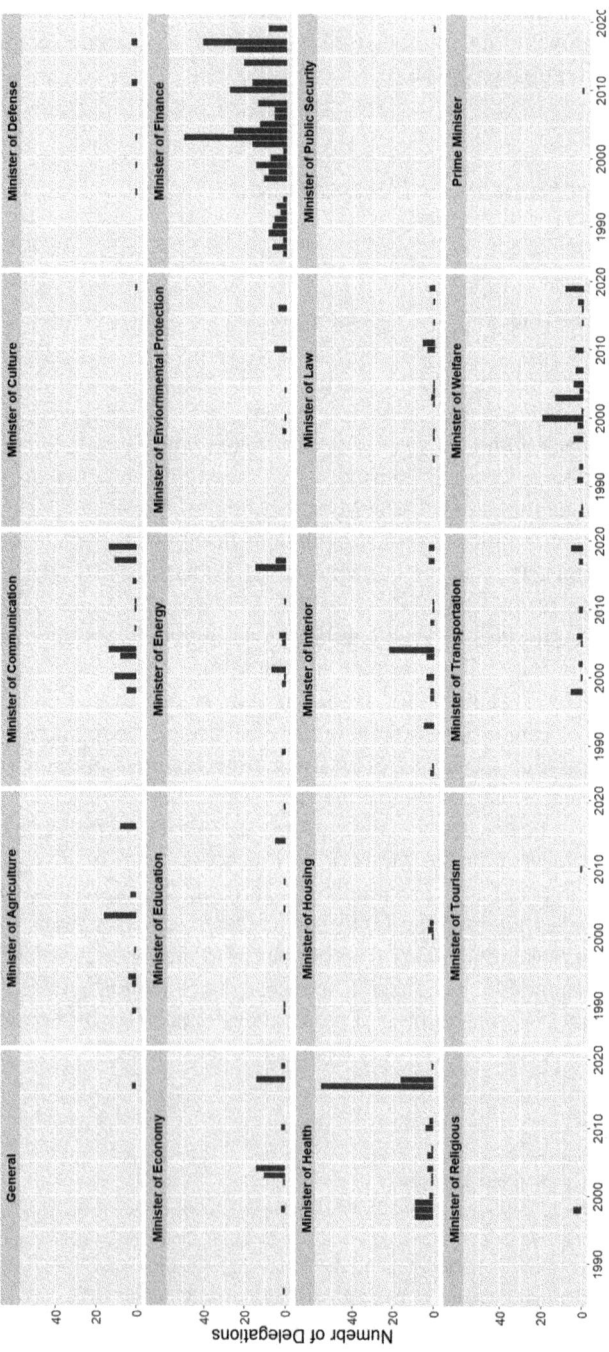

Fig. 2 Delegations by ministers in the arrangements laws, 1985–2019

Interestingly, among the 179 authorities the Minister of Finance granted to create regulations alone (the rest were shared with other ministers), many of them were included as part of laws whose implementation was under the responsibility of other ministries. These laws included the National Insurance Law, the Postal Authority Law, The Mines Ordinance, the Veterinary Doctors Law, the Shipping and Ports Authority Law, the Natural Gas Sector Law, etc. While these authorities can be seen as the MOF's attempt to exercise its budgetary powers in controlling other ministries' budgetary resources, they do have a real impact on policy decisions. As an illustration in this regard, an amendment of the Public Libraries Law in 2003 in the Law for Economic Recovery in Israel (Legislative Amendments to Achieve Objectives Regarding the State Budget and Economic Policy for the Fiscal Years 2003 and 2004) can be taken as an example:

> The Minister of Finance, in consultation with the Minister of the Interior and the Advisory Committee, and with the approval of the Education and Culture Committee of the Knesset, shall set conditions and criteria for determining the rate of participation of the State Treasury in the maintaining and management of a public library, considering the geographical location of the library.

Additionally, the MOF has also granted new authorities for making regulations under laws whose implementation was under its own responsibility. These laws include the Income Tax Ordinance, the Value Added Tax Law, the Civil Service (Pensions) Law, the Fuel Excise Law, the Control of Financial Services (Regulated Financial authorities) Law, the Supervision of Financial Services Law (Provident Funds). Such authorities, however, are exclusively in the MOF domain, and do not directly correspond to other ministries. Including them in the Arrangements Laws provides the MOF with additional powers, but not necessarily at the expense of other ministries.

Beyond the authorizations granted to the MOF, the Minister of Health was authorized to make regulations through the arrangements 183 times. As shown in Fig. 2, numerous authorities were granted to the Minister of Health in 2015, as part of the Public Health Protection Law, (Food), that was included in the Arrangements Laws of 2015. Additionally, other authorities were granted to the Minister of Health as part of the National Health Insurance Law, as well as other laws including the Pharmacists' Ordinance, the People's Health Ordinance. Among the 183 authorities, the Ministry of health granted 114 of them alone, while the rest included a few dozens authorities that were constrained by other ministries.

Apart from the Minister of Health, other ministers also granted a relatively large number of authorities over the years. They included the Minister of Interior, the Minister of Social Affairs, the Minister of Communication, and the Minister of Economy—each one of which were delegated authority to make regulations at least 50 times. While some authorities were either shared or constrained by the MOF, we can still argue that the fact that the MOF itself formulated the laws allowed it to gain some control over the outcomes of those authorities.

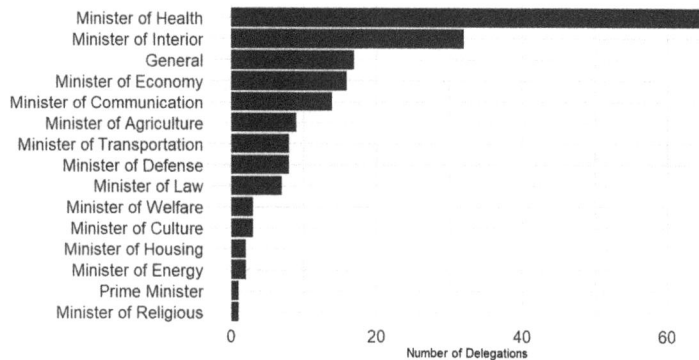

Fig. 3 Co-authority granted to the minister of finance and other ministers

5.2.2 Co-authority

An examination of all delegations included in the Arrangements Laws revealed that 22 percent of them (207) granted authorities to more than one minister. In such cases of co-authority, both players have had equal powers in the process of designing and making a regulation. This means that both players must have reached an agreement during the regulatory process, and that both have had large veto powers over each other's decisions. In other words, one of five delegation in the Arrangements Laws provided extensive veto powers to ministries in designing and creating the regulations of other ministries. Yet, these veto powers were not shared equally by all the ministries. In fact, almost 90 percent of them (185) were shared by the MOF and another ministry.

Figure 3 presents the amount of delegation of authorities shared between the Minister of Finance and other ministers. As illustrated, 65 delegations were shared with the Minister of Health. The large authorities given to the Minister of Finance in the health sector, and especially concerning the National Health Insurance law, have already been described in the academic literature.[47] In fact, 72 percent of the legislative amendments in the National Health Insurance law during the first decade of its implementation were part of the Arrangements Laws.[48]

No previous study has investigated, however, how the Arrangements Laws have given the MOF a dominant position in everyday health policymaking by sharing authority with the Minister of Health to create regulations on certain topics. This position has made the MOF, de facto, a powerful veto player in the Ministry of Health's regulatory duties. Such duties include the management and funding of

[47] Asiskovich (2011); Cohen (2013); Horev and Babad (2005); Horev T, Kedar N, *Light and Shadow in the Development and Implementation of the National Health Insurance Law: Reflection of the Reform from Fifteen Years of Legislation*, 2010.

[48] Horev T, Kedar N, *Light and Shadow in the Development and Implementation of the National Health Insurance Law: Reflection of the Reform from Fifteen Years of Legislation*, 2010.

Health Maintenance Organization, health tax, medication oversight, pharmaceuticals and drugs regulation, etc.

Such use of co-authorities points to the influence the MOF gained on the everyday policy making decisions in various policy domains. Another notable example comes from delegation of authorities the MOF shared with the Minister of Interior. Many of these delegations dealt with municipal taxes, an issue that was originally under the sole responsibility of the Minister of Interior. This can be exemplified by an authority granted to the Minister of Finance and the Minister of Interior in the Economy Arrangements (Legislative Amendments for Achieving Budgetary Goals) Law of 1993:

> The Ministers will make by regulations, with the approval of the Knesset Finance Committee, minimum amounts and maximum amounts for the general property tax imposed by the local authorities on each type of property, and rules on updating the general property tax amounts, and may also determine the ratio between the amounts that will be levied on each type of property for each financial year.

5.2.3 Consent

Another mechanism of centralization apprent in the Arrangements Laws is the mechanism of consent. Laws sometimes demand that regulations be approved by certain players before publication. These players include ministers, parliamentary committees, or other public actors. The obligation to receive the consent of certain players give them the status of veto players, as their consent is a necessary condition before regulation can come into effect.

The Arrangements Laws included 164 delegations with an obligation to recieve consent in advance. Of these delegations, 113 involved the consent of the MOF (approximately 70 percent of all delegations). This means that the MOF has not only gained domination in everyday policymaking through authorities to create new regulations (either alone or with another ministry), but it also obtained large powers that allows it to forestall regulations of other ministers.

As illustrated in Fig. 4, the MOF had veto powers over delegations of 14 different ministers. In other words, the MOF could potentially prevent 14 other ministers from installing regulation, at least once. These ministers were the Minister of Social Affairs, the Minister of Health, the Minister of Economy, and the Minister of Communication—the four ministers that were mostly affected by this mechanism. For example, an amendment to the Foreign Workers Act in the State Economy Arrangements (Legislative Amendments for Achieving Budgetary Goals) Law of 2000 provided the MOF a veto power on medical insurance of foreign workers:

> The employer arranged, at his expense, medical insurance for the foreign worker for the duration of his employment, which would include a basket of services set by the Minister of Health in an order; The Minister of Health may, with the consent of the Minister of Finance, determine whether a medical insurance will include additional health services over those prescribed in the basket of services.

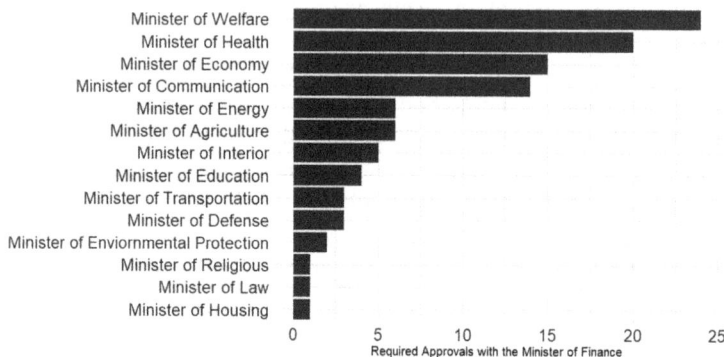

Fig. 4 Delegations required the consent of the MOF by minister

Interestingly, only 23 delegations of authorities to the MOF required the consent of other ministers. In other words, while the MOF has become a veto player in regulatory decisions of many other ministries, very few restrictions were actually set on the MOF itself as a regulatory player.

5.2.4 Consultation

Additional mechanism of centralization is the mechanisms of consultation. Laws sometimes require that before ministries issue regulations they ought to consult with other players. Consultation requirements are different than consent, because they do not require the agreement of these players on the final decisions.

According to the Attorney General Guidelines on Secondary Legislation (2003, p. 21), "the consultation shall be conducted at a stage and in a manner that allows the advisory body to comment on the regulations...". Since the player who promotes the regulation does not have to accept the position of the player with whom he consult, this mechanism seems much less effective than the mechanism of consent.

Evidently, this mechanism was far less common than the first three mechanisms. In fact, only 89 delegations required that before a player install a regulation, he must consult with other players. Out of these 89 delegations, 30 involved a consultation with the MOF, while in other 27 cases, the MOF was required to consult with another minister prior to publication.

This evidence suggests that when the MOF imposed restrictions on its own authority to make regulations, those constraints were far less restrictive than the restrictions imposed on other ministries. At the same time, the MOF has required that its consent on other ministries' regulations be accepted in advance much more than it demanded that it be taken into account in the form of consultation.

6   Conclusions

Delegation of legislative powers from legislatures to bureaucracies is a remarkable feature of contemporary governments. Those powers are translated into day-to-day regulatory activities of the executive. While this phenomenon usually reflects a process of decentralization of powers to various bureaucratic actors, this chapter suggests that the MOF has used the Israeli Arrangements Laws to centralize its powers in the everyday process of regulation.

Based on a unique dataset, this chapter investigated almost 900 delegation provisions included in 38 arrangements laws. Overall, out of all delegations included in the Arrangements Laws, the MOF was involved in nearly 60 percent of them through four mechanisms of centralization: (1) having new authorities to create regulation (20 percent); (2) Sharing authority to create regulation with another ministry (21 percent); holding a veto power over new regulations of other ministers either by requiring its (3) consent (14 percent) or (4) consultation (4 percent) prior to publication.

Altogether, while the literature on delegation mostly provides functional explanation for the delegation of legislative powers, this chapter argues that the process of delegation is highly politicized. In the Israeli context, the MOF uses the Arrangements Laws to gain excessive control over the regulatory powers of other ministers on a day-to-day basis. In other words, the process of centralization via delegation does not end with the legislation of the Arrangements Laws once a year. Rather, it allow the MOF to hold excessive control over parts of the government's day-to-day work. A quote made by Yoram Gabay, a former head of State Revenues Division in the MOF, reflects these findings squarely:[49]

> Since 1985, after the economic stabilization program, we, the Ministry of Finance officials, have taken control of the state, because the plan has succeeded so well, inflation has fallen from 400 percent to 20 percent, we have succeeded in streamlining the entire economy, and then the Knesset has decided on the Arrangements Law. We have been granted authority not only over the budget, but also over legislation and reforms. But over the years... the Ministry of Finance slowly increased its powers in government ministries until each change requires the approval of the Ministry of Finance; At the same time, the Ministry of Finance has lost its confidence in the ministers and their ability to restrain spending. This creates a split of responsibility and authority.

Yet, several questions remain unanswered at present. First, this research is part of our broader research agenda that aims to bring together the study of primary and secondary legislation.[50] While the academic literature has mostly studied delegation

---

[49] Amsterdamski S (2012) 'We, the Ministry of Finance Officials, have Taken over the Country' (Hebrew). In: Calcalist. https://www.calcalist.co.il/local/articles/0,7340,L-3575841,00.html. Accessed 27 December 2018.

[50] Kosti and Levi-Faur (2019).

to provide a better understanding of how politicians use it to shape their control over the bureaucracy,[51] the scope of its actual use is poorly understood.[52]

In the context of the Arrangements laws, it may be assumed that not all delegations deliberately aimed to result in regulation. In fact, the use of co-authorization and consent might have been intended to restrain future actions by other ministers. In line with the difficulties in implementing secondary legislation in Israel where more than one bureaucratic actor is involved,[53] it might be possible to observe the extent to which these delegations eventually yielded regulations.

Second, there is abundant room for further progress in determining to what extent the process centralization via delegation is limited to the Arrangements Laws. While the Arrangements Laws differ notably from the ordinary legislative process, investigation of delegations outside the Arrangements Laws were beyond the scope of this study. A future investigation will need to take into account delegations made under the ordinary legislative process to strengthen the validity of the findings.

Third, the practice of omnibus legislation is not an Israeli invention as this book illustrates. An important issue for future research may be the extent to which the process of centralization via delegation is limited to the Israeli arena.

Appendix 1: Laws Included in the Dataset

	Title of law	Date	Year of implementation[a]
1	Emergency Arrangements in the State Economy Law, 5746-1985	1.10.1985	1986
2	Economic Stability Law (Various Provisions), 5747-1987	9.4.1987	1987
3	Arrangements Law in the State Economy (Legislative Amendments for the Attainment of the Budget Goals), 5748-1988	17.4.1988	1988
4	Arrangements Law in the State Economy (Legislative Amendments), 5749-1989	7.4.1989	1989
5	Arrangements Law in the State Economy (Legislative Amendments), 5750-1990	6.4.1990	1990
6	Arrangements Law in the State Economy (Levies and Property Taxes), 5751-1991	31.1.1991	1991
7	Arrangements Law in the State Economy (Legislative Amendments), 5751-1991	27.3.1991	1991

(continued)

---

[51]Epstein and O'Halloran (1999), Franchino (2007), Huber and Shipan (2002) and Huber et al. (2001).

[52]Yackee and Yackee (2016).

[53](2003) Attorney General Guidelines on Secondary Legislation; *Annual Report 65c for the Year 2014 and for Fiscal Year*, 2015.

	Title of law	Date	Year of implementation[a]
8	Arrangements Law in the State Economy (Creating Conditions for Growth and Aliyah and Integration), 5751-1991	27.3.1991	1991
9	Arrangements Law in the State Economy (Legislative Amendments for the Attainment of the Budget Goals), 5752-1992	2.1.1992	1992
10	Arrangements Law in the State Economy (Legislative Amendments for the Attainment of the Budget Goals), 5753-1993	7.1.1993	1993
11	Arrangements Law in the State Economy (Legislative Amendments for the Attainment of the Budget Goals), 5754-1994	9.1.1994	1994
12	Arrangements Law in the State Economy (Legislative Amendments), 5755-1995	27.1.1995	1995
13	Arrangements Law in the State Economy (Legislative Amendments for the Attainment of the Budget Goals), 5756-1996	8.1.1996	1996
14	Arrangements Law in the State Economy (Legislative Amendments for the Attainment of the Budget Goals), 5757-1996	7.1.1997	1997
15	The Law for Enhancing the Growth and Employment for the Attainment of the Budget Goals for the Fiscal Year 1998 (Legislative Amendments), 5758-1998	15.1.1998	1998
16	Arrangements Law in the State Economy (Legislative Amendments for the Attainment of the Budget Goals and Economic Policy for the Fiscal Year 1999), 5759-1999	15.2.1999	1999
17	Arrangements Law in the Israeli State Economy (Legislative Amendments for the Attainment of the Budget Goals and Economic Policy for the Fiscal Year 2000), 5760-2000	10.1.2000	2000
18	Arrangements Law in the State Economy (Legislative Amendments for the Attainment of the Budget Goals and Economic Policy for the Fiscal Year 2001), 5761-2001	4.4.2001	2001
19	Arrangements Law in the State Economy (Legislative Amendments for the Attainment of the Budget Goals and Economic Policy for the Fiscal Year 2001), (Amendment, Repeal, and Postponent of Private Member's Bills) 5761-2001	4.4.2001	2001
20	Arrangements Law in the State Economy (Income Tax Discounts), (Temporary Order) 5761-2001	4.4.2001	2001
21	Arrangements Law in the State Economy (Legislative Amendments for the Attainment of the Budget Goals and Economic Policy for the Fiscal Year 2002), 5762-2002	17.2.2002	2002
22	Arrangements Law in the State Economy (Legislative Amendments for the Attainment of the Budget Goals and Economic Policy for the Fiscal Years 2002 and 2003), 5762-2002	16.6.2002	2002
23	Arrangements Law in the State Economy (Legislative Amendments for the Attainment of the Budget Goals and Economic Policy for the Fiscal Year 2003), 5763-2002	29.12.2002	2003

(continued)

	Title of law	Date	Year of implementation[a]
24	Recovery Program for the Israeli Economy 2003 (Legislative Amendments for the Attainment of Budget Goals and Economic Policy for Fiscal 2003–2004), 5763-2003	1.6.2003	2003
25	Economic Policy Law for the Fiscal Year 2004 (Legislative Amendments), 5764-2004	18.1.2004	2004
26	Economic Policy Law for the Fiscal Year 2005 (Legislative Amendments), 5765-2005	11.4.2005	2005
27	Arrangements Law in the State Economy (Legislative Amendments for the Attainment of the Budget Goals and Economic Policy for the Fiscal Year 2006), 5766-2006	15.6.2006	2006
28	Arrangements Law in the State Economy (Legislative Amendments for the Attainment of the Budget Goals and Economic Policy for the Fiscal Year 2007), 5767-2007	11.1.2007	2007
29	Arrangements Law in the State Economy (Legislative Amendments for the Attainment of the Budget Goals and Economic Policy for the Fiscal Year 2008), 5768-2008	1.1.2008	2008
30	Economic Efficiency Law (Legislative Amendments to for Implementing the Economic Plan for 2009–2010), 5769-2009	23.7.2009	2010
31	Economic Policy Law for the Years 2011 and 2012 (Legislative Amendments), 5771-2011	6.1.2011	2011
32	The Law for Changing National Priorities (Legislative Amendments for the Attainment of the Budget Goals for 2013–2014), 5773-2013	5.8.2013	2014
33	Economic Efficiency Law (Legislative Amendments for the Attainment of the Budget Goals for the Budget Years 2015–2016), 5775-2015	30.11.2015	2016
34	Economic Efficiency Law (Legislative Amendments for Implementing the Budget Goals for the Budget Years 2015–2016), 5775-2015	30.11.2015	2016
35	Economic Efficiency Law (Legislative Amendments for the Attainment of the Budget Goals for the Budget Years 2017–2018), 5777-2016	29.12.2016	2017
36	Economic Efficiency Law (Legislative Amendments for Implementing the Budget Goals for the Budget Years 2017–2018), 5777-2016	29.12.2016	2017
37	conomic Efficiency Law (Legislative Amendments for Implementing the Economic Policy for the Budget Year 2019), 5778-2018	22.03.2018	2019
38	Economic Efficiency Law (Legislative Amendments for the Attainment of the Budget Goals for the Budget Year 2019), 5778-2018	22.03.2018	2019

[a]Round

Appendix 2: Number of Words in the Arrangements Laws, 1986–2019

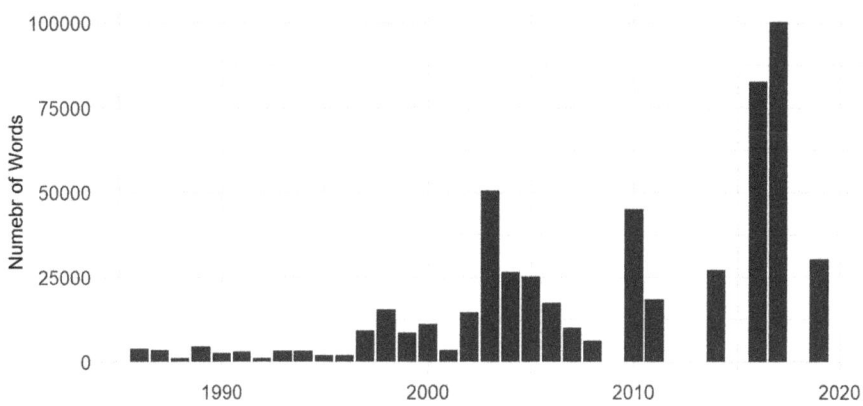

References

Anastasopoulos J, Bertelli AM (forthcoming) Understanding delegation through machine learning: a method and application to the European Union. Am Polit Sci Rev

Asiskovich S (2011) Life has a price: the political economy of the national health insurance reform in Israel (Hebrew). Jerusalem

Baldwin R (1995) Rules and government. Clarendon Press, Oxford

Bar-Siman-Tov I (2015) The role of courts in improving the legislative process. Theory Pract Legis 3:295–313

Ben-Bassat A, Dahan M (2006) The balance of power in the budgeting process (Hebrew). The Israeli Democracy Institute, Jerusalem

Cohen N (2013) The power of expertise? Politician–bureaucrat interactions, national budget transparency and the Israeli health care policy. Policy Stud 34:638–654. https://doi.org/10.1080/01442872.2013.804174

Croley SP (1998) Theories of regulation: incorporating the administrative process. Columbia Law Rev 98:1–168. https://doi.org/10.2307/1123396

Epstein D, O'Halloran S (1999) Delegating powers: a transaction cost politics approach to policy making under separate powers. Cambridge University Press, Cambridge

Franchino F (2007) The powers of the union: delegation in the EU. Cambridge University Press, Cambridge

Frickey PP, Farber D (1991) Law and public choice. The University of Chicago Press, Chicago

Gilad S, Cohen N (2018) Bureaucratic politics in Israel. In: The Oxford handbook of Israeli politics and society. Oxford University Press

Golan E (2008) The democratic deficit of the arrangements law and the erosion of the Israeli Welfare State (Hebrew). Law Gov 11:243–331

Horev T, Babad YM (2005) Healthcare reform implementation: stakeholders and their roles: the Israeli experience. Health Policy 71:1–21. https://doi.org/10.1016/j.healthpol.2004.05.001

Huber JD (2000) Delegation to civil servants in parliamentary democracies. Eur J Polit Res 37:397–413. https://doi.org/10.1023/A:1007033306962

Huber JD, Shipan CR (2002) Deliberate discretion? The institutional foundations of bureaucratic autonomy. Cambridge University Press, Cambridge

Huber JD, Shipan CR, Pfahler M (2001) Legislatures and statutory control of bureaucracy. Am J Polit Sci 45:330–345. https://doi.org/10.2307/2669344

Kerwin CM (2010) Rulemaking: how government agencies write law and make policy, 4th edn. CQ Press, Washington, DC

Kop Y (2010) A sting in its tail: 1985 Israel economic stabilization plan and the arrangements law method that accompanied it. In: Lissak M, Hacohen D (eds) Critical decisions in Israel. Ben-Gurion University Publisher, Beer-Sheva, pp 238–261

Kosti N, Levi-Faur D (2019) The co-production of primary and secondary legislation: Israel as a case study. Law Policy 41:432–457

Kosti N, Levi-Faur D, Mor G (2019a) Legislation and regulation: three analytical distinctions. Theory Pract Legis 7:169–178

Kosti N, Shpizman I, Levi-Faur D (2019b) The Israeli Agendas Project. In: Baumgartner FR, Grossman E, Breuning C (eds) Comparative Agendas Project. Oxford University Press, Oxford, pp 114–119

Maor A, Bar Nir D (2008) Implications of the sweeping use of the economic arrangements law on social gaps in 2002–2005 (Hebrew). Soc Secur 77:95–124

Miers D, Page AC (1982) Legislation. Sweet & Maxwell, London

Nahmias D, Klein E (1999) The arrangements law: between economics and politics [Hebrew]. The Israel Democracy Institute, Jerusalem

Page EC (2001) Governing by numbers: delegated legislation and everyday policy-making. Hart Publishing, Portland

Page EC (2012) Policy without politicians: bureaucratic influence in comparative perspective. Oxford University Press, Oxford

Rose-Ackerman S (2019) Executive rulemaking and democratic legitimacy: 'Reform' in the United States and the United Kingdom's Route to Brexit. Chic-Kent Law Rev 94:267

Slapper G, Kelly D (2012) The English legal system: 2012–2013. Routledge, London

Sperling D, Cohen N (2012) The influence of the Israeli state economy arrangement law and Supreme Court decisions on health policy and the right to health in Israel – neo-institutional analysis. Hukim- Isr J Legis 4:153–236

Taggart M (2005) From 'parliamentary powers' to privatization: the chequered history of delegated legislation in the twentieth century. Univ Tor Law J 55:575–627. https://doi.org/10.1353/tlj.2005.0030

Thatcher M, Sweet AS (2002) Theory and practice of delegation to non-majoritarian institutions. West Eur Polit 25:1–22. https://doi.org/10.1080/713601583

Tsebelis G (1995) Decision making in political systems: veto players in presidentialism, parliamentarism, multicameralism and multipartyism. Br J Polit Sci 25:289–325. https://doi.org/10.1017/S0007123400007225

Tsebelis G (1999) Veto players and law production in parliamentary democracies: an empirical analysis. Am Polit Sci Rev 93:591–608. https://doi.org/10.2307/2585576

Yackee J, Yackee S (2016) From legislation to regulation: an empirical examination of agency responsiveness to congressional delegations of regulatory authority. Adm Law Rev 68:395–443

Nir Kosti PhD candidate, the Department of Political Science, the Hebrew University of Jerusalem.

When Rationalisation of Bureaucracy De-rationalizes Laws and Legislatures: 'Monster Bills' in France

Olivier Rozenberg

Abstract The last decade has seen the development of the so-called 'monster bills' in France, that is too say remarkably long laws, putting together heterogeneous elements. Among the notorious examples of them, we investigate the 'Grenelle laws' aiming at protecting the environment field (2009) and the 'Macron Law' aiming at liberalizing the economy (2015). The development of these laws is interpreted as resulting from two factors: a. the willingness of the executive power to send a diversity of messages to a diversity of audiences through visible legislation, b. pressures from bureaucracies of state departments cyclically willing to promote their reforms in a context of limited access to the legislatures' agenda. The paper presents this process as well as it consequences for the functioning of the parliament in terms of work-overload, lobbying and MPs influence. The paper supports the view that the inner-logic of rationalization within the State paradoxically lead to de-rationalize the legislative procedure, i.e. a greater complexity and legal as well as political uncertainty in the passing of such bills.

Keywords Law · Law-making · France · French National Assembly · Monster laws · Omnibus laws

1   Introduction

Strictly speaking, there are no omnibus laws in France. Finance bills constitute the closest legal instruments to them. When the government wants to modify significantly public spending, it should be done through Finance bills, either during fall with the usual budgetary procedure or at other periods of the year with a corrigendum to the Finance law. Any type of provisions holding financial consequences can be integrated whatever their topic. Since 1995, provisions related to the Welfare

O. Rozenberg (✉)
Center for European Studies & Comparative Politics, Sciences Po, Paris, France
e-mail: olivier.rozenberg@sciencespo.fr

© The Author(s), under exclusive license to Springer Nature Switzerland AG 2021   95
I. Bar-Siman-Tov (ed.), *Comparative Multidisciplinary Perspectives on Omnibus Legislation*, Legisprudence Library 8, https://doi.org/10.1007/978-3-030-72748-2_5

State financing are passed through a specific budgetary instrument. Despite the great heterogeneity in their content, Finance bills cannot be considered as genuine omnibus laws as they should deal with financial issues.

All other kinds of law require having a minimal homogeneity in terms of topics covered. These topics can be defined widely—for instance 'economic growth' or 'health'—but it should be defined. Each law has a leading minister who hold the responsibility for preparing the bill and for its passing in parliament which also strengthen its homogeneity. Arguably, the government can insert provisions that are totally unrelated to the topic of the bill but it runs the risk of being blamed for that. If the adding of new provisions of that kind is realised through amendments during the passing in parliament, the Constitutional Council may also censure them for being too remote from the initial content of the bill.

Despite the lack of genuine omnibus laws in France, close phenomenon can be observed during the recent period. There is first an increase in the size of some bills resulting both from their important size at the governmental stage and from the amendments during the parliamentary phase. Second, we observe a multiplication of bills that cover a large number of policy fields.[1] Despite being defined by a given topic, these bills address, usually on purpose, a variety of issues. Some bills are characterised by both aspects: they are long and multi-field. We propose to name them 'monster bills' following a naming which is sometimes used in the media and by practitioners—'catch-all bill' or 'tote bill' (*loi fourre-tout*) being also used.

Big bills, heterogeneous bills, monsters bills: this chapter offers an in-depth investigation of these legal instruments over the last decade. It supports the view that their significance has to do with two unrelated factors. First, the fact that laws are signal sent to third parts, and second the scarcity of plenary time. The paper presents this process as well as it consequences for the functioning of the parliament in terms of work-overload, lobbying and MPs influence. The paper supports the view that the inner-logic of rationalization within the State paradoxically lead to de-rationalize the legislative procedure, i.e. a greater complexity and legal as well as political uncertainty in the passing of such bills.

This chapter first present the main characteristics of big laws, heterogeneous laws and monster laws in France. The second section discusses the rationales for their development. The third develops the examples of two recent bills related to environment and economy. A fourth section questions the democratic quality of these monster bills seen from a diversity of perspectives.

---

[1] Existing studies point to the increase in the bills size (Hispalis 2005; Council of State 2016, 2018). To our knowledge, the trend regarding the heterogeneity of the bills has not been considered so far. Our data cover the 2008–2018 period only and do not enable us therefore to compare with the previous one.

2 Big Bills, Heterogeneous Bills and Monster Bills

Our investigation requires to identify which texts fall into the categories defined in introduction. This supposes to give precise criteria for selecting bills.[2] From 2008 to 2018, about one thousand bills became laws in France.[3] Nearly half of them deal with international agreements (400 out of 925). It is indeed a French specificity that bilateral or multilateral diplomatic agreements should be incorporated into domestic legislation through a parliamentary act.[4] These bills have a limited, if not null, political significance: they cannot be amended and are passed through a specific fast-track procedure. Once these bills as well as budgetary texts are put aside, there remains 469 ones adopted during the 2008–2018 decade.

These texts vary greatly in terms of numbers of initial (i.e. before the parliamentary procedure) number of characters from 112 to 437,712. The 5% of these bills that are the longest form the 'long bills' category. The identification of heterogeneous bills is realized through legal codes. French legislation is indeed categorised according to codes that gather pieces of legislation according to policy fields—the most famous one being the Penal Code often called the Napoléon Code by the name of its founder. The main codes deal with labour (11,007 articles in 2019), building and housing (3523), civil matters (2873), tax (2398) and urbanism (2285).[5] Bills passed in France from 2008 to 2018 made references to one to 38 codes. The 5% of the bills that make reference to the highest numbers of codes cited more than 22 codes. These are considered as heterogeneous bills.

Table 1 provides descriptive statistics for several kinds of bills.

Table 1 indicates that big laws, heterogenous laws and the yearly budget are close to each over in terms of size and of cited codes. Yet, big laws are systematically multi-dimensional while some multidimensional laws are not always long. When crossing the 25 longest laws and the 25 more heterogeneous ones, a list of twelve texts belonging to both group—the monster laws—logically appears. These laws are listed in Table 2.

Table 2 shows a diversity of the issues addressed by 'monster bills'. Economy, a major source of concern for citizens, is present through two texts which cover a high diversity of policy fields. But many other types of issues are addressed, including some that are remote from citizens concerns, such as the simplification of law. We also note that these bills are not proposed just after the arrival of a new parliamentary

---

[2]Source for all the figures from this chapter: lafabriquedelaloi.fr. This work is supported by a public grant overseen by the French National Research Agency (ANR) as part of the "Investissements d'Avenir" program LIEPP (reference: ANR-11-LABX0091, ANR-11-IDEX-0005-02). My warmest thanks to the lafabrique team and especially the Regards Citoyens hacktivists and Damien Marié.

[3]Only bills that finally became laws are considered which excluded the rare governmental texts that are abandoned and the numerous private members bills that are tabled but not considered on the floor of the assemblies.

[4]Brouard et al. (2009).

[5]Source: Secrétariat général du gouvernement (2019).

Table 1 Types of laws adopted in France (2008–2018)

	Number	Initial number of words	Initial number of characters	Mean number of cited codes
All laws	469	3847	25,718	6
Big laws	25	30,662	190,864	27
Heterogenous laws	25	19,920	119,330	29
Finance laws	10	36,212	237,288	29

Note: the main and single text voted yearly has been considered for Finance laws, international agreements excluded
Source: https://www.lafabriquedelaloi.fr/

Table 2 'Monster bills' in France (2008–2018)

Title	Year start	Duration (days)	Initial size (charac.)	Cited codes
Modernisation of economy	2008	99	178,679	38
Environment ('Grenelle II')	2009	547	287,569	36
Simplification of law	2011	239	138,880	32
Agriculture, food & forest	2013	335	193,796	26
Growth, activity… ('Macron')	2014	239	162,280	37
Organisation of regional governments	2014	416	174,237	28
Energy transition	2014	384	171,811	33
Health	2014	469	222,488	33
Architecture and patrimony	2015	366	123,968	23
Labour	2016	138	294,969	25
Equality and citizenship	2016	290	115,621	33
Local housing	2018	234	255,481	32

Note: duration = total duration in days of the examination in parliament
Source: https://www.lafabriquedelaloi.fr/

majority, which was the case in that period in 2012 with a left-wing President, François Hollande, and 2017 with a centre-right one, Emmanuel Macron. This may be explained by the duration of the passing of these texts in parliament—as a mean 313 days, nearly one year—which can discourage a new majority willing to obtain quick results.

Two of these laws will be especially considered in the rest of the text. The text called 'Grenelle 2' deals with a diversity of environmental issues.[6] More than one hundred articles are organised around six headings related to housing, transport, energy, biodiversity, recycling and the institutional governance of environmental issue. The so-called Marcon Law is even more diverse in its content.[7] The bill took in

---

[6]Law n° 2010-788 of 12 July 2010 for a national commitment for environment. This law came after a first one the previous year who defined the general objectives of environmental policies.

[7]Law n° 2015-990 of 6 August 2015 for Growth, activity and equality of economic chance.

Table 3 Initiative of laws adopted in France (2008–2018, %)

	Government	National Assembly	Senate
All laws	57	24	18
Big laws	92	8	0
Heterogeneous laws	88	8	4
Finance laws	100	0	0

Note: international agreements not included
Source: https://www.lafabriquedelaloi.fr/

the press the name of Hollande's young minister for Economy, Emmanuel Macron, who proposed it two years before betraying Hollande and being elected President of the Republic. The bill contains a diversity of measures aimed at strengthening economic growth, mainly through deregulation. The provisions touch issues as diverse as: coach transportation, building permits, driving licences, law jobs deregulation (especially notaries), Sunday working... The initial bills contained no less than ten chapters grouped around three titles ('free activity', 'invest' and 'work').

3 A Twofold Rational

Table 3 identifies the background of the different kind of bills adopted in France.

The high share of governmental bills among big and heterogeneous laws means that the rational for them has to be found on the executive side. The exceptions are indeed not numerous: we find only one-private member bill among the 25 'monster bills' listed in Table 2.[8] Why do ministers propose long and heterogeneous bills? We support the view that this process obeys to a twofold strategy which respective strength varies from a project to another.[9]

---

[8]Law n° 2016387 of 22 March 2012 on the Simplification of law and lightening of administrative procedures which originated from the chair of the powerful law committee of the National Assembly.

[9]This contribution seeks to explore the rationales for 'monster bills', i.e. bills that are both long and heterogeneous, rather than one of the two aspects separately. The analysis of the length of the bills only points indeed to a diversity of specific factors. Some are technical as the requirement to precise the status for over-seas territories, the on-going codification process or the frequent adding of reports to bills (see Hispalis 2005). Other are political and has to do with agency issues as theorised by Huber and Shipan (2002). Ministers may include details into their bills because they do not trust the administration in charge of the implementations, be it a strong minister afraid to be betrayed by her bureaucracy (typically the minister for Economy) or a weak minister afraid to lose future inter-ministerial battles (typically the minister for Environment).

3.1   A Public Signal Through Law and Law-Making

First, 'monster bills' constitute a signal sent to external actors. Arguably, each bill can be considered as a public signal sent for a diversity of reasons, beyond defining what can and cannot be done from a legal standpoint. Making laws is indeed a way of seducing voters or other actors given the general public attention for legislation and more generally the societal aura of laws as instruments of government.[10] If this claim is universalistic, there are reasons to believe that it is all the more relevant in France, a country where the 1789 Revolution was first realised through adopting laws and where the notions of law, willingness of people (*la volonté générale*) and States are intimately interconnected.[11] It has been demonstrated for instance that French governments occasionally take the risk to be censured by the Constitutional Council, should they held the benefice of demonstrating that public concerns are taken into account.[12] Legal scholars and practitioners also regularly complain about the lack of normative direct or obvious consequences of many symbolic legal provisions.[13] Therefore, we support the view that the very fact of proposing long and heterogeneous bills is assumed and staged by the executive power as a communication strategy. In other words, the monstrosity of these bills is turned into a proof of the government capability and willingness.

A diversity of audience can be targeted by such signalling strategy: public opinion in general, voters from a specific social group or from a region, stakeholders and the international community. Some bills are especially focussed towards one of these audiences but most of them tend to address signals to a diversity of publics which also contribute to extend their content. Examples are provided below.

3.2   A Procedural Opportunity

Second, ministers tend to propose long and/or heterogeneous bills for procedural reasons. Three elements may be distinguished here. The most important one is the scarcity of plenary time in parliament. Ministers and their administration know that

---

[10]The signal sent by law-makers does not principally result from the unequal information between actors as supposed by the game theory literature (for instance Banks 2001) but from the general uncertainty of all actors concerning the middle-terms consequences of a new law. Most of the time, it is unsure what new legal provisions will produce. Therefore, it is all the more important for law-makers to send the message that they are acting rightly. In addition, the message they sent when legislating can be, on some occasions, totally unrelated to the content of the law. It has been said for instance that President Hollande decided to merge French regions in 2014 to show 'Brussels' he was undertaking structural reforms.

[11]For a classical view of this issue: Carré de Malberg (1984).

[12]For a general model see Rogers (2001) and for the French case Brouard (2009).

[13]For instance Carcassonne (2005), Hispalis (2005) and reports of the Council of State regularly complaining about law inflation.

the opportunities to have a bill passed in parliament are rare. Anecdotal evidences indicate that governmental departments are in competition with each other to obtain from the President and Prime minister to draft legislative projects.[14] Putting many provisions in their bill is both a way to weight in these tense bargains ('take my bill, there is much in') and a consequence of the limited access to parliament. Ministers and bureaucrats are indeed aware of the uniqueness of the opportunity to prepare a bill. Major departments can expect to do about once every 2 years and minor ones at best once a parliamentary term (i.e. 5 years). In both cases, they want to make the most of this procedural opportunity by adding numerous and heterogeneous provisions. Furthermore, it may also be difficult for a minister to resist to the legislative input of her services for a variety of reasons, including her willingness to maintain good relations with senior civil servants.

The scarcity of floor time is confirmed from a comparative standpoint by the duration of plenary sessions. The National Assembly and the Senate often meet more than one thousand hours a year—which locate both assemblies among the first in Europe both in absolute and relative terms.[15] Everything seems to indicate that the assemblies have reached a maximum of duration and that it would be difficult to extent it further. The major reform of the Constitution in 2008 contributed to exacerbate the issue of the scarcity of floor time—especially from the government standpoint.[16] It has been indeed forbidden to pass legislation during one week out of four. Half of the agenda is also defined by the assemblies. Although exceptions are significant (and despite the fact that governmental bills can be considered during the weeks decided by the assemblies), this provision departs from the previous monopoly of the executive in defining the agenda and has led to an increase in the number of private members bills adopted since. A specific additional element linked to the 2008 constitutional reform may also lead to 'monster bills'. The famous article 49.3 of the French Constitution enables the National Assembly to pass a bill without voting it.[17] Once the government decides to use it, the only possibility for MPs to oppose the bill is to censure the government. This highly controversial instrument has been drastically limited in 2008 as the government can use it only once a year.[18] Given this institutional constraint, it is rational for the government, given that institutional constraint, to put all controvesial elements in the same text and use

---

[14]Meetings are regularly organised by the Prime minister services (Secrétariat général du gouvernement) to decide of the legislative agendas. Despite the usual commitments made by the executive power, the middle-term programing established during these meetings is more than often perturbed by on-going events, especially in a vertical and reactive political system such as French one (Brouard et al. 2009).

[15]Alke et al. (2021) and Rozenberg (2016).

[16]De Montis (2016).

[17]The procedure is sometimes called the guillotine in the literature. See Huber (1996).

[18]More exactly for one bill as it may be used at the different readings of the same bill. No restriction applies for Finance Bill and Social Security Financing Bill. The records of the procedure since 1959 indicate that the 49.3 is used either to bypass an unstable or relative majority or to circumscribe filibustering. More 'monster bills' should be therefore expected under these two circumstances.

Table 4 The analytical grid for 'monster bills' applied to the Grenelle 2 and Macron laws

		Grenelle 2 (2010)	Macron (2015)
Signalling strategy	Public opinion	Image of environment supporters	Modernity, action, anti-conservatism
	Stakeholders	Pro-environment NGOs	Private actors: pro-business image
	International actors	–	EU institutions & financial markets: pro structural reforms
Procedural strategy	Administrative input	Opportunity for a weak administration	Ambitious agenda of a strong administration
	Ex-ante consultations	Yes	No
	Hidden tracks	Yes indirecty: nothing on nuclear energy	Yes: several small provisions

the 49.3 without waiting for the following year. It is also rational to limit its occurrences as this procedure is especially costly within public opinion.[19]

There are two other, and less significant, procedural reasons for the existence of long and heterogeneous bills. First, the government has developed over the last years, vast ex-ante consultations of stakeholders and the large public. This trend illustrates the crisis of legitimacy of the executive power that seeks to rest on interested parts and/or citizens at an early stage. It is fed both by neo-corporatist and participative democracy inputs and has taken a great variety of shapes, including in 2019–2020 after the Yellow Vest protest, a committee of citizens on environment partly selected randomly. Whatever their shapes, these kinds of forums tend to open the Pandora legislative box. The usual lack of precision of the issues treated by these forums, the diversity of their participants, log-rollings between them or the search for consensus may result in longer and more heterogeneous bills. These forums may also constitute a trap for the government given the difficulty to departure from the conclusion of a participatory process that the government itself has decided to initiate. Second, from a more cynical standpoint, complex bills may also be a way from the government to hide difficult decisions or even non-decisions. The visibility of the measures that the minister want to adopt or to put aside may indeed be lower when lost within the legislative forest, especially as some other measures will attract (public and/or stakeholders) attention.

4   The Examples of the Grenelle 2 and Macron Laws

Table 4 offers an illustration of the analytical framework developed in the case of two 'monster bills' already evoked: Grenelle 2 on environment (2010) and Macron (2014–15) on economy.

---

[19]Becher and Brouard (2020).

4.1 The Signalling Strategy in Both Laws

The communicational aspect is significant for both laws. Elected in 2007, President Sarkozy originates from the Gaullist family which is closer to the productivist world then to environmental concerns. In a context where environmental issues gained ground in public opinion, he wanted to show both to specialised NGOs and to the general public that his majority was now seriously dealing with this issue. He organised a series of meetings involving no less than 1.500 actors that prepared two bills voted in 2009 and 2010.[20] The very word 'Grenelle' used by the authorities to name the whole process is illustrative of the communicative strategy. In the French political culture, 'Grenelle' refers indeed to a meeting organised in 1968 with labour and business representatives to increase wages in a building located in the street of Grenelle in Paris. By extension, the Grenelle format refers to large stakeholders consultations. The audiences targeted by the majority were both the general public and NGOs that had developed for the first time during the 2007 presidential campaign an active strategy for obtaining commitments from all candidates.[21] An international audience cannot be identified as that time but, a decade latter, the signatories of the Paris agreement on climate of 2015 and the Intergovernmental Panel on Climate Change (IPCC) would have certainly been targeted by this kind of law.[22]

The communicational aspect is also present in the Macron bill as illustrated by the first sentences of the explanatory memorandum that preceded the bill: 'To return to sustainable growth, the French economy must be modernized and the brakes on activity removed. To achieve these objectives, the law for activity and growth aims to ensure confidence, to simplify the rules that hamper economic activity and to strengthen the capacities to create, innovate and produce of French people and in particular the youth'.[23] This neo-Blairist message is framed for different targets. First, the general public. President Hollande may want to break with the reputation of limpness which he suffered from during the first months of his presidency. His minister Macron, who gave his name to the law in the press releases, also wanted to be perceived as modern and full of energy. Unknown in the public when he was named minister in late August 2014, he knew that this bill was a unique opportunity for developing an image of courageous and pragmatist politician willing to fight domestic taboos that were considered as drags for economic activity. There is indeed a willingness to stage his personal bravery in Macron's attitude. Most of the citizens knew for instance that facilitating Sunday work would immediately provoke

---

[20]See Boy et al. (2012) for a general presentation of the whole process.

[21]The 'Pacte écologique' promoted by a popular former TV-program presenter, Nicolas Hulot, had been signed during the campaign by Sarkozy.

[22]This was the case for the main environmental law passed during Holande's years: law n° 2015-992 of 17 August 2015 on the 'energy transition for green growth' which very name illustrates the signalling aspect of law-making.

[23]My translation of the explanatory memorandum (exposé des motifs) of the law.

demonstrations by trade unions. Despite repeated warnings, the ambitious minister deliberately decided to include this controversial provision.[24]

The government also wanted to address a pro-business message to domestic and foreign private actors. The socialist majority, who had tried in 2017 to introduce surtaxes on high incomes, had to improve its reputation vis-à-vis private business. The official discourse of the authorities also let understood that they considered that the 'confidence' of private actors was a key factor in their decision to invest. As said in the above mentioned sentence, the Macron law actually aimed to 'ensure confidence'. Last but not least, this law, as other adopted during Hollande's presidency, was also targeted at international organisations, the European Union and financial rating agencies. In May 2013, the European Council had given two years to France to balance its budgetary accounts. The passing of the Macron bill in parliament close to the deadline was actually a way of saying to the Commission and Northern Europe that the French government was finally implementing the so-called structural reforms.[25] The international pressure does not only originate from Brussels but also (and above all?) from financial markets. From January 2012 to July 2013, the three main financial rating agencies removed the 'triple A' for France. In a globalized economy where reputation (and not only macroeconomic balances) is taken into account by investors, a salient law was also a message sent to international economic circles.

4.2   The Procedural Strategy in Both Laws

There is as well a procedural aspect to both bills. From an administrative standpoint, the minister for Environment that prepared the Grenelle laws and the minister for Economy in charge of the Macron one are in opposite situation which both contributed nevertheless to draft these 'monster bills'. The former is heading a weak administration that is often defeated in the government internal bargains.[26] The opportunity to prepare a major bill was unique and led all services to make the

---

[24]A televised portray of the minister shows the negative reaction on this issue from his personal advisors (France 2 TV Chanel, 26 February 2015). A documentary on Hollande also indicates that senior majority backbenchers complained about it (Un temps de president by Yves Jeuland, 2015).

[25]Several decisions adopted at the EU level during the previous years targeted more precisely notaries. In a decision of 24 May 2011, the EU Court of Justice estimated the notaries were not participating to the exercise of 'public authorities' (C-50/08, Commission c/ France (Rec. I.04195)). In the 2012 recommendation of the European Council to France, a list of professions for which restrictions and barriers to entry should be removed mentioned: 'veterinarians, taxis, health sector, legal professions including notaries' (Recommendation for a COUNCIL RECOMMENDATION on France's 2012 national reform programme and delivering a Council opinion on France's stability programme for 2012-2016 /* COM/2012/0313 final */).

[26]For instance on the regulations relative to hunting for which the minister is in competition with the agriculture department. See Rozenberg (2020a, chapter 4).

most of it. The latter by contrast is a major pillar of the French State.[27] 'Bercy', as it is called, is used to play the role of referee during budgetary bargains and is therefore well-placed to obtain from the Prime minister to include a maximum of provisions in the bill. Some of them were a source of inter-ministerial tensions[28] but in most cases Macron succeeded in imposing his administration' views. The detailed chronology of the preparation of the bill also indicates the high degree of agency enjoyed by Bercy senior civil servants.[29] In March 2013, an internal body of the minister drafted a secret report on regulated professions calling for the liberalisation of some of them, particularly in the legal sector.[30] In July 2014, the then minister for Economy, Arnaud Montebourg, announced a bill on 'growth and purchasing power'. The view of this leftist politician, who will be fired one month later, were not similar to Macron's ones. Yet, his project already foresaw to deregulate partly different professions including notaries and bailiffs. This does not mean that the identity of the minister does not matter but that senior civil servants belonging to powerful State bodies typically sail them their pre-existing 'receipts'. The discretion given to these bureaucrats certainly is a classical phenomenon. What is more specific to Bercy is the mix between the internal divisions of its services and the global strength of this administration[31]—a cocktail that contributes to produce long and complex bills.

Other procedural aspects also played in the case of both laws. There has not been large consultations in the case of the Macron bill—quite the opposite. It was the case at an unprecedented level for the Grenelle. The multiplicity of actors embedded in the bargains was huge from NGOs to private business or local government representatives. The number of actors, the division in their talks between different groups, the large publicity of their debates lead the government to prepare two bills instead of one at the end, the second one being especially long and heterogeneous. In depth-analysis of the whole process confirms that 'Given its great complexity and its innovative dimension, built into action, the Grenelle drives a dynamic that partly escapes its designers and participants'.[32] The government was also all the more induced to follow the main results of the Grenelle that the process had created strong expectations among environment activists.

Regarding last the 'hidden track' aspect, both laws obey to different logics. There are indeed some 'hidden tracks' within the Macron law. Some provisions clear for

---

[27] See the special issue of the journal Pouvoirs (2019).

[28] For instance with the Justice ministers regarding the partial liberalisation of notaries, with the Labour minister regarding Sunday working and with the Home affairs ministers regarding driving licenses procedures.

[29] These senior civil servants belong to the 'programmatic elites' conceptualised by Genieys and Hassenteufel (2012). See also Genieys (2010).

[30] Inspection générale des finances (2012).

[31] See Bezes et al. (2019).

[32] My translation from Halpern and Pollard (2017, p. 125). Comparing two sectors from the Grenelle, waste and housing, they observe both that the bargains within each of these fields followed their own logics and that log-rolls and equilibrium were sought at the level of each field rather then globally—a trend that undoubtedly leads to 'monster bills'.

instance environmental protective rules in housing and urbanism with the hope that lowering regulation could stimulate economic growth. Strictly speaking, embedding such provisions within a bill as complex as this one does not hide them. Environmental NGOs were actually critical about the project. Yet, their views received lower echoes than if the articles had been presented in a dedicated legislative text. The press, the unions and the extreme left were focussed on Sunday working. The right was massively lobbied by notaries. Important regional leaders were concerned by airports privatisations. In this tense context, environmental issues arrived second, if not third. The case for the Grenelle is different. Contrary to Angela Merkel in 2011, Sarkozy decided since the beginning that the bargains will not question what was one of the main source of concern for environmentalists: France's past choices in favour of civil nuclear energy. For Greenpeace and other, this was a major source of disappointment. From that perspective, adding a long series of provisions within the text was a way to compensate for this initial choice. It is not a controversial article that was hidden within a monster bill as for Macron's one. It is the monstrosity of the bill that hide a major non-decision.

5   A Mixed Democratic Assessment

The very wording of 'monster bills' or 'tote bills' seems to imply that these bills are not good for democracy. A detailed assessment based on empirical evidences lead to a less clear-cut conclusion. We distinguish in the section the democratic quality of these bills according to three criteria: the legitimacy brought by the parliamentary procedure, the capacity of elected representatives to influence the bill content and the quality of the final product, i.e. the law itself.[33]

5.1   A Chaotic Parliamentary Procedure

The parliamentary procedure used to pass monster bills raises three legitimacy issues. First, it takes a lot of time and may be therefore a source of frustration. Second, it is often somehow chaotic given the size of the bills. Third, these bills often raise strong opposition that is circumscribed by using special and unpopular procedural arrangements. Before coming back to these three points, an overview of the comparative duration of the procedure is provided at Table 5.

Despite the frequent use of the accelerated procedure,[34] it takes, on the average more than ten months to adopt longest and heterogeneous laws versus eight and a

---

[33]On the discussed democratic virtues of parliamentarism, see Rozenberg (2020b).

[34]The government uses it at it offers the possibility to call the conciliation committee after one reading instead of two.

Table 5 Duration and parliamentary procedures for several kinds of French laws (2008–2018)

	Duration of the procedure	Accelerated procedure	Number of texts produced	Number of floor sessions
All laws	261	61%	8	9
Big laws	316	64%	11	43
Heterogeneous l.	315	76%	11	27
Finance laws	93	*Specific*	8	98

Note: number of texts = changed version of the bill after its examination by a committee or on the floor in one of the assembly
Source: https://www.lafabriquedelaloi.fr/

half for the whole sample. As considered in Table 2, the delays are sometimes much longer, the record among monster bills being one year and a half for Grenelle 2. The number of floor sessions (usually 3 h) is significantly more important for the longest laws given the number of articles, and therefore amendments, to be discussed. The greater duration of the passing in parliament also results from the more frequent lack of agreement with the Senate: in the French unequal bicameral system, the last word has been given to 13% of the laws over the last decade versus one third for the heterogeneous laws and 40% for big ones.[35]

The duration of the procedure is a source of frustration for both the government that typically wants to obtain quick results and the interested parts. Those in favour of the provisions may not understand why they are not implemented. For those opposed to them, the uncertainty of a long procedure may be a source of tension as well. Arguably, the compatibility of law-making procedures to the contemporary acceleration of time is a general and of prime-order challenge for legislatures. It is all the more raised in the case of monster bills that they take longer to be passed and given their visibility in the public sphere.

Second, the precise passing of complex bills in parliament is often chaotic. For MPs, clerks and assistants, the length of the bills and the duration of the procedures are a source of mistakes as, after days and nights of sittings, tired actors may make confusions between amendments. For the Macron law for instance, the special committee met seven consecutive days, more than 10 h a day. The internal division of labours between MPs and clerks makes difficult to keep an overview on both the general equilibrium of the bill and the state of the parliamentary procedure. A senior chief clerk in the Senate admitted for instance to be unable to identify all parliamentary civil servants in charge of reviewing the Macron law.[36]

---

[35]Source: https://www.lafabriquedelaloi.fr/ International agreements excluded. The bicameral system foresees that a conciliation committee composed of representatives from both assemblies can be called after one or two readings. In case of disagreement during this meeting, the National Assembly may have the last word after an ultimate reading in both chambers. Assemblies have able to vote the same bill without a conciliation committee for half of all bills but only 12% of the most heterogeneous ones and none of the biggest ones.

[36]Interview in Paris, 12 December 2005.

Table 6 Change of the bills during the legislative procedure and faith of the amendments (2008–2018)

	Number of tabled amendments	Number of tabled amendt from MNAs	Share of adopted amendt from MNAs	Share of modified text
All laws	526	365	32%	54%
Big laws	5134	3649	23%	58%
Heterogeneous l.	3391	2421	29%	62%
Finance laws	4275	3533	23%	58%

Note: MNAs = Members of the National Assembly
Source: https://www.lafabriquedelaloi.fr/

Third, these bills often raise strong oppositions given their substantial significance or the political one that the government wants to give them. It is indeed an established result that the opposition focusses first and foremost on salient texts.[37] Opposition MPs are tempted to use all possible filibustering tactics not only in order to slow down the review but also to show to their electorate how mobilized they are. Again, external signals matter in law-making. As a result, the government and the majority may use all the negative agenda control devises at their disposal: one reading instead two with the accelerated procedure (see Table 5), a priori limitation of the plenary time (allowed since 2008) or even the above-mentioned article 49.3. These procedural arrangements may share the feeling that there is something illegitimate in the procedure.

More importantly, the heterogeneous nature of the monster bills often contribute to raise opposition against them. The Macron bill offers a perfect example of that as it faced a left-wing opposition against Sunday work but also a conservative one against the liberalisation of law professions. The coalition of nays may make it more difficult to find a majority in parliament. Faced with rebel majority backbenchers ready to vote against him, the Prime minister finally decided to use the 49.3 in 2005—a decision that was perceived as a major political failure.

5.2   MPs Influence Between Opportunities and Constraints

Is the parliament active and influential during the examination of the big and heterogeneous bills? Table 6 provides mix quantitative evidences on that point.

Long and heterogeneous bills provoke an intense amending activity. On the average, members of the National Assembly table ten times more amendments than for the whole sample of laws. The share of adopted amendments remains closed to the average despite this important increase. As a result, both kinds of laws come

---

[37] As exemplified for France by Milet (2010) or Lascoumes (2009).

out seriously modified. The share of modified text, calculated on the base of the number of characters added or deleted when comparing the initial and final version, is indeed higher than for other kinds of law[38]—especially in the case of heterogeneous bills. In part, these changes originate from the government which is allowed to amend its bills anytime but some are also imposed or negotiated by majority backbenchers.

The Macron law provides a relevant example of what the passing in parliament change to a bill. None of the major initial orientations of the bills have been modified at the parliamentary stage despite hours of debates.[39] Yet, the debates made a lot to amend, specify and even modify the details of numerous provisions. Regional transportation by cars is allowed but local governments are given the right to ban some journeys. The possibility for shops to open for 12 Sundays by year (versus five previously) is voted as Macron wanted but the mayors will still decide when and if shops are open on Sunday (Macron wanted to by-pass them for five Sundays) and wage compensations are more clearly defined. Dozens of examples of that kind could be provided. The patterns of influence of backbenchers for monster bills are equivalent to those generally observed in France: the President and the government decide of the main legislative lines, they refuse to change them during the parliamentary procedure considering that their reputation is at stake but they accept many detailed and less visible modifications. What is more specific to monster bills is that, as public attention is by definition focussed on a limited number of issues, there are more room of manoeuver for MPs to amend the remaining and numerous other provisions of these bills.

There are also drawbacks to the monster bills for the parliament influence. First, special committees are frequent. The French Constitution stipulates that a bill can be considered either by one of the standing committees or by an ad hoc one, especially created to that end as in the British system. Given their heterogeneous nature and their political significance, monster bills often require to create an ad hoc committee. This is rather detrimental to the parliament for two reasons. Ad hoc committees do not beneficiate from the accumulated expertise of standing committees as well as their members sociability which may facilitate compromises and internal cooperative strategies.[40] Parliamentary party group chairs may also exclude from the ad hoc structure disloyal members. This possibility was especially useful for the socialist majority group under Hollande presidency (2012–17) as rebellion progressively reached an unprecedented level.[41]

Second, the greater use of negative agenda control procedure mentioned above constitutes a source of constraint for all MPs and not only opposition ones. It shows

---

[38]This ratio is more precise than the comparison of the simple size of the two versions of the bill. See Sieberer et al. (2016).

[39]For the first reading in the National Assembly, the special committee met during 72 h and plenary sessions for 111 h.

[40]As well established by the legislative studies literature, for instance Martin (2014).

[41]Lecomte et al. (2017).

how, in details, the so-called rational parliamentarianism procedures are in the hands of the government. For instance, as indicated, it is possible since 2009 to decide in advance of the maximal plenary time of each group at the National Assembly. For backbenchers, the so-called programmed legislative time (*temps législatif programmé*) suffers no exception: it is not possible to speak to support a tabled amendment for an MP which group has used all its speaking quotas. By contrast, there is not such limitation on the government side. Thus, during the passing of the Macron bill in 2015, the young minister was committed to answer at length to each amendment when backbenchers faced strict constraints.

The unbalance between the executive and legislative powers regarding monster bills is also exacerbated by the law-case of the Constitutional Council. As considered, at the proposal stage, the government has the possibility to gasp a great variety of issues with a minimal of coherency between them. Once the review in parliament has started, the legislative agenda is progressively reducing itself. In theory, it is not possible to introduce riders (*cavaliers législatifs*), that is to say new and unrelated topics. After one reading, articles that have been approved by both assemblies cannot be modified any more—what is called the funnel principle (*règle de l'entonnoir*). Since the years 2000s, the Constitutional Council has decided to be stricter in the implementation of both rules.[42] Arguably, its procedural review applies to all types of amendments: those introduced by MPs but also by the government. Yet, the case-law of the Constitutional Council is specifically detrimental to the parliament as the government sets the initial agenda: a minister can add a title on animal well-being to a draft bill on agriculture at the preparatory stage but a MP cannot do so once the bill is under review. Thus 17 of the 308 articles of the Macron law were censured for being regarded as riders. In 2017, 36 of the 124 articles of Equality and citizenship (listed as a 'monster' law in Table 2) were censured for the same reason.

With the multiplication of participatory forums before the legislative process, the limitation of MPs capacity to amend becomes crueller. In 2018, a sort of Grenelle was organised regarding the economics of the food sector. The government did not take back some of its conclusions in a bill proposed then.[43] Some were latter re-introduced by backbenchers during the legislative procedure but the Constitutional Council regarded no less than 23 articles out of 98 as riders.[44] The parliament adopted amendments may have been unrelated to the initial bill articles but they had been tabled in the follow up of the participatory forum.

---

[42]The first censure based on this claim dates back to 1989. The introduction in 2008 in the constitution that amendments with an 'indirect link' to the text were valid has not modified the Constitutional Council case-law. According to Chamussy (2014), 30% of the decisions of the Council were based on procedural issues in 1986–88 vs. 62% in 2007–12. The censure based on riders are especially numerous for the Finance Bill and Social Security Financing Bill. See also Marin (2018).

[43]Law n° 2018-938 of 30 October 2018 for the balance of trade relations in the agricultural and food sector and healthy, sustainable and accessible food for all, also called Egalim.

[44]Decision n° 2018-771 DC of the Constitutional Council of 25 October 2018. See Crevel (2019).

Table 7 Constitutional review of French bills before they came into force (2008–2018)

	Constitutional Council not ceased	Bills judged conform with the Constitution	Partial or total unconformity	Proportion of censured articles
All laws	67%	14%	18%	8%
Big laws	24%	4%	72%	5%
Heterogeneous l.	52%	No	48%	6%
Finance laws	No	No	100%	5%

Note: Proportion of censured articles = average share of censured articles out of all articles of the bills that are reviewed by the Council

Source: https://www.lafabriquedelaloi.fr/

5.3 A Perfectible Legislative Quality

It is difficult to identify shared and neutral criteria for the notion of legislative quality. The decisions taken by the Constitutional Council provides at least a proxy for their constitutional quality—an important but incomplete part of the picture. Table 7 indicates if the Council has been ceased, what its decision has been and the proportion of censure articles.

Sixty MNAs or senators may cease the Constitutional Council once the bill has been passed and before its enactment. The opposition does it for politically important laws[45] which explain the figures of Table 7 for big and heterogeneous laws. In proportion yet, these two kinds of laws are not more censured than other since 5 to 6% of their articles are censured.[46] Beyond these figures, the anecdotal evidences point toward a lower quality of the 'catch-all laws'.

Often, the length of the review in parliament and the parallel use of filibustering tactics and negative agenda control procedures created attention losses. The first articles tend to be better discussed and amended than the ones arriving after two weeks of debate. MPs may lack the supplementary information brought in theory by parliamentary debates to make their judgment. This trend is not only an opportunity for MPs willing to pass their amendments, as considered, but also for lobbyists. All indicates, that private actors beneficiate indeed from the complexity of the bill and the length of the procedure. Parliament, as intuited by Bentham,[47] is an institution operating under the eyes of public opinion. With monster bills, eyes tend to be close.

The length of the procedure may also enter in tension with politicians attention shifting.[48] Within a year, the saliency of the input that initially led to propose

---

[45]Brouard (2009).

[46]In volume, it represents yet more censures as these bills are composed of a higher number of articles.

[47]Schofield (1989).

[48]Studies comparing policy fields have established how punctuated political attention is. See Jones and Baumgartner (2005).

legislation may have changed drastically. For instance, the law resulting from a severe industrial accident will be very different if adopted a few months after when public emotion is still high or if years have passed.[49] Similarly, the government may have to face unforeseen events during the legislative procedure and be tempted to introduce last-minutes amendments which could be remote from the initial purpose of the bill.

6 Conclusion

In conclusion, this chapter has sought to demonstrate that big and/or heterogeneous bill were drafted in view of sending messages to external actors and/or as a result of the scarcity of floor time in parliament. The precise examples of two 'monster' bills as well as the final assessment of the democratic quality of these kinds of bills points to the limits of both strategies. Regarding the signal sent, the duration, difficulties and complexity of the law-making procedure often contribute to cloud the message. The government may create deceptions regarding one of the numerous issues treated by the bill—a deception that may frame the whole presentation of it.[50] It may be accused to follow lobbies on this or that issue. The use of procedural arrangements may also create a feeling of injustice vis-à-vis the opposition or division vis-à-vis the majority. Regarding the procedural opportunity, there is an obvious adverse effect: the scarcity of plenary time contributes to inflate bills—bills which need more time to be reviewed in parliament given their size which reduce the availability of plenary time...

From both rationales, monster bills are therefore far from being the perfect answer. Yet, they are passed. Ultimately, the government resorts to them first because politicians share the belief that laws matter. This has not only to do with the symbolic place of laws in the French political culture but also with the reduced governing capacity in a globalized economy and Europeanised polity. Politicians may not be able to 'change life' any more, to take back on old socialist slogan. They also operate under strong financial constraints. From that perspective, they compensate for this perceived loss through proposing monumental laws—and possibly, monuments through laws.

The second reason has to be found in the deepness of the process of State rationalisation. The ever-growing departmentalisation of bureaucracy is a well-known phenomenon that hold consequences in law-making: each department tends to produce its own norms (including ones of legal nature) and seeks to influence other policy fields to its interest. Long and heterogeneous bills are a product of that trend which questions Max Weber's classical view (1994) according to which

---

[49]The example is borrowed from Bonnaud and Martinais (2013).

[50]This happened for the above mentioned Egalim law in 2018 which originally mainly aimed at ensuring a fair price to farmers and ended being focussed on the use of pesticides.

parliaments constitute essential counterweights to the phenomena of bureaucratisation. For him, parliaments indeed should counter the structural tendency of bureaucracy to specialise and to follow its own internal logic. Only their constant, meticulous, pluralist, public and deliberative oversight of bureaucracy can protect basic freedoms and avoid the rigidity of a society ruled by experts and bureaucrats. The tale of 'monster' bills in France rather illustrates an opposite trend. Instead of containing the rationalization of bureaucracy, the French parliament and legislation appear to be victim of it. The chaos of the legislative procedure and the complexity of the final products seem to indicate that the rationalisation of State bureaucracy paradoxically lead to de-rationalize laws and legislatures.[51]

References

Alke L, Brouard S, Rozenberg O (2021) France: talkative MPs under control. In: Bäck H, Debus M, Fernandes J (eds) The politics of legislative debates. Oxford University Press, Oxford

Banks J (2001) Signalling games in political science, reprint. Routledge, Abon

Becher M, Brouard S (2020) Executive accountability beyond outcomes: experimental evidence on public evaluations of powerful prime ministers. Am J Polit Sci. https://doi.org/10.1111/ajps.12558

Bezes P, Descamps F, Viallet-Thévenin S (2019) Bercy : empire ou constellation de principautés ? Pouvoirs 168:9–28

Bonnaud L, Martinais E (2013) Une catastrophe au Parlement. La contribution des débats parlementaires à l'écriture du droit. In: de Galembert C, Rozenberg O, Vigour C (eds) Faire parler le Parlement. LGDJ, Paris

Boy D, Halpern C, Lascoumes P, Brugidou M (2012) Grenelle de l'environnement: acteurs, discours, effets. Armand Colin, Paris

Brouard S (2009) The politics of Constitutional Veto in France: Constitutional Council, Legislative Majority and electoral competition. West Eur Polit 32(2):384–403

Brouard S et al (2009) Comparer les productions législatives : enjeux et méthodes. Revue internationale de politique comparée 16(3):381–404

Carcassonne G (2005) Penser la loi. Pouvoirs 114:39–52

Carré de Malberg R (1984) La Loi, expression de la volonté générale, 1st ed. 1931. Economica, Paris

Chamussy D (2014) La procédure parlementaire et le Conseil constitutionnel. Nouveaux Cahiers du Conseil Constitutionnel 38

Crevel S (2019) La loi EGALIM : à boire et à manger pour les Sages. Revue de droit rural 472:14–17

De Montis A (2016) La rénovation de la séance publique du Parlement français. Étude sur l'efficacité de la séance publique du Parlement français. Dalloz, Paris

Genieys W (2010) The new custodians of the state. Programmatic elites in a French society. Transactions Books, Rutgers

Genieys W, Hassenteufel P (2012) Qui gouverne les politiques publiques ? Par-delà la sociologie des élites. Gouvernement et action publique 1(2):89–115

---

[51]In that sense, monster bills participate to a more general trend of denationalization that affects many different aspects of the French parliament. See Rozenberg (2019).

Halpern C, Pollard J (2017) Les effets du Grenelle de l'environnement sur l'action publique. Analyse comparée entre deux secteurs : déchets et bâtiment. Gouvernement et action publique 6(2):107–130

Hispalis G (2005) Pourquoi tant de loi(s) ? Pouvoirs 114:101–115

Huber J (1996) Rationalizing Parliament, Legislative institutions and party politics in France. Cambridge University Press, Cambridge

Huber J, Shipan C (2002) Deliberate discretion? The Institutional. Foundations of Bureaucratic Autonomy. Cambridge University Press, New York

Jones B, Baumgartner F (2005) The politics of attention: how the government prioritizes problems. University of Chicago Press, Chicago

Lascoumes P (2009) Les compromis parlementaires, combinaisons de surpolitisation et de sous-politisation. Revue française de science politique 59(3):455–478

Lecomte D, Bouvard H, Perez D, Boelaert J (2017) Le respect de la boutique. L'étiolement de la discipline partisane dans le groupe parlementaire socialiste au cours de la 14e législature (2012-2017). Politix 117:171–199

Marin M (2018) La prohibition des cavaliers législatifs. Les Petites Affiches 9 July 137(4):55

Martin S (2014) Committees. In: Martin S, Saalfeld T, Strom K (eds) The Oxford handbook of legislative studies. Oxford University Press, Oxford, pp 353–368

Milet M (2010) Pour une sociologie législative du pouvoir des parlementaires en France. Revue française d'administration publique 135:601–618

Pouvoirs (2019) Bercy. Special issue 168

Rogers JR (2001) Information and judicial review: a signaling game of legislative–judicial inter-action. Am J Polit Sci 45(1):84–99

Rozenberg O (2016) Un petit pas pour le Parlement, un grand pour la Vème République. LIEPP Working Paper 61

Rozenberg O (2019) De la difficulté d'être un Parlement normal. In: Duhamel O, Foucault M, Fulla M, Lazar M (eds) La Ve République démystifiée. Presses de Sciences Po, Paris, pp 47–65

Rozenberg O (2020a) The French Parliament and the European Union. Backbenchers Blues. Palgrave Macmillan, Basingstoke

Rozenberg O (2020b) On the concepts of parliament, parliamentarianism and parliamentary democracy. In: Benoît C, Rozenberg O (eds) Handbook of parliamentary studies: interdisciplinary approaches to legislatures. Edward Elgar, Cheltenham

Schofield P (1989) First principles preparatory to constitutional code. The collected works of Jeremy Bentham. Oxford University Press, Oxford

Sieberer U, Meissner P, Keh J, Müller W (2016) Mapping and explaining parliamentary rule changes in Europe: a research program. Legis Stud Q 41(1):61–88

Weber M (1994) Political writings, 1st edn. 1917. Cambridge University Press, Cambridge

Reports

Council of State (2016) Etude annuelle. Simplification et qualité du droit. La Documentation française, Paris

Council of State (2018) Mesurer l'inflation légilative

Inspection générale des finances (2012) Les professions réglementées. Report of the Ministry of Economy and Finance, M057 03

Secrétariat général du gouvernement (2019) Indicateur de suivi de l'activité normative

Omnibus Legislation in Germany: A Widespread Yet Understudied Lawmaking Practice

Klaus Meßerschmidt

Abstract Omnibus legislation (aka 'Artikelgesetz') is widespread in Germany and encounters only a few constitutional and other legal constraints. Efficiency of law-making, in particular by avoiding separate legislative procedures, the implementation of European directives and the growing sophistication of the statutory systems are strong reasons for legislative packaging. Moreover, by linking different regulations, omnibus legislation may serve as a tool to achieve consensus, though the U.S. debate on riders does not translate into the German legal context. Opaque omnibus bills, however, are a challenge to democratic decision-making. The worst example so far of non-transparent law-making by an omnibus bill was the de facto amnesty of tens of thousands Nazi criminals by the Regulatory Offences Act of 1968, which apparently only concerned traffic violations. This conspiracy-like aberration, however, did not fuel the small-scale German debate on omnibus legislation, which revolves around follow-up problems only comprehensible in the particular context of German constitutional law (relating to the issue of federalism on the one hand and the relationship of parliamentary bills and executive regulations on the other hand). Consequently, this doctrinal debate hardly contributes to the general analysis of omnibus legislation while the constitutional constraint on omnibus legislation in the field of budgetary legislation (Article 110.4 GBL) may attract attention abroad. Moreover, some provisions with no special focus on omnibus legislation, such as Federal Council participation in the legislative process depending on the subject matter, may create a deterrent effect in that they suggest avoiding provisions that trigger a high level of involvement of the Second Chamber. Irrespective of the identified problems, omnibus legislation is not intrinsically wrong. Codes of conduct, however, may be necessary to avoid abuses. The alternative to omnibus legislation is not myriads of miniscule statutes but codification and the answer to the lack of accountability is reason-giving requirements. Imposing the obligation to rationality on the legislator can tackle the excesses of the omnibus method at the root.

K. Meßerschmidt (✉)
Department of Tax Law and Public Law, University of Erlangen-Nürnberg, Nürnberg, Germany
e-mail: klaus.messerschmidt@fau.de

© The Author(s), under exclusive license to Springer Nature Switzerland AG 2021
I. Bar-Siman-Tov (ed.), *Comparative Multidisciplinary Perspectives on Omnibus Legislation*, Legisprudence Library 8, https://doi.org/10.1007/978-3-030-72748-2_6

Keywords Abuse · Article bill · Budget law · Packaging ban · Transparency

1 Terms and Concepts

The notion of omnibus legislation exists neither in German law nor in German legal doctrine and only in one place does the German Basic Law (*Grundgesetz*) approach the thinking underlying omnibus legislation. This is not an ideal starting point for a report that deals with omnibus legislation in Germany. However, bills and statutes, which one can assign to this category, *are* an integral part of German legislative practice. Therefore, addressing the topic presupposes a definition. First, we have to decide whether we want a universally applicable definition[1] or one that is specific to the national legal order. Since this study is intended to convey the legal situation in Germany and I do not want to prejudge the comparative view, I will focus on the German approach and begin with a consideration of the pertinent terminology. Unfortunately, it will soon become clear that most German contributions revolve around trivial or technical matters. I nevertheless hope that the country report will contain some ideas for the overall analysis of omnibus legislation.

Like the term itself, literal translations of 'omnibus legislation' are largely unknown in Germany.[2] Legal terminology is different. Not even the romantic metaphor 'Christmas tree bills'[3] is sufficiently attractive for Germans.[4] Legal officers, drafters and legal scholars address the phenomenon of omnibus legislation mostly by the sober term *'Artikelgesetz'*.[5] This term has advantages and

---

[1]Some operational definitions are suitable for the performance of empirical analyses, while giving from the legal point of view the impression of arbitrariness. See, e.g., Krutz (2000), p. 539: 'Omnibus Bill: any piece of major legislation that: (1) spans three or more major topic policy areas OR ten or more subtopic policy areas, AND (2) is greater than the mean plus standard deviation of major bills in size.' On the controversial U.S. practice of combining disparate measures in one massive bill, see in more detail Krutz (2001a).

[2]The use of the term by some authors and courts (references at Lachner 2007, pp. 25–26) does not prove its full inclusion into legal terminology. According to Lachner (2007), pp. 25–26, the term has a negative connotation and evokes the impression of boarding passengers at a bus stop (*'Zusteigen von Reisegästen in einen Omnibus'*). Others see it as a joke, cf. Lachner, id., with further references, whereas the Federal Finance Court (*Bundesfinanzhof*) applies the term '*Omnibusgesetz*' in a neutral manner, see BFH, Deutsches Steuerrecht (DStR) 1997, 486 (487) and BFHE 198, 493 (495) {III R 22/01}.

[3]Cf. Nightingale (2016)

[4]House of Commons Committee on political and constitutional reform (2013), p. 7. 'Portmanteau' (id.) is also unknown.

[5]Kluth (2014), p. 32; Schulze-Fielitz (1988a), pp. 49–50. See for further references, Lachner (2007), p. 27, and for a short definition in German, Creifelds (2017), p. 91. In the adjudication of the German Federal Constitutional Court (*Bundesverfassungsgericht*) the term appears in several judgments, cf. BVerfGE 38, 348 (348); 72, 175 (191); 101, 297 (302, 307, 308). The German abbreviation 'BVerfGE' used here and below stands for *'Entscheidungen (Decisions) des Bundesverfassungsgerichts'* which are the official Reports of Judgments and Decisions.

disadvantages over 'omnibus bill'. One advantage is the greater clarity of the term. The formal-technical character,[6] however, is both a blessing and a curse. It gives an idea of the structure of the law, but no idea of its content, whereas 'omnibus legislation' conveys the idea that the legislation covers a multitude of issues.

'*Artikelgesetz*' in turn raises a translation problem. The word 'Amendment Act', as proposed in Romain German-English legal dictionary,[7] addresses the close relationship between the growing number of legislative changes[8] and the turn to omnibus legislation,[9] but does not grasp the specific character of amendments effectuated by the omnibus method. Regardless of the translation issue, the term refers to a merely technical aspect. In legal terms, the word means the same as 'Article' in English; it is a basic unit of the law. Using this term to denote a piece of omnibus legislation, however, only makes sense against the background of common legal language in Germany. In federal law and the majority of state laws the word 'Paragraph' and the corresponding icon '§' substitute the word 'Article'. This means that a regular law or ordinary statute and even the majestic Civil Code consist of paragraphs, not Articles. This may be confusing for foreigners who apply the word 'paragraph' to the subdivisions of an Article (in German: '*Absatz*'). Only the Articles of the German Constitution, European and Bavarian legislation, ratifying legislation and introductory acts are designated by the word '*Artikel*'. Against this background, the word '*Artikelgesetz*' is specific in that it refers to Articles as prime structural subdivisions of the omnibus act. In federal legislation, the legislator makes use of this extended classification almost exclusively in omnibus legislation. Omnibus bills consist of several levels. The '*Artikel*' represents the newly introduced or amended Bill and is, as a rule, subdivided by numbers and letter abbreviations, which refer to the individual Articles (*'Paragraphen'*) of the Bill. The thus restricted application of the word '*Artikel*' and its specific meaning with respect to omnibus bills build the base for the identification of omnibus bills as '*Artikelgesetze*'. It is thus quite easy to identify the German type of omnibus bills and there is no need to signal the omnibus character of a law by its legal title. Sometimes, however, the legislator makes the effort to indicate both the principal subject of the law and the attachment of amendments to other laws not mentioned individually.[10] Miscellaneous Statutes Amendment Acts are common in Germany, though the legislator is under no obligation to disclose this content in the legal title.[11]

This formal-legal explanation matters since it reveals the German understanding of omnibus legislation. It is, at first sight, a purely technical device. Moreover, unlike

---

[6]Lachner (2007), p. 27.

[7]Romain et al. (2002), p. 75.

[8]See Xanthaki (2014), pp. 45 and 223–241; Brandner (2004).

[9]The handbook on legislative drafting issued by the German Ministry of Justice emphasises the proximity of omnibus bills and amendments (Bundesministerium der Justiz 2008, p. 147).

[10]E.g. Gesetz zur Auflösung der Bundesmonopolverwaltung für Branntwein und zur Änderung weiterer Gesetze (Branntweinmonopolverwaltungs-Auflösungsgesetz – BfBAG) vom 10. März 2017 (BGBl. I S. 420).

[11]This may be the fact in some Canadian provinces, see Massicotte (2013), p. 13.

omnibus legislation in the North American context, no further delimitation is required. Each law that encompasses more than one new bill or alteration to a bill meets the formal definition of *'Artikelgesetz'*. Thus German 'omnibus legislation' ranges from a law consisting of only three Articles (the third one deals with the entry into force),[12] which Americans or Canadians will hardly view as 'omnibus', to monstrous compilations of dozens or hundreds of Articles, each of which stands for one separate bill created or altered by the omnibus bill. A German author once called an omnibus act containing 41 Articles a 'Mammoth' article act[13] and this latter is what Americans are much more likely to recognise as an omnibus bill. The average German omnibus act contains at least one principle bill, accompanied by consequential amendments[14] 'to be made in other laws or statutory instruments if this is necessary to preserve the consistency of the remaining body of law with the provisions amended or newly created in the omnibus act'.[15] However, departing from the standard model, omnibus bills may confine themselves to a compilation of various amendments to different bills. Again, this is far from any meaningful characterisation of omnibus legislation[16] and as no legal definition of omnibus bill exists, we may choose a nominal definition, which is tailored specifically to the problems to be examined.

Irrespective of the preferences of the official drafting manual,[17] the synonymous term *'Mantelgesetz'*, which may be translated literally by 'coat law'[18] or 'cloak act', is used less frequently nowadays.[19] While it does not depend on the denomination of Articles, it still refers to the technical aspect of bundling together a series of legal acts. Typically, *'Mantelgesetze'* consist of several statutes that could exist autonomously.[20] Omnibus legislation may constitute an overarching framework, though few words will often suffice to link the different parts. *'Mantelgesetz'* cannot be equated with 'umbrella laws'. In contrast to omnibus legislation, an 'umbrella law',

---

[12]The lowest threshold of three Articles results from the existence of bills consisting of two Articles: the first one contains the bill and the second lays out its entry into force. It obviously would be misleading to call such a bill 'omnibus legislation'. The second Article may also contain an enabling act for a recast regulation while the third Article determines its entry into force.

[13]Zeh (1982), p. 963. However, much longer article acts exist. See Einführungsgesetz zum Gesetz über Ordnungswidrigkeiten (EGOWiG) vom 24. Mai 1968 (BGBl. I S. 503), consisting of 167 Articles and extending over 44 pages of the Official Journal.

[14]On consequential amendments, Xanthaki (2014), pp. 239–240. See, as a recent example, Gesetz zur Fortentwicklung der haushaltsnahen Getrennterfassung von wertstoffhaltigen Abfällen vom 5. Juli 2017 (BGBl. I S. 2234) containing the new packaging law *(Verpackungsgesetz)* and approximately 25 consequential amendments in Article 2.

[15]Federal Ministry of Justice (2008), p. 226.

[16]Perhaps this is why Schulze-Fielitz (1988a), p. 50, warns against equating this type of *'Artikelgesetzgebung'* with genuine omnibus legislation *('Artikelgesetz')*.

[17]Bundesministerium der Justiz (2008), p. 191.

[18]Cf. Karpen (2017), p. 14.

[19]See, however, Smeddinck (2014), p. 84; preceding Müller (1963), pp. 277–279; Hugger (1983), p. 298.

[20]Müller (1963), p. 277.

which is mainly an instrument of implementation of EU directives, is not an all-encompassing regulation but will be supplemented by separate amendments to individual legal texts.

The German concept of '*Artikelgesetz*' may be criticized because of the underlying formal-legal approach that faces the risk of replacing legal issues with statistics while in the international scene some scholars of omnibus legislation extend the term to multi-topic bills or 'big laws' in general.[21] There seems to be consensus among international experts that omnibus bills differ from typical major bills in their scope (number of substantive policy areas spanned), size and, hence, complexity.[22] In this context, the relationship between omnibus legislation and the concept of 'holistic regulation'[23] needs clarification. Another characteristic of the German approach to omnibus legislation is pragmatism,[24] which stands in the way of comprehensive analysis despite its advantages.

The neglect of omnibus legislation in German law and German legal doctrine[25] may also be due to the lack of any counterparts. The single-subject rule known in the U.S. and some other countries[26] does not exist in Germany. Notwithstanding this discrepancy, the well-established German term '*Artikelgesetz*' shall be denoted as omnibus legislation hereinafter.[27]

2 Examples

Omnibus legislation, as a way of making laws, is routine in Germany. Consequently, the Manual for Drafting Legislation by the Federal Ministry of Justice devotes a separate, though short, chapter to omnibus acts.[28] Insufficient resources prevent me from providing statistical information on the number of composite bills, what

---

[21] House of Commons Committee on political and constitutional reform (2013), p. 7.

[22] Krutz (2000), p. 539. In the same vein, Gluck et al. (2015), p. 1804. On complexity and length as features of omnibus bills Sinclair (2011), pp. 112–113.

[23] Xanthaki (2014), p. 236.

[24] Schulze-Fielitz (1988a), p. 49.

[25] As Hebeler and Schröder (2018), p. 641, have correctly noted, German constitutional law and legal theory textbooks as a rule do not even mention 'article acts'.

[26] On this centuries-old rule in most U.S. State Constitutions and the litigation amounting to up to 8,000 cases, see Huefner (2017), pp. 212–213; Lowenstein (2002); Gilbert (2006); Kaminski and Hart (2012). Further information at https://ballotpedia.org/Single-subject_rule (accessed 5 November 2018). The idea that different negotiating matters should not be treated as a single entity is, incidentally, also the basis for the revision of Swiss Law Governing Corporations. Cf. Neue Zürcher Zeitung, 24 November 2018, p. 12.

[27] In this I am in good company with the Federal Ministry of Justice Manual for Drafting Legislation (2008), pp. 226–232: 'omnibus acts', while the original German text refers to '*Artikelgesetze*'.

[28] Bundesministerium der Justiz (2008), pp. 226–232.

percentage of legislation they form, or their evolution over the course of time.[29] Nonetheless, it is safe to say that sometimes it seems easier to find omnibus bills in Germany than single-issue bills. Key areas of applications are the budget, environment and social legislation.[30] In addition to omnibus bills (*'Artikelgesetze'*), omnibus regulations on the level of executive law-making also exist in Germany. Recently, a regulation amended 626 Federal statutes and regulations, which is tantamount to more than one tenth of Federal law.[31] Omnibus regulations, however, must not be equated with the notorious emergency regulations *(Notverordnungen)* of the Weimar Republic, i.e. regulations enacted by the President with the force of parliamentary law.[32]

In general, omnibus legislation often relates to a type of legislation based on the idea that statutes should organise specific changes in administration and society, focussing on the attainment of specific goals. German legal scholarship has coined the term *'Massnahmegesetz'* for this kind of legislation,[33] conveying the idea that the legal act is both a law and a measure.

The extraordinary variety of omnibus legislation in Germany stems both from variations in size and, more importantly, from the range of issues it encompasses. The distinction between homogeneous and heterogeneous omnibus bills is less a strict contrast than the endpoints of a scale. Homogeneous omnibus bills are defined by the convergence of issues whereas heterogeneous omnibus bills unite loosely connected items[34] or issues that are exclusively linked by the regulation in the composite bill. Borderline cases are by no means a rarity. Omnibus acts may even touch upon a variety of legal fields.[35]

3 Motives and Reasons

Underlying motives of the widespread practice of omnibus legislation are various. Some are universal and some reflect the specific conditions of legislation in Germany.

---

[29]Lachner (2007), pp. 79–80, provides some data which support the conclusion that the share of legislation of omnibus acts rose from 13.1% in the 1950s to almost 50% by the end of the 14th parliamentary term (1998–2002). On the U.S. Gluck et al. (2015), pp. 1800–1803.

[30]Due to lack of space, no references can be provided.

[31]Zehnte Zuständigkeitsanpassungsverordnung vom 31. August 2015 (BGBl. I S. 1474). This regulation, however, was no challenge to the legal system because its sole objective was to adapt references to changes in departmental responsibilities or to adopt new department names.

[32]Schneider (2002), p. 144.

[33]For references, see Meßerschmidt (2000), pp. 71 and 137.

[34]See BVerfGE 72, 175 (191).

[35]Cf. Lachner (2007), pp. 64–65, referring to the example of anti-discrimination law (Gesetz zur Beendigung der Diskriminierung gleichgeschlechtlicher Gemeinschaften: Lebenspartnerschaften vom 16. Februar 2001 [BGBl. I S. 266]) which addresses both civil and public law.

3.1 General Considerations

Necessary amendments to bills play a major role in omnibus legislation, for instance the introduction of a new bill often requires consequential amendments. Generally, the rise of omnibus bills results from the high degree of 'connectivity' typical of a mature Continental European legal system. The amount and importance of omnibus legislation increase depending on the sophistication of the statutory system. The network character of legislation and the systematic approach of continental jurisprudence are closely related. Therefore, any new legislation almost inevitably results in the need to change various other bills.[36] This kind of 'legislation by reference'[37] often coincides with omnibus legislation.

Another reason for omnibus legislation results from the implementation of EU Directives. EU Directives often affect a multitude of national laws and because they usually concern several laws, omnibus legislation is the method of choice.[38] Although implementation can be managed by a series of single-issue laws, omnibus legislation is not only efficient but also transparent, thus satisfying watchful EU institutions. In German federalism, omnibus legislation may be useful for similar reasons.

Besides planned omnibus acts, spontaneous omnibus legislation of inferior structure and quality may occur due to the dynamics of parliamentary deliberation.[39] In one case, the number of Articles doubled.[40] Another reason for omnibus addenda may be time limitations, e.g. the imminent expiration of implementation deadlines.[41]

Some of these reasons differ from the reasons reflected in the international debate while most 'universal' reasons play a role in German omnibus legislation as well. Bundling multiple legal measures into a single legal package, in general, facilitates the law-making process in Germany as it probably does everywhere. The law-making procedure has to be completed only once. Efficiency of lawmaking, in particular by avoiding separate law-making procedures,[42] thus is a strong reason for legislative packaging in most countries, Germany included.

The compilation of various legislative measures serves, in addition to the procedural benefits, to keep related regulations and their flanking measures together, and to take care of the impact of the main rule on other laws (consequential amendments).

Legislative packages[43] moreover increase the chances of enacting controversial pieces of legislation. First, omnibus legislation may help to neutralize political

---

[36]See on amendments in general, Duprat and Xanthaki (2017), pp. 122–123.

[37]Cf. Irresberger and Jasiak (2017), pp. 174–175.

[38]See for details and examples, Lachner (2007), pp. 66–73.

[39]Cf. Lachner (2007), pp. 45–46.

[40]Id. with further details.

[41]See Lachner (2007), pp. 82–83.

[42]Cf. Hebeler and Schröder (2018), p. 642.

[43]Cf. Goertz (2011).

opposition by connecting controversial issues. In this case, packaging is 'an agenda-control and coalition-building tool'[44] and an instrument of political compromise.[45] One faction or interest group may swallow the toad in return for getting its favourite regulation and vice versa. This may be horse trading and tantamount to vote trading,[46] but this is politics and true of all kinds of legislation, though omnibus legislation admittedly allows for a wider array of 'deals'. From the point of view of German legal officers and drafters, omnibus legislation even serves the opposite purpose since legislative packaging is meant to prevent Members of Parliament from cherry picking.[47] This, however, stands in stark contrast to U.S. and Canadian experiences and is apparently influenced by the idea of executive law-making.

Second, unpleasant measures can be inconspicuously submerged in an omnibus bill.[48] Unlike the case of compromise packages, where everybody is aware of what is going on, omnibus legislation—this time—turns into clandestine legislation.[49] Therefore, omnibus legislation is often suspected of being an instrument of streamlining legislation (e.g. environmental legislation).[50] This feature has given rise to fierce debates in Northern America whereas Germans seem to accept the practice. Perhaps they are right from the legal point of view because the mere proposal of an omnibus bill does not put Parliament under any obligation to accept it fully; Members are free to change proposals before enacting them. It is true, however, that in most instances they do not make this effort and nor are they successful if they do attempt it.

This leads to the most problematic point: omnibus legislation reduces the transparency of the contents and procedure of legislation. It provides ample opportunity to hide debated or onerous provisions in a complex setting.[51] If I may borrow from the language of railway companies, 'One train may hide behind another'. The bigger the law and the more heterogeneous its agenda, the greater the risk of opacity. Therefore, focusing on 'massive bills with component measures from disparate substantive policy areas'[52] helps identify hard cases.

---

[44]Krutz (2000), p. 533.

[45]On the importance of compromise in politics and law, Schulze-Fielitz (1988b); Lachner (2007), p. 110, referring especially to omnibus legislation. The capacity of the omnibus method to facilitate the finding of compromises was also noticed by the Federal Constitutional Court. See BVerfGE 70, 69 (88–89). For a more sophisticated analysis in light of public choice theory, see Gilbert (2006), pp. 831–849 with a focus on the single subject rule and the advantages and disadvantages of logrolling.

[46]Gilbert (2006), p. 831, referring, in particular, to Buchanan and Tullock.

[47]Müller (1963), p. 277.

[48]Schneider (2002), p. 144. In the same vein from the overseas point of view, Gluck et al. (2015), p. 1805: 'mask transparency for certain objectives'.

[49]See, generally, Bryde (1998). In this vein, newspapers have addressed a recent omnibus draft as a 'secret agency style operation' ('Geheimdienstoperation'), cf. Süddeutsche Zeitung of November 27, 2018, p. 5.

[50]Kirchhoff and Tsuji (2014).

[51]Schneider (2002), p. 144. In the same vein, Hebeler and Schröder (2018), p. 642.

[52]Krutz (2000), p. 533.

3.2   Cases of Abuse

A typical example of hiding (a presumably) controversial provision is the tax privilege of aviation fuel in the context of a comprehensive tax reform act.[53] A shameful historic example of the abuse of omnibus legislation is the Introductory Act of 1968 to the Regulatory Offences Act.[54] This Act consists of four Titles and 167 Articles and is thus a prime example of an omnibus bill. The first section deals with amendments to the Penal Code, the Criminal Procedure Code and Road Traffic Law. With regard to the Penal Code, Article 1 includes 23 amendments and insertions, of which the amendment of Article 50.2 of the Penal Code (§ 50 Abs. 2 StGB) was the most important by far. It said:

> In the event that special personal characteristics which constitute criminal liability of the offender are not present in the abettor or aider, his sentence is to be mitigated according to the rules applying to a punishable attempt.[55]

This clause had a devastating effect on the extraordinarily reluctant criminal prosecution of Nazi criminals by the German courts.[56] Since the courts found it difficult to prove that the personal features of (first degree) murder were present in the accessory i.e. secondary participant—note that most offenders were qualified as 'accessories'—they only applied the lower penalty. Because of this, these crimes profited from shorter periods of limitation that depend on the maximum term of imprisonment, which, at that time, had already expired. Against a background of intense dispute around the extension or abolition of the statute of limitations with regard to cases of murder and genocide during the Nazi regime,[57] no sober-minded observer[58] believed the protestations of the then Federal Minister of Justice that this

---

[53] Art. 24 Steuerreformgesetz 1990 vom 25. Juli 1988 (BGBl. I S. 1093).

[54] Einführungsgesetz zum Gesetz über Ordnungswidrigkeiten (EGOWiG) vom 24. Mai 1968 (BGBl. I S. 503).

[55] Unauthorized translation of the following provision: 'Fehlen besondere persönliche Eigenschaften, Verhältnisse oder Umstände (besondere persönliche Merkmale), welche die Strafbarkeit des Täters begründen, beim Teilnehmer, so ist dessen Strafe nach den Vorschriften über die Bestrafung des Versuchs zu mildern.' Recently the German Federal Ministry of Justice issued a slightly different translation, available at https://www.gesetze-im-internet.de/englisch_stgb/englisch_stgb.html#p0156 (accessed 5 November 2018).

[56] The German Supreme Criminal Court has applied this law without reservation. See BGH 22 Neue Juristische Wochenschrift (NJW) 1969: 1181 {5 StR 658/68}. This conforms with the general attitude of German courts. See for a short summary, Sambale (2002), pp. 212–217.

[57] See Arndt (1965); Baumann (1969); Asholt (2016), pp. 51–56; Sambale (2002). Section 78 (2) (Period of Limitation) reads: 'Serious criminal offences under Section 220a (genocide) and Section 211 (murder) are not subject to a statute of limitations.' Asholt's Ph.D. thesis (2016) of 785 pages dedicates only one line to the 'mishap' ('Panne') of 1969.

[58] See Frommel (2001), Gehrling (1969), Glienke (2011), Greve (2000), Görtemaker and Safferling (2016, 2017), Rottleuthner (2001) and Samson (1969). Representative for the counter opinion Schröder (1969), p. 132.

was the result of an 'unintended error'.[59] It is inconceivable that the previous Act of 13 April 1965, which *did* allow for further criminal prosecution, should have been buried in oblivion within the space of 3 years. It is equally unlikely that legal officers and drafters would be unfamiliar with the basics and details of the pertinent law.[60] Since the ministerial bureaucracy was a stronghold of former members of the Third Reich elite,[61] the senior official was known as an outstanding expert and the most widely read commentator of the time on criminal law,[62] the intention to introduce an amnesty for Nazi criminals by the back door is beyond doubt. Consequently, a 15-year statute of limitations was applied and the Act had retroactive effect from 8 May 1960. The timing of this surely did not escape experts of the time. It was a cunning move to insert such a politically risky (though presumably popular) change of law into the trivial context of traffic regulation offences. Borrowing from American terminology, this was a rider and a straightforward case against riders.[63]

3.3   Preliminary Conclusion

Can one draw a more general lesson from this incident? Probably yes. Omnibus legislation should not be related exclusively to political and parliamentary bargaining; it is sometimes a masterpiece of legislative bureaucracy. Moreover, incidents similar to the Introductory Act to the Regulatory Offences Act (1968) demonstrate that the risks of omnibus legislation result from the correspondence with another more fundamental problem i.e. the suboptimal state of parliamentary law-making. A final issue bears mentioning. Putting the blame one-sidedly on omnibus legislation overlooks the opportunities of this type of law-making. A strong point of omnibus bills is that they can deal with the overall context simultaneously whereas separated legislative projects may run the risk of tearing apart and obfuscating existing legal relationships.[64] Because of the complexity of omnibus legislation, there is no simple answer about how to manage it. As Gilbert has rightly noted, 'allowing several measures to be combined in one act may improve legislators' information by helping them to recognize political bargains and compromises. For

---

[59]Statement on June 11, 1969 to the German Parliament (Bundestag, 5th legislative term, session 236, Protokoll vom 11. Juni 1969, p. 13055). Ehmke emphasised that the draft was elaborated under his predecessors, but admitted that the impact escaped his notice when he was State Secretary.

[60]Note the caustic comment of a former (Conservative) Federal Minister of Justice, Richard Jaeger (Bundestag, 5th legislative term, session 236, Protokoll vom 11. Juni 1969, p. 13062).

[61]Braunbuch (1965) and Görtemaker (2018).

[62]Kramer (2004) and Braunbuch (1965), pp. 147–148. Last edition of 1968 accessible in the internet https://archive.org/stream/braunbuchBRD/braunbuch_djvu.txt.

[63]See, in general, Gilbert (2006), pp. 858–859.

[64]Kluth (2014), p. 32: 'Der Vorteil der Artikelgesetze besteht darin, dass der Gesamtzusammenhang des Gesetzgebungsvorhabens deutlicher wird, als dies bei parallelen Gesetzgebungsakten der Fall ist.'

the same reason, reducing the number of provisions in a bill does not necessarily make it easier for citizens to monitor their representatives.'[65] This suggests as a preliminary conclusion that omnibus legislation, irrespective of the problems, is not intrinsically wrong and its contribution to efficient law-making should be acknowledged. Codes of conduct, however, are necessary to avoid abuses.

4 Evaluation of the German Approach

Given the small number of practical comments on and academic contributions related to the conference theme (which is unusual in the generally overcrowded German legal literature),[66] it would be an exaggeration to refer the existing scholarship on omnibus legislation as a 'debate'. Nevertheless, I shall try to briefly summarise the scattered information.

The spectrum of opinions range from diffuse scepticism[67] to full endorsement.[68] According to the prevailing opinion, omnibus acts are a practical and necessary means of ensuring up-to-date legislation.[69] Although the German Federal Constitutional Court has never had to decide on the constitutionality of omnibus acts, some *obiter dicta* indicate a positive assessment.[70] At least, no author or court has gone so far as to claim a constitutional duty to omnibus legislation. In sum, omnibus acts are, in principle, constitutionally unobjectionable in Germany.[71]

The formal, essentially quantitative definition of omnibus legislation in the German context has assets and drawbacks as compared to the international concept. Its main asset is its simplicity and clarity; the definition applies but one criterion, which is easy to handle. The international notion, on the contrary, relies on at least dual criteria. On the one hand, the implication of a multitude of single laws characterises omnibus legislation and, on the other, the importance of the subject matters. Some authors call an important piece of legislation 'omnibus' even if it is a singular, though complex, bill whereas the German definition sticks to the packaging together of different laws.

The technical approach clearly dominates the German perception of omnibus bills. The main drawback of the technical understanding of omnibus legislation is that it runs the risk of ignoring the political controversies and fundamental legal problems of this type of legislation. From the German point of view, omnibus legislation is rather a matter of drafting than a political vehicle, yielding minimal

---

[65] Gilbert (2006), p. 846.

[66] Cf. Hebeler and Schröder (2018), p. 641.

[67] See Schulze-Fielitz (1988a), p. 39 and, for further references, Lachner (2007), p. 97.

[68] Cf. Lachner (2007), p. 81.

[69] See Lachner (2007), p. 81.

[70] BVerfGE 68, 193 (225); 70, 69 (88–89).

[71] Hebeler and Schröder (2018), p. 643.

legal problems and never stirring political debate. The ban on omnibus legislation in some U.S. States is alien to the German legislative system where no relevant proposals have been made to curb omnibus legislation. German legal theory and adjudication do not deny the legal problems of omnibus bills but nor do they fully tackle the issue of omnibus legislation; they refer to the problems that occasionally result from omnibus legislation but do not address omnibus legislation as such. Therefore, I mention the two most debated problems but do not discuss them in detail. First, the German Federal Constitutional Court has faced the problem of legislative powers after the enactment of an omnibus bill, namely where does competence lie if only part of an omnibus bill needs to be amended? Second, given that omnibus legislation covers both parliamentary legislation and changes to government regulations—an accepted practice in Germany—can changes to regulations be passed by regulation or must there be a new piece of omnibus legislation? The Court has previously decided that the legal status of an amendment, both its competence base and procedure, depend on its contents and not its reference to a preceding omnibus bill.[72] Its answer to the second question, therefore, is that amendment by law does not change the legal status of a regulation.[73] This short summary is only meant to give a picture of the kind of debates on omnibus legislation taking place in Germany. Note that there is no debate on the legitimacy of omnibus legislation, its accountability or its impact on parliamentary decision-making as may be witnessed in the United States and Canada. Given the German debate about the obligation to good legislation,[74] this disregard of omnibus legislation is amazing.

Stating the obvious shortcomings of the German view of omnibus legislation does not mean that omnibus legislation must meet a universal standard. The legal problems and risks of omnibus legislation depend in the first place on the legal setting of each country. The fierce debate in Northern America stems from the traditional prohibition of omnibus legislation in most State Constitutions. Moreover, awareness of the practice of logrolling and 'pork barrelling' and the threat of special interest legislation contribute to the critical perception of omnibus legislation.

The German law-making system differs from the Northern American by the inferior role of Members of Parliament as compared to Members of Congress. Although half of the Members of the German Parliament are directly elected in constituencies whereas the rest are nominees on party lists, the typical German MP does not need to seek popular support and sponsorship in the way his U.S. colleague does.[75] He is much more dependent on the party organisation and usually hesitates to

---

[72]BVerfGE 37, 363 (379–383) and 39, 1 (33–35). See for a short explanation, Hebeler and Schröder (2018), p. 643.

[73]BVerfGE 114, 196 (234–240) {2 BvF 2/03}. Consequently, the oft-practiced insertion of the so-called *Entsteinerungsklausel* is redundant. See for a short explanation, Hebeler and Schröder (2018), p. 644; Lachner (2007), pp. 38–39. The term '*Entsteinerung*' is difficult to understand even for Germans; it means the opposite of 'petrification'. Cf. Sendler (2001) and Uhle (2001).

[74]See, among many others, Schuppert (2003) with further references.

[75]On the impact on omnibus legislation, see Krutz (2001b), p. 211.

openly follow his own political agenda. Therefore, he is less inclined to endorse legislative projects on his or her own initiative.[76] While the role of individual MPs in the law-making procedure is not on an equal footing with that of a U.S. Congressman or Senator, the role of German Departments/Ministries is much stronger. Omnibus riders may be easily introduced in the pre-parliamentary draft of a law. Against this background, the idea that the omnibus method generally improves the productivity of law-making by giving coalition leaders a tool to get around gridlock,[77] is of far less importance in Germany than in the United States, and nor does an explanation of the use of omnibus legislation in the context of the Congress-President relationship[78] have any bearing on Germany. Moreover, the frequency of omnibus bills in Germany does not depend on political circumstances, at least not in the same way as in the United States,[79] although it is conceded that legislative activism resulting from a policy reform agenda may inflate the number of omnibus bills in Germany. Being unaware of any research carried out in Germany on the chances of omnibus bills surviving the legislative procedure, I assume that the omnibus method has neither a positive nor a negative effect. If a bill fails in Germany, there are other reasons for its failure. However, the backwardness of the theory of legislation in Germany, in particular its empirical branch, comes once again to the fore.

Although the danger of omnibus legislation being abused by political horse-trading may be less marked in Germany, we must be cautious not to confound the intensity of the debate with the gravity of the problem. Whereas skepticism overseas toward omnibus legislation partially reflects its link with stakes, special interest legislation is still a taboo in Germany.[80] This does not mean, however, that German omnibus legislation is immune to lobbyist interference.[81] The channels of influence are less obvious and more various, though not specifically related to omnibus legislation. The telling story of Article 50 para 2 of the Penal Code shows the multifaceted character of omnibus legislation and the role of political string-pullers in Germany.

There is one fundamental question, which arises in all countries who pride themselves on having a democratic process of law-making. Must omnibus bills be justified or are they an expression of parliamentary sovereignty? Although the idea of parliamentary sovereignty for varying reasons never conquered Germany in the

---

[76]This statement is not to deny the dignified status of German MPs, as enshrined in Article 38 para 1 GBL, nor is it downplaying the individual activities of Members—an aspect which von Bogdandy (2000), pp. 96–100, has emphasised.

[77]Krutz (2000), p. 537.

[78]Krutz (2001b), p. 212.

[79]On the influence of a tough budgetary situation and divided government on the likelihood of omnibus usage, Krutz (2001b), p. 221.

[80]There is almost no open academic debate on the influence of special interests on the law-making process. See, however, Meßerschmidt (2019).

[81]Lobbyism often addresses the law-making bureaucracy. Outsourcing of drafting and placing external staff are gateways for lobbyist influence. Cf. Maisch (2015) and Meßerschmidt (2012).

way of the British tradition,[82] the preference for omnibus legislation is part of parliamentary discretion and parliamentary self-government, which includes the choice of political priorities and legislative procedures ('Geschäftsordnungsautonomie'). Against this background, the analysis must turn to the pertinent constitutional constraints on omnibus legislation.

5 Constraints

Omnibus legislation is so widespread in Germany that it cannot be associated with 'unorthodox lawmaking'.[83] Nor can the law-making process justify a special label because omnibus legislation does not display distinctive procedural features. Law-making procedures in Germany do not lay down specific rules for omnibus bills; German law neither privileges nor discourages omnibus legislation, it simply does not refer to it. The question is dealt with at the subordinate level of official drafting manuals in the form of recommendations on when and how to enact 'Article bills'[84] whereas German constitutional law is silent on omnibus legislation in general and regulates but one special case. The joint rules of procedure of the Federal Ministries (Gemeinsame Geschäftsordnung/GGO), at least, recommend integrating consequential amendments into draft bills (§ 42.2 (2) GGO).[85] Paradoxically, the failure to acknowledge omnibus legislation may promote its proliferation.

5.1 The Exception of the Budget Law

Mechanisms in German constitutional law, which restrict the use of omnibus legislation, are rare. The sole exception concerns budgetary legislation. Article 110.4 GBL contains the so-called budget law packaging ban ('haushaltsrechtliches Bepackungsverbot'):

> The Budget Act may contain only such provisions as relate to federal revenues and expenditures and to the period for which it is enacted.

---

[82] See Meßerschmidt (2000), pp. 443–543.

[83] See Gluck (2015).

[84] Bundesministerium der Justiz (2008), pp. 191–195. English translation available, cf. Federal Ministry of Justice (2008), pp. 226–231. According to § 42.4 GGO the official draft manual is binding on the drafters ('Für die rechtsförmliche Gestaltung von Gesetzentwürfen gelten das vom Bundesministerium der Justiz herausgegebene Handbuch der Rechtsförmlichkeit und die vom Bundesministerium der Justiz im Einzelfall gegebenen Empfehlungen').

[85] 'Gesetzentwürfe sollen die notwendigen Folgeänderungen in anderen Gesetzen und, zum Zweck der Rechtsbereinigung, die Aufhebung überholter Vorschriften vorsehen.'

This provision intends to prevent abuse of the budget appropriation power. Without this prohibition, Parliament might be tempted to make budget approval conditional on it being able to enforce other non-budgetary concerns.[86] Thus, the budgetary laws mentioned above may be omnibus bills only within narrow limits and the amendment of other laws must relate to federal revenues and expenditures. Therefore, social spending cutbacks or tax increases may be part of such legislation, but no other issues, and the legislator must demonstrate that complementary amendments have an impact on the budget although delimitation may be difficult.[87]

Considering the important role of so-called money bills including omnibus appropriation bills and budget bills in the American discussion,[88] it is amazing that the German provisions are considered antiquated.[89] Even though it is true that the original motivation of this provision with roots going back to the German Empire and its anti-parliamentarian orientation have become obsolete due to the changed legal situation, the proscription of arbitrary linking, far from being alien to constitutional law, must be taken seriously and merits present-day justification.[90]

5.2 Implementation of International Law

Another, albeit less strict, case of rejecting article laws is the implementation of international law treaties. Consent laws on international treaties should not be passed in a joint legislative process with regulations for their national implementation. Although Article 59.2 of the Basic Law makes no such statement, there is a good reason for the two-stage procedure preferred by the legislative directives.[91] In view of the narrowing of parliamentary freedom of decision-making in the case of consent laws, the government should not profit from this special situation by implementing related national legislative proposals in an omnibus law.[92] In contrast, the ratification of several international treaties in one omnibus bill is not objectionable.

As these are narrow exceptions limited to the Budget law and implementation of international treaties, the reverse conclusion, that omnibus legislation in general is admissible in Germany, can be inferred. This comes as no surprise given that Germany in contrast to the U.S.[93] has never adopted a truth-in-legislation clause.

---

[86]Schneider (2002), p. 154.

[87]References can be found in Lachner (2007), pp. 99–103.

[88]Gluck et al. (2015), p. 1804; Tollestrup (2010). On 'omnibudget bills' in Canada Dodek (2017), pp. 11–14 and 19–21.

[89]Cf. Lachner (2007), p. 102. Due to restricted space availability, I waive further specific references.

[90]Cf. Sachs (2018), Art. 110 n. 87–88 and Kube (2013), Art. 110 n. 182.

[91]See Funke (2010), p. 17.

[92]Schneider (2002), p. 157.

[93]For an overview, see Denning and Smith (1999), p. 957.

5.3 Other Considerations

However, there is a growing awareness that omnibus bills in general and heterogeneous bills in particular create the risk of unpredictability for the norm addressees
and thus violate the European-wide recognized principle of transparency of law.
This criticism must, however, be reduced to its reasonable core. First, a distinction
should be drawn between the transparency of laws and the transparency of
law-making. Omnibus legislation concerns much more the process of law-making
than the content of laws. The problem of the lack of transparency, which may
overshadow legislative proceedings, ends at the very moment of legislative resolution. The numerous amendments made by omnibus bill are automatically integrated
into the pertinent laws and whilst it used to be necessary to wait to access published
laws, modern information technology and legal databases have considerably facil-
itated and speeded up access to the law.[94] Moreover, the transparency gap is not
necessarily related to omnibus legislation. Though some legal scholars in Germany
expect each omnibus bill to specify its components,[95] their argument is not fully
convincing. After all, we are not talking about food or medicines where the ingre-
dients must be disclosed. In the case of a law, you just have to read it. Thus, opaque
omnibus legislation is above all a challenge to democratic decision-making and less
to the rule of the law. Outside Germany, many people are concerned that large pieces
of omnibus legislation challenge Parliament's ability to properly scrutinize legislation[96] and we Germans should be too.

A more intricate problem results from referential amendments, i.e. the indirect
changes to laws by referenced provisions.[97] The nested legislative amendment[98] is
based on the following principle: Law A refers to Law B. The legislator changes Law
B and due to the intersection of Law A and Law B, changes to B may or even
primarily affect A. This can go so far as to limit the scope of application of Law A via
Law B.[99] Impact on Law A may escape notice because the law as such remains
apparently unaltered. While editors of collections of laws incorporate the amendments to the pertinent law by any omnibus bill, such a revision is unlikely to happen

---

[94] As Hernandez Ramos and Heydt correctly remark (Hernandez Ramos and Heydt 2017), p. 137.

[95] Kirchhof (2002), p. 2760 and Klein (2004) pp. 16–17, 26.

[96] Wherry (2014), referring to 2000 pages of legislation passed by the House (Canada) without a change.

[97] See on indirect amendments, in general, Xanthaki (2014), pp. 235–239. However, the selected example may exceed the definition. On a similar indirect amendment BVerfGE 37, 363 (383).

[98] See, generally, Müller (1963), pp. 251–252.

[99] The following example is revealing: under Article 6 of the Asylum Procedures Acceleration Act (Asylverfahrensbeschleunigungsgesetz) of 20 October 2015 (BGBl. I S. 2015), which amended several laws (thus meeting the definition of an omnibus bill), Paragraph 16 was added to Article 246 of the Building Code (Baugesetzbuch) making it clear that the assumption of approval in cases where the Nature Conservation Authority had not delivered an opinion within the 1 month time limit, applies to the construction of hostels for asylum seekers in protected areas. See for details, Meßerschmidt (2017), § 18 no. 64a.

in the case of hidden law changes via reference chain. Thus, the intelligibility and accessibility of laws[100] should be improved in many areas and ways, and should not be treated as a particular problem of omnibus legislation. Without prejudice to the (process-related) transparency problem, so far no infringement of the (product-related) principle of legal certainty by omnibus acts has been demonstrated.[101]

Whilst there are no provisions that specifically and deliberately restrict this practice of law-making, there are other provisions that make omnibus legislation less attractive, even though they pursue different goals and serve the implementation of other constitutional law concepts. First, the participation of Germany's Second Chamber (the *Bundesrat*, or Federal Council) may complicate or deter omnibus bills. The Second Chamber, which consists of representatives of the sixteen governments of Member States of the German Federation, contributes to the legislative process. However, two types of participation exist, depending on the subject matter of the legislation. Type I (law appeal or 'objection bill') basically grants consultation via the Mediation Committee *(Vermittlungsausschuss)* while the Second Chamber can only delay legislation *(Einspruchsgesetz)*. Type II (consent bill or act of assent, not to be confused with consent to international agreements) gives veto power to the Second Chamber *(Zustimmungsgesetz)*. Note that the requirement of approval resulting from one singular part of the law affects the law in total. Due to special country interests or diverging political majorities, the Second Chamber may torpedo or amend legislative proposals. Against this background, a major legislative maxim is to avoid all regulations that trigger a need for approval by the Second Chamber.

Consequently, the Federal Government and the First Chamber of the German Parliament *(Bundestag)* carefully avoid integrating provisions into a legislative draft, which might trigger the need for strong Second Chamber participation. This happens with singular legislation and, *a forteriori*, with omnibus legislation.[102] However, if major parts of the legislation require approval, there are fewer motives to avoid flanking regulations for the very reason of undesirable strong *Bundesrat* participation. On the contrary, the legislature retains the right to split up the legal project into separate laws[103] as far as this is not abusive,[104] without being obliged to do so.

The related, but more specific, issue of amendments by the Mediation Committee of the *Bundestag* and *Bundesrat* warrant consideration. This practice, which may be driven by the same motivation as omnibus legislation and may result in omnibus amendments, is controversial because it threatens to undermine the right of legislative initiative of the *Bundestag.* Therefore, the German Federal Constitutional Court accepts such proceedings only on condition that the pertinent provision has been

---

[100]Reimer (2012), § 9 no. 111.

[101]On the legal certainty of omnibus bills *(Rechtsstaatsprinzip, Gesetzesbestimmtheit* and *Gesetzesklarheit)* Lachner (2007), pp. 119–136 with further references.

[102]Schneider (2002), p. 145.

[103]BVerfGE 34, 9 (21); 37, 363 (382); 39, 1 (35). Undecided BVerfGE 24, 184 (199–200).

[104]Relevant discussion can be found in Schulze-Fielitz (1983), p. 715.

debated at the first reading of the draft bill and its contents are closely related to the context of the law.[105]

6 Conclusions

Even though it is highly desirable that German legal officers, drafters, courts and academia stop neglecting the problems of omnibus legislation, a radical shift cannot reasonably be expected. In contrast to many U.S. States where Constitutions and Truth-in-Legislation Acts outlaw statutes that embrace several subjects and do not express subjects in their title,[106] a general ban on omnibus legislation is not on the German agenda or seems even utopian and excessive. Although fierce criticism of legislation, referring to both quantity and quality, is part of the repertoire of political debates, nobody would call omnibus bills a 'crying evil'.[107] The same is true of political comments holding omnibus bills 'fundamentally undemocratic'.[108] On the contrary, omnibus legislation is often regarded as contributing to the production of high-quality laws and, thus, as a convenient tool for the management of legislation.[109] It is, in general, institutionally and technically efficient. Thus, the difficulty of omnibus legislation largely depends on the general conditions and political circumstances. A far greater threat to the democratic decision-making process than omnibus bills nowadays seem to be international agreements discussed outside the democratic forum.[110]

Although we expect German (and European Union) legislators to meet the calls for clarity and truthfulness in laws ('Gesetzesklarheit und Titelwahrheit')[111] no specific strategy on omnibus legislation exists yet. The Better Lawmaking Agenda of the European Union touches upon this topic only indirectly. Their favourite instrument of codification as a means to improve EU law, however, focuses on existing law and is no remedy against future laws. Besides European Union law, Directives in particular, do not indulge in omnibus legislation. The focus of EU law is on single issues and piecemeal acts,[112] which creates another problem and contributes to the patchwork character of EU law. This may explain why EU

---

[105]BVerfGE 72, 175 (191–192) and 101, 297 (308). See for details and further references, Lachner (2007), pp. 106–110.

[106]See Massicotte (2013), pp. 14–15 with further references.

[107]Quoted in Massicotte (2013), p. 15.

[108]See for references, Massicotte (2013), p. 17.

[109]See on the management of legislation in general, Popelier (2017).

[110]The UNECE Aarhus Convention and the UN International Migration Pact provide good examples.

[111]Merten (1984).

[112]See Robinson (2017), p. 247.

legislative quality policies[113] do not focus on the perils of omnibus legislation. Omnibus legislation comes into play mainly at the national level, when national legislators feel the need to make all pieces of the puzzle fit together.

Addressing the problem of omnibus legislation requires a better understanding of the overall nature of law. Law in itself is complex and sometimes confusing and omnibus bills and omnibus attachments are not the first 'fall from grace'. On one hand, we might wish for remedies against the excessive use of omnibus attachments but we should be clear about what annoys us most about omnibus legislation. Do we dislike long and complex laws or rather hasty and confusing amendments that open the doors to lobbyist influence? With respect to point one, the question arises whether the hyper-complexity of some regulations does not suggest that one should better not regulate the questions regulated there.[114] With point two, the main problem results from legislative 'dawn raids'. These are legislative strategies which are incompatible with the idea of 'due process of lawmaking',[115] and that reflect a malfunctioning of contemporary parliamentarianism and the absence or weakness of parliamentary opposition. Moreover, legislative surprise attacks may occur also by means other than via omnibus legislation. On the other hand, some forms of omnibus legislation appear to be indispensable under the rule of law. Replacing omnibus legislation by a patchwork of clear and true single-issue laws would create a similar kind of confusion. Therefore, the alternative to omnibus legislation is not a myriad of minuscule statutes. It could be vigorous codification,[116] provided that the era of codification is not over and the instrument of codification may be adapted to an ever faster changing world.[117] Irrespective hereof, one of the main criticisms of omnibus legislation is its lack of accountability. The answer to this—and thus also to the discontent with omnibus legislation—would be the placing of reason-giving requirements on the legislator.[118] An example of this is the

---

[113]See Voermans (2017), pp. 30–32; Robinson (2017), pp. 250–255; Xanthaki (2017).

[114]The extremely detailed provisions of some German energy laws serve primarily to perfect a subsidy system and only secondarily, indirectly the environmental protection and climate protection goal. See Meßerschmidt (2020), pp. 541–570.

[115]For an overview, see Rose-Ackerman et al. (2015), who do not however mention the problem of omnibus legislation.

[116]Schulze-Fielitz (1988a), p. 51, contrasts omnibus legislation with codification. Codification is based on the compilation of diverse single-issue laws and provisions, which are reorganized according to a uniform systemic structure, resulting from preparatory works and taking into account case law and often associated with ideas of legal reform. The German and continental concept is more demanding than the definition of codification as part of the EU Better Regulation Agenda. See on codification in general, Duprat and Xanthaki (2017), pp. 113–116; on consolidation and codification in the EU, European Commission (2015), pp. 35–37; Irresberger and Jasiak (2017), pp. 183–184; on consolidation in particular De Benedetto (2017), p. 224.

[117]Cf. Schmidt (1985).

[118]Oliver-Lalana (2005, 2013) and Shapiro (1992). On the German debate Lücke (1987) and Waldhoff (2016). Although German Constitutional Law privileges justifiability over justification and I therefore hesitate to place on the legislator the obligation to state reasons from the unspecific provisions of German Constitutional law (cf. Meßerschmidt 2000, pp. 920–924), I have developed a

proposed UK legislative standard in relation to large multi-topic bills which requires 'an explanation as to how the parts of the bill bring into effect the bill's central policy purpose and why it cannot be separated into individual bills'.[119] By imposing the obligation of rationality on the legislator,[120] the excesses of omnibus legislation could be tackled at root. This leads to my final point, which is to emphasise that it is not sufficient to discuss the problems of omnibus legislation from a politico-legal point of view; it also requires a cross check from a decision-theoretical perspective. Thus, my contribution ends by apologizing for a severe deficit.

References

Arndt A (1965) Zum Problem der strafrechtlichen Verjährung. Juristenzeitung (JZ) 20:145–149

Asholt M (2016) Verjährung im Strafrecht. Mohr Siebeck, Tübingen

Baumann J (1969) Vorsicht bei der Verjährung von NS-Gewaltverbrechen. Neue Juristische Wochenschrift (NJW) 22:1279–1282

Brandner T (2004) Gesetzesänderung. Berlin Verlag Arno Spitz, Berlin

Bryde B-O (1998) Geheimgesetzgebung. Juristenzeitung (JZ) 53:115–120

Bundesministerium der Justiz (ed) (2008) Handbuch der Rechtsförmlichkeit, 3rd edn. Bundesministerium der Justiz, Berlin. (see also English translation *sub* Federal Ministry of Justice)

Creifelds C (2017) Rechtswörterbuch, 22nd edn. C.H. Beck, München

De Benedetto M (2017) Maintenance of rules. In: Karpen U, Xanthaki H (eds) Legislation in Europe. A comprehensive guide for scholars and practitioners. Hart, Oxford, pp 215–227

Denning BP, Smith BR (1999) Uneasy riders: the case for a truth-in-legislation amendment. Utah Law Rev 51:957–1004

Dodek AM (2017) Omnibus bills: constitutional constraints and legislative liberations. Ottawa Law Rev 48:1–42

Duprat J-P, Xanthaki H (2017) Legislative drafting techniques/formal legistics. In: Karpen U, Xanthaki H (eds) Legislation in Europe. A comprehensive guide for scholars and practitioners. Hart, Oxford, pp 109–127

European Commission (2015) Commission Staff Working Document 'Better Regulations Guidelines' COM(2015) 215 final

Federal Ministry of Justice (2008) Manual for drafting legislation, 3rd revised edn. Berlin

Frommel M (2001) Taktische Jurisprudenz – Die verdeckte Amnestie von NS-Schreibtischtätern 1969 und die Nachwirkung der damaligen Rechtsprechung bis heute. In: Mahlmann M (ed) Festschrift für Hubert Rottleuthner zum 65. Geburtstag. Gesellschaft und Gerechtigkeit. Nomos, Baden-Baden, pp 458–473

Funke A (2010) Umsetzungsrecht. Mohr Siebeck, Tübingen

Gehrling R (1969) Nochmals § 50 Abs. 2 StGB n.F. und die Verjährung für Teilnahme an Mord. Juristenzeitung (JZ) 24:416–418

---

conciliatory procedural model of obligations related to the allocation of the burden of proof, and thus serving the self-interest of the legislator. This approach comes close to the 'onus model' as proposed by Gilbert (2006), p. 863.

[119]House of Commons Committee on political and constitutional reform (2013), p. 50.

[120]See Meßerschmidt and Oliver-Lalana (2016).

Gilbert MD (2006) Single subject rules and the legislative process. Univ Pittsburgh Law Rev 67:803–870

Glienke SA (2011) Die De-facto-Amnestie von Schreibtischtätern. In: Perels J, Wette W (eds) Mit reinem Gewissen. Wehrmachtrichter in der Bundesrepublik und ihre Opfer. Aufbau Verlag, Berlin, pp 262–277

Gluck AR (2015) Imperfect statutes, imperfect courts: understanding congress's plans in the era of unorthodox lawmaking. Harv Law Rev 129:62–111

Gluck AR, Joseph O'Connell A, Po R (2015) Unorthodox lawmaking, unorthodox rulemaking. Columb Law Rev 115:1789–1865

Goertz JM (2011) Omnibus or not: package bills and single-issue bills in a legislative bargaining game. Soc Choice Welfare 36:547–563

Görtemaker M (2018) Die heile Welt der Rosenburg. Das Bundesministerium der Justiz und die NS-Vergangenheit. In: Creuzberger S, Geppert D (eds) Die Ämter und ihre Vergangenheit. Ministerien und Behörden im geteilten Deutschland 1949 – 1972. Ferdinand Schöningh, Paderborn, pp 47–70

Görtemaker M, Safferling C (2016) Die Akte Rosenburg. Das Bundesministerium der Justiz und die NS-Zeit. C.H. Beck, München

Görtemaker M, Safferling M (2017) The Rosenburg files – the federal ministry of justice and the Nazi Era. Federal Ministry of Justice and Consumer Protection, Berlin. Bmjy.de/geschichte series

Greve M (2000) Amnestierung von NS-Gehilfen – eine Panne? Die Novellierung des § 50 Abs. 2 StGB und dessen Auswirkungen auf die NS-Strafverfolgung. Kritische Justiz 33:412–424

Hebeler T, Schröder K (2018) Das Artikelgesetz – Gesetzestechnik, Gesetzesrecherche, verfassungsrechtliche Fragestellungen. Juristische Ausbildung (JA) 50:641–647

Hernandez Ramos M, Heydt V (2017) Legislative language and style. In: Karpen U, Xanthaki H (eds) Legislation in Europe. A comprehensive guide for scholars and practitioners. Hart, Oxford, pp 129–143

House of Commons Committee on political and constitutional reform (2013) 'Ensuring standards in the quality of legislation'. First Report of Session 2013-14. The Stationery Office Ltd., London

Huefner SF (2017) Legislation and regulation in a Nutshell. West Academic Publishing St, Paul, MN

Hugger W (1983) Gesetze – Ihre Vorbereitung, Abfassung und Prüfung. Nomos, Baden-Baden

Irresberger K, Jasiak A (2017) Publication. In: Karpen U, Xanthaki H (eds) Legislation in Europe. A comprehensive guide for scholars and practitioners. Hart, Oxford, pp 165–185

Kaminski S, Hart EL (2012) Logrolling versus the single-subject rule, In: Bloomberg BNA (The Bureau of national Affairs) The United States Law Week 2-28-12: 1–6

Karpen U (2017) Introduction. In: Karpen U, Xanthaki H (eds) Legislation in Europe. A comprehensive guide for scholars and practitioners. Hart, Oxford, pp 1–16

Kirchhof P (2002) Sprachstil und System als Geltungsbedingung des Gesetzes. Neue Juristische Wochenschrift (NJW) 55:2760–2761

Kirchhoff D, Tsuji LJS (2014) Reading between the lines of the 'Responsible Resource Development' rhetoric: the use of omnibus bills to 'streamline' Canadian environmental legislation. Impact Assess Project Appraisal 32:108–120

Klein E (2004) Gesetzgebung ohne Parlament? De Gruyter, Berlin

Kluth W (2014) Entwicklung und Perspektiven der Gesetzgebungswissenschaft (§ 1). In: Kluth W, Krings G (eds) Gesetzgebung. C.F. Müller, Heidelberg, pp 3–39

Kramer H (2004) Eduard Dreher: Vom Sondergerichtsdezernenten zum führenden Strafrechtler der Bundesrepublik. In: Justizministerium NRW (ed) Zwischen Recht und Unrecht. Lebensläufe deutscher Juristen. Justizakademie Printing Office, Recklinghausen, pp 101–103

Krutz GS (2000) Getting around gridlock: the effect of omnibus utilization on legislative productivity. Legislative Stud Q 25:533–549

Krutz GS (2001a) Hitching a Ride. Omnibus Legislating in the U.S. Congress. The Ohio State University Press, Columbus

Krutz GS (2001b) Tactical maneuvering on omnibus bills in congress. Am J Political Sci 45:210–223

Kube H (2013) Kommentar zu Art. 110 GG. In: Maunz T, Dürig G (eds) Grundgesetz Kommentar, Supplement December 2013. C.H. Beck, München

Lachner TM (2007) Das Artikelgesetz. Duncker& Humblot, Berlin

Lowenstein DH (2002) Initiatives and the new single subject rule. Election Law J 1:35–48

Lücke J (1987) Begründungszwang und Verfassung. Zur Begründungspflicht der Gerichte, Behörden und Parlamente. Mohr Siebeck, Tübingen

Maisch A (2015) Der Einsatz externer Mitarbeiter in Bundesministerien. Springer VS, Wiesbaden

Massicotte L (2013) Omnibus Bills in Theory and Practice. Can Parliamentary Rev Spring 36:13–17

Merten D (1984) Gesetzesklarheit und Titelwahrheit. In: Gesellschaft für Rechtspolitik (ed) Festgabe zum 10jährigen Jubiläum der Gesellschaft für Rechtspolitik. C.H. Beck, München, pp 295–314

Meßerschmidt K (2000) Gesetzgebungsermessen. Berlin Verlag Arno Spitz, Berlin

Meßerschmidt K (2012) Private Gesetzgebungshelfer – Gesetzgebungsoutsourcing als privatisiertes Regulierungsmanagement in der Kanzleiendemokratie? Der Staat 51:387–415

Meßerschmidt K (2017) Bundesnaturschutzrecht Kommentar, supplement 135 of July 2017. Rehm, München

Meßerschmidt K (2019) Special interest legislation and legislative capture. In: Oliver-Lalana D (ed) Conceptions and misconceptions of legislation. Springer, Dordrecht, pp 243–272

Meßerschmidt K (2020) Immissionsschutz und Klimaschutz (§ 46). In: Ehlers D, Fehling M, Pünder H (eds) Besonderes Verwaltungsrecht, vol 2, 4th edn. C.F. Müller, Heidelberg

Meßerschmidt K, Oliver-Lalana AD (eds) (2016) Rational lawmaking under review. Legisprudence according to the German Federal Constitutional Court. Springer, Dordrecht

Müller H (1963) Handbuch der Gesetzgebungstechnik. Carl Heymanns Verlag, Köln

Nationalrat der nationalen Front des demokratischen Deutschland (ed) (1965) Braunbuch. Kriegs- und Naziverbrecher in der Bundesrepublik. Staatsverlag der DDR, Berlin

Nightingale RL (2016) How to trim a christmas tree: beyond severability and inseverability for omnibus statutes. Yale Law J 125:1675–1743

Oliver-Lalana AD (2005) Legitimacy through rationality: Parliamentary argumentations as rational justification of laws. In: Wintgens LJ (ed) The theory and practice of legislation: essays in legisprudence. Ashgate, Aldershot, pp 239–258

Oliver-Lalana AD (2013) Rational lawmaking and legislative reasoning in parliamentary debates. In: Wintgens LJ, Oliver-Lalana AD (eds) The rationality and justification of legislation: essays in legisprudence. Springer, Dordrecht, pp 135–134

Popelier P (2017) Management of legislation. In: Karpen U, Xanthaki H (eds) Legislation in Europe. A comprehensive guide for scholars and practitioners. Hart, Oxford, pp 53–72

Reimer F (2012) Das Parlamentsgesetz als Steuerungsmittel und Kontrollmaßstab (§ 9). In: Hoffmann-Riem W, Schmidt-Aßmann E, Voßkuhle A (eds) Grundlagen des Verwaltungsrechts, vol 1, 2nd edn. C.H. Beck, München, p 585–675

Robinson W (2017) EU-legislation. In: Karpen U, Xanthaki H (eds) Legislation in Europe. A comprehensive guide for scholars and practitioners. Hart, Oxford, pp 229–256

Romain A, Byrd S, Thielecke C (2002) Wörterbuch der Rechts- und Wirtschaftssprache, vol. 2: Deutsch – Englisch, 4th edn. C.H. Beck, München

Rose-Ackerman S, Egidy S, Fowkes J (2015) Due process of lawmaking. The United States, South Africa, Germany and the European Union. Cambridge University Press, Cambridge

Rottleuthner H (2001) Hat Dreher gedreht? Über Unverständlichkeit, Unverständnis und Nichtverstehen in Gesetzgebung und Forschung. Rechtshistorisches J 20:665–679; revised edition in: Lerch KD (ed) (2004), Die Sprache des Rechts, vol. 1: Recht Verstehen. De Gruyter, Berlin, pp 307–320

Sachs M (2018) Kommentar zu Art. 110 GG. In: Sachs M (ed) Grundgesetz Kommentar, 8th edn. C.H. Beck, München

Sambale A (2002) Die Verjährungsdebatte im Deutschen Bundestag. Verlag Dr. Kovac, Hamburg

Samson E (1969) § 50 II n. F. StGB und die Verjährung. Zeitschrift für Rechtspolitik (ZRP) 2:27–29

Schmidt K (1985) Die Zukunft der Kodifikationsidee. C F. Müller, Heidelberg

Schneider H (2002) Gesetzgebung, 3rd edn. C.F. Müller, Heidelberg

Schröder H (1969) Der § 50 StGB n. F. und die Verjährung beim Mord. Juristenzeitung (JZ) 24:132–134

Schulze-Fielitz H (1983) Gesetzgebung als materiales Verfassungsverfahren. Die Befugnisse des Vermittlungsausschusses und die Aufspaltung von Gesetzen. Neue Zeitschrift für Verwaltungsrecht (NVwZ) 2:709–717

Schulze-Fielitz H (1988a) Theorie und Praxis parlamentarischer Gesetzgebung. Duncker & Humblot, Berlin

Schulze-Fielitz H (1988b) Der politische Kompromiß als Chance und Gefahr für die Rationalität der Gesetzgebung. Jahrbuch für Rechtssoziologie und Rechtstheorie 13:290–326

Schuppert GF (2003) Gute Gesetzgebung. Zeitschrift für Gesetzgebung 18 Sonderheft (special issue). C.F. Müller, Heidelberg

Sendler H (2001) Verordnungsänderung durch Gesetz und 'Entsteinerungsklausel'. Neue Juristische Wochenschrift (NJW) 54:2859–2861

Shapiro M (1992) The giving reasons requirement. Univ Chicago Legal Forum 8:179–220

Sinclair B (2011) Unorthodox lawmaking, 4th edn. Sage, Los Angeles

Smeddinck U (2014) Gesetzestypen (§ 3). In: Kluth W, Krings G (eds) Gesetzgebung. C.F. Müller, Heidelberg, pp 69–93

Tollestrup J (2010) Omnibus appropriation acts: overview of recent practices, Congressional Report Services Report for Congress, August 25, 2010

Uhle A (2001) Verordnungsänderung durch Gesetz und Gesetzesänderung durch Verordnung? Die Öffentliche Verwaltung (DÖV) 54:241–247

Voermans WJM (2017) Legislation and regulation. In: Karpen U, Xanthaki H (eds) Legislation in Europe. A comprehensive guide for scholars and practitioners. Hart, Oxford, pp 17–32

von Bogdandy A (2000) Gubernative Rechtsetzung. Mohr Siebeck, Tübingen

Waldhoff C (2016) The constitutional duties to give reasons for legislative acts. In: Meßerschmidt K, Oliver-Lalana AD (eds) Rational lawmaking under review. Springer, Dordrecht, pp 129–151

Wherry A (2014) The omnibus question. Could something be done to limit omnibus legislation?, March 31, 2014 http://www.macleans.ca/political/the-omnibus-question/. Last accessed 31 July 2018

Xanthaki H (2014) Drafting legislation. Art and technology of rules for regulation. Hart, Oxford

Xanthaki H (2017) Emerging trends in legislation in Europe. In: Karpen U, Xanthaki H (eds) Legislation in Europe. A comprehensive guide for scholars and practitioners. Hart, Oxford, pp 275–296

Zeh W (1982) Asylrecht und kommunale Selbstverwaltung. Die Öffentliche Verwaltung (DÖV) 35:957–963

Israel's Economic Arrangements Law and Similar Omnibudget Laws in Other Countries

Susan Hattis Rolef

Abstract This paper deals with the question whether there is anything Israel can learn from other countries that contend with omnibudget legislation such as its Economic Arrangements Law. The paper is divided into three sections. The first describes the history of the EAL, and efforts to deal with its worst abuses such as its length, the diversity of subjects contained in it, many of which have no direct relation to the budget or economic reforms program which the law is supposed to support, the expedited procedures with which it is dealt, which prevent the Knesset from fulfilling its scrutinizing role of government legislation. The second deals with omnibus and omnibudget laws in other countries, and how each has (or has not) tried to cope with them. The third section deals with the various measures that can be taken to deal with such legislation, based on the experience of other countries. The main conclusion is that countries where such legislation exists, find it impossible to get rid of it altogether and permanently, but that if there is political will some of its worst abuses can be modified.

Keywords Economic arrangements law · Omnibus bills · Budget law · Single subject rule · Oversight · Constitutionalism · Legislative process

1 The Israeli Economic Arrangements Law

1.1 Background

The Economic Arrangements Law (EAL) is an omnibudget law first introduced in Israel in 1985, within the framework of the Economic Plan for the Stabilization of the Economy, launched by the National Unity Government under Prime Minister Shimon Peres (Labor Alignment) and Minister of Finance Yitzhak Modai (Likud), to

S. H. Rolef (✉)
Jerusalem, Israel
e-mail: susan-sheila@bezeqint.net

deal with an acute economic crisis, which required drastic measures, including major and highly unpopular amendments to numerous existing laws, such as labor laws, and new legislation, and was originally passed by means of emergency regulations.[1]

The EAL is a law of vast dimensions, that is formally supposed to amend existing legislation, or enact new laws on a variety of usually unrelated subjects, allegedly in order to enable the implementation of the budget and the Government's economic reform program, which is passed in parallel with the Budget Law, in an expedited timetable.[2]

Originally there was no intention to continue using such omnibus legislation after the economic crisis was over, but the Ministry of Finance discovered its advantages, and started using it on an annual basis.

Over the years the dimensions of the EALs kept growing, and they started to contain a growing number of chapters that were not directly connected either to the budget, or to economic reforms, as the Government began including in it legislation that it was having difficulty enacting as ordinary Government bills, and using it to put off the implementation of legislation approved by the Knesset, that had originated in Private Members' Bills (PMBs) of which the Ministry of Finance disapproved, mostly for financial reasons.[3]

By the 1990s there was growing criticism of the EALs over the dimensions and diversity of issues raised in them, and the expedited manner in which they were dealt with by a single Knesset committee—the Finance Committee—which did not enable proper consideration and scrutiny by the MKs of the Bills' content. An additional problem concerns the fact that since one is speaking of a single law that contains many unrelated pieces of legislation, an MK might find himself/herself being forced to choose between voting in favor of the law, even though he/she objects to some of its chapters, or against the law, even though he/she supports some of them.[4] While some called for banning this form of legislation, others called for major changes in its content, and the procedures by which it is enacted.

It was only towards the end of the 1990s that concrete measures were considered for dealing with some of these issues.

1.2 Distribution of the Various Chapters in the Arrangements Bill for Deliberation in the Relevant Subject Committees

The demand that the various chapters of the EAL be divided among the relevant Knesset committees for preparation towards second and third readings rather than

---

[1]For a detailed analysis of the history of the Economic Arrangements Law, see Rolef (2006).

[2]Dodek (2017), p. 6.

[3]Rolef. op. cit. pp. 18–19.

[4]See, for example, MK Haim Oron (Meretz) in the meeting of the Knesset House Committee on July 6, 2004.

the Finance Committee alone, first emerged in the late 1980s, but came across opposition from the Ministry of Finance on the one hand, and doubts on the part of the Legal Advisor to the Knesset at the time—Attorney Zvi Inbar—as to whether under the Rules of Procedure, the House Committee was entitled to divide up a single bill among several committees.[5]

It was only during the 15th Knesset (1999–2003), that the problem was partially resolved. In November 2001 Knesset Speaker Avraham Burg (Labor), in collaboration with the Chairmen of the House and Finance Committees, proposed that the chapters in the Arrangements Bill be divided into three categories: *the first* would include chapters directly connected to the current budget proposal, which would be dealt with in the Finance Committee and approved by the plenum by December 31; *the second* would include all those chapters that are important for the implementation of the budget but are not directly linked to it, which would be separated from the EAL, and dealt with as separate bills by the relevant permanent committees, which would undertake to get them approved in second and third readings by December 31; *the third* would include all the chapters of the original Bill that were not connected to the budget, and would be dealt with as separate ordinary government bills.

This proposal was disbanded due to a change of Government in March 2001. A compromise was finally worked out in November 2002, to the effect that the House Committee would refer parts of the Arrangements Bill to the Finance Committee, and other parts to the subject committees, or joint committees in which the Finance Committee and subject committees would be represented, but that the Arrangements Bill would remain a single bill, and be brought as such for second and third readings.[6]

At this stage the idea of enabling the House Committee to take articles out of the Arrangements Bill and turn them into independent bills was dropped, and the option of taking sections out of the Arrangements Bill as originally submitted, was left to informal negotiations between the Knesset and the Ministry of Finance, either before or after the Arrangements Bill is approved in first reading, and before it reaches the House Committee for distribution among the various committees. To the present day, this is the procedure followed—a time consuming ritual, which starts off with the Ministry of Finance including numerous chapters in the Bill that it knows will not remain in it. There are years when the Knesset is more successful in reducing the size of the Arrangements Bills, and others when it is less successful, all depending on the political circumstances and the identity of the persons involved in the negotiations.

---

[5]Rolef. op. cit. p. 13.
[6]Ibid. pp. 14–15.

1.3   Attempts to Reduce the Dimensions
of the Arrangements Laws

The greatest efforts to deal with the dimensions of the EALs were made in the course of the 17th Knesset (2006–2009). The ruling of the HCJ in the Poultry Growers case in 2004 (see below), which dealt with certain chapters in the EAL for that year, had a significant effect, but so did the efforts of the Legal Advisor to the Knesset at the time (Attorney Nurit Elstein), the Chairperson of the House Committee [MK Ruhama Avraham (Kadima)], and the Secretary General of the Knesset (Eyal Yinon).

Both Elstein and Avraham organized symposia in the Knesset in which the future of the EALs was deliberated. When the Arrangements Bill for 2007 was submitted to the Knesset the two embarked on a battle to cut the number of chapters in the Bill from 84 to 4, turning the remaining chapters into separate bills. However, under pressure from the coalition chairman the House Committee voted in favor of leaving most of them in the Bill, and the number of chapters was reduced to 53 only.[7]

The following year, the Arrangement Bill for 2008 was reduced from the original 90 to 22 chapters, but Avraham's plan to head a committee that would introduce procedural changes in the treatment of the Arrangements Law by means of an amendment to the Knesset Rules of Procedures, and by law, came to naught, as she joined the Government, and her successor lacked her reformist drive.

In February 2009, around the time of the elections to the 18th Knesset, Yinon and the Government Secretary, Oved Yehezkel, presented a document to the outgoing Prime Minister Ehud Olmert, and Knesset Speaker Dalia Itzik, titled "Mutual relations between the Knesset and the Government". The document included proposals and recommendations that *inter alia* combined the issues of PMBs, the EALs and the Knesset treatment of government legislation, in a sort of package deal. This package deal was to drastically reduce the number of provisions in the EALs submitted by the Government, in return for a cut in the number of PMBs submitted by MKs (which stood at around 1000 per annual session).[8]

On July 20, 2009, a week after the Budget Law and EAL for 2009 had been approved by the Knesset, Yinon, with the backing of the new Knesset Speaker, Reuven Rivlin (Likud), sent a letter to the Ministry of Finance Budgets Director, in which he explained why the whole situation regarding the EALs was intolerable, ending with the following proposal:

"I propose that a professional team be set up by the Ministry of Finance and the Knesset, to examine the existing working arrangements in the process for approving the Budget Law and the Arrangements Law in the Knesset, and to attempt to formulate agreements to be approved by the Prime Minister, the Knesset Speaker,

---

[7]Meeting of the House Committee held on December 5, 2006.

[8]Yehezkel and Yinon (2009), pp. 13–15.

and the Finance Minister, with the goal of implementing them towards the approval of the State Budget for 2011".[9]

However, since the newly elected Prime Minister, Binyamin Netanyahu, was an enthusiastic supporter of EALs from the time that he had served as Minister of Finance in the years 2004–2005,[10] neither proposal had any chance of being adopted.

1.4   Rulings of the High Court of Justice

Petitions relating to specific chapters in the EAL are frequently submitted to the HCJ. The policy of the HCJ has been not to deal with such petitions if the law has not been approved in third reading, with the actual content of the various chapters, or with the question whether these chapters should remain in the Arrangements Bill.

Two rulings that dealt with the allegedly faulty procedures under which particular chapters in EALs have been passed are of particular interest: the popularly called "Poultry Growers" case (HCJ 4885/03), and the popularly called "Tax-on-the-third-apartment" case (HCJ 10042/16). In each of the two cases the Court gave rulings that emphasized the importance of the MKs' "participation in the legislative process".

The HCJ's ruling in the Poultry Growers case given on September 27, 2004, which dealt with structural changes in several agricultural branches that were included in Chapter 11 of the EAL for 2004, was a landmark in the approach to the procedure by which EALs are approved, even though the court declared such laws to be constitutional, and did not declare the relevant chapter null and void, since it felt that the procedural faults that occurred had not "gone down to the root of the process".

What the court did was to lay down the basic principles of the legislative process in democratic parliamentary regimes, the breach of which might justify judicial intervention. However, it refused to apply the concept of "legislative due process", which goes into details of the actual application of the principles, which is recognized by the Israeli courts when they deals with the decisions of administrative authorities, but not in the case of the Knesset's legislative process, due to the "Knesset's special status".[11]

In her ruling, Supreme Court Justice Dorit Beinish listed as the four basic principles of the legislative process in a constitutional, parliamentary regime the principle of *decision by the majority*, the principle of *equality in the legislative process*, the principle of *publicity* (or openness), and the principle of *participation*, and decided to concentrate on the latter.

---

[9]Thanks to Yinon, who provided a copy of the letter.

[10]Zerahia (2005).

[11]HCJ 4885/03, articles, 26–29.

"The principle of participation, according to which every MK has the right to participate in the legislative process, constitutes [. . .] a basic principle in the legislative process in parliamentary regimes. The principle of participation is nothing more than the development of the representational democracy approach, and its implementation on the parliamentary law.(art.18) [. . .] [I]n order that the Knesset shall be able to perform its functions by force of the democratic representation principle, it is necessary to enable all the Knesset members to participate in the parliamentary procedures that are required for the fulfillment of these functions. (art. 22)"

After pointing out that the participation principle is recognized in other countries as well, Beinish continued to discuss what is to be included in the principle of participation beyond the "appropriate and proper opportunity [for the MK] to participate in voting on the Bill", the breach of which would justify the intervention of the Court.(art. 24) Relating to the claim of the appellants that in the case under review the MKs had been denied the ability to formulate a position with regards to the Bill due to the expedited procedure with which it was dealt, Beinish ruled that in the current case, while the procedure had been problematic, this did not justify the intervention of the court. (art. 25).

In her conclusion Beinish emphasized that the Knesset ought to consider the problems, from a democratic point of view, involved in the legislative apparatus of the EAL, and should ensure that minimal use be made of this apparatus. (art. 31)

Twelve years after this ruling, once again serious procedural faults occurred during the deliberations in the Finance Committee on December 15, 2016, on Chapter 12 in the Arrangements Bill attached to the biennial budget for 2017–2018. The chapter dealt with taxation on the owners of multiple apartments, from the third apartment upwards.[12] The Committee's Legal Advisor, Attorney Sagit Shafik, announced at the beginning of the all-night deliberation of the chapter, that the legal department of the Knesset had received a new version of this chapter from the Ministry of Finance only minutes before the deliberation was to begin, and that she was therefore unable to express an opinion on it.

The Legal Advisor to the Knesset, (former Knesset Secretary General) Attorney Eyal Yinon, tried to intervene in order to ensure that an appropriate deliberation take place, but failed. The law was approved on December 21, 2016, and once again various bodies petitioned the HCJ.

This time the court decided to go one step further than it had done in 2004. In his verdict of August 6, 2017, Supreme Court Justice Noam Solberg, returned to the principle of 'participation', deciding to concentrate on the question whether the MKs had been denied "any practical possibility to formulate an opinion regarding a bill", rather than whether the MKs we denied "any practical possibility to know what they are voting about", as Beinish had done. In article 59 of his verdict he wrote:

---

[12]This was done within the framework of measures to reduce the price of housing for first time house owners.

"[I]t is not sufficient that the legislative process is designed to enable the MKs 'to know what they are voting about'—to read the Bill, to hear about it and superficially understand the law that is to be voted on. The legislative process must enable the MKs to formulate a basic position, even if in a very limited manner, regarding the law before them. The formulation of a position is not merely a 'passive' act, but requires a certain thinking process, an independent processing of information handed over to the MK, the adoption of a thought-out decision in favor or against a bill. Only when the MKs have been given such an option, can one say that they had been given an opportunity to participate in the legislative process in an active and real manner."

Solberg ruled that in the preparation of the said chapter in the EAL for the second and third readings a defect had occurred, which "goes down to the root of the process", and that consequently the suitable result falls within what is known as the *relative nullity* doctrine, which in practical terms meant that the said chapter should be returned to the Finance Committee and prepared again for second and third readings.

As it were, the relevant chapter was not returned to the Knesset, and a request by the State that the court review the principle it had laid down, did not occur.[13]

1.5   Intervention by Attorney Generals

On December 31, 2003 the Attorney General, Eliakim Rubinstein, tried to bring about a change in what the Ministry of Finance includes in the EALs which it submits, in an instruction he issued on "Government decisions within the framework of the deliberations on the budget and economic plans".[14] In the section concerning the EALs he suggested an alternative to the current practices, that would reduce the size of the EAL itself to a bare minimum, and enable the Government to bring all the economic and structural reforms it seeks to introduce separately from the budget, but by means of effective procedures.

A year later Menachem (Meni) Mazuz, who succeeded Rubinstein, continued what the latter had begun. In an interview in 2008[15] he described procedural changes, that he started to introduce after his appointment, as to how the Ministry of Finance prepares and submits its proposals for the Arrangements Bill to the Government, and how the Government deliberates them. The purpose of the procedural changes was to get the Government itself to be more selective in what it included in the EAL—a law which he considered extremely importance in enabling the Government to implement its economic policy—by laying down several criteria for deciding what belongs in the EAL and what does not, including the direct link of the subject to the budget and economic policy, serious prior preparation and

---

[13]For a legal discussion of this issue see Daniel (2017).

[14]See Appendix 6 in Rolef (2006).

[15]Mazuz (2008).

deliberation by the Ministry of Finance with the relevant factors of each measure to be introduced in the Law, and keeping the number of issues included in the law down to what the Government can effectively deal with.

Neither Attorney General left behind any permanent change in the way EALs are prepared, while the two following Attorney General—Yehuda Weinstein and Avihai Mandelblitt—showed no special interest in the subject.

It should be noted that steps taken by Attorney Generals concern the Government rather than the Knesset.

1.6   Legislative Initiatives to Deal with the Problems of EALs

Over the years numerous efforts were made to bring about change in the nature and legislative process of EALs by means of legislation submitted by MKs. These bills proposed amendments to the Budget Foundations Law, or Basic Law: the State Budget and/or the Knesset Rules of Procedure. Only one such PMB (2434/15), submitted by MK Haim Katz (Am Ehad) towards the end of the 15th Knesset, actually reached preparation for second and third readings, but following the elections to the 16th Knesset in 2003, the new Government decided to disband it. None of the other bills proposed over the years got beyond Preliminary Debate, largely because of Government opposition.

It should be noted that in the course of the 16th Knesset (2003–2006), within the framework of the deliberations of the Constitution, Law and Justice Committee chaired by MK Michael Eitan (Likud), on the subject of "a Constitution by Consensus", the idea of including provisions regarding EALs in the chapter on legislation was raised. However, work on the constitution was discontinued during the 17th Knesset (2006–2009).

2   Omnibus and Omnibudget Laws in Other Countries

2.1   "Such Things Don't Exist Anywhere in the World"

Within and outside the Knesset there has traditionally been wariness about admitting that omnibudget laws exist in other countries. The main reason for this is a general inclination to say about every phenomenon in the Knesset that is considered negative or problematic, that it is unique to Israel. Over the years the notion that the EAL is a phenomenon unique to Israel received backing from several renown academics. In a paper they presented on EALs at the Caesarea Conference in 2005, economics professors Avi Ben-Bassat and Momi Dahan from the Hebrew University, stated that they had discussed the issue with representatives of the OECD, and with senior officials in the Finance Ministries of Ireland, the Netherlands and Denmark, and found that usually, the budget Law in industrialized countries does not include legislative amendments of direct budgetary significance. These legislative amendments are made in the usual legislative manner. Those states that attach legislative amendments of direct budgetary ramifications to the Budget Law, do so with care.[16]

They were right in pointing out that Ireland the Netherlands and Denmark, do not have omnibudget legislation, but as we shall see below, quite a few other members of the OECD do, and do not necessarily deal with them "with care".

One of the reasons why the Knesset prefers to ignore the existence of omnibudget legislation in other democratic countries, is that the Ministry of Finance wards off complaints by the Knesset about the abuses of the EAL by arguing that such laws exist in other countries[17] and are considered a legitimate tool in an era when Governments find it increasingly difficult to get their economic plans and reforms approved in parliament, as is also the case in Israel.

2.2 Canada

Canada's Budget Implementation Act (BIA) is very similar to Israel's EAL The main difference between the Canadian and Israeli experience is that Canada has had omnibus legislation since the late nineteenth Century.

Omnibus bills were always criticized in Canada for being a problematic form of legislation well before the first BIA was submitted in 1994, primarily due to the large number of subjects included in these bills, which had no connection to the bills' titles, thus making it difficult for MPs to properly scrutinize their content.[18]

Despite the criticism, Speakers of the Canadian House of Commons have been traditionally conservative in their treatment of abusive omnibus legislation, and most of them have been wary of intervening, acting only under extreme pressure to break up omnibus bills. Nevertheless, Lucien Lamoureux, Speaker in the years 1966–1974, expressed his concerns about the dimensions and diversity of the 1971 Government Organization Act (Bill C-207) and stated "[W]here do we stop? Where is the point of no return? [. . .] we might reach the point where we would have only one bill, a bill at the start of the session for the improvement of the quality of life in Canada which would include every single proposed piece of legislation for the session".[19]

The BIAs, designed to help implement certain aspects of the government's annual budget by means of the amendment or repeal of existing legislation, and the enactment of new legislation, aggravated the situation. Though the first Budget

---

[16]Ben-Bassat and Dahan (2008).

[17]They usually quote my 2005 document on this.

[18]Dodek (2017), p. 9.

[19]Ibid.

implementation Act in 1994 was only 24 pages long, it contained all the maladies associated with this type of legislation.[20]

Over the years the BIAs have become progressively longer.[21] For example the 2010 BIA contained 883 pages of varied and unrelated legislative provisions, which amounted to around 50% of Parliament's legislative output for 2010.[22] Since the turn of the millennium in most years *two* Budget Implementation bills have been submitted—both relating to the same annual budget. Another development has been that while in the first years "budget implementation bills tended to be slimmed down markedly between first reading and Royal Assent, [. . .] in recent years they [have] kept their initial size throughout".[23]

Neither the Canadian Constitution nor the Parliament of Canada Act say anything on the subject of omnibus legislation that might instruct the two House of Parliament to take a more active stance. Though the *House of Commons Procedure and Practice,*[24] deals quite extensively with the phenomenon of omnibus bills, this is in a descriptive rather than an instructive sense.

I found one PMB from 2015, which sought to reduce the use of omnibus legislation on the federal level. The Bill provided for the addition of article 13.1 to the Parliament of Canada Act,[25] but since it was submitted towards a general election it wasn't even debated.

In the 2015 general elections the Liberal Party, under Justine Trudeau, promised to do something about the use of omnibus bills. Two years later the Liberal Government added article 69.1. to the Standing Orders of the House of Commons, which gave the Speaker the power to break up the voting on omnibus bills, thus enabling the House of Commons to reject certain sections of such bills. However, this did not stop the Liberal Party from continuing to introduce and pass massive BIAs,[26] though both in 2017 and 2018 the Speaker did act upon article 69.1.[27]

While it is generally assumed in Canada that the Senate performs the role of "a chamber of sober second thought",[28] in the case of omnibus legislation this is rarely the case. In fact, the Senate has avoided taking any drastic measures over BIAs, though in its Report on the 528 page Budget Implementation Act for 2009, the Standing Senate Committee on National Finance, published Recommendation 9, to the effect that "the Government [should] cease the use of omnibus legislation to

---

[20]See speech delivered by MP Stephen Harper during the Second Reading of the Bill on March 25, 1994. Canada, House of Commons Debates, Official record, First Session, 35th Parliament, Vol. III, 1994, p. 2775.

[21]Massicotte (2013), pp. 16–17.

[22]Franks (2010).

[23]Massicotte op. cit.

[24]Bosc and Gagnon (2017).

[25]https://openparliament.ca/bills/41-2/C-654/.

[26]Wherry (2016).

[27]Wherry (2017).

[28]Massicotte op. cit. p. 26.

introduce budget implementation measures", to which was added Observation 5, which called upon the Senate to divide BIAs into coherent parts and deal with them separately, allowing committees to do their jobs properly; to delete all non-budgetary provisions and proceed to consider only those parts of the bill that are budgetary by nature; to defeat the bill at second reading on the grounds that it is an affront to Parliament; and to establish a new Rule of the Senate prohibiting the introduction of budget implementation bills that contain non-budgetary measures.[29]

Nothing came of the Committee's initiative.

The courts in Canada have used the principle of 'parliamentary privilege' to shield virtually all internal legislative proceedings, including the legislative process, from judicial review. This principle explains why the courts refuse to scrutinize how bills are made, introduced, or considered as long as the legislative process complies with the terms of the Constitution—i.e. three readings in both Houses of Parliament, and Royal Assent. It also explains why even the most abusive omnibus and omnibudget bills have never been legally challenged.[30]

2.3 The United States

2.3.1 Omnibus legislation has featured in the United States on the federal level, since the middle of the 19th century, but significantly expanded at the beginning of the Reagan Administration in 1980/81.

Though many omnibus bills introduced to Congress are made up of large numbers of unrelated, legislation initiated by individual congressmen, the congressional parties and the President, and lumped together as package deals, a significant number are related to the budget approving process, in the form of Appropriation Bills[31] or Reconciliation Legislation.[32]

The main difference between such legislation in the U.S., with its presidential system, and parliamentary democracies where such legislation exists, is that in the latter it is the executive branch, which is responsible for the formulation and submission of omnibus bills with parliament contending with them as best it can,

---

[29]Standing Senate Committee on National Finance, "Report on the Budget Implementation Act, 2009", June 2009, pp. 42–43.

[30]Dodek (2017), pp. 33–37.

[31]Appropriations Bills are legislation designed to allocate federal funds to specific federal government departments, agencies, and programs. (Saturno and Tollestrup 2016; Saturno et al. 2016).

[32]Reconciliation Bills are designed to reconcile, where necessary, spending, revenue and debt limits in existing legislation to those appearing in the Budget Resolution passed by Congress after the budget proposal is presented to Congress. The purpose of the reconciliation process is to allow Congress to use an expedited procedure in both congressional Houses in the course of preparing and passing the required legislation. [Lynch and Saturno (2017)].

while in the U.S. it is the party and committee leaders, in collaboration with top executive officials, who are responsible for compiling these bills. Whether an omnibus bill is a hodgepodge of unrelated legislative initiatives or more coherent Appropriation Bills, Congressmen are requested to approve vast pieces of legislation that they have no time to study in advance.[33] For example, towards the end of March 2018, the two Houses of Congress passed a 2232 page, $1.3 trillion Appropriations Bill, less than 48 h after being submitted to them to prevent a federal government shutdown.[34] To the present no serious attempt has been made by Congress to tackle this problem, though occasionally there are proposals by proponents of "small government" to apply the 'single subject rule' (see below) to the federal level.[35]

In the case of Reconciliation Bills attempts are frequently made at the committee stage to use the reconciliation process to add policy clauses that are not connected to the budget as presented in the Budget Resolution. In response to this phenomenon in 1985 Senator Byrd initiated the addition of article 313 to the Congressional Budget Act, known as the Byrd Rule, which aims at preventing the addition of subjects that are extraneous to the content of the Reconciliation Directives, by laying down six tests that determine the criteria for deciding which provisions are to be considered extraneous and left out of the Reconciliation Bill.[36]

The Federal Courts refuse to deal with the highly problematic legislative process involved in the passage of some of the Omnibus Bills.[37] In fact, the courts are only willing to review legislative procedures if basic constitutional conditions are broken, such as the requirement that the laws are passed by both Houses, and signed by the President.[38]

Despite complaints about the frequently undemocratic manner in which omnibus legislation is prepared and passed, there are many who defend the practice, on grounds that it is necessary for the smooth running of the political system, arguing that without omnibus legislation in certain situations the whole legislative system could be totally paralyzed, especially in periods in which the President does not control one or both Houses of Congress.[39]

2.3.2 The Single Subject Rule in the U.S.

The Single Subject Rule (SSR), which declares that bills must contain a single subject only, appears in one form or another in the constitutions of 43 of the

---

[33]Curry (2015).

[34]Kaplan (2018).

[35]See Dodek (2017).

[36]Heniff (2016).

[37]Linde (1976).

[38]Rose-Ackerman et al. (2016).

[39]Sinclaire (2017), deals extensively with this subject.

50 U.S. States. In most of the States the subject of the bill must appear in its title. [40] In 37 States Appropriation Bills are excluded from the rule, and in a few the rule does not apply to some other types of bill as well.

The SSR was first introduced into North America in the beginning of the eighteenth century, during British colonial rule, and was subsequently adopted by most of the States, after gaining independence. In a 1901 judgment of the Commonwealth Court of Pennsylvania that dealt with omnibus legislation, the following explanation was provided for why the SSR had been adopted in Pennsylvania:

"Bills, popularly called *omnibus bills*, became a crying evil, not only from the confusion and distraction of the legislative mind by the jumbling together of incongruous subjects, but still more by the facility they afforded to corrupt combinations of minorities with different interests to force the passage of bills with provisions which could never succeed if they stood on their separate merits. So common was this practice that it got a popular name, universally understood, as *logrolling*.

A still more objectionable practice grew up, of putting what is known as a *rider* [. . .] on the appropriation bills, and thus coercing the executive to approve obnoxious legislation, or bring the wheels of the government to a stop for want of funds.

These were some of the evils which the later changes in the constitution were intended to remedy."[41]

However, most writers on the subject of the SSR agree that the implementation of the rule is partial and problematic, especially because of the different ways in which the courts have interpreted the term 'single subject'.[42]

2.4   The United Kingdom

It was the British Empire, which introduced the SSR into North America. In 1695, the Committee of the Privy Council in London complained that diverse acts in the North American colony of Massachusetts were "joined together under ye same title, whereby it has been necessary for the repealing of such of them as have not been thought fit to be confirmed to vacate such others as have been comprehended under such titles".[43] More specifically, the Privy Council wanted to prevent colonial legislatures from attaching riders to bills submitted by the administration concerning the funding of the salaries of crown officials in the colonies.[44]

The first known application of this principle was in 1702, when Queen Anne sent the Governor of New Jersey an instruction, to the effect that "You are also, as much

---

[40]Most of the information on the Single Subject Rule is taken from Gilbert (2006).

[41]*Commonwealth v. Barnett*, 199 Pa. 161 (1901), quoted in Massicotte (2013), p. 15.

[42]Kaminski and Hart (2012).

[43]Luce (1922), pp. 549–550.

[44]Email from Dr. Seth Barrett Tillman, dated September 3, 2018.

as possible, to observe in the passing of all laws that whatever may be requisite upon each different matter be accordingly provided for by a different law without intermixing in one and the same act such things as have no proper relation to each other".[45] In subsequent years the Privy Council turned this instruction into a standing order to all the Governors of its colonies and dominions throughout the world.[46] On January 1, 1932, a similar instruction was sent to the High Commissioner of Palestine, Sir Arthur Wauchope, even though Palestine was not a colony, and did not have a legislative council.[47]

Unlike the British Empire the U.K. is not commonly associated with omnibus legislation. However, according to the Hansard Society, omnibus bills did start to appear in the U.K. after the Labour Party assumed power in 1997, and were continued by the Conservative Party after it replaced Labour in 2010.[48] The Hansard Society mentioned two particular "Christmas-tree" bills (as such legislation is referred to in the U.K.), which brought together "an array of 'miscellaneous provisions'", and in effect constituted several bills in one, some of which were so large they had to be published in two parts, such as the Criminal Justice Act 2003, and the Coroners and Justice Act 2009.

2.5 New Zealand

New Zealand was one of the British dominions, whose Governor received a Royal Instruction to the effect that bills should include but a single subject. However, from a resolution passed in the Legislative Council of New Zealand on December 17, 1887 we learn that the instruction was not strictly followed. The resolution stated that "this Council, considering it of the highest importance that, in passing of all laws, each different matter should be provided for by a different law, without intermixing in one and the same law such things as have no proper relation to each other, will refuse to sanction any proposed legislation of the nature of the Special Powers and Contracts Act" (which was the background for the resolution being raised).[49]

In fact, even after independence, New Zealand continued to employ omnibus legislation. According to former Clerk of the of the New Zealand Parliament David MacGee (1985–2007), by the 1950s there were five types of omnibus bills (often referred to as 'washing-up' bills) that were introduced in most years: local legislation

---

[45]Gilbert (2006), p. 811.

[46]Luce, op. cit.

[47]Drayton (1933), p. 2664.

[48]See Fox and Korris (2010), pp. 30–31, and Evidence of Dr. Ruth Fox of the Hansard Society to the House of Commons Political and Constitutional Reform Committee 2013, pp. ev.41–47.

[49]New Zealand Parliamentary Debates (1887).

bills, reserves and other lands disposal bills, statutes amendment bills, Mäori purposes bills and finance bills.[50]

In 1955 a new procedure was introduced to deal with a statutes amendment bill under which the omnibus bill was divided at the committee stage into separate bills amending the several Acts to which its provisions related, and these separate bills were then passed as separate Acts. In 1974 the procedure started being applied to other types of omnibus legislation.

However, the new technique did not discourage the Government from submitting omnibus bills. On the contrary. in 1983 a new type of omnibus bill was devised—the Law Reform (Miscellaneous Provisions) Bill, which consisted of a miscellaneous collection of unrelated statutory provisions, whose only common feature was that they were too controversial to go into a Statutes Amendment Bill. For the next 12 years Parliament was plagued by miscellaneous law reform bills, whose lack of any discernible common content left them open to blatant abuse of any good law-making process.

Finance bills, that like the Canadian BIAs were supposed to contain amendments to existing legislation related to the Budget, also started growing out of hand, and in 1995 Parliament added provisions to its Standing Orders to constrain the use of omnibus bills, though the House of Representatives' Business Committee can unanimously decide to approve the introduction of a bill which is in breach of the Standing Orders.[51]

To the present day the Standing Orders are very clear about what can and what cannot be included in Omnibus laws. The basic principle is however (clause 260) that as a general rule bills are to relate to one subject area—in other words, the SSR is provided for. Clause 262 enumerates, in great detail, the types of omnibus bills that may be introduced, while clause 263 speaks of "other omnibus bills".

It should be noted that in the Chapter on development and approval of bills in the Cabinet Manual issued by the Department of the Prime Minister and Cabinet in New Zealand, there is a section on omnibus bills, in which Ministers are referred to the Standing Orders of the House of Representatives on the subject, and instructed on how to act when they intend to submit omnibus legislation of one sort or another, including consultations with the Office of the Clerk of the House.[52] In the case of Statute Amendment Bills the Ministers are referred to the latest Cabinet Office circular on the subject, which provides detailed instructions on how to draft such bills, and what may be included in them.[53]

---

[50]Unless otherwise stated all the information about New Zealand originates in McGee (2007).

[51]McGee (2017). Chapter 26, footnote 456.

[52]https://dpmc.govt.nz/our-business-units/cabinet-office/supporting-work-cabinet/cabinet-manual/7-executive-legislation-6.

[53]See Cabinet Office circular CO (17) 5: Statues Amendment Bill for 2018.

2.6 *Australia*

Section 55 of the Australian Constitution requires that laws imposing taxation, or customs and excise duties shall deal with these only.

In addition, in 1999 information about omnibus legislation started to appear in a Legislative Handbook published by the Department of the Prime Minister and Cabinet in Canberra. The handbook goes into great detail on when bills should include a single subject only, when they can be multi-issued, and when they can take the form of portfolio and omnibus bills.[54] The current issue of the handbook, was published in February 2017.[55]

I have not managed to establish how the provisions for each type of legislation works in practice, and have not found any academic or parliamentary literature on the subject of portfolio and omnibus legislation in Australia on the federal level. Furthermore, even though many federal bills include the word 'omnibus' in their title, I found no official definition of what is considered an omnibus bill in Australia.

However, the case of the Budget Savings (Omnibus) Bill 2016, involving 6.3 billion Australian dollars (around 4.5 billion U.S. dollars) budget savings spread over 24 schedules, which was over 250 pages long, was submitted on August 31, 2016, and finally approved on September 15, 2016 (within half a month), suggests that the situation is not as straight forward as the handbook might suggest.[56]

Omnibus amendment bills feature also in the State (or sub-federal) level, and provide additional insights into the Australian approach to the issue. The issue was investigated in the Australian Capital Territory (ACT) in 2017 by the Standing Committee on Administration and Procedure of the ACT Legislative Assembly.

The Committee's report was published in May 2017,[57] and included submissions by the Parliamentary Counsel's Office, which is responsible for drafting bills; by the Government of the ACT; and by the Green Party that had requested the investigation.

While the Council's Office provided a detailed description of the current guidelines and practices as provided in the ACT Cabinet and Legislation Handbooks; the Government recommended that it should be able to include more significant items in omnibus bills—not only minor and uncontroversial matters, as provided for in the handbooks—whenever the need may arise, so that it might be able "to efficiently implement [its] agenda"; while the Green Party reiterated its complaints about the abuse of the current procedures by the Government, which made effective oversight very difficult.

---

[54]Portfolio bills are bills that emanate from a single ministry, but include a variety of subject that are either not related or only loosely related to each other.

[55]Department of the Prime Minister and Cabinet (2017).

[56]*SBS Radio*, "Senate sits into night to pass omnibus bill". September 10, 2016 and Budget Savings (Omnibus) Bill 2016, Bills Digest no. 7, 2016–2017.

[57]The two documents are produced in full in the report.

The Committee did not reach revolutionary conclusions, merely suggesting that the guidelines and practice note provided by the Parliamentary Counsel on the subject be observed and developed.

2.7   Belgium[58]

For many years Belgium has had a law that is very similar to the EAL in Israel. The intention of the law, called *loi programme*, is to assist in the implementation of the budget. The law includes both legislative amendments and new legislation. In the past the bilingual (Flemish/French) law was usually 100–200 pages long, but was occasionally much longer. The 2005 *loi programme* included 505 articles, and 20% of its content was unrelated in any way to the budget, while another 25% was only marginally related. The Belgian Government introduced by means of the program laws around a quarter of the total legislation it brought to parliament. In the Chamber of Representatives the Bill was dealt with in numerous subject committees.

In the past there was heavy criticism of the *Loi Programme*, due to its dimensions and content. On March 18, 2005, it was agreed to add paragraph 4 to article 72 in the Rules of Procedure, according to which every parliamentary group is entitled to demand the convention of the Presidents Conference, and bring to the vote a proposal to delete from the *Loi Programme* articles that are not directly related to the budget. Since this amendment was adopted, the dimensions of the *Loi Programme* have been reduced, as well as the number of subjects in the law that have nothing to do with the budget.

2.8   Italy[59]

Until the budgetary reforms of the last decade, Italy's Budget Bill was accompanied by a Financial Bill (*Disegno di legge finanziaria*) that included new legislation and legislative amendments, required for the smooth implementation of the budget, and after 1999, to ensure compliance with the EU Stability and Growth Pact that was directed towards the enforcement of fiscal discipline. The two bills were supposed to be approved together by December 31—a goal that was not always met.

Over time the financial bill turned into a vast omnibudget bill, and attempts were made over the years to deal with its excessive size and problematic content by procedural means. For example until 1988, when the Budgetary Procedure Law was

---

[58]The original section about Belgium was based on an extensive correspondence with the Legal Advisor of the Belgian House of Representatives at the time, Mr. Marc Van der Hulst, and a visit to the lower house of the Belgian parliament on April 12, 2005.

[59]Unless otherwise stated, the section on Italy is based on Pisauro (2003).

passed—the budgetary balance (or deficit) was set only after the Budget Law and Financial Law were passed, which meant that there were few constraints on the number of amendments included in the 'must pass' Financial Law. The 1988 Law also laid down that the budgetary balance (or deficit) must be decided <u>before</u> The Budget and Financial Laws were passed. Another change introduced concerned limitations to the content of the Financial Law, laying down that complex policy changes would be left out and included in separate accompanying laws, to be passed simultaneously with the Budget and Financial Laws in December. However, neither change helped reduce the size of the Financial Law. In the case of the Accompanying Laws, these laws were eventually integrated into a single law, which in 1995 was reintegrated into the Financial Law.[60]

Following the financial crisis of 2008, the Financial Law for 2009 included only 4 articles.[61] The main reason for this appears to have been the adoption of two laws, Nos. 112/2008 and 133/2008 which laid down an economic planning range of 3 years, so that the process of approving the annual Budget Law and the accompanying Financial Law changed.[62] A further change in the budgetary process and its timetable began in 2012 and was fully implemented in 2016. In the new process the former Budget and Financial Bills were united into a single Budget Bill that includes two sections—one being the budget itself, and the second the legislative amendments and additions required for the implementation the budget. It is not clear whether the second section of the Budget Bill today is more compact and less varied in its content than was the old Financial Bill.[63]

Incidentally, since 1989 Italy passes an annual *legge communitaria*, which includes all EU directives which must be enacted on the national level. This law takes the form of an omnibus law. This practice began as a result of Italy's poor record in complying with Community directives.[64]

2.9 Spain[65]

Since the 1980s Spain has had two types of omnibus legislation: omnibus decree laws, and laws similar to Israel's EAL, known in Spanish as *Ley de Acompañamiento*.

---

[60]Pisauro (2003), and information from Mr. Riccardo Ercoli of the Economic Planning and Budget Committee in the Italian Senate on June 17, 2005.

[61]Altalex (2008).

[62]Cottone (2009). Il Sole 24 Ore.

[63]Many thanks to Prof. Giuseppe Pisauro for a brief description of the current situation in an email dated July 8, 2018.

[64]La Pergola (1994).

[65]Most of section up to 2005 is based on del Campo (1997). and on information received from the director Research and Documentation Department in the Senate, Mr. Fernando Santaolalla López, and the director of the Research and Documentation Department in the Congress, Mrs.

Until 1993 the Budget Law in Spain contained legislative amendments that were directly connected to the budget. However, in fact these amendments were, in the words of the Spanish Constitutional Court: "leftovers of the year's legislation". The court ruled in 1992 (case No. 76), that even if this practice is not contrary to article 134 in the Constitution, which deals with the budget, it should be condemned. In fact, the court set a rule, according to which the budgetary legislation must be coherent.

Following the Court's ruling, legislative amendments were taken out of the Budget Law, and the Accompanying Law, which was attached to the 1994 Budget Law, emerged. The content of this law was fiscal, administrative and social means to enable the implementation of the economic goals laid out in the Budget Law. Unlike the Budget Law, this was an ordinary law, to which the Constitution did not relate, but since it was attached to the Budget Law, it was passed in an expedited procedure, that prevented any deep deliberation of it.

The first Accompanying Law included 43 articles. The second 81, and the third 150 articles. There were those who pointed out that instead of a carriage carrying the remains of the previous year's legislation, now one had a train with many cars, performing the same task. Others used the image of "a tailor's drawer" (*cajón de sastre*), which contains all sorts of haberdashery.

In the general elections held in Spain in 2004 the leader of the Socialist Party, José Luis Rodriguez Zapatero, promised that if elected he would disband the Accompanying Law. And indeed, after the elections in which his party won, the law was dropped, but not prohibited.[66]

However, the disbandment of the law left a void, and when the new Government presented the 2005 budget, part of the content of the Accompanying Law was returned to the Budget Law itself, while some issues were added to a separate tax law. According to the director of the Research and Documentation Department in the Spanish Senate at the time: "We need time to consider the outcome of all this mess".[67]

Following the threat of the Popular Party to return the issue to the Constitutional Court the Government started limiting the number of legislative amendments in the Budget Law to the necessary minimum, and brought amendments connected to structural changes in the economy as separate, ordinary bills. [68] The Popular Party, on its part, promised that when it returned to power it would return the Accompanying Law.[69] And indeed, when Mariano Rajoy of the People's Party became Prime

---

Maria Rosa Ripolles Serrano. Most of the post-2005 material was generously recommended by Prof. Daniel Oliver-Latana.

[66]The *Cinco Dias* news website, article No. 20040910, September 10, 2004.

[67]Emails from Mr. Fernando Santaolalla López, past Director of the Research and Documentation Department in the Spanish Senate, received on January 31and April 28, 2005.

[68]Email from Ms. Sylvia Marti Sanchez from Congress of Deputies, received on July 28, 2009.

[69]Email received from Member of the Congress of Deputies of the Popular Party, Jaime Garcia Legaz on July 20, 2009.

Minister in December 2011, he immediately introduced a new Accompanying Law, and such a bill continues to be submitted with the budget law every year since then.[70]

In September 2011 the Spanish Constitutional Court issued a verdict on an appeal regarding the constitutionality of the Accompanying Law for 1998.[71] The Court reiterated its traditional position that the Spanish constitution does not ban such laws. The Court also laid down the principle that such a law could be considered unconstitutional if its object was not clearly defined and published in the Official Gazette, and if accepted parliamentary procedure was not followed with regards to the report presented together with the Bill, the process in the committee stage, or even in the emergency procedure followed—all this to ensure the right of participation of members of parliament in the legislative process. This was a rather surprising comment, since the case-law of the Constitutional Court indicates that it is wary of imposing its opinion over that of parliament in case of procedural irregularities involved in its decisions.[72]

Academic circles in Spain appear to support a fundamental change in the way the legislative amendments are dealt with, especially in light of the most recent comments by the Constitutional Court.[73]

According to Oliver-Lalana,[74] the phenomenon in Spain is a result of "political expediency", the academic reaction to it is "doctrinal condemnation" based on the principle of "legal security", and the approach of the Spanish Constitutional Court is generally one of "indulgence". The approach of the Spanish Constitutional Court to the subject is similar to that of the Israeli High Court of Justice,[75] which makes it an interesting example for comparative purposes in Israel.

The Spanish case is also interesting because Spain, like Israel, has not laid down any rules on the subject of omnibus legislation in its constitution or parliamentary rules of procedure.

2.10   Austria[76]

The Austrian case is of interest because Omnibudget laws are used only occasionally, when absolutely necessary.

---

[70]For an article on the 2017 law see *Europa Press,* December 31, 2016.

[71]The constitutional ruling was No 136/2011, given on September 13, 2011.

[72]Tribunal Constitutionnel de L'Espagne, 2011 and Martinez Lago (2016).

[73]Thanks to Professor Daniel Oliver-Lalana for sending several relevant articles, especially Enériz Olaechea (2014).

[74]Oliver-Lalana (2019).

[75]Comment by Professor Suzie Navot in reaction to the paper submitted by Professor Danel Oliver-Lalana, at the Bar-Ilan Workshop, on January 3, 2019.

[76]Most of the information about Austria was provided in 2005 by Dr. Günther Schefbeck, who was head of the Documentation Department in the Austrian Nationalrat.

When the 2005 document was written, Austria's Budget Law was regularly accompanied by several legislative amendments and/or new laws that had some sort of connection to the Budget, each of them approved separately by an ordinary, even if somewhat expedited legislation procedure. However, from time to time, especially when there was a significant change in policy (for example, after the formation of a new Government), all the amendments and new laws were introduced within the framework of a single omnibus bill. Examples of two such bills that were especially large, were the Structural Adaptation Law (*Strukturanpassungsgesetz*) of 1996, that included 98 articles, and was 365 pages long, and the Budget Accompanying Law (*Budgetbegleitgesetz*) of 2001, which included 87 articles.

However, in Austria, as in many other member states of the EU, following the financial crisis of 2008-9, extensive budgetary reforms were introduced, and it is not clear whether the new procedures have affected the legislative amendments accompanying the budget law.

2.11 Malta[77]

Malta is an example of a country where there is an annual budget implementation law, but which does not diverge from what such a law is supposed to do: namely to implement amendments to existing laws that are necessary for the implementation of the budget. Most of these amendments are of a fiscal nature, though there are no formal limitations as to what may be included, and during the Committee stage additional amendments may be added to any Act. At the Committee stage each and every article is debated. The time frame for the Budget Measures Implementation bill is the same as for the Budget. The Bill must be passed within six months from the First Reading, and if it is passed after the new financial year has begun, it is applied retroactively from January 1.

All the bilingual (Maltese/English) laws that I saw were around 80 pages long, but there is no limit to their length, which depends on the nature of the measures included in the budget. The Law for 2018 amended the Customs Ordinance, the Income Tax Law, the Cash Control Regulations, the Motor Vehicles Registration and Licensing Law, the Income Tax management Act, the Excise Duty Act, and the Arbiter for Financial Services Act.[78] The Government does not use the Law for the purpose of legislating major structural reforms, though at least in theory it could.

---

[77]The information on the Maltese Budget Measures Implementation Act was received from the Maltese Ministry of Finance, and emailed to me by Dr. Steffi Borg from the Legislation Unit at the Maltese Attorney General's Office on October 25, 2018.

[78]The Budget Measures Implementation Act for 2018 may be seen at: https://parlament.mt/media/93630/act-vii-budget-measures-implementation-act.pdf.

In his budget speech the Minister of Finance mentions additional legislation that the Government plans to pass in order to implement the Government's policy goals, but the actual bills are submitted separately.[79]

3 Some Conclusions Regarding Means of Contending with Omnibus Legislation

The first conclusion that emerges from looking at what happens in other countries in which omnibus legislation exists is that getting rid of the phenomenon, once it comes into existence, seems to be impossible, even though where there is political will, one can try to get rid of some of its worst manifestations.

3.1 The Single Subject Rule

The importance of the SSR is that it is one of the few legal, rather than procedural means by which one may completely proscribe, or drastically limit the use, dimensions, or number of omnibus laws. The origin of the rule is a Roman law of 98 B.C., known as *Lex Caecilia Didia*, which prohibited the practice of *lex satura*—i.e. the proposal of laws that include provisions unrelated to each other.[80]

It is a provision that prevails mainly in U.S. States, and was first introduced there by the British Empire at the beginning of the eighteenth century. Today, the Single Subject Rule appears also in the constitutions of Greece (art. 74(5), Chile (art. 69),[81] Columbia (art.158), Ecuador (art. 136), and Tonga (an island state in the southern Pacific) (art. 81). The history and practice of this rule in these countries is yet to be studied.

The case of New Zealand is interesting in that the Standing Orders of parliament include several articles, added in 1995, which deal with the application of the single subject rule, followed by a list of exceptions.

Israel did not adopt the single subject rule as it existed in the Royal Instruction sent to the British High Commissioner in Palestine in 1932, and never considered it. If Israel were to adopt the principle in one form or another, the suitable place to introduce it would be in Basic Law: Legislation, if and when such a basic law is enacted.

---

[79]The budget Speech of the Maltese Minister of Finance for 2018 in English may be seen at https://mfin.gov.mt/en/The-Budget/Documents/The_Budget_2018/Budget_speech_English_2018.pdf.

[80]For a fuller description of the Roman law see Luce (1922), pp. 548–549.

[81]Chile does not have the single subject rule as such, but prohibits riders that are not directly related to the subject of a bill. Email from Prof. Eduardo Alemán, dated April 10, 2020.

3.2   Changes in Rules of Procedure, and Other Sources of Procedure

As we saw in Chapter 1, there are no provisions relating to EALs in the Knesset Rules of Procedure. We have seen that several countries that suffer from the problem of omnibus legislation have tried to deal with it by means of their Rules of Procedure/Standing Orders.

New Zealand introduced clear rules on the issue of omnibus legislation into its Standing Orders in 1995. Belgium introduced an amendment to its Rules of Procedure in 2005, which enables parliamentary groups in its House of Representatives to have greater influence on what is included in the Belgian Program Law, which has apparently helped deal with the problem. In Canada the Standing Orders were amended in 2017 to give the Speaker greater power to deal with omnibus laws, and even though since the new clause was introduced several omnibus bills were divided, the change does not appear to be sufficiently significant to make a real change in the way the House of Representatives deals with such legislation.

In Israel we have seen that at least one former Attorney General, Eliakim Rubinstein, tried to use the Attorney General's occasional instructions to lay down rules on how the Government deals with EALs, which had an only marginal effect. In Australia the Legislative Handbook published by the Department of the Prime Minister and Cabinet in Canberra, lays down very clear instructions regarding various forms of omnibus legislation, but it is not clear how effective these instructions are.

The Byrd rule in the U.S. might not be directly relevant for states with a parliamentary system of goernment, but its content is nevertheless interesting in terms of how it defines what may and what may not be included in omnibus reconciliation bills.

3.3   Dealing with Omnibus Laws by Means of Legislation

In Israel there has apparently been the largest number of attempts to deal with the problem of omnibus bills by means of designated legislation—all PMBs. We found at least one PMB in Canada and one in the United States at the federal level, that intended to introduce the Single Subject Rule into the law book by means of proposed bills. None of the bills had any chance of getting enacted due to government opposition and general apathy.

3.4 Political Decisions to Deal with Omnibus Legislation

While there is no doubt that bringing about a change in the way omnibus legislation is dealt with requires political will, depending exclusively on political will, without backing it up with some significant legislative or administrative action, might bring about a temporary change, but not a permanent one. The example of Spain, described above, is a case in point.

The case of Canada is also telling. Strong words by the Liberal Party during the 2015 election campaign, were followed up by weak provisions in the Standing Orders.

3.5 The Role of the Courts

In several countries the issue of omnibus legislation has reached the courts. In the U.S. States, which have the SSR in their constitutions, the State courts are usually asked to deal with the definition of "single subject".

Of the countries that have omnibus legislation but no SSR, if the issue reaches the courts the question is usually whether omnibus legislation is constitutional, which in all the cases examined in this article—Canada, Israel, Spain and the U.S.—the answer given was affirmative as long as constitutional provision for the approval of laws is kept. The second question that the courts have been asked to deal with is whether alleged procedural disorders in the passage of the said laws invalidate the laws.

The Canadian courts have been unwilling to deal with the issue on grounds of "parliamentary privilege". We have seen that in Spain it was the Constitutional Court that was responsible in 1994 for the appearance of the Accompanying Law in the first place. We have also seen that in 2011 the Court laid down the principle that the Accompanying Law could be considered unconstitutional if its object is unclear or not published in the Official Gazette, and if accepted parliamentary procedure— especially that concerning the right of participation of MPs in the legislative process, was not followed.[82]

The issue of whether the courts should or should not intervene in procedural issues concerning law and rulemaking, both at the parliamentary and executive levels, is a subject that is getting growing attention. The basic approach to the issue depends on whether the state has a presidential or a parliamentary system of government, and on various provisions in the constitution, or constitutional laws.[83]

In Israel the High Court of Justice, which has time and again ruled that EALs as such are not unconstitutional, has gone into great detail in discussing the principle of

---

[82] In the case it was dealing with, the Court did not find that there had been any infringement of the proper legislative process.

[83] See Rose-Ackerman et al. (2015).

what constitutes appropriate participation by MKs in the legislative process. However, it was only in 2017 that it actually took action when it considered that "a defect, which goes down to the root of the [legislative] process" had taken place with regards to such participation, and actually returned one chapter in the EALfor the years 2017–2018 to the Knesset for reenactment from the stage at which the defect had taken place—i.e. the preparation in the Knesset Finance Committee of the chapter on the Taxation on the Third Apartment Law for Second and Third Readings.

There are those who feel that the court went too far in this decision. However, this verdict constitutes an international precedent in court rulings dealing with the problem of bills that are approved in parliament in hasty procedures, that do not allow for proper scrutiny by MPs, thus contributing to the democratic deficit of how the system works.

References[84]

Altalex (2008) "Legge Finanziaria 2009 pubblicata sulla Gazzetta Ufficiale" Legge, 22/12/2008 n° 203, G.U. 30/12/2008

Ben-Bassat A, Dahan M (2008) The balance of forces in the budgeting process. Israel Democracy Institute, Jerusalem. (H)

Bosc M, Gagnon A (2017) House of commons procedure and practice, 3rd edn. https://www.ourcommons.ca/About/ProcedureAndPractice3rdEdition/index-e.html

Cottone N (2009) L'abc della Finanziaria 2009. Il Sole 24 Ore

Curry JM (2015) Legislating in the dark - information and power in the house of representatives. The University of Chicago Press

Daniel L (2017) An additional deliberation of the cancellation of the tax on the third apartment - what stands behind the State's move? The Takdin Website. (H)

del Campo LG (1997) Nuevos problemas en torno al ejercicio de la potestad presupuestaria por el parlamento. In: Francesc Pau I Vall (coord.), Parlamento y Justicia Constitucional, Aranzadi editorial, 1997, pp 573–592

Department of the Prime Minister and Cabinet (2017) Legislation Handbook. Canberra

Dodek AM (2017) Omnibus bills: constitutional constraints and legislative liberations. Ottawa Law Rev 48(1):5–48

Drayton RH (1933) The laws of palestine, vol III. Government Printer, South Africa

Enériz Olaechea FJ (2014) La persistencia del legislador en no respetar los límites materiales de las Leyes Generales de Presupuestos de Estado. Revista Aranzadi Doctrinal, Número 1

Fox R, Korris M (2010) Making better law - reform of the legislative process from policy to act. Hansard Society, London

Franks CES (2010) Omnibus bills subvert our legislative process. The Globe and Mail, 14 July 2010

Gilbert MD (2006) Single subject rules and the legislative process. Univ Pittsburgh Law Rev 67 (4):803–870

Heniff Jr B (2016) The budget reconciliation process: the senate's 'Byrd Rule'. Congressional Research Service

---

[84](H) – Hebrew.

House of Commons Political and Constitutional Reform Committee (2013) Ensuring standards in the quality of legislation. First Report of Session 2013–2014, Vol I. The Stationary Office Ltd., London

Kaminski SR, Hart EL (2012) Log rolling versus the single subject rule. Bloomberg Bureau of National Affairs

Kaplan T (2018) Congress Approves $1.3 Trillion Spending Bill, Averting a Shutdown. New York Times, 22 March 2018

La Pergola A (1994) Italy and European integration: a lawyer's perspective. Indiana Int Comp Law Rev 4(4):259–275

Linde HA (1976) Due process of lawmaking. Nebraska Law Rev 55(2):197–249

Luce R (1922) Legislative procedure; parliamentary practices and the course of business in the framing of statutes. Houghton Mifflin Company, Boston

Lynch MS, Saturno JV (2017) The budget reconciliation process: stages of consideration. CRS, January 4, 2017

Martinez Lago MA (2016) Los límites de la justicia constitucional: la interpretación constitucional y la técnica jurídica en las 'leyes de contenido heterogéneo'. Revista española de derecho constitucional 36(106):17–71

Massicotte L (2013) Omnibus Bills in theory and Practice. Canadian Parliam Rev 36:12–17

Mazuz M (2008) Interview with the Attorney General, Meni Mazuz in Ma'asei Mishpa, Vol A, January 2008, pp 41–42. (H)

McGee D (2007) Concerning legislative process. Otago Law Rev 11(3):417–432

McGee D, Harris M, Wilson D (eds) (2017) Parliamentary practice in New Zealand, 4th edn. Oratia Books, Oratia

New Zealand, Parliamentary Debates, First Session of the Tenth Parliament, Legislative Council and House of Representatives, Fifty-ninth Volume, November 25 to December 22, 1887

Oliver-Lalana AD (2019) Omnibus legislation in Spain: Between political expedience, doctrinal condemnation, and judicial indulgence. Paper presented at the Bar-Ilan workshop Rearranging the Arrangements Law: Comparative, Multidisciplinary, Empirical and Normative Perspectives on Omnibus Legislation, on January 3, 2019

Pisauro G (2003) The Central State Budget Process in Italy. International Forum for Macroeconomic Issues, Tokyo, 17–19 February 2003

Rolef SH (2006) The Arrangements Law: Issues and International Comparisons. The Knesset Research and Information Center. (Translation of a document originally written in Hebrew in 2005)

Rose-Ackerman S, Egidy S, Fowkes J (2015) Due process of lawmaking: the United States, South Africa, Germany, and the European Union. Cambridge University Press

Rose-Ackerman S, Egidy S, Fowkes J (2016) The law of lawmaking: positive political theory in comparative public law. In: Bignomi F, Zoring D (eds) Comparative law and regulation - understanding the global regulatory process. Edward Elgar, pp 353–382

Saturno JV, Tollestrup J (2016) Omnibus appropriations acts: overview of recent practices. Congressional Research Service (CRS)

Saturno JV, Heniff B Jr, Lynch MS (2016) The congressional appropriation process: an introduction. CRS

Sinclaire B (2017) Unorthodox lawmaking: new legislative processes in the U.S., 5th edn. CQ Press, Washington D.C

Tribunal Constitutionnel de L'Espagne (2011) SENTENCIA 136/2011, de 13 de septiembre

Wherry A (2016) New Liberal budget bill raises old concerns about omnibus legislation. CBC News, 24 April, 2016

Wherry A (2017) Speaker splits up Liberal omnibus budget bill, thanks to new Liberal rule. CBC News, 11August 2017

Yehezkel O, Yinon E (2009) Mutual relations between the Knesset and the government - proposals and recommendations. Document presented to Prime Minister Ehud Olmert, and Knesset Speaker Dalia Itzik. (H)

Zerahia Z (2005) Netanyahu: 'cancelling the Arrangements Law means sentencing the State to poverty, distress and absence of growth. Haaretz, July 29, 2005 (H)

Susan Hattis Rolef is a retired researcher of the Knesset Research and Information Center, who lives in Jerusalem. She recently published a book in Hebrew on "The Job of the Knesset Member: an Undefined Job". which will be published in English by Routledge.

Part II
Regulating the Use of Omnibus Legislation

The Single-Subject Rule: Uncertain Solution for Omnibus Legislation

Richard Briffault

Abstract The requirement found in many constitutions of the states of the United States that a legislative bill must be limited to a single subject has been proposed as a means of preventing legislatures from passing omnibus laws. This chapter reviews the experience of American state courts in enforcing single-subject requirements. Courts have had difficulty defining and applying the concept of "subject" or the allied idea of germaneness. Proposals to apply the rule to logrolls or riders have, similarly, had difficulty in determining whether a provision is a logroll or rider or simply the product of legitimate legislative compromise. Single-subject rule cases have been marked largely by a mix of judicial deference and intermittent, sometimes inconsistent, enforcement. In short, the American states' experience has been that the single-subject rule does not provide an effective, judicially-enforceable tool against omnibus legislation.

Keywords Courts (or state courts) · Germaneness · Legislative process · Legislatures (or state legislatures) · Logrolling · Riders (or legislative riders) · Subject (or legislative subject) · State constitutions (or state constitutional law)

1 Introduction

Could a constitutional requirement that legislation be limited to a single subject be used to prevent legislatures from passing omnibus laws? The constitutions of most of the states in the United States contain such a requirement. In many states the requirement dates back to the middle of the nineteenth century, and has long been a fertile source of litigation. However, in practice the single-subject rule has been a

---

An earlier version of this chapter appeared as "The Single-Subject Rule: A State Constitutional Dilemma," 82 Albany L. Rev. 1629 (2018/2019). It has been revised for this publication.

R. Briffault (✉)
Columbia University School of Law, New York, USA
e-mail: Rb34@columbia.edu

© The Author(s), under exclusive license to Springer Nature Switzerland AG 2021
I. Bar-Siman-Tov (ed.), *Comparative Multidisciplinary Perspectives on Omnibus Legislation*, Legisprudence Library 8, https://doi.org/10.1007/978-3-030-72748-2_8

very uncertain constraint on legislative behavior. Courts have been unable to come up with and enforce a consistent definition of "subject," with the case law consisting in large part of unpredictable "I know it when I see it" decisions, and courts frequently defer to the legislature's determination that a bill contains just a single subject.

Some courts and commentators have suggested that the elusiveness of "subject" can be sidestepped by using the rule to target logrolling and riders. But determining whether a law is the product of logrolling, or whether a provision should be treated as a rider, is also often be difficult. Moreover, it is debatable whether logrolls and riders are as pernicious as proponents of more vigorous enforcement of the single-subject rule assume. So, too, the more aggressive use of the single-subject rule urged by advocates as a means of thwarting "legislative chicanery"[1] and "backroom politics"[2] could also undo the cooperation and compromise necessary to get difficult but important legislation enacted.

This chapter first briefly reviews the history and purposes behind the single-subject rule. It then examines how state courts have applied the single-subject rule, with particular attention to cases decided in the last decade. It considers the arguments for reframing enforcement on preventing logrolling or riders. It concludes by reflecting on the significance of the mixed history of the rule for the more general project of constitutional limits on omnibus legislation.

2   The History and Purposes of the Single-Subject Rule

2.1   History

Every American state has its own constitution, which sets up the structure of state government and often imposes both substantive and procedural restrictions on state legislatures. The procedural restrictions, in particular, go well beyond the limitations the United States Constitution places on Congress. The state constitutional procedures dealing with state legislative procedure were first adopted in the early and middle years of the nineteenth century in response to such abuses as "[l]ast-minute consideration of important measures, logrolling, mixing substantive provisions in omnibus bills, low visibility and hasty enactment of important, and sometimes corrupt legislation, and the attachment of unrelated provisions in the amendment process."[3] The single-subject limit was part of this legislative reform movement. Illinois in 1818 required that bills appropriating salaries for government officials be limited to that subject. Michigan in 1843 limited laws authorizing the borrowing of

---

[1]Denning and Smith (2011), p. 832.

[2]Note (2007), p. 1389.

[3]Williams (1987), p. 798.

money or the issuance of state stock to a single object. In 1844, New Jersey adopted the first general single-subject requirement.[4] Thereafter, the idea spread quickly. Today, forty-three states, including every state entering the Union after 1844, includes some version of the single-subject rule in its constitution.[5]

There are some variations across the states in the language and scope of the rule. Two states apply the requirement only to appropriations bills, and another two states limit it to bills adopting special or local laws.[6] Conversely, a few states exempt appropriations bills;[7] others exclude bills "for the codification, revision, or rearrangement of laws."[8] A handful of states use the term "object" rather than "subject," although that does not appear to have had any legal significance.[9] Notwithstanding these variations, some version of the single-subject requirement applies in most states to most state legislation. It is probably the "most significant and most litigated procedural requirement" in state constitutions.[10] The language of the Ohio Constitution is typical: "No bill shall contain more than one subject, which shall be clearly expressed in its title."[11]

2.2 Purposes

The purposes of the single-subject rule are briefly stated and often repeated: the prevention of logrolling and riders; the promotion of informed legislative decision-making and public accountability;[12] and, less frequently, the protection of the governor's veto power.[13] Logrolling and riders, in particular, have been most frequently cited as the "evils" against which the single-subject rule" is aimed.[14] The two terms are sometimes blurred together,[15] but they refer to somewhat different

---

[4]Ruud (1958), pp. 389–390.

[5]Catalano (1990), p. 80.

[6]Id.

[7]Ruud (1958), p. 416.

[8]Ill. Const., art IV., §8(d).

[9]Ruud (1958), pp. 394–396.

[10]Kasper (2009), p. 848.

[11]Ohio Const. Art II, § 15(D).

[12]Ruud (1958), pp. 390–391.

[13]Evans and Bannister (2014), pp. 151–152; In re Initiative Petition No. 382, 142 P.3d 400, 405 n. 11 (Okla 2006); Dragich (2001), pp. 114–115; Migdal v. State. 747 A.2d 1225, 1229 (Md. 2000); Hammerschmidt v. Boone Co., 877 S.W.2d 98, 102 (Mo. 1994); Figinski (1998), p. 366.

[14]Ruud (1958), p. 398; Hoffer and McDade (2004), p. 557 (2004); In re Title, Ballot Title and Submission Clause for 2005–2006 #74, 136 P.3d 237, 243 (Coats, J., dissenting)

[15]Fent v. State, 214 P.3d 799, 804 (Okla. 2009); Porten Sullivan Corp. v. State, 568 A.2d 1111, 1116 (Md. 1990); State ex rel Ohio AFL-CIO v. Voinovich, 631 N.E.2d 582, 604 (Ohio 1994) (Francis E. Sweeney, Sr., J., dissenting in part and concurring in part); Dragich (2001), p. 161 ("hard to say" whether a single-subject violation involved a logroll or a rider).

forms of legislative action. "Logrolling" is used to describe what occurs when two or more separate proposals, none of which is able to command majority support, are combined so that the minorities behind each measure aggregate to make a majority capable of passing the resulting bill.[16] A "rider" is a provision which could not pass on its own but is attached to a bill considered likely to pass and so "rides" on that more popular measure to enactment.[17]

Both logrolling and riders have been sharply criticized as leading to the adoption of measures that do not enjoy true majority support within the legislature, and, if legislators accurately represent the views of their constituents, within the state as a whole. Logrolls and riders also arguably interfere with the freedom of legislators by presenting them with the "Hobson's choice" of being "forced to assent to an unfavorable provision to secure passage of a favorable one, or conversely, forced to vote against a favorable provision to ensure that an unfavorable provision is not enacted."[18]

Many courts and commentators also assert that the rule improves legislative deliberation and promotes transparency.[19] As the Illinois Supreme Court asserted, the single-subject rule "promote[s] an orderly legislative process. . ... 'By limiting each bill to a single subject, the issues presented by each bill can be better grasped and more intelligently discussed.'"[20] The Missouri Supreme Court similarly claimed that by limiting each bill to a single subject, the rule enables bills to "be easily understood and intelligently discussed, both by legislators and the general public."[21] The Pennsylvania Supreme Court has urged that the general aim of the rule is to "encourage an open, deliberative, and accountable government."[22] The assumption is that when a bill is limited to a single subject, it is easier for legislators to more fully understand its ramifications and for the public to know what their legislators are up to. That can facilitate public input while the measure is pending, and voter efforts to hold legislators accountable after enactment. Proponents have also contended it will "prevent surprise and fraud upon the people and the legislature"[23] by barring special interest groups from hiding deals or giveaways in long and complex multi-subject measures.

---

[16]Comm. v. Neiman, 84 A.3d 603, 612 (Pa. 2013).

[17]Schuck (2000), p. 901.

[18]In re Initiative Petition No. 382, 142 P.3d at 405. Accord, Porten Sullivan, 568 A.2d at 1121 ("to avoid the necessity for a legislator to acquiesce in a bill he or she opposes in order to secure useful and necessary legislation").

[19]Kasper (2009), pp. 848–849; Schuck (2000), p. 903; Ruud (1958), pp. 391, 449–450.

[20]Wirtz v. Quinn, 953 N.E.2d 899, 905 (Ill. 2011).

[21]Rizzo v. State, 189 S.W.3d 576, 578 (Mo. 2006). See also Missouri Roundtable for Life, Inc. v. State, 396 S.W.3d 348, 351 (Mo. 2013).

[22]Pennsylvanians Against Gambling Expansion Fund ("PAGE") v. Commonwealth, 877 A.2d 383, 395 (Pa. 2005).

[23]Otto v. Wright Co., 920 N.W.2d 446, 456 (Minn. 2018); Stroh Brewery Co. v. State, 954 S.W.2d 323, 325 (Mo. 1997) (the rule serves to "facilitate orderly procedure, avoid surprise, and prevent 'logrolling'").

3 The Single-Subject Rule in the Courts

3.1 Defining "Subject"

Courts have regularly recognized that "subject" is inherently difficult to define. As the Utah Supreme Court recently acknowledged, a "precise formula may well be impossible to craft."[24] Other courts have agreed that "[f]or purposes of legislation, 'subjects' are not absolute existences to be discovered by some sort of a priori reasoning, but are the result of classification for convenience of treatment and for greater effectiveness in attaining the general purpose of the particular legislative act."[25] A "subject" can be very specific or very general: "[A]ny collection of items, no matter how diverse and comprehensive will fall 'within' a single (broad) subject if one goes high enough up . . . and, on the other hand, the most simple and specific idea can always be broken down into parts, which may in turn plausibly be regarded as separate (narrow) subjects."[26]

Some courts have read "subject" broadly. The Utah Supreme Court has emphasized that "there is no constitutional restriction as to the scope or magnitude of the single subject of a legislative act."[27] The Illinois Supreme Court agreed that "[t]he subject may be as broad as the legislature chooses," albeit not "so broad that the rule is evaded as a meaningful constitutional check on the legislature's actions"[28]—perhaps not the most helpful formula. Indeed, some state courts have approved as constitutionally permissible subjects such broad topics as "land,"[29] "education,"[30] "transportation,"[31] "utilities,"[32] "state taxation,"[33] "public safety,"[34] "capital projects,"[35] and "operations of state government."[36]

---

[24]Gregory v. Shurtleff, 299 P.3d 1098, 1112 (Utah 2013).

[25]Washington Ass'n for Substance Abuse and Violence Prevention v. State, 278 P.2d 632, 642 (Wash. 2012).

[26]Lowenstein (1983), p. 941.

[27]Gregory v. Shurtleff, 299 P.3d at 1112.

[28]Wirtz v. Quinn, 953 N.E.2d at 905.

[29]State v. First Nat'l Bank of Anchorage, 660 P.2d 406 (Alaska 1982).

[30]Kansas Nat'l Educ. Ass'n v. State, 387 P.3d 795, 808-09 (Kans. 2017).

[31]Yute Air Alaska, Inc. v McAlpine, 698 P.2d 1173, 1181 (Alaska. 1985); Wass v. Anderson, 2452 N.W.2d 131, 137 (Minn. 1977); C.C. Dillon v. City of Eureka, 12 S.W.3d 322 (Mo. 2000).

[32]Kansas One-Call Sys. v. State, 274 P.3d 625 (Kan. 2012).

[33]North Slope Borough v. SOHIO Petroleum Corp., 585 P.2d 534 (Alaska 1978).

[34]Townsend v. State, 767 N.W.2d 11, 13-14 (Minn. 2009).

[35]Wirtz v. Quinn, supra, 953 N.E.2d at 907 ("capital projects is a legitimate single subject").

[36]Otto v. Wright Co., supra, 910 N.W.2d at 457 ("'the operation of state government'—is not too broad to pass constitutional muster"). But see People v. Reedy, 708 N.E.2d 1114 (Ill. 1999) (rejecting subject of "governmental matters").

Other courts, however, reject "any broad, expansive, approach,"[37] and have ruled out certain relatively broad topics. The Maryland Court of Appeals concluded that the purpose of "generally regulating corporations is too broad and too tenuous" to satisfy the single-subject requirement."[38] The Pennsylvania Supreme Court held that "municipalities" is "too broad to qualify for single-subject status"[39] and, similarly, that "refining civil remedies or relief" and "judicial remedies and sanctions" are "far too expansive" to satisfy the single-subject requirement[40]—although the same court also held that the "regulating of gaming" was sufficiently narrow as to be a constitutionally permissible subject.[41]

A good example of the indeterminacy of "subject" is the division among state courts over whether comprehensive tort reform constitutes a single subject. The Alaska Supreme Court upheld a tort reform law that imposed caps on noneconomic and punitive damages, required payment of half of all punitive damages awards to the state, created a statute of repose, adopted a comparative allocation of fault between parties and nonparties, provided for a revised offer of judgment procedure, and gave hospitals partial immunity from vicarious liability for some physicians' actions. The court acknowledged that the law's provisions "concern different matters" but concluded that "they are all within the single subject of 'civil action.'"[42] The Ohio and Oklahoma Supreme Courts, however, rejected similar measures, finding, respectively that "tort and other civil actions,"[43] and "lawsuit reform"[44] could not be sustained as constitutionally permissible single subjects of legislation.

Courts have similarly struggled over the significance of the length or number of sections of a bill or the number of articles or titles of the state code that the measure amends. Although longer, more complex bills are certainly more likely to be found to violate the single-subject constraint, the fact that the bill amends only a single article or title will not save it,[45] and the fact that it runs over one hundred pages, with dozens of chapters and multiple sections, need not be fatal.[46]

Courts have acknowledged the inconsistency in their single-subject jurisprudence. The Pennsylvania Supreme Court has candidly written that in its decisions "the line between what is constitutionally acceptable and what is not is often blurred."[47] Many of the most prominent recent cases in Pennsylvania and Ohio—

---

[37]Fent v. State ex rel. Okla. Cap. Imp. Auth. ("OCIA"), 214 P.3d 799, 806 (Ok. 2009).

[38]Migdal v. State, 747 A.2d at 1231.

[39]City of Philadelphia v. Comm., 838 A.2d 566, 589 (Pa. 2003).

[40]Comm. v. Neiman, 84 A.3d at 613.

[41]PAGE, 877 A.3d at 396.

[42]Evans v. State, 56 P.3d 1046, 1070 (Alaska 2002).

[43]State ex rel Ohio Academy of Trial lawyers v. Sheward, 715 N.E.2d 1062, 1101 (Ohio 1999).

[44]Douglas v. Cox Retirement Props., Inc., 302 P.3d 789, 793 (Okla. 2013).

[45]See, e.g., Comm. v. Neiman, 84 A.3d at 612-13; Migdal, 747 A.2d at 1230.

[46]See, e.g. Wirtz v. Quinn, 953 N.E.2d at 905-07, PAGE, 877 A.2d at 392 (bill was 145 pages and included seven chapters and 86 sections).

[47]Id. at 400.

two states which have witnessed considerable single-subject rule litigation—have been marked by sharp dissents,[48] with one Ohio dissenter pointing out that in one case each state supreme court justice authored a separate opinion demonstrating "that there was little consensus among the justices on the rule's meaning."[49] A dissenting justice of the Colorado Supreme Court similarly lamented "an unmistakable lack of uniformity in our treatment of the single-subject requirement."[50] Even when there are no dissents, it can be hard to see how a court's treatment of "subject" holds together. The Oklahoma Supreme Court, which has had a heavy docket of single-subject cases in recent years,[51] invalidated a law authorizing a single state agency to incur debt to finance three different projects,[52] then a few years later upheld a law authorizing a different state agency to issue bonds to finance four different projects—both times without dissent. The second decision sought to distinguish the first by finding the common theme of turnpike construction and maintenance linked the multiple projects,[53] but the tension between the decisions remains.

3.2   Applying a Germaneness Test

As the Oklahoma turnpike decision indicates, the question in many single subject cases is not the definition of "subject" *per se*, but whether the different topics, sections, or parts of a bill are sufficiently closely connected that they can be treated as dealing with a single subject. As the Ohio Supreme Court put it, the rule "allows a plurality of topics" even as it bars a "disunity of subjects."[54] Indeed, most single-subject disputes involve laws that, as enacted, consist of multiple provisions. Courts have developed a range of tests for determining whether the multiple parts of a bill are sufficiently related so that when combined they constitute but a single subject, including whether they are "rationally related;"[55] whether there is a "unifying

---

[48]See, e.g., Comm. v. Neiman; Penn. State Ass'n of Jury Comm'rs v. Comm., 64 A.2d3d 611 (Pa. 2013); Spahn v. Zoning Bd. of Adjustment, 977 A.2d 1132 (Pa. 2009); State ex rel Ohio Civ. Serv. Emp. Ass'n v. State Emp. Rel. Bd. ("CSEA v. SERB"), 818 N.E.2d 688 (Ohio 2004); Simmons-Harris v. Goff, 711 N.E.2d 203 (Ohio 1999); Sheward; Voinovich.

[49]CSEA v SERB, 818 N.E.2d at 705 (dissenting opinion of Lundberg Stratton, J., joined by O'Connor, J.).

[50]In re Title, Ballot Title and Submission Clause, 136 P.3d at 244 (Coats, J., dissenting).

[51]Matter Oklahoma Turnpike Auth., 389 P.3d 318 (Okla. 2017); Burns v. Cline, 382 P.3d 1048 Okla. 2016); Fent v. Fallin, 315 P.3d 1023 (Okla. 2013); Douglas; Thomas v. Henry, 260 P.3d 1251 (Okla. 2011); Nova Health Sys. v. Edmondson, 233 P.3d 380 (Okla. 2010); OCIA; In re Petition No. 382, 142 P.3d 400 (Okla. 2006).

[52]Fent v. State.

[53]Matter of Okla Tpke Auth at 320–321.

[54]State ex rel Hinkle v. Franklin Co. Bd. of Elec. 580 N.E.2d 767, 770 (Ohio 1991).

[55]State ex rel Ohio Civ. Serv. Emp. Ass'n v. State, 56 N.E.3d 913, 922 (Ohio 2016).

principle,"[56] "natural and logical connection,"[57] or a "common purpose or relation-ship . . . between the topics;"[58] "whether they have a nexus to a common purpose;"[59] whether they "fairly relate to the same subject"[60] or "relate, directly or indirectly, to the same general subject and have a mutual connection;"[61] whether there is a "common thread"[62] or "filament"[63] linking them to each other, or—from the oppo-site perspective—whether they are "distinct and incongruous"[64] or "dissimilar and discordant."[65] The most commonly used judicial standard is whether they are "germane" or "reasonably germane" to each other or to some general subject.[66]

But "reasonable germaneness" is not much more precise or determinate than "subject" itself.[67] The body of law the courts have produced as they have grappled with the question of whether the different parts of a bill are germane to each other or to some overarching subject is not much more consistent than the jurisprudence concerning permissible subjects.

Thus, courts have found sufficient germaneness in laws that combine a tax on motor vehicle fuels with authorization of bonds to finance highway construction;[68] add an authorization of a park district to acquire land to a bill making appropriations for state government;[69] combine an authorization of the privatization of liquor sales with funding for public safety;[70] combine provisions dealing with asbestos abate-ment, leaking underground storage tanks, and water well drilling under the rubric of "environmental control;"[71] combine local regulation of billboards with funding for the state transportation department;[72] add a program for the privatization of child support enforcement to a bill dealing with welfare reform;[73] add an authorization for counties to hire private accounting firms to audit their books to the state government

---

[56]McIntire v. Forbes, 909 P.2d 846, 855-56 (Pre. 1996).

[57]People v. Cervantes, 723 N.E.2d 265, 267 (Ill. 1999).

[58]Hoover v. Bd. of Franklin Co. Comm'rs, 482 N.E.2d 575, 580 (Ohio 1985).

[59]Neiman, 84 A.3d at 612.

[60]Hammerschmidt v. Boone Co., 877 S.W.2d 98, 102 (Mo. 1994).

[61]Ex parte Jones, 440 S.W.3d 628, 632 (Tex. 2014).

[62]Beagle v. Walden, 676 N.E.2d 506, 507 (Ohio 1997).

[63]Blanch v. Suburban Hennepin Reg. Park Dist., 449 N.W.2d 150, 154-55 (Minn. 1989).

[64]Porten Sullivan Corp. v. State, 568 A.2d 1111, 1121 (Md. 1990).

[65]Kansas Nat'l Educ. Ass'n v. State, 387 P.3d 795, 805 (Kans. 2017).

[66]Unity Church of St. Paul v. State, 694 N.W.2d 585, 593 (2005); Kastorf (2005). at 1660.

[67]Cooter and Gilbert (2010), p. 710 ("[g]ermaneness provides no clear guidance to the level of abstraction").

[68]Wass v. Anderson, 252 N.W.2d 131, 135-36 (Minn. 1977).

[69]Blanch v. Suburban Hennepin Reg. Park Dist., 449 N.W.2d 150 (Minn. 1989).

[70]Washington Ass'n for Substance Abuse v. State, 278 P.3d 632 (Wash. 2012).

[71]Corvera Abatement Tech. v. Air Conservation Com'n, 973 S.W.2d 851 (Mo. 1998).

[72]C.C. Dillon Co. v. City of Eureka, 12 S.W.3d 322, 327-29 (Mo. 2000).

[73]Maryland Classified Emp. Ass'n v. State, 694 A.2d 937, 942-46 (Md. 1997).

finance omnibus bill;[74] include provisions regulating the sale of prisons to private operators in the state budget bill;[75] and combine funding for emergency medical services with a prohibition on the use of tax increment financing in flood plains (on the theory that the financing restriction would reduce the need for emergency services).[76]

On the other hand, courts have rejected measures that sought to combine: regulation of long-term care with authorization of the state attorney general to enforce regulation of advertising by nursing homes;[77] multiple anti-crime and neighborhood safety provisions with provisions regulating (including but not limited to criminal punishments for fraud) private providers of public welfare services;[78] payment of prevailing wage requirements for both publicly and nonpublicly financed school construction and remodeling projects added to an omnibus tax relief bill;[79] a ban on persons convicted of a felony from running for elected office in the state with a general regulation of political subdivisions including local elections;[80] changes to a state's public utilities regulatory fund with changes in the public service commission's rule-making process;[81] a provision relating to resident agents of corporations and a provision governing directors of investment companies;[82] and changes to the state's workers' compensation system with an exemption from the state's child labor laws and provision for an intentional workplace tort.[83] There may be a principle that explains the different findings of connection or germaneness across the cases, but it is not easy to discern.

3.3 Judicial Deference

Most courts have declared that they will take a deferential approach to the legislature's determination that a bill addresses only a single subject. The Pennsylvania Supreme Court has explained that "[i]n more recent decisions . . . Pennsylvania courts have become extremely deferential toward the General Assembly in

---

[74]Otto v. Wright Co., 910 N.W.2d 446, 455-57 (Minn. 2018).

[75]State ex rel Ohio CSEA v. State, 56 N.E.3d 913 (Ohio 2016).

[76]City of St. Charles v. State, 165 S.W.3d 149, 151-52 (Mo. 2005).

[77]Missouri Health Care Ass'n v. Attorney General, 953 S.W.2d 617 (Mo. 1997).

[78]People v. Cervantes, 723 N.E.2d 265 Ill. 1999).

[79]Assoc. Bldrs & Contrs. v. Ventura, 610 N.W.2d 293 (Minn. 2000).

[80]Rizzo v. State, 189 S.W.3d 576 (Mo. 2006). See also Hammerschmidt v. Boone, 877 S.W.2d 98 (Mo. 1994) (rejecting a bill combining provisions allowing certain counties to adopt, by election, a county constitution with general regulation of local elections); State ex rel Hinkle v. Franklin Co. Bd. of Elec. 580 N.E.2d 767 (Ohio 1991) (rejecting combination of judicial elections and local option elections).

[81]Delmarva Power & Light Co. v. Public Service Comm., 809 A.2d 640 (Md. 2002).

[82]Migdal (Md. 2000).

[83]State ex rel Ohio AFL-CIO v. Voinovich, 631 N.E.2d 582 (Ohio 1994).

[single-subject] challenges" and have upheld laws as long as "the court can fashion a single, over-arching topic to loosely relate the various subjects included in the statute under review."[84] High courts in Alaska,[85] Illinois,[86] Kansas,[87] Maryland,[88] Missouri,[89] Minnesota,[90] Ohio[91] and other states have similarly held they will strike down laws on single-subject grounds only if the violation is "clearly, plainly, and palpably so," "manifestly gross and fraudulent," or shown "beyond a reasonable doubt."[92]

Deference demonstrates respect for a coordinate branch of government. Moreover, if few laws are struck down on single-subject grounds, that minimizes the need for the court to articulate a clear and consistent standard for determining the meaning of "subject" or "germaneness" or to rationalize the different treatment of different cases. And it avoids the extremely knotty question of what to do when a law is determined to violate the rule—strike the whole law down; or sever the section or sections not germane to the other provisions, strike those down, and sustain the rest.[93] But judicial deference threatens to undermine the single-subject principle and to render a provision of the state constitution a "dead letter."[94] If the purpose of the single-subject requirement is to reform the operations of the state legislature, it may be odd to leave enforcement of the requirement to the legislature itself. Nor is it clear that enforcement of the rule would be so disrespectful of the legislature. Like other process reforms, the single-subject requirement does not limit the objects of state

---

[84]City of Philadelphia at 576–577.

[85]Evans at 1069 ("only a 'substantial and plain' violation of the one subject rule will lead us to strike down legislation on this basis").

[86]Wirtz at 905 ("we construe the word 'subject' liberally in favor of upholding the legislation;" a law violates the rule only "when it contains unrelated provisions that by no fair interpretation have any legitimate relation to the single subject").

[87]Kansas NEA at 808 ("the underlying policy of liberally construing the one-subject rule").

[88]Porten Sullivan at 1118 ("the 'general disposition of [this] Court has been to give the section a liberal construction, so as not to interfere with or impede legislative action'").

[89]C.C. Dillon Co. at 327 (no violation unless the act "clearly and undoubtedly violates" the rule).

[90]Unity Church at 594 ("because of the liberal deference given to the legislature, Minnesota courts have rarely invalidated laws for a lack of germaneness").

[91]Ohio CSEA at 919 ("To accord deference to the General Assembly's law-making function, we must liberally construe the term 'subject' for purposes of the rule").

[92]Dragich (2001), pp. 105–106.

[93]On the difficulty of the severability question, see Ruud (1958), pp. 396–400; Dragich (2001), at 154–163; Voinovich at 587 (ordering severance); id. at 599–600 and 600–604 (opinions concurring in finding of single-subject violation, dissenting from remedy of severance); Comm. v. Neiman at 613–615 (generally rejecting severance because "discerning the 'main' purpose of a piece of legislation becomes an untenable exercise in conjecture when the legislation has metamorphosed during the legislative process to include a panoply of additional and disparate subjects"); Ohio CSEA v. State at 920 ("the appropriate remedy when a legislative act violates the one-subject rule is generally to sever the offending portion of the act;" to cure the defect and save the portions" of the act that do relate to a single subject).

[94]Porten Sullivan at 1118.

legislation or the goals of state policy, but only the form of the legislation used to achieve those ends. There would be no restriction on the legislature enacting separately those measures it could not enact together, and some findings of single-subject violations have been followed by just such separate enactments.[95]

In any event, nearly all the courts that have declared themselves committed to a deferential, liberal interpretation of subject have at one time or another struck down laws on single-subject grounds.[96] "There must be limits"[97]—"[t]here comes a point"[98]—the courts complain, but the rule of liberal-interpretation-up-to-a-point fails to provide a very predictable or neutral principle, and contributes to concerns that application of the rule is driven by the policy or political views of the judges.[99]

3.4 Some Recent Cases

A brief review of cases from the 2010s from a half-dozen state supreme courts around the country may give a fuller sense of the difficulty inherent in applying the rule. Although some readers—and this author—may conclude that in some of the cases the "single-subject" question was pretty easy and that the court got it right, in others the issue was far more difficult and the wisdom of the decision far more debatable.

To begin, there are at least two cases involving what seem to be easy violations of the rule. In 2016, in *Leach v. Commonwealth*,[100] the Pennsylvania Supreme Court struck down a law that consisted of four substantive sections addressing: trespass for the purpose of unlawfully taking secondary metal[101] from a premises; theft of secondary metal as an independent offense; state police disclosure of records; and standing for individuals or organizations to challenge local gun regulations. The

---

[95]See, e.g., Rev. Stat. Mo. 290.528 (H.B. 1194 of Laws of 2017), preempting local minimum wage laws, adopted in response to the invalidation of a similar preemptive measure invalidated on single-subject grounds in Cooperative Home Care, Inc. v. City of St. Louis, 514 S.W.2d 571 (Mo. 2017); Dooley (2014), pp. 262–263 (following Oklahoma Supreme Court's invalidation of tort reform law on single-subject grounds, governor called a special session of the legislature which passed 23 separate bills which had been part of the invalid comprehensive measure).

[96]See, e.g., for Illinois, People v. Cervantes, People v. Reedy; for Maryland, Porten Sullivan, Migdal, Delmarva Power & Light; for Minnesota, Unity Church; for Missouri, Cooperative Home Care, Missouri Roundtable for Life, Inc.; for Ohio, Sheward, Simmons-Harris v. Goff; for Pennsylvania, Comm. v. Leach, Comm. v. Neiman, Penn. State Ass'n of Jury Comm'rs, Spahn, City of Philadelphia.

[97]City of Philadelphia, at 578.

[98]Sheward.

[99]Gilbert (2011), p. 355; Downey (2004), pp. 593–596; Hoffer and McDade (2004), p. 569 (Ohio Supreme Court's *Sheward* decision "as much a political shake-up as a judicial pronouncement").

[100]141 A.3d 426 (Pa. 2016).

[101]"Secondary metal" refers to metal such as copper and aluminum or wire and cable used by utilities and transportation agencies. Id. at 427.

provisions could be linked only if, as the legislative leaders contended, they addressed "the subject of amending the Crimes Code."[102] Such a "subject" would pass constitutional muster only at a very high level of abstraction, which conceivably might have sufficed if the law was a comprehensive revision of the criminal code, which it wasn't. Similarly, in 2017, the Missouri Supreme Court held in *Cooperative Home Care, Inc. v. City of St. Louis* that a law combining "the establishment, proper governance, and operation of community improvement districts" with a prohibition on municipalities setting a minimum wage higher than that set by the state violated Missouri's single-subject rule. It's not clear what "single subject" could have held these two parts together since the party defending the local minimum wage ban argued only that an earlier decision barred the city from raising the statute's invalidity as a defense, and the court simply declared without analysis that the minimum wage preemption was "not connected to, related to, or germane to" the regulation of community improvement districts.[103]

On the other hand, two cases from Kansas and Utah dealing with laws broadly addressing education issues reached the seemingly reasonable conclusion that they dealt with a single subject, education. The Utah law addressed a number of education issues ranging from the state's school aid formula, to the funding of charter schools, requirements regarding educational materials, teacher salaries, a number of pilot programs, and appropriations for the pilot programs, pupil transportation, classroom supplies, and arts education. Not only could many of these measures have been enacted as separate laws, but in fact the bill was an amalgamation of what had originally been fourteen separate bills.[104] It is possible that some legislators supported some of these measures and not others and, as a result, had to cast votes inconsistent with their topic-by-topic preferences. Nonetheless, if the single-subject rule is to permit comprehensive approaches to legislative subjects, this would appear to be such a case. The Kansas education case, *Kansas NEA v. State*,[105] arguably pushes the envelope a bit more. Adopted in response to a state supreme court decision invalidating portions of the state's public school finance laws, the challenged law "had a sweeping scope" including the appropriation of new state school aid, the cancellation of prior appropriations for non-education purposes to fund the new school aid, "substantive and technical changes to the state's public school financing statutes," appropriations and transfer of land to state universities, a tax credit for businesses that contribute to organizations that provide scholarships to low-income students, changes to high school teacher licensing requirements, "performance-based incentives for GED and career education matriculation and enrollment at state universities," and most controversially, changes to the Teacher Due Process Act to remove protections from many elementary and secondary public

---

[102]Id. at 431.

[103]514 S.W.3d at 580–581.

[104]Gregory v. Shurtleff, 299 P.3d 1098, 1115, 1118 (Utah 2013).

[105]387 P.3d 795 (Kans. 2017).

school teachers concerning the termination or nonrenewal of their contracts.[106] As the court acknowledged, the law contained multiple topics affecting the operations of public schools, benefits for students, and state universities, and touched many different government agencies.[107] Those who favored increased school funding might have opposed the elimination of teacher due process. Yet, applying the "policy of liberally construing the one-subject rule," the Court concluded that all the measures were germane to education and "the term 'education' is not so broad that it fails to limit the area in which the legislature may operate."[108]

Turning to closer cases, in *Wirtz v. Quinn*,[109] the Illinois Supreme Court sustained a complex, multi-part law intended to authorize and fund a massive capital projects program. Its provisions included, *inter alia*, raising and reallocating the proceeds of a range of different taxes and fees; authorizing a pilot program allowing individuals to purchase state lottery tickets on the internet, reallocating the proceeds of the state lottery, and directing a named state university to conduct a study of the effects on Illinois families of purchasing lottery tickets; increasing the weight limits for vehicles and loads; and authorizing, regulating, and taxing video gaming. On its face this would seem to include multiple subjects. But the Illinois court rationalized that they were all related to financing the capital program. The authorizations of video gaming and of the on-line purchase of lottery tickets were intended to generate funds for the capital program, and the study of the impact of the lottery on families was a response to the expansion of the lottery program. The increased weight and load limits for motor vehicles was an offset to the increase in motor vehicle fees and fines for overweight vehicles—which was one of the many sources of funds for the capital program. The court made a plausible case that it all hung together, although other commentators sharply disagreed.[110]

Less persuasive—to this author, at least—are two other state court decisions that concluded that budget bills that also included substantive policy measures satisfied the single-subject requirement. In 2016 in *State ex rel Ohio Civil Service Employees Ass'n v. State*,[111] the Ohio Supreme Court held that the inclusion in the biennial budget bill of provisions changing the law governing the terms for the privatizing of prison operations and authorizing the operation, management, and sale of five prison facilities did not violate the single-subject rule. The privatization of prison operations and the sale of prison facilities would save costs and generate revenue for the state and thus fell within the subject of "budgeting for the operation of the state government."[112] On that theory, any law with state fiscal implications could be

---

[106]Id. at 798, 803–804.

[107]Id. at 808–809.

[108]Id. at 808–809.

[109]953 N.E.2d 899 (Ill. 2011).

[110]Id. at 904–911; Block (2012), p. 246; Apadula (2013), p. 634 ("render[s] the single subject rule a dead letter").

[111]56 N.E.3d 913 (Ohio 2016).

[112]Id. at 922.

considered part of the subject of budgeting for the operation of state government—certainly, an enormous subject. Similarly, in *Otto v. Wright County*,[113] the Minnesota Supreme Court in 2018 determined that including in the State Government Omnibus Finance Act a provision enabling counties to choose to have their required annual audit performed by a CPA firm instead of by the state auditor did not violate the single-subject rule because that was "clearly germane to the subject of state government operations," which was the subject of the Act.[114] Although the county audit option could potentially reduce the workload of the state auditor, the amendment seems to be really far more about the powers and duties of counties than the operations of state government.

Finally, there is the divided Oklahoma Supreme Court's decision in *Douglas v. Retirement Properties, Inc.*,[115] invalidating that state's Comprehensive Lawsuit Reform Act. The majority stressed that the law contained ninety sections that included multiple amendments to the civil procedure code plus many new acts dealing with, *inter alia* emergency volunteer health practitioners, asbestos and silica claims, mandatory seat belt use, livestock activities liability, firearm manufacturers liability, and school discipline.[116] Without much analysis[117] the majority simply concluded that the multiple provisions were "unrelated" to each other and that "[m]any . . . have nothing in common."[118] By contrast, the two dissenters found a unifying theme: "the legislature and the public understood the common themes and purposes understood in the legislation; it was tort reform." They also pointed out the legislature had previously enacted, without successful single-subject objection, such broad measures as the ten-article and 368-section Uniform Commercial Code, and a 78-section Evidence Code, and that the majority's treatment of the tort reform law would create "substantial difficulty" for the legislature to pass "comprehensive legislation including any uniform codes that are generally adopted among the states." In their view, the "majority opinion gives little guidance" for distinguishing between impermissibly sweeping multi-part laws and acceptable comprehensive ones.[119]

Both opinions in *Douglas* considered the single-subject rule's anti-logrolling purpose in their analyses. Without citing any specific instances of logrolling in the legislative history, the majority concluded that in a bill with so many different sections and topics, legislators were inevitably "faced with an all-or-nothing choice" which would require them to vote for provisions they did not want "to ensure the

---

[113]910 N.W.2d 446 (Minn. 2018).

[114]Id. at 457.

[115]302 P.3d 789 (Ok. 2013).

[116]Id. at 793–794.

[117]The majority devoted five paragraphs to the discussion of the law and the application of the single-subject rule to it, including one that focused solely on whether severance rather than complete invalidation was a possible remedy. Id.

[118]Id. For an argument that it is inconsistent with Oklahoma single-subject precedents, *see* Dooley (2014).

[119]302 P.2d at 802–803.

passage of favorable legislation."[120] The dissent, however, saw the range of multiple provisions in the bill as evidence of legislative compromise. In any complex measure, "[i]t is likely that some of the legislators who voted in favor of the bill compromised to secure its passage." But in the dissent's view that is a feature and not a bug as "[l]egislation requires some compromise."[121]

The division in *Douglas* points to the possibility of anti-logrolling and the other purposes behind the single-subject rule in providing a more workable standard than the text of the rule itself for applying the rule, as well as the difficulties in doing so. That is the focus of the next Part.

4 From Text to Purpose: Anti-Logrolling and Anti-Riders as Standards for Enforcement

Like the Oklahoma judges in *Douglas*, many courts and commentators have sought to resolve the intractable question of how to define "subject" by turning to the purposes that arguably explain and justify the single-subject rule: prevention of logrolling and riders, and, more generally, protection of the legislative process from improper manipulation.[122] Logrolling, in particular, has long been condemned. Indeed, "in the United States at least, . . . this word has always had pejorative connotations."[123] By definition, an act put together by logrolling consists of measures which, considered individually, lacked majority support. Hence, its enactment is often seen as inconsistent with majority rule. Logrolling has been particularly criticized for facilitating the passage of wasteful "Christmas tree" bills and pork-barrel legislation, that is, laws that provide concentrated benefits—typically, subsidies; tax breaks; restrictive licensing requirements; tariffs; and roads, harbors and other highly targeted infrastructure investments—to a small number of interests but impose broader costs on consumers and taxpayers.[124] Some courts, like the Oklahoma Supreme Court and the Maryland Court of Appeals, have also emphasized that a logroll coerces legislators to vote for provisions they do not actually support or against a provision they would otherwise support because it has been combined with measures they oppose.[125]

---

[120]Id. at 793.

[121]Id. at 803.

[122]See, e.g., Comm. v. Heiman at 611–12; Wirtz at 905-05; Rizzo at 578.; Simmons-Harris v. Goff at 214 ("logrolling . . . was the very evil the one-subject rule was designed to prevent"); Denning and Smith (1999), p. 968; Schuck (2000), p. 901 (prevention of logrolling as the "primary and generally recognized purpose" for the single-subject rule); Hoffer and McDade (2004), p. 558.

[123]Riker and Brams (1973), p. 1235.

[124]Mueller (1979), p. 51.

[125]Thomas v. Henry, 260 P.3d 1251, 1260 (Ok. 2011) (logrolling means "many of those voting on the law would be faced with an unpalatable all-or-nothing choice"); Porten Sullivan at 1121.

An early application of the single-subject rule by the Michigan Supreme Court to strike down an act that appropriated state funds for the improvement of three different state roads is a classic example of the anti-logrolling philosophy at work. As Chief Justice Thomas Cooley explained, the roads were

> distinct objects of legislation which might, with entire propriety, have been provided for by separate acts, and indeed, ought to have been, in view of the care which is taken by the Constitution to compel each distinct object of legislation to be considered separately. These objects have certainly no necessary connection, and being grouped together in one bill, legislators are not only preclude[d] from expressing by their votes their opinion on each separately; but they are so united, as to invite a combination of interests among the friends of each, in order to secure the success of all, when, perhaps, neither could be passed separately. The evils of that species of omnibus legislation which the constitution designed to prohibit, are all invited by acts thus framed.[126]

In contrast to this longstanding judicial hostility to logrolling, modern scholarship has recognized that logrolling—or, less pejoratively, vote-trading—may be socially desirable because it recognizes that legislators have different intensities of preference for different measures. A proposal may enjoy only minority support not so much because the majority is actively hostile to it but rather because the majority is largely indifferent or only weakly opposed. Logrolling allows legislators to obtain passage of the measures they more strongly support at the modest price of voting for measures they are apathetic about or only mildly oppose. As a result, logrolling can make more legislators better off. To the extent legislators accurately represent the interests of their constituents, logrolling can enhance the overall well-being of the community. Moreover, logrolling may be particularly beneficial to certain legislative groups, particularly weaker parties or representatives of minority ethnic groups, that ordinarily lack the votes to get the measures they care most about passed. By being able to make vote-trading deals with some members of the majority, there is at least some prospect they can advance some items of their legislative agenda. Moreover, as some commentators have noted, logrolling need not involve only pork-barrel legislation but may embrace "what are truly pure public goods, e.g., defense, education, and the environment."[127]

To be sure, there is no guarantee that logrolling will be welfare-enhancing. The ability of a legislative minority to advance its goals through logrolling will depend on the skills, information, and resources of the legislators.[128] And the majority put together by logrolling might still impose costs on the community as a whole that are greater than the benefits to the logrolling coalition. But it is fair to say that there is no reason to assume that majorities put together by logrolling categorically impose net

---

[126]People ex rel Estes v. Denahy, 20 Mich. 349, 351–352 (1870).

[127]Mueller (1979), pp. 51–52.

[128]Wieting (1964), p. 93.

social costs or that they are more net costly than majorities composed of a single group.[129] It is even more unlikely that courts will be able to tell the difference.[130]

Even if logrolling is considered to be a problem, the real difficulty is distinguishing it from the deal-making and compromises that are "pervasive" in collective bodies and "normally characteristic of representative assemblies."[131] Such deal-making is often a critical means for contending groups to compromise their differences and reach a collective decision.[132] Although the Illinois Supreme Court once asserted "there is a difference between impermissible logrolling and the normal compromise which is inherent in the legislative process,"[133] it is not clear that's correct. Even a close review of the legislative history behind a bill[134] may not help as the question is less one of fact and more of interpretation and acceptance of legislative practices.

As the Utah Supreme Court explained, "the line between forbidden log-rolling and mere horse-trading may be a fine one."[135] The Minnesota Court of Appeals went further in defending a challenged bill against the claim that it was the result of impermissible logrolling: "If the historical nature of legislation was that every single provision of a larger bill had to be able to pass both houses of the legislature and obtain the governor's signature on its own merits, little if any legislation would ever be signed into law. . . . The practice of bundling controversial, volatile provisions with germane and less-controversial laws is not impermissible logrolling. Rather it is the nature of the democratic process. . . . The negotiations and the constant give and take are historical, purely legal, and purely permissible."[136] Indeed, courts have defended the "liberal" approach to interpreting the single-subject rule as essential "to accommodate a significant range and degree of political compromise that necessarily attends the legislative process in a healthy, robust democracy."[137]

The concern that bills that result from logrolling somehow improperly coerce legislators into voting against their preferences seems even weaker than the claim that bills composed of provisions that might not have passed on their own violate proper legislative norms. Compromise necessarily involves votes at odds with one's ideal position. As Professor Dan Lowenstein crisply put it: "Most choices in life involve trade-offs."[138] Or as one member of Congress noted in early February 2019

---

[129]Riker and Brams (1973), p. 1246.

[130]Kastorf (2005) pp. 1663–1665.

[131]Buchanan and Tullock (1962), p. 134; cf. Easterbrook (1983), p. 548 (logrolling an "accepted part[] of the legislative process").

[132]Kastorf (2005), p. 1647 (logrolling "the necessary lubrication to overcome collective action problems").

[133]Wirtz 911.

[134]The *Wirtz* court engaged in such a close review. See id. at 909–911.

[135]Gregory at 1116.

[136]Defenders of Wildlife v. Ventura, 632 N.W.2d 707, 714-15 (Minn. App. 2001).

[137]MCEA at 943.

[138]Lowenstein (1983), p. 958.

in explaining his vote for the bill that prevented the recurrence of a second partial government shutdown, "When you strike a deal you get some things you want and you get some things that you don't like."[139]

In theory, the case against riders may be stronger than the case against logrolling. By definition, a rider is attached to a bill that already enjoys majority support so that the bill's backers should not have had to vote for the rider in order to get their measure enacted. One commentator speculates that riders are likely to result from the ability of powerful individual legislators to manipulate rules and procedures to get their particular proposals attached to a popular bill and to block efforts to strip the rider out. As such, riders are anti-majoritarian as a majority of legislators would have preferred to vote for the bill in question without the rider. He would reframe the single-subject rule exclusively around the prevention of riders.[140] Yet, in practice, it may be difficult to distinguish a rider from a logroll. As the earliest study of the single-subject rule found, determining whether a provision is a rider is a "troublesome question."[141] Before enactment, a bill's proponents may be unsure whether the measure actually enjoys majority support or is, instead, a few votes short of passage and so is willing to accept an amendment that brings along a few more votes. Is such a provision a logroll or a rider?[142] Assessing the provisions of an act after enactment, a court trying to distinguish a logroll from a rider "would have to make unseemly, and possibly difficult, judgments about the relative popularity of various provisions and the motivations of the sponsors."[143] Indeed, a close assessment of Illinois's *Wirtz* decision concluded that "the attempt to distinguish between the two [logrolling and riders] may be futile."[144] The fact that a provision, subsequently folded into a bigger bill, did not pass on its own does not make it a rider.[145] And even critics of riders recognize that, like logrolls, they can be socially beneficial and make net contributions to social well-being.[146]

Several judges taking a legislative-process-focused approach to the single-subject rule have emphasized that the troublesome sections of a bill—whether logroll or rider—were added at the "last minute" or the "eleventh hour."[147] This underscores

---

[139]Paul Kane, "The bill to avert a shutdown has few eager to claim parentage," Wash. Post, Feb. 13, 2019 (quoting Rep. Gregory Meeks (D-NY)).

[140]Gilbert (2006), pp. 836–843.

[141]Ruud (1958), p. 400.

[142]Kastorf (2005), p. 1646. See also Briffault (1993) pp. 1189–1194 (considering the difficulties courts have distinguishing between improper riders and acceptable conditions in item veto cases).

[143]Lowenstein (1983), p. 963; Dragich (2001), pp. 161–162 (2001) (analyzing two Missouri single-subject cases and finding it "hard to say" whether the laws at issue involved logrolls or riders).

[144]Block (2012), p. 250.

[145]Gregory at 1112; Ex parte Jones, 440 S.W.3d 628, 634 (Tex. 2014); Cf. Defenders of Wildlife at 714 ("the fact that a controversial bill could not pass as a stand-alone bill, while not irrelevant, is not conclusive proof of impermissible logrolling").

[146]Gilbert (2006), p. 839.

[147]Delmarva at 645–646; Porten Sullivan at 1114–1115; Voinovich at 601–602 (concurring opinion); Leach at 430; Spahn at 1146.

the single-subject rule's purposes of making sure legislators are able to understand and deliberate what they are voting on, and that the legislative process is transparent to the broader public. A last-minute surprise also implies some kind of legislative chicanery that would support a judicial decision to strike down a measure. However, many state legislatures operate under requirements of time-limited legislative sessions.[148] Some of these are as short as twenty to thirty legislative days or sixty to ninety calendar days;[149] in four states, the legislature meets only for a limited number of days every other year.[150] Frequent amendments to pending legislation are surely a part of the legislative process to begin with.[151] But tight session limits put a lot of pressure to get the legislative business done in a very short period and make it even more likely that there will be a rush of amendments, combinations of previously separate measures into bigger bills, and a surge of deal-making as the end of the legislative session approaches. From the perspective of an idealized, orderly and deliberative legislative process, this is surely unfortunate. But, as one Ohio Supreme Court justice observed, however "distasteful" and "ugly" the process may be, that does not make it unconstitutional.[152]

It is difficult—probably impossible—to quarrel with the goals of improved deliberation, transparency, and accountability norms. The real issues are whether attention to those concerns, and the logrolls and riders said to violate them, helps determine what is a subject and when the single-subject rule is violated. There can be logrolls and riders within a single subject, and omnibus or multi-part bills which are put together for convenience or for the comprehensive treatment of a subject. In at least some circumstances, legislative deliberation, effective law-making, transparency and public accountability may be better served by multi-part bills that comprehensively address a complex or multifaceted problem[153] than by narrower measures that address the issues piecemeal. Improper manipulations of the legislative process—if they can be judicially identified—may be evidence that a new law goes beyond a single subject, but it is not clear that even a close review of the legislative process can resolve the meaning of "subject."

---

[148]See Nat'l Conf. of State Legs., "Legislative Session Length," (noting that 39 state legislatures are under state constitutional, statutory, or other restrictions on the length of the legislative session).

[149]Id.

[150]Nat'l Conf. of State Legs., "Annual vs. Biennial Legislative Sessions."

[151]PAGE at 395.

[152]Beagle v. Walden, 676 N.E.2d 506, 510 (Ohio 1997) (Pfeifer, J., concurring in part).

[153]State ex rel Ohio CSEA v. State at 919 (a large number of topics may be combined "for the purposes of bringing greater order and cohesion to the law"); Wirtz at 911 (rejecting single-subject challenge to a "diverse and complex" enactment); MCEA at 943. Cf. Gellert v. State, 522 P.2d 1120, 1122 (Alaska 1974) (if the rule were interpreted too narrowly, "statutes might be restricted unduly in scope and permissible subject matter, thereby multiplying and complicating the number of necessary enactment[s] and their interrelationships").

5   Conclusion

The single-subject rule presents a paradox. It is "part of the fundamental structure of legislative power articulated in [the] constitution"[154] of the vast majority of states, and it reflects and seeks to promote a noble vision of deliberative, majoritarian, and accountable law-making. But it has proven all but impossible to consistently implement, or even to consistently define. Although some commentators have criticized the courts for excessive deference to the legislatures and have urged that more aggressive enforcement will improve legislative performance, that seems unlikely to occur. The problems of subject definition and consistent application would only get worse with more aggressive enforcement efforts. Nor is it clear that more aggressive enforcement would affect legislative behavior. The Oklahoma Supreme Court has taken a more stringent approach than many other state courts and has frequently struck down laws on single-subject grounds but the legislature continues to pass laws the court finds objectionable, leading the court to complain of "growing weary of admonishing the Legislature for so flagrantly violating the Oklahoma Constitution."[155]

The single-subject rule's view of relatively tidy, separate topic-by-topic deliberation and enactment is often in tension with the coalition-building and deal-making characteristic of the legislative process in practice. Comprehensive, multi-topic legislation will often be necessary, if not desirable, in order for the legislature to act at all, and a proliferation of small, piecemeal single-subject measures would not improve legislative efficiency or, given the time limits many legislatures are under, legislative deliberation.

The experience of the states suggests that the single-subject rule is unlikely to be an effective constraint on omnibus legislation. That experience indicates that courts will typically embrace a broad definition of subject and defer to the legislature, with only the occasional invalidation of the most egregious combinations of seemingly unrelated subjects. This seems likely to occur, paradoxically, not in the large, complex omnibus measures that advocates of the rule decry, but with smaller laws that combine just a handful of laws or amendments on discrete topics, and which can be claimed as single subject at only the highest level of abstraction, such as "amending the crimes code" or "judicial remedies and sanctions." General deference with intermittent enforcement in the most egregious cases—with the meaning of "egregious" left open—is in tension with the rule of law values of consistency and predictability but reflects the general judicial preference to accommodate the actual functioning of the legislative process.

The purposes of the single-subject rule—majority rule, deliberation, transparency, orderly procedure, public accountability—are surely desirable legislative

---

[154]Gregory at 1108.

[155]Nova Health Systems v. Edmondson, 233 P.3d 380, 382 (Ok. 2010). At the time of the Nova Health decision, the Oklahoma court had found seven violations of the rule over the preceding two decades. Since then, the court has found at least four more violations.

process goals. But the experience of the state constitutional single-subject rule indicates that a constitutional requirement—even if judicially enforceable—may not be an effective way to achieve these ends.

State Constitutional Provisions and State Statutes

Illinois Const., Art IV, §8(d).
Ohio Const. Art II, §15(D).

Rev. Stat. Mo. 290.528 (H.B. 1194 of Laws of 2017)
Cases (Alphabetically by State)

Alaska

Gellert v. State, 522 P.2d 1120, 1122 (Ak. 1974)
North Slope Borough v. SOHIO Petroleum Corp., 585 P.2d 534 (Ak. 1978)
State v. First Nat'l Bank of Anchorage, 660 P.2d 406 (Ak. 1982)
Yute Air Alaska, Inc. v McAlpine, 698 P.2d 1173 (Ak. 1985)
Evans v. State, 56 P.3d 1046 (Ak. 2002)

Colorado

In re Title, Ballot Title and Submission Clause for No 2005-2006 No. 74, 136 P.3d
   237 (Co. 2006)

Illinois

Johnson v. Edgar, 680 N.E.2d 1372 (Il. 1997)
People v. Reedy, 708 N.E.2d 1114 (Il. 1999)
Arangold v. Zehnder, 718 N.E.2d 191 (Il. 1999)
People v. Cervantes, 723 N.E.2d 265 Il. 1999)
Wirtz v. Quinn, 953 N.E.2d 899 (Il. 2011)

Kansas

Kansas One-Call Sys. v. State, 274 P.3d 625 (Ks. 2012)
Kansas Nat'l Educ. Ass'n v. State, 387 P.3d 795 (Ks. 2017)

Maryland

Porten Sullivan Corp. v. State, 568 A.2d 1111 (Md. 1990)
Maryland Classified Employees Ass'n, Inc. v. State ("MCEA"), 694 A.2d 937 (Md. 1997)
Migdal v. State. 747 A.2d 1225 (Md. 2000)
Delmarva Power & Light Co. v. Public Service Comm., 809 A.2d 640 (Md. 2002)

Michigan

People ex rel Estes v. Denahy, 20 Mich. 349 (Mi. 1870).

Minnesota

Wass v. Anderson, 252 N.W.2d 131 (Mn. 1977)
Blanch v. Suburban Hennepin Reg. Park Dist., 449 N.W.2d 150 (Mn. 1989).
Assoc. Bldrs & Contrs. v. Ventura, 610 N.W.2d 293 (Mn. 2000)
Defenders of Wildlife v. Ventura, 632 N.W.2d 707 (Mn. App. 2001)
Unity Church of St. Paul v. State, 694 N.W.2d 585 (Mn. 2005)
Townsend v. State, 767 N.W.2d 11 (Mn. 2009)
Otto v. Wright Co., 920 N.W.2d 446 (Mn. 2018)

Missouri

Hammerschmidt v. Boone Co., 877 S.W.2d 98 (Mo, 1994)
Missouri Health Care Ass'n v. Attorney General, 953 S.W.2d 617 (Mo. 1997)
Stroh Brewery Co. v. State, 954 S.W.2d 323 (Mo. 1997)
Corvera Abatement Tech. v. Air Conservation Com'n, 973 S.W.2d 851 (Mo. 1998)
C.C. Dillon Co. v. City of Eureka, 12 S.W.3d 322, 327-29 (Mo. 2000)
City of St. Charles v. State, 165 S.W.3d 149 (Mo. 2005)
Rizzo v. State, 189 S.W.3d 576, 578 (Mo. 2006)

Missouri Roundtable for Life, Inc. v. State, 396 S.W.3d 348 (Mo. 2013)
Cooperative Home Care, Inc. v. City of St. Louis, 514 S.W.3d 571 (Mo. 2017)

Ohio

State ex rel Hinkle v. Franklin Co. Bd. of Elec., 580 N.E.2d 767 (Oh 1991)
State ex rel Ohio AFL-CIO v. Voinovich, 631 N.E.2d 582 (Oh 1994)
Beagle v. Walden, 676 N.E.2d 506 (Oh. 1997)
Simmons-Harris v. Goff, 711 N.E.2d 203 (Oh. 1999)
State ex rel Ohio Academy of Trial lawyers v. Sheward, 715 N.E.2d 1062 (Oh. 1999)
State ex rel Ohio Civ. Serv. Emp. Ass'n v. State Emp. Rel. Bd. (SERB"), 818 N.E.2d 688 (Oh. 2004)
State ex rel Ohio CSEA v. State, 56 N.E.3d 913 (Oh. 2016)

Oklahoma

In re Initiative Petition No. 382, 142 P.3d 400 (Ok. 2006)
Fent v. State, 214 P.3d 799 (Ok. 2009)
Nova Health Systems v. Edmondson, 233 P.3d 380 (Ok. 2010)
Thomas v. Henry, 260 P.3d 1251 (Ok. 2011)
Douglas v. Cox Retirement Props., Inc., 302 P.3d 789 (Ok. 2013)
Fent v. Fallin, 315 P.3d 1023 (Ok. 2013)
Burns v. Cline, 382 P.3d 1048 (Ok. 2016)
Matter Oklahoma Turnpike Auth., 389 P.3d 318 (Ok. 2017)

Pennsylvania

City of Philadelphia v. Comm., 838 A.2d 566 (Pa. 2003)
Pennsylvanians Against Gambling Expansion Fund ("PAGE") v. Commonwealth, 877 A.2d 383 (Pa. 2005)
Spahn v. Zoning Bd. of Adjustment, 977 A.2d 1132 (Pa. 2009)
Commonwealth v. Neiman, 84 A.3d 603 (Pa. 2013)
Leach v Commonwealth, 141 A.3d 426 (Pa. 2016)

Texas

Ex parte Jones, 440 S.W.3d 628, 634 (Tx. 2014)

Utah

Gregory v. Shurtleff, 299 P.3d 1098 (Ut. 2013)

Washington

Washington Ass'n for Substance Abuse and Violence Prevention v. State, 278 P.2d 632 (Wash. 2012)

References

Apadula G (2013) State constitutional law – single subject rule – The Illinois Supreme Court adopts an irrebutable presumption of constitutionality for legislation challenged by the single subject rule, Wirtz v. Quinn, 953 N.E.2d 899 (Ill. 2011). Rutgers Law J 43:617–634

Block E (2012) Broke: the pocketbook of Illinois and the single subject rule after Wirtz v. Quinn, 953 NE.2d 899 (Ill. 2011). So Ill Law J 37:237–252

Briffault R (1993) The item Veto in State Courts. Temp Law Rev 66:1173–1204

Buchanan JM, Tullock G (1962) The calculus of consent: logical foundations of constitutional democracy. University of Michigan Press

Catalano MW (1990) The single subject rule: a check on anti-majoritarian logrolling. Emerg Iss State Const Law 3:77–90

Cooter RD, Gilbert MD (2010) A theory of direct democracy and the single subject rule. Colum Law Rev 110:687–730

Denning BP, Smith BR (1999) Uneasy riders: the case for a truth-in-legislation amendment. Utah Law Rev 1999:957–1026

Denning BP, Smith BR (2011) The truth-in-legislation amendment: an idea whose time has come. Tenn Law Rev 78:831–838

Dooley SA (2014) Comment, It's still a peanut butter cookie: a comment on Douglas v. Cox Retirement Properties, Inc. Okla City Univ Law Rev 39:243–264

Downey R et al (2004) A survey of the single subject rule as applied to statewide initiatives. J Contemp Leg Issues 13:579–627

Dragich MJ (2001) State constitutional restrictions on legislative procedure: rethinking the analysis of original purpose, single subject, and clear title challenges. Harv J Legis 38:103–172

Easterbrook F (1983) Statutes' Domains. Univ Chicago Law Rev 50:533–552

Evans JW, Bannister MC (2014) The meaning and purpose of state constitutional single subject rules: a survey of states and the Indiana example. Val Univ Law Rev 49:87–154

Figinski MA (1998) Maryland's constitutional one-subject rule: neither a dead letter nor an undue restriction. U Baltimore Law Rev 27:363–394

Gilbert MD (2006) Single subject rules and the legislative process. Univ Pitt Law Rev 67:803–870

Gilbert MD (2011) Does law matter? Theory and evidence from single-subject adjudication. J Leg Stud 40:333–366

Hoffer S, McDade T (2004) Of disunity and logrolling: Ohio's one-subject rule and the very evils it was designed to prevent. Clev St Law Rev 51:557–580

Kasper MJ (2009) Using Article IV of the Illinois Constitution to attack legislation passed by the general assembly. Loy Univ Chicago Law J 40:847–878

Kastorf KG (2005) Logrolling gets logrolled: same-sex marriage, direct democracy, and the single-subject rule. Emory Law J 54:1633–1670

Lowenstein DH (1983) California initiatives and the single-subject rule. UCLA Law Rev 30:936–975

Mueller DC (1979) Public choice. Cambridge University Press

Nat'l Conf. of State Legs., "Annual vs. Biennial Legislative Sessions", http://www.ncsl.org/research/about-state-legislatures/annual-vs-biennial-legislative-sessions.aspx. Accessed 15 Apr 2020

Nat'l Conf. of State Legs., "Legislative Session Length", http://www.ncsl.org/research/about-state-legislatures/legislative-session-length.aspx. Accessed 15 Apr 2020

Note (2007) Tipping Point: Missouri's Single Subject Provision. Missouri Law Rev 72:1387–1410

Paul Kane (2019) The bill to avert a shutdown has few eager to claim parentage. Wash Post, Feb. 13, 2019. https://www.washingtonpost.com/powerpost/the-bill-to-avoid-a-shutdown-has-few-eager-to-claim-parentage/2019/02/13/b3f61658-2fd6-11e9-86ab-5d02109aeb01_story.html. Accessed 15 Apr 2020

Riker WH, Brams SJ (1973) The paradox of vote trading. APSR 67:1235–1247

Ruud MH (1958) No law shall embrace more than one subject. Minn Law Rev 42:389–452

Schuck JP (2000) Returning the one to Ohio's one-subject rule. Capital Univ Law Rev 28:899–921

Wieting HL Jr (1964) Philosophical problems in majority rule and the logrolling solution. Ethics 76:85–101

Williams RF (1987) State constitutional limits on legislative procedure: legislative compliance and judicial enforcement. Univ Pitt Law Rev 48:797–827

Unorthodox Lawmaking and Legislative Complexity in American Statutory Interpretation

Abbe R. Gluck

Abstract The traditional legislative process is dead in the U.S. Statutes are increasingly long and complex omnibus efforts rushed through at the end of congressional sessions. Yet American statutory interpretation remains largely unchanged, with judges generally uninterested in the realities of the legislative process, despite claiming our dominant interpretive approach reflects Congress or is in conversation with it. Omnibus statutes pose challenges for judges who read statutes with assumptions of linguistic perfection and consistency—as American judges do—and the truncated legislative process results in more gaps and mistakes, problems that lack coherent doctrinal approaches in our courts. And American judges have never been willing to strike down federal statutes for lack of deliberation or process, preferring instead indirect nudges toward more "due process in lawmaking." This chapter documents the rise of unorthodox modern lawmaking in the U.S., including omnibus lawmaking, and details its causes, costs and benefits. These developments are not unmitigated negatives; they are adaptations to the changing complexities of the American political system. It has been 50 years since the last congressional reorganization and another revolution may be coming. There is a burgeoning legal movement among scholars and some American jurists, including several Supreme Court justices, to bring understanding of the legislative process, and how it has changed, into our theories and doctrines of statutory interpretation.

Keywords Legislation · Interpretation · Lawmaking · Statutes · Omnibus · Statutory interpretation · Congress

In the United States, the textbook, "Schoolhouse Rock!" legislative process is dead. Statutes have grown in length, are increasingly large omnibus efforts rushed through at the end of congressional sessions, and are documents of dizzying complexity that often cannot be understood, or even really read, from cover to cover.

A. R. Gluck (✉)
Yale Law School, New Haven, CT, USA
e-mail: abbe.gluck@yale.edu

© The Author(s), under exclusive license to Springer Nature Switzerland AG 2021   195
I. Bar-Siman-Tov (ed.), *Comparative Multidisciplinary Perspectives on Omnibus Legislation*, Legisprudence Library 8, https://doi.org/10.1007/978-3-030-72748-2_9

The American courts barely have seemed to notice. The judicial approach to statutory interpretation has been generally uninterested in the realities of our legislative process, even as many judges claim either that their interpretive approach approximates how Congress drafts, reflects a set of conventions shared by the judiciary and the legislature, or captures Congress's purposes. Nor does American jurisprudence embrace a concept like "due process of lawmaking," as was first suggested in a famous 1976 article by Oregon Supreme Court Justice Hans Linde, which entails scrutinizing the particulars of a statute's legislative process and pegs statutory legitimacy to proper deliberation or other process safeguards.[1]

And yet big legislative changes have been afoot. Consider, for instance, that omnibus legislation has comprised approximately 11% of major legislation in recent Congresses.[2] Only about 1% (!!) of enacted laws went through the standard legislative process set out by Congress's own rules (the modern basses for many of which have been in place since the 1970s[3] and in the case of some rules, for much longer[4]), which includes committee consideration and vote, full debate and vote within each chamber, and an inter-chamber "conference committee" to reconcile differences across chambers and put the final touches on legislation. Almost 18% of enacted bills did not go through the committee process at all in either chamber—even though committees are the primary loci of expertise, engagement and deliberation in Congress; rather, these bills were sent straight to the floor by party leadership or by the White House. Another approximately 38% were initially reported to committee only to be discharged directly to the floor for management before the committee vote to report the bill to the floor. Major bills, including the important 2017 tax cut, have been provided to legislators just hours before the vote, making reading and understanding them—much less deliberating over them—impossible. Statistics like these have grown decade by decade. These departures from what congressional experts call "regular order" have become the norm, not the exception.

In addition, the U.S. Code also is now significantly more complicated than it was decades ago. Its length has grown exponentially over the past 40 years, as has its complexity, including the number of delegations to agencies and other implementers, and the skyrocketing use of internal cross-references. These changes make it impossible to read a statute cover to cover, even if one wanted. Omnibus laws in particular, which are on the rise, are particularly non-narrative: they bring together a variety of subjects in a sea of cross references and often lack key explanatory materials, like legislative history, that usually help staff and elected Members—

---

[1]Linde (1976).

[2]Sinclair (2017).

[3]Standing Rules of the Senate, S. Doc. No. 113–18 (2013); Rules of the One Hundred Sixteenth Congress, H. Res. 6 (2019); Cong. Research Serv., Reorganization of the House of Representatives: Modern Reform Efforts (2003); Cong. Research Serv., R30862, The Budget Reconciliation Process: The Senate's "Byrd Rule" (2016), https://www.everycrsreport.com/files/20161122_RL30862_ce42dbc9f4a53acdf63bcb8097c7392495568965.pdf.

[4]*Cloture Rule*, U.S. Senate, https://www.senate.gov/artandhistory/history/minute/Cloture_Rule.htm.

and down the line, courts, agencies and the public—understand what the statutes are doing.

At the same time, the U.S. Congress is in a period of historic gridlock. Without these deviations from regular order, and without omnibus legislation, Congress would get little done. To wit, Congress often uses a special legislative process known as reconciliation to pass omnibus laws. Reconciliation is attractive because it bypasses the supermajority rule in the Senate that requires 60 votes to close debate and move to a vote,[5] but reconciliation also has complex rules about statutory content, which must be budget-related and cannot include any extraneous provisions.[6] These rules often result in "slicing and dicing" statutory language, or putting unrelated provisions together, in ways that make statutory language even more difficult than usual to parse. What's more, not all content can be included in reconciliation rules, making the resulting laws even more unwieldly.

The American federal courts, for their part, have barely acknowledged the changes in Congress through the years. In addition to the challenges that modern omnibus statutes pose for judges who like to read statutes with assumptions of linguistic perfection and consistency—as American federal judges do—the truncated legislative process results in more gaps and mistakes. The process also produces less legislative history, fewer amendments in the course of enactment, and more drafting decisions made specifically to clear procedural hurdles.

These changes pose real problems for judicial interpreters. American judges have never been willing to strike down federal statutes on the basis that legislative deliberation was lacking or defective. They only very rarely even strike down statutes, in general, for vagueness, preferring instead to "interpret" "gaps" as "ambiguities" that courts or agencies can fill—a fictional concept of the judicial role that prominent appellate Judge Richard Posner recently exposed in an important concurrence at the end of his career.[7] Nor does our bench have a coherent doctrine of how to deal with a statutory mistake. Instead, in cases that implicate serious mistakes, like the major 2015 healthcare case that was heard by the U.S. Supreme Court,[8] courts often refuse to admit that Congress made a mistake and instead interpret around it. In more minor cases, however, without open acknowledgment of the different treatment courts give less salient statutes, the courts will often enforce mistakes as written. This is a strange indirectness. Instead of telling Congress that it must be more careful or deliberate in these minor cases, courts often read mistakes literally—a "tough love" approach to send a message.

Other times, our courts try to "nudge" Congress gently into better lawmaking through default rules of statutory interpretation. American courts adore those so-called "canons of statutory interpretation", the interpretive presumptions that courts apply to statutory questions. The canons can be pushy: they protect, enforce

---

[5]Standing Rules of the Senate, S. Doc. No. 113–18, R. XXII (2013).

[6]2 U.S.C. § 644.

[7]*See* Hively v. Ivy Tech Cmty. Coll., 853 F.3d 339, 352 (7th Cir. 2017) (Posner, J., concurring).

[8]*See* King v. Burwell, 135 S. Ct. 2480 (2015).

and implement coherence and consistency, and may sometimes enforce other substantive commitments like federalism, presumptions favoring arbitration, and Indian rights. These canons enforce these values even when Congress has not contemplated them, perhaps in an effort to remind Congress that it should do so next time. But there is no canon that openly protects the basic legislative value of deliberation or due process in lawmaking.

Given this book's focus on omnibus legislation across the globe, the question also arises: Are these changes—and the judicial responses to them—universal? Have omnibus legislation, and attending departures from regular legislative order, multiplied across the globe, and if so why? Do the same circumstances give rise to them in each country? Have statutes become similarly and increasingly complex across the countries? And have other courts paid insufficient due to the changes—like the U.S. courts—or are some jurisdictions more attuned to new legislative processes?[9]

This chapter begins with some jurisprudential background—where do the rules of statutory interpretation come from and how might they change as lawmaking itself changes? It then describes the rise and implications of omnibus lawmaking in the United States, as well as some other kinds of unorthodox lawmaking. It concludes with implications for judicial review.

1   Brief Jurisprudential Background

For those who study interpretation and how its rules change over time, a key jurisprudential question is where those rules come from. What is interesting is how often principles of statutory interpretation are described as "universal" law—law that applies across many jurisdictions in the same way, rather than being tied to any particular sovereign government and how that particular government operates. My research comparing civil and common law interpretation reveals more similarities than differences, and some surprising twists that have relevance here. Most notably, in civil code countries there is less literal formalism and much more purposive interpretation when it comes to the Code than we have with respect to our statutes in the United States. Justice Antonin Scalia's most famous essay—the one that announced the now-dominant textualist methodology that he advanced in the United States—was written almost a quarter-century ago, and entitled *Common Law Courts in a Civil Law System: The Role of United States Federal Courts in Interpreting the Constitution and Laws*.[10] Scalia used this same comparison to the civil code systems to suggest that an increasingly statutory United States landscape is an argument *for* a literal textualism. But Justice Scalia may have got it exactly backwards.

My hypothesis is that the civil courts understand their role to protect the Code as their primary source of law—to keep it functional and rational—and so unforgiving

---

[9]See Bar-Siman-Tov (2021).

[10]Scalia (1997).

formalism cannot work given how much law is codified. If this hypothesis has any truth to it, one takeaway might well be that similar adjustments are required for countries like the United States, even with a common-law tradition, in the face of what is truly no longer a common-law system given the dominance of statutes. And yet American courts have barely changed their interpretive practice since the founding of our government; the famous eighteenth-century English judge William Blackstone's rules of interpretation still are the norm rather than the exception.

The other jurisprudential question is about the judicial role. What is the role of the judge, for example, to respond to changes in the legislative process when interpreting statutes? In the United States this debate is largely smoke and mirrors. Virtually all federal judges and legislation scholars *claim* that the judicial role in statutory interpretation is to act as a "faithful agent of the legislature." They claim the debate is merely over *how* that role is to be implemented—for instance, whether being a "faithful agent" means looking only to the words Congress enacted, or whether it means that courts should be purposive partners of the legislature, and so on—and not what the role *is*.

But this kind of pervasive talk masks a fundamental incoherence in the American jurisprudence of statutory interpretation. In reality, both "textualists" and "purposivists" in the United States toggle among a variety of approaches without explicit acknowledgement or justification—that is, they toggle among different conceptions of the judicial *role*. What is more, most of their approaches have no empirically defended link to how Congress actually works.[11]

Both sides sometimes approach statutory interpretation with the goal of reflecting how Congress drafts. But the linguistic default presumptions, like presumptions of word consistency across the U.S. Code, do not actually reflect Congress's own practice. Neither side acknowledges that these seemingly neutral linguistic tools actually are quite active in their imposition of perfection and coherence on legislative work-product that was not drafted that way.

Both sides sometimes also interpret using the default linguistic canons, arguing that those canons are "shared conventions" that both the judicial and legislative branches know and under which they operate. My own empirical work, however, has largely disproved that Congress knows or shares those canons. Still other times, interpreters apply policy canons without ever acknowledging that those canons are judge-created law that impose external, judge-driven values on Congress and its work-product.

All this might be well and good if our courts were upfront about what they were doing, if they acknowledged their larger and more active role than claiming to merely mirror Congress when they interpret. But American courts do not do this, instead shrinking behind the false shield that legislative supremacy prevents them from doing anything active when it comes to statutes, when of course they are doing exactly that.

---

[11]Gluck (2015).

The relevance of these jurisprudential problemsfor this volume is that, ultimately, the rise of omnibus legislation and the increasing complexity of the legislative landscape matters little to the theories and doctrines of judicial statutory interpretation if courts are not going to pay attention to *any* of the realities of the legislative process or to differences across kinds of statutes. But, if we are to take courts at their word, then modern legislative complexities should call into major question many of the operative doctrines of American statutory interpretation. Those doctrines assume the very opposite of what happens with much legislation today, including omnibus laws. Those doctrines depend on congressional omniscience, intra-congressional communication, legislative perfection and uniformity across statutory types—a world that no longer exists, if it ever did. The complexities of the modern landscape raise the stakes of the question as to how important it is for interpreters to think about and understand the legislative process and whether we need a modern approach—as opposed to a Blackstonian approach or something more universal and global—to statutory interpretation for the U.S. legal system.

The rest of the chapter documents some of the increasing complexities of our legislative process and the recent empirical work that illustrates the disconnect between Congress and the courts.

2   Unorthodox Lawmaking in the United States

The phenomenon of "unorthodox lawmaking" was first brought to the attention of the academy by political scientist Barbara Sinclair, in her eponymous book.[12] Subsequent editions empirically documented the increase in legislative-process deviations, a phenomenon elaborated on by this author, with co-authors, for legal audiences, in several previous articles.[13]

Not all unorthodox policymaking is the same, and omnibus laws are only one type. For example, omnibus actions are different from emergency actions, not only in motivation and in final product, but also in the distinct challenges each poses for courts. Utilizing the budget reconciliation process to push through statutes poses its own challenges for understanding the final law. Outsourcing difficult legislative and regulatory questions to special processes, commissions, and unconventional delegates is yet another kind of unorthodox legislation raising its own set of questions for law, as do the simultaneously regulatory and legislative roles of the modern President. Direct democracy is another type of lawmaking whose differences from the norm courts seem to prefer to ignore.

These tools are not new; but rather they are being used in many instances for different purposes than those for which they were initially introduced, and often with increasing frequency.

---

[12]Sinclair (2017).

[13]Gluck et al. (2015) and Gluck and Bressman (2013, 2014).

Perhaps the primary example of the way in which old legislative tools are being used for new purposes is Congress's penchant now for legislating substantively through the omnibus budget process. Legislative bundling through omnibus vehicles has increased dramatically, both for substantive legislation and for appropriations. Although variable by year, process deviations, as noted, are prevalent. Legislation bypassed the regular committee process much more in the 1990s and 2000s than in the preceding decades.

As traditional legislation becomes rarer and gridlock cripples lawmaking, the unorthodox President also emerges. The President now uses more executive memoranda and directives for major policy moves previously thought to be legislative terrain. New unorthodox delegations outside of traditional federal actors to states, private, and quasi-private actors also have been widely observed by scholars. Unorthodox workarounds introduced in recent decades that outsource controversial issues, once the providence of legislatures, to boards and commissions include base realignment and closure, cutting Medicare, and the fast-track trade and budget processes.[14] State initiatives have become extremely popular. From 1904 through 2008, according to one study, 2306 statewide initiatives were put to a vote, and voters approved 936 of them—more than half of these proposed initiatives dated since the 1970s.[15]

2.1 Omnibus Legislation

Omnibus legislation is the most familiar type of unorthodox lawmaking and the one to which this chapter will devote the most attention. Omnibus vehicles are marked by their length, complexity, and the way in which they often bring together multiple congressional and administrative stakeholders to cover various unrelated subject areas and thus garner broader support. In addition, they transfer power away from conventional lawmakers on both sides. The need to coordinate among multiple committees, stakeholders, and agencies has given a heightened role to party leaders and the White House to coordinate or even direct this kind of policymaking.

From a statutory interpretation standpoint, omnibus bills pose particular challenges for common doctrinal assumptions regarding legislative perfection. These are often long and messy bills. They may have errors or linguistic inconsistencies that statutory interpretation doctrine does not usually tolerate. Legislative history for omnibus bills is also often outdated, because parts of such bills often are drafted years before—as part of earlier, failed bills that later are bundled into an omnibus package as part of a bigger deal.[16] The Gluck/Bressman study found that even when omnibus legislative history does exist, it is often "confused" as a result of this hasty

---

[14]*Ibid.*, p. 1802.

[15]*Ibid.*, p. 1803.

[16]*Ibid.*

compilation.[17] Sometimes omnibus legislative history is simply nonexistent, because many omnibus bills bypass the committee stage, where reports are typically produced. In recent years, as the process has become more rushed, Congress's professional drafters have reported far fewer opportunities to clean up language and correct errors before passage.

There is no single definition of omnibus legislation, but there is consensus that legislation that "packages together several measures into one or combines diverse subjects into a single bill" fits the label, as do so-called "money bills," including omnibus appropriations bills and budget bills. Some experts, including Sinclair, include in this definition legislation that is "usually highly complex and long" and that takes on numerous issues, even within a single subject area—for example the 800-page Clean Air Act and the 2700-page Affordable Care Act health reform statute.[18]

Omnibus bills, particularly in their length, are very different from the majority of bills that are passed in Congress. For example, in the past three Congresses, 40% of the 917 enacted bills were only one page long and approximately 80% of enacted bills were just six pages or under. These short one-page bills typicallu accomplish simple administrative or ministerial tasks; for example, 162 enacted bills renamed post offices after famous individuals. Omnibus bills in the past three Congresses, on the other hand, averaged about 350 pages, with several close to 1000 pages, and contained upwards of, on average, six thousand sections. The most common type of omnibus bill still appears to be appropriations legislation. Other common topics for omnibus bills include trade, health care, defense authorization acts, and bills passed in response to national emergencies like the coronavirus epidemic.

Omnibus legislation often comprises "mini-bills"—separate pieces of legislation, or at least separate topics within a single subject, drafted by different committees and linked together. As noted, some parts of an omnibus bill might have been drafted years earlier. The 2008 financial bailout legislation, for example, included the Paul Wellstone and Pete Domenici Mental Health Parity and Addiction Equity Act of 2008, which was originally introduced but failed to make it through Congress in 2007. Even an omnibus bill that is drafted at once and deals with a single subject can have a wide array of authors. The 1990 Clean Air Act, initially drafted by the Bush I Administration, ultimately included the work of at least nine different congressional committees.[19]

Omnibus vehicles also sometimes mask transparency for certain objectives. The 2008 budget bailout, for instance, had a variety of individual goodies attached to it, ranging from subsidies for wooden arrow makers to those for racetrack owners. Omnibus bills also sometimes quietly *reverse* both legislation and delegation. A recent omnibus spending bill undid a controversial Dodd-Frank mandate. With respect to undoing delegation, omnibus bills often contain appropriations riders,

---

[17]Gluck and Bressman (2013), p. 979.

[18]Gluck et al. (2015), p. 1804.

[19]*Ibid.*

which prevent agencies from using funding to carry out previously delegated authority. As another example from the recent spending bill, a rider prohibited the Secretary of the Interior from using congressional appropriations to "issue further rules to place sage-grouse on the Endangered Species List."[20] On the other hand, in 2020, the Supreme Court did reject a congressional effort to halt promised payments to insurers under the Affordable Care Act through use of an appropriations rider.[21]

Omnibus lawmaking leads to what I and co-authors have called omnibus administrative implementation.[22] Several agencies are often made jointly responsible for implementing a single piece of very long legislation. This complicates interpretation down the road for courts trying to determine which agency, if any, deserves control. The rise of omnibus legislation has also given rise to parallel regulatory workarounds. Both the ACA and Dodd-Frank required unprecedented amounts of agency action under tight timelines and intense political scrutiny. That pressure made timely use of the ordinary administrative process impossible and led agencies to themselves innovate unorthodoxly outside formal processes.

Escalating gridlock has made omnibus lawmaking more attractive, both because omnibus laws are bundles of deals and also because of the general sense that anyone interested should get their bill onto any "train leaving the station."

Not only are these omnibus bills growing in length and in statutory and subject complexity, but they are different from ordinary bills for interpretive purposes precisely because of the multitude of drafters and topics. The word "hospital" used on page three of an omnibus bill is unlikely to mean the same thing as the word "hospital" on page 500, because the inserts are coming from different committees, different subjects and different pieces of legislation.

As noted, budget-related legislation has become an ever-more- popular moving legislative train thanks to the special procedural rules that exempt such legislation from the Senate filibuster and the 60-vote-cloture rule. But to the extent that substantive lawmaking is happening in appropriations bills (something congressional rules ostensibly prohibit), there are additional quirks. For example, Congress's rules provide that appropriations legislation mention only the financial outlays, and reserve substantive directions to special legislative history. The U.S. Supreme Court has never acknowledged this special rule and refuses to treat appropriations legislative history differently—that is, it often refuses to look at it—even though Congress treats it uniquely. These gaps are all casualties of a judicial approach that fails to acknowledge legislative realities and a changing legislative process.

---

[20] *Ibid.*, p. 1805.

[21] Maine Community Health Options v. United States, 140 S. Ct. 1308, 1319 (2020).

[22] *Ibid.*, p. 1806.

2.2   Other Kinds of Unorthodox Lawmaking

By way of comparison, it is helpful to understand that omnibus are not the only unorthodox vehicles. For example, emergency legislation—statutes passed under unusual time pressure, often in reaction to a system shock—pose different (indeed, in some ways opposing) challenges down the road than omnibus practices, but are just as unusual.

Unlike potential governance challenges posed by the length and detail of omnibus bills, emergency practices bring challenges in their brevity and generality. There are risks of imputing the same level of attention to detail to legislation enacted under harried circumstances as to legislation that passes through months of deliberation in committee. Consider the September 14, 2001 Authorization for the Use of Military Force (AUMF). Despite its brevity and the unique pressures under which it was enacted—in the wake of the September 11 attacks—the AUMF has (controversially) served as the legal foundation for nearly every dimension of U.S. counterterrorism policy since its enactment, although Congress was almost certainly not thinking ahead to future uses of the AUMF at the time. Emergency financial legislation provides a more recent example; scholars have argued that lawmaking in the shadow of financial crises leads to particularly poor financial policy.[23] In another recent example, the original vehicle for the coronavirus stimulus package, the CARES Act, was a tax bill introduced in the House more than a year earlier. The Senate "hijacked" that bill as a vehicle to circumvent the constitutional requirement that revenue bills must originate in the House.[24]

Like omnibus bills, emergency legislation often bypasses conventional process, including committee deliberation and report writing. The AUMF, for example, passed Congress just 3 days after the September 11 attacks, without going through the foreign relations committees in the House and Senate. Instead, the majority and minority leaders of both chambers conducted the negotiations, and the AUMF was drafted jointly by White House and congressional lawyers beginning just hours after the attacks. As a result, there is no formal legislative history for the AUMF that can be found in committee reports or conference reports, and there was minimal floor debate.[25]

The Hurricane Katrina Relief legislation came on September 2, 2005, just 4 days after the hurricane hit land, under circumstances so rushed there was not even a quorum of senators present for the vote. The Troubled Asset Relief Program (TARP)—the "bailout" legislation responding to the financial crisis—was a 450-page bill that was drafted first by the Secretary of the Treasury as a three-page, $700 billion request, then given to Congress to flesh out the details, and brought to a vote just 14 days after Lehman Brothers filed for bankruptcy. The initial version did not pass the House, but a revised version—sweetened with

---

[23] *Ibid.*, pp. 1807–1808.

[24] Wolfensberger (2020).

[25] Gluck et al. (2015), pp. 1808–1809.

additional pieces of legislation, including the Wellstone Mental Health Parity Act and provisions for rural schools—passed just 4 days later. After watching the Dow Jones industrial average drop more than 700 points after the bill's failure to pass the House for the first time, the House moved quickly on the second turn. In the 113th Congress, many of the bills that were enacted in less than a month were appropriations bills.[26]

For the CARES Act, the COVID-19 relief bill, no formal committee action was taken on the bill, which passed by voice vote in the House, and subsequent relief packages have been waved through by unanimous consent in the Senate.[27] Commentators have criticized various omissions and oversights in the CARES Act, which may be a result of its hurried passage, in particular the lack of restrictions put in place to prevent big businesses from securing relief funds.[28]

As another example, sometimes there is non-emergency fast-track lawmaking. The House can "suspend" its rules; the Senate has "unanimous consent" agreements; these procedures allow for expedited proceedings to bypass conventional process if two-thirds of House members or all Senators agree. Unlike the case in which process is bypassed to fight a true emergency, unanimous consent is usually (but not always) deployed for mundane and non-urgent legislation.

In my work with O'Connell and Po, we detail many other kinds of unorthodoxies.[29] For example, "unorthodox outsourcing" occurs when Congress pushes lawmaking outside of itself and even outside the federal government. "Automatic" lawmaking occurs when Congress establishes procedures that effectively make law without Congress having to do anything other than set up the initial framework. These procedures both overcome the structural veto gates that Congress has created for itself to intentionally slow down lawmaking in most instances—veto gates such as the multistage legislative process or specialized debate and amendment rules—and also allow legislators to avoid having to engage with particularly controversial issues.

The Base Realignment and Closure Commissions (BRAC) of the 1990s are common examples; the ACA's Medicare cost-cutting board, the Independent Payment Advisory Board (IPAB), is a more recent one (now defunct). In both cases, Congress enacted a statute that charges an outside board to decide a difficult question—after all, no Member would agree to closing a naval base in her own state and cutting Medicare is similarly a political third rail. The recommendations of the board take effect automatically unless Congress adopts a joint resolution of disapproval, in the case of BRAC, or a substitute provision to reduce Medicare spending, in the case of IPAB. This mechanism conveniently prevents any legislator from having to say that he or she voted *for* the unpopular policy decision.[30] Fast

---

[26]*Ibid.*, p. 1809.

[27]*Ibid.*

[28]O'Connell et al. (2020).

[29]Gluck et al. (2015).

[30]*Ibid.*, p. 1813.

track-type rules—such as the special rules for the budget process and fast-track trade deals—are related unorthodox workarounds: they likewise push Congress to act more quickly than otherwise possible. These special quick procedures often are salutary pre-committing devices, helping to ensure that Congress gets important work done in a timely fashion.

Statutory waivers are a different kind of unorthodox delegation. The delegates are conventional—federal agencies—but their power is not. Waiver authority gives agencies broad powers to determine whether Congress-made law should effectively be dispensed with altogether. Of late, these waivers have become a common regulatory strategy and have been deployed in a more unorthodox fashion, in part to work around Congress itself. A prominent recent example is President Obama's announcement—expressly motivated by the inability of Congress to pass adequate reforms to the No Child Left behind Act—directing the Department of Education to offer statutory waivers from that Act to states that could devise a better policy plan. The waiver process itself is also a legal black box. For the most part, there are no laws, procedures, or assurances of transparency that regulate the state–federal negotiations that result in these large exemptions from federal statutory mandates.[31]

Tahe President is also an unorthodox legislator. In the textbook account of American legislation, the President is understood as the last stop (the signature) in the U.S. Constitution's Article I, Section 7 path to formal law. In contrast, the unorthodox President takes on aspects of Congress himself, shaping legislation and sometimes using executive tools to manipulate the congressional process. Indeed, today, the White House is often the first, not the last, step in the legislative process. It frequently initiates and drafts legislation—as it did, for example, with the Dodd-Frank financial reform legislation; or intervenes with high-level summits during the drafting process to save legislation—as it did, for example, with the ACA.

The White House can also take less direct administrative action that sometimes is overtly aimed at affecting the legislative process. Sometimes such efforts are aimed at spurring Congress itself to legislate. President Obama's directive on cybersecurity provides one example. Issued because Congress had failed to legislate in the area, the directive itself—as intended—galvanized the business community to push Congress to pass its own law, because the business community could shape and influence legislation in ways it could not shape an executive directive. Conversely, the President may use such tools to preempt legislation. For instance, President Reagan's famous Executive Order 12,532, imposing sanctions on South Africa headed off a stronger proposal with congressional momentum that would have frustrated his policy of "constructive engagement." In such contexts, presidential action can, often intentionally, take the wind out of the sails of related congressional efforts.[32]

Modern Presidents also have increasingly used executive orders and memoranda as substitutes for failed domestic-policy legislative efforts. President Obama's "We

---

[31] *Ibid.*, pp. 1817–1818.The Affordable Care Act offer an important exception, with novel process requirements for Medicaid waivers.

[32] *Ibid.*, p. 1820.

Can't Wait" initiative—a self-proclaimed campaign of unilateral executive action in the face of historic gridlock—espoused this philosophy.

Finally, at the state level, ballot referenda and initiatives, are another increasingly utilized workaround to legislative inertia.

2.3 Drivers and Tradeoffs

In the United States, some drivers of unorthodox lawmaking are obvious, like legislative gridlock.[33] Sinclair's path-breaking work identifies a hostile political climate and gridlock as key causal factors that have altered the context in which Congress functions.[34] The Gluck/Bressman study of congressional drafters corroborates that leaders have been forced to modify traditional legislative practices to achieve their goals in the current hyper-partisan environment.[35]

Institutional structures also have enormous influence on the modern lawmaking context and are often underappreciated by legal scholars. The increasingly overlapping jurisdictions of congressional committees likely contributes to the rise in omnibus policymaking. Although Congress heavily consolidated its committee structure in the Legislative Reorganization Act of 1946, since then, subcommittees have proliferated, and existing committees have fought to expand their turf. For instance, approximately eighty committees and subcommittees have jurisdiction over some part of homeland security.

This horizontal complexity not only spurs omnibus policymaking, but also opens the door to strong, often-unorthodox coordinators. The Gluck/Bressman study documents how multiple committees working on a single bill are often not in communication with one another; committees even have different drafting practices from one another.[36] Party leadership has taken on the critical coordinating role as a result, but the increased involvement of party leadership has generally also meant less emphasis on traditional committees and traditional process.

With respect to tradeoffs, the main benefit is that *policy actually gets made*. Of course, not everyone agrees that more laws are a benefit, but most of the unorthodoxies I have identified—including omnibus deals, workarounds, and emergency policy—can be viewed at least some of the time as increasing social welfare in this way, and as overcoming barriers to doing so in difficult political or institutional circumstances. Sinclair herself, although originally critical of unorthodox lawmaking, became more favorably disposed for precisely this reason.

In at least some instances, unorthodox practices may promote better policymaking. Outsourcing policy to states, private actors, and

---

[33]Binder (2015).

[34]Sinclair (2017).

[35]Gluck and Bressman (2013).

[36]*Ibid.*, p. 750.

congressionally-created commissions like the IPAB or BRAC can be an act of delegating to entities with deeper expertise, and fewer regulatory constraints—although it could alternatively empower special interests.

Of course, there may be substantial quality costs to rushed or log-rolled policymaking. Among these costs are concerns about excessive mistakes and the inability of the professional analysts and drafters inside of Congress to do their work. For example, the Offices of Legislative Counsel, Congress's professional drafters, did not have a chance to clean up the Affordable Care Act before passage. The Congressional Budget Office, Congress's budget scorers, did not have a chance to provide a financial estimate for the CARES Act until after the bill had passed.[37]

Legitimacy values also come into play. The values that are common currency for courts—public participation, transparency, and accountability—are all implicated here and pose some of the biggest challenges for unorthodox practices. When lawmakers bypass committees, floor debate, and other stages of the process, they skip typical opportunities for public and expert input or move them earlier in the process and behind closed doors. Moreover, the paucity or confused nature of the legislative history for many unorthodox laws also deprives both the general public and experts working in a field of important explanatory reports about complicated legislation. The textbook process of approving and amending bills has largely been replaced by the practice of working out conflicts before bills hit the floor. Congressional staff routinely use a new term—"preconference"—to describe the now-common practice of resolving differences between House and Senate versions of bills before any votes. These behind-the-scenes efforts to evolve legislation are designed to reduce the number of votes that must be taken (for instance, any differences between bills enacted by the House and Senate must be resolved in conference and voted on again). But without this public record of discussion and amendment, judges tasked with interpreting statutes have less information about what was animating Congress in its work.

With respect to accountability, legislation and regulations that rely on workarounds or nonfederal and nonpublic processes are not subject to the same transparency and accountability checks as government agencies. Presidential directives making policy are sometimes unreviewable in court.[38] Finally, from the perspective of the public and democratic accountability, because omnibus bills are aggregations of different committees' work, individual policy decisions also may be less accountable, and the final piece of legislation, as a whole, may be impossible for any member of Congress or the public to completely absorb or answer for.

---

[37]Elis (2020).

[38]Stack (2010).

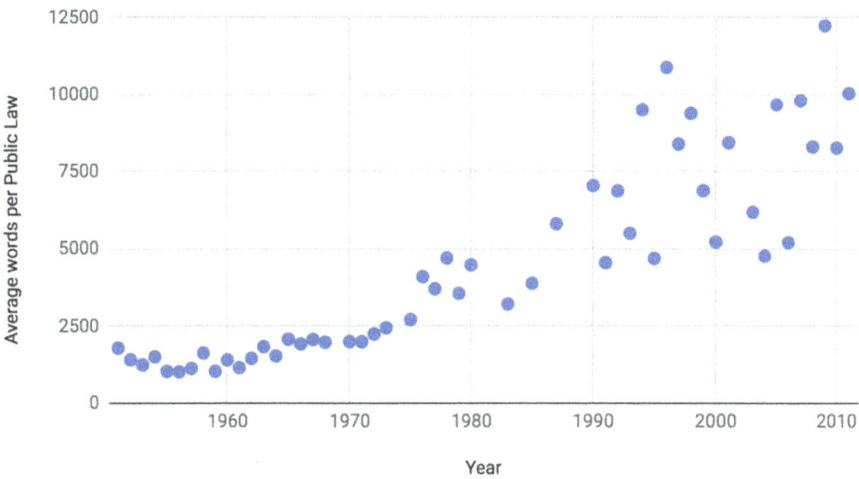

Fig. 1 Average words per public law over time

3 The Increasing Complexity of the U.S. Code

Statutes have grown steadily and exponentially in in the United States (Fig. 1).

According to a Brookings report, the number of bills introduced in the House in the 115th Congress (2017–2018) was 7542, compared with over 10,000 in the years from 1953 to 1978.[39] The highest was more than 22,000 bills in 1967, at the height of the "Great Society" legislative period.[40] Numbers remained over 15,000 for the next decade and then gradually declined to current levels. The Senate story is in parallel in terms of the trends, but the absolute numbers are lower, most likely due to the Senate's smaller size and more significant procedural barriers to legislation. The 115th Congress saw 3,874 bills introduced in the Senate, compared with over 4000 in most of the years from 1953 to 1976.[41]

The same report details that in the 80th Congress (1947–1948), 906 public bills were enacted, averaging 2.5 pages each. The highest was the 84th Congress (1955–1956) with 1028 bills passed averaging 1.8 pages each. In the 112th Congress, 283 bills were passed at 15.6 average pages each and in the 115th Congress, 442 bills were passed averaging 17.81 average pages each.[42] The number of pages of statutes in the 115th Congress, 7872, was significantly higher as compared with the 80th Congress, in which total pages of statutes numbered around 2000. Pages in the Federal Register—which includes legislative debates and administrative

---

[39]Reynolds (2019).

[40]*Ibid.*

[41]*Ibid.*

[42]*Ibid.*

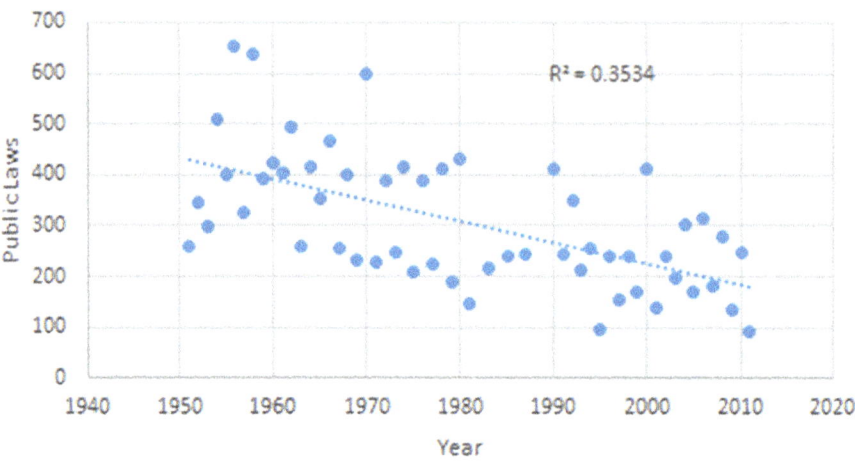

Fig. 2 Number of public laws per year

rulemaking—skyrocketed from 14,736 in 1946 to 97,069 in 2016.[43] These statistics indicate that we now have fewer, but longer, statutes.

Trying to get at the same story in a different way, with different search methodology, we found the number of public laws per year has decreased in amount and variance in a somewhat linear fashion; however, the average words per public law has increased seemingly exponentially in amount, and has increased in variance, suggesting an increase in statutory complexity (Fig. 2).

A different measure is the absolute number of internal cross references in a statute in a given year, because one important manifestation of this complexity is that statutes have become impossible to understand as narratives. For countries, like the U.S., that adopt "text-only" approaches as the dominant mode of interpretation and assume that courts can read the law, the rise of cross references is a critical development interfering with that project. As with average word per statute, the number of absolute cross references appears to have exponentially increased in amount and in variance (Fig. 3).

A similar, even clearer pattern, appears for the number of cross references per public law (Fig. 4).

Breaking the data out over different periods, the major shift appears to have happened in 1975—a few years after the Legislative Reorganization Act of 1970, which invigorated the committee system (Fig. 5).

---

[43] *Ibid.*

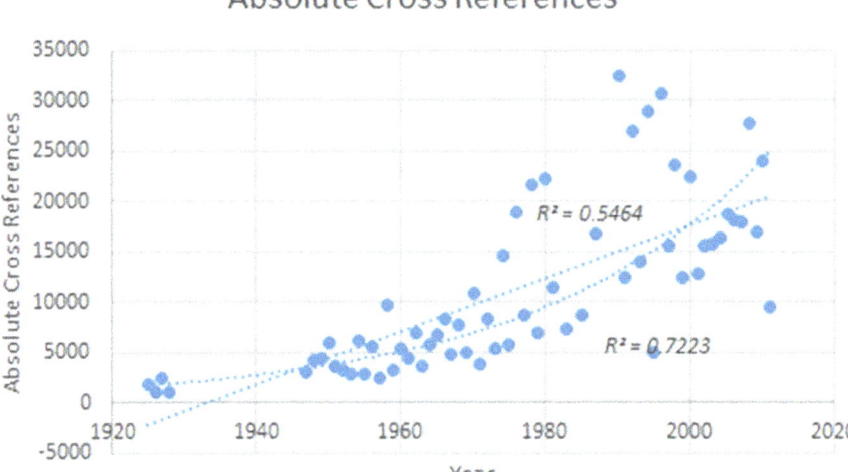

Fig. 3 Absolute cross-references. The higher R-squared values for the exponential trend line and the lower for the linear trend line

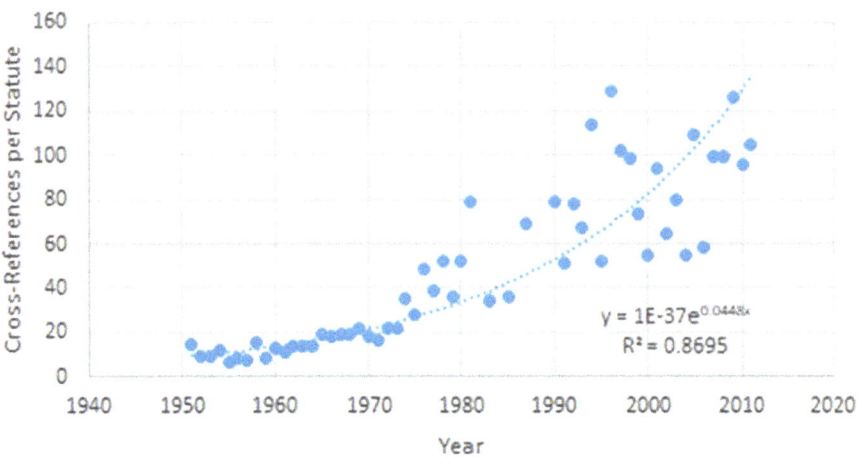

Fig. 4 Cross-references per statute

3.1 Drivers

The use of the filibuster in the Senate is one potential driver of changes in statutory complexity. Catherine Fisk and Erwin Chemerinsky note that as filibusters have led to a decline in committee power, activity by non-committee members has

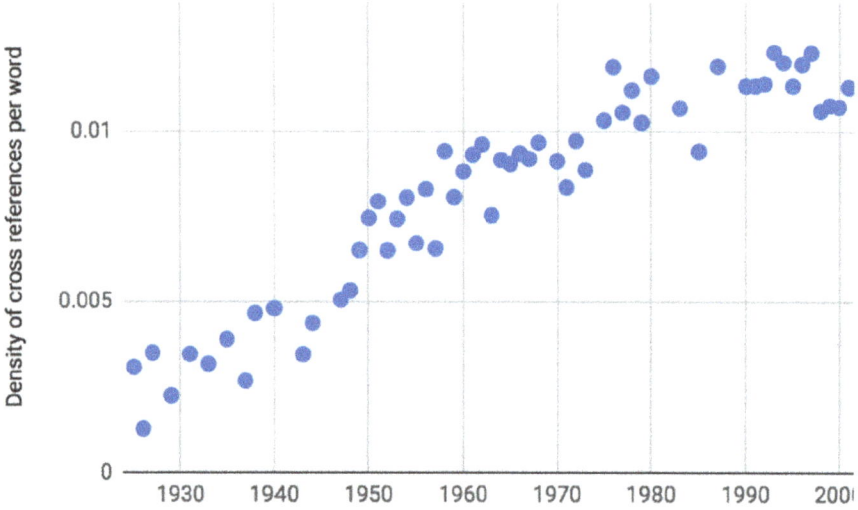

Fig. 5 Cross references per word over time

increased.[44] Non-committee members now more frequently introduce significant amendments to legislation, which in turn creates more statutory complexity.

By contrast, since the budget process is exempt from the filibuster process, budget reconciliation bills have become more complicated as senators try insert substantive provisions into those bills (despite the requirement that reconciliation bills be germane to the federal budget).

Gregory Koger documented the incidence of filibusters in the Senate over the course of the twentieth century. He found sharp peaks during the debates surrounding the passage of the Civil Rights Act of 1964 and during President Clinton's first 2 years in office (Fig. 6).[45]

We looked at more recent data and found a sharp rise in the number of cloture motions, which are required to close debate. This may be a good proxy for the rise of filibusters (Fig. 7).

The number of Unanimous Consent Agreements (UC agreements), which limit debate, has also risen in the latter half of the twentieth century. Steven Smith and Marcus Flathman equate the increased use of UC agreements with an increase in closed-door bargaining and the advent of a more individualistic, as opposed to communitarian, Senate.[46]

---

[44]Fisk and Chemerinsky (1997).

[45]Koger (2010).

[46]Smith and Flathman (1989).

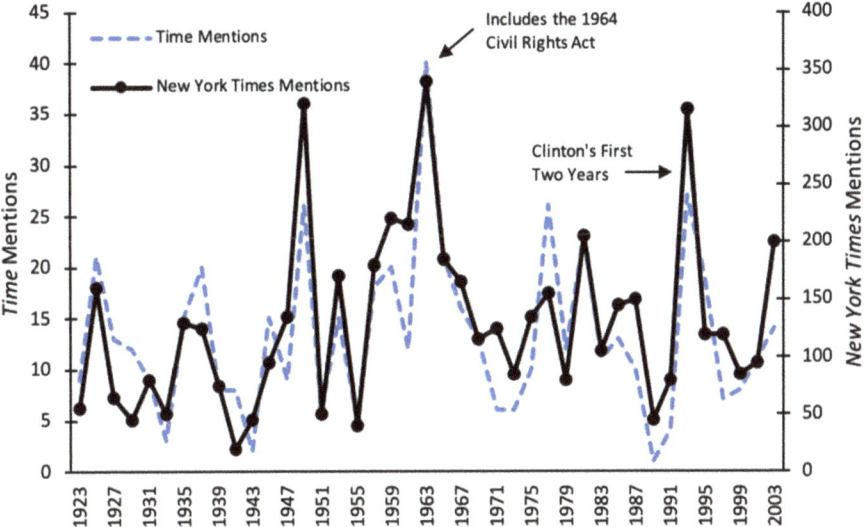

Fig. 6 Koger (2010)

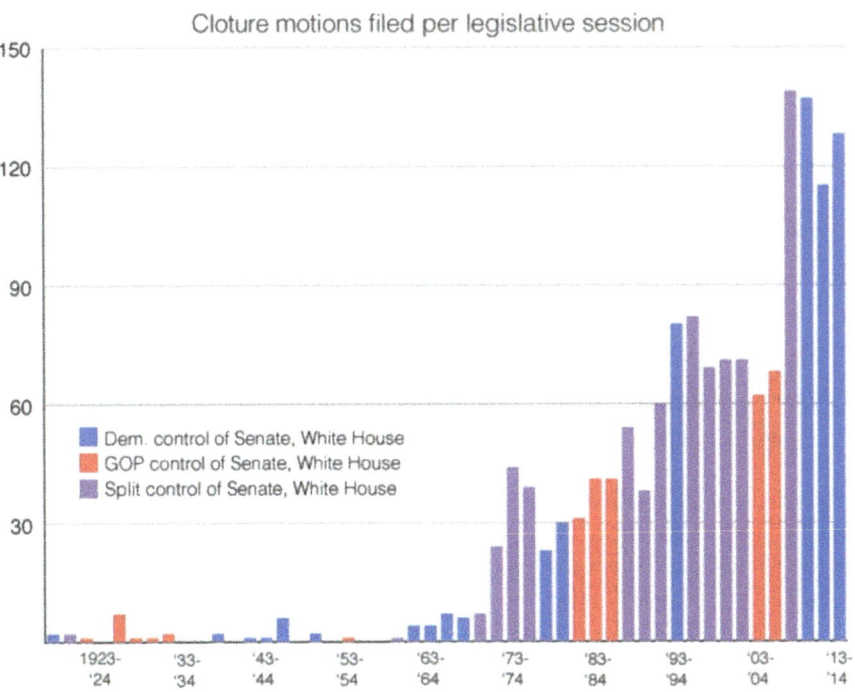

Fig. 7 Rise of the filibuster

4   The Advent of Professional Drafters

The underappreciated role of the Offices of Legislative Counsel in the House and the Senate—which were founded in 1919 and have since readily expanded—was first theorized and studied in the Gluck/Bressman empirical study of congressional drafting and further explored in the Gluck/Cross study of the congressional bureaucracy. The effect of the creation of these drafting offices on the increased complexity of legislation remains something of an open research question.

A 1975 report by the House Commission on Information and Facilities regarding the House Office of Legislative Counsel, concluded that the Office of Legislative Counsel's assignments from committees nearly doubled from the 91st Congress to the 93rd Congress (roughly 1970–1975).[47] Assignments from members of Congress also increased nearly 20% in that short timespan.[48] This explosion in workload closely tracks the second Legislative Reorganization Act. Indeed, the Commission's report noted, "there is clear consensus of opinion . . . that the increased workload is attributable to the increase in the number of professional staff of the committees and subcommittees and the autonomy of the latter."[49] This expansion was part of a broader trend during the 1970s when Congress, seeking to reclaim its lawmaking power from the executive, allocated greater resources to the growth and development of its own nonpartisan support institutions.[50] Here we see a confluence of process- and people-based changes that likely had significant ramifications for drafting and statutory complexity at the inflection point of the early 1970s (Fig. 8).

4.1   Implications for Judicial Review

Finally, what follows are the implications of these changes for judicial statutory interpretation.

4.1.1   New Empirical Work on the Relationship Between the Courts and Congress

Jurists and academics on all sides of the American debate over statutory interpretation lay claim to the notion that their method best reflects congressional process or reflects a set of shared conventions of which Congress is aware and in whose shadow Congress drafts. None of those claims has ever been supported with empirical proof

---

[47]H. Comm'n on Immigration and Facilities, Staff Requirements of the House Legislative Counsel, H. Doc. 94-327 at 4.

[48]*Ibid.*

[49]*Ibid.* at 5.

[50]Gluck and Cross (2020).

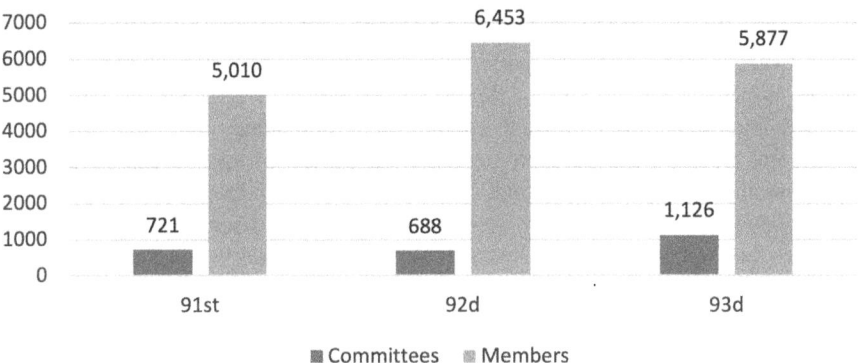

Fig. 8 H. Comm'n on immigration and facilities, staff requirements of the House Legislative Counsel, H. Doc. 94-327 at 4

and recent studies have proved them incorrect. In fact, the courts generally have not considered how Congress works, or how Congress has changed.

The Gluck/Bressman 2011–2012 survey of 137 congressional counsels across different committees, offices, and political parties is the first and still only major study to evaluate the empirical validity of these claims.[51] Every counsel was asked 171 questions, which aimed to examine the drafters' knowledge and use of canons of interpretation applied by the courts and legislative history. The questions also sought to elicit information about the legislative process and drafters' views of the role of courts in interpretation.[52]

Gluck and Bressman did not inquire into Congress's self-organization—including the committee system, unorthodox lawmaking or other nonpartisan, expert support offices inside of Congress like legislative counsel. Even so, these structural and organizational influences on legislative drafting were repeatedly volunteered by interviewees as significant. For instance, 45% of respondents emphasized the committee system as the fundamental organizing principle of congressional drafting that is critical in understanding a range of matters—from agency delegation to obstacles to linguistic consistency.[53] Similarly, more than 83% of staffers volunteered comments that understanding the role of the Offices of Legislative Counsel—the nonpartisan drafting offices in the House and the Senate that turn policy deals into statutory language—is essential to understanding how statutes are written and what

---

[51] Gluck and Bressman (2013).

[52] *Ibid.*

[53] *Ibid.*, p. 748.

is often the distance between the big-picture statutory policy decisions made by Members and high-level staff and the individual words that wind up on the page.[54]

The majority of respondents confirmed that omnibus bills are different from appropriations bills, which are different from ordinary legislation. They reported the pervasiveness of unorthodox lawmaking processes, and how these processes shift power from committees to party leadership. Respondents also noted that statutes shepherded through by party leaders had less and lower quality legislative history because leadership lacks the policy expertise of committee leaders and bundled legislative deals are less conducive to producing legislative history.[55] House and Senate rules prohibit regulatory language in appropriations text, so directions about how to use the funds have to be included in the legislative history.[56] Appropriations legislative history, on the other hand, was described as more important than any other legislative history. Tellingly, Legislative Counsel drafts no legislative history except in the appropriations context—a signal of its significance.[57] The study also corroborated the concern that unorthodox processes lead to more gaps and errors that may arise later.[58]

Most respondents emphasized the increasingly frequent departures from the regular order. Most of the canons employed by the courts—ranging from federalism canons that protect areas of traditional state authority from intrusion by the national government, to consistency presumptions, to presumptions against repetitive language—were not familiar or salient to congressional drafters, and were deemed by the drafters to reflect unrealistic assumptions about the legislative process. Accordingly, these canons fail to capture drafting practices as they actually are. For instance, organizational barriers like the committee system, lengthy multi-drafter statutes, and bundled legislative deals prevent consistency across statutes.[59] In addition, congressional committees and nonpartisan support staff—including the Congressional Research Service, the Joint Tax Commission, Legislative Counsel, and the Government Accountability Office—are largely organized into groups by subject-matter specialty. As a result, staff is not focused on whole-code consistency.

More recent empirical work by Gluck and Jesse Cross extends the Gluck/Bressman story deeper into what we call the "*congressional bureaucracy*," utilizing an interview study of high-level staff from all of the nonpartisan support institutions in Congress that play a role in the drafting process. That study corroborates the Gluck/Bressman findings about the impact of unorthodox lawmaking procedures on how statutes are created and ultimately read. Legislative Counsels confirmed that unorthodox processes like foregoing conference make it more difficult to fix problems in bills.[60] Respondents vividly described the process of ripping apart budget

---

[54]*Ibid.*, p. 739.

[55]Gluck and Bressman (2013), p. 757.

[56]Gluck and Bressman (2013), p. 761.

[57]Gluck and Bressman (2013), p. 980.

[58]Gluck and Bressman (2013), p. 763.

[59]*Ibid.*, p. 936.

[60]*Ibid.*

reconciliation bills to comply with the Byrd rule, with the result that remaining language may seem incoherent or inconsistent.[61] Other features of the legislative process, like the cost and revenue analyses produced by the Congressional Budget Office and the Joint Tax Committee, were emphasized as critical inputs that Members rely on in assessing statutory meaning. But these inputs are largely ignored by courts when interpreting statutes.

4.1.2 Utilizing Knowledge of Congress's Process in Doctrine and Theory

These institutional features, including the new unorthodoxies canvassed, are Congress's own creations. Congress organizes itself into committees. It has created a variety of statutory vehicles—omnibus, appropriation, and single-subject bills—that differ significantly from one another in structures, linguistic conventions, and legislative processes. The U.S. Constitution explicitly gives Congress control over its own procedures.[62] But courts smooth over the effects of the very institutional structures that Congress itself has erected when they impose perfection and uniformity on statutes that the legislative process does not in fact reflect.

What would an approach more tethered to the realities of modern American lawmaking actually look like? We have seen a few tantalizing glimmers of what judicial review in Congress's shadow might amount to in the small handful of exceptional cases that have indeed paid some attention to Congress. Most of these cases involve President Obama's major health care law, the Affordable Care Act (ACA). This is largely because the ACA is an extremely consequential law, went through an unorthodox process, and has been challenged in the Supreme Court an unprecedented number of times—seven—in less than a decade.

Of these challenges to the ACA, the 2015 *King v. Burwell* case is most important.[63] The case involved, at best, sloppy legislative drafting and, at worst, an error in amalgamating two drafts of the law produced by different committees without the chance for cleanup. That error, read literally, would have rendered the ACA's insurance markets dysfunctional. The case posed the greatest test yet to the modern Supreme Court's approach to statutory interpretation—a hyper-literal approach that does not account for the vagaries of the legislative process and has no consistent approach to statutory mistakes. ACA opponents hoped to take advantage of the Court's unrealistic presumptions about legislation to impose perfection on a very imperfect statute—one that went through a highly unorthodox process and so did not have the opportunity to be reviewed for errors before the final vote.

In a watershed moment for the Court, Chief Justice Roberts' opinion acknowledged the statute's unusual legislative process and therefore refused to read the text literally, instead saying that the Court must "do its best" to read the statute in line

---

[61]*Ibid.*

[62]U.S. Const. art. I, § 5.

[63]King v. Burwell, 135 S. Ct. 2480 (2015).

with Congress' broader "plan."[64] The Court still got some things wrong, however: Most importantly, the characterization of the ACA's legislative process as unusual specifically because a portion of the statute went through the reconciliation process—and also the charge that the ACA was undeliberated. Not so. Many statutes before the ACA had gone through reconciliation (and only a small piece of the ACA did); and although the ACA was rushed at the end, prior to that point it had been exceedingly deliberated, for 2 years across an unprecedented five congressional committees, and drafted with the close assistance of Legislative Counsel.[65]

King was the first open rejection of textualism in favor of legislative realism in modern American interpretive history. Whether *King* was a one-off special case for a special law is still unclear, although the Court has since seemed to return to its textualism-as-usual approach. But *King* provides a window into what could be. Indeed, as noted, in 2020, the Court again applied a legislative-realist approach in yet another ACA case concerning the interpretation of an appropriations rider, and held that language buried in a later rider should not be read to repeal by implication an earlier mandate in the ACA's initial authorizing legislation.[66]

Justice Sotomayor has cited the new empirical studies of Congress as evidence that committee reports are a particularly reliable source of legislative history, including in the view of legislative staffers themselves.[67] Justice Kagan likewise cited this empirical work to rebut an interpretive presumption—the presumption against redundancy—to suggest that Congress might have intentionally used redundant language across two different sections of the U.S. Code "to satisfy audiences other than courts."[68] And the newest Justice, Brett Kavanaugh, wrote an important opinion while still on the lower federal appellate court citing empirical evidence about Congress as a reason to disfavor the presumption against redundant language.[69] He has continued to indicate this view in one of his recently authored Supreme Court opinions.[70] Then Judge-Kavanaugh also cited the new empirical work in support of the administrative law doctrine that Congress does not intend to delegate questions of major political or economic significance to administrative agencies.[71]

The lower federal courts also have begun to absorb the empirical findings. Several judges on the D.C Circuit—the court of second highest importance to the Supreme Court—have explicitly relied on these empirical studies of congressional drafting to

---

[64]*Ibid.* at 2492.

[65]Gluck and Cross (2020).

[66]Maine Community Health Options, supra.

[67]*See* Digital Realty Tr., Inc. v. Somers, 138 S. Ct. 767, 782–83 (2018) (Sotomayor, J., concurring).

[68]*See* Yates v. United States, 574 U.S. 528, 562 (2015) (Kagan, Scalia, Kennedy & Thomas, JJ., dissenting).

[69]*See* Loving v. I.R.S., 742 F.3d 1013, 1019 (D.C. Cir. 2014).

[70]*See* Barton v. Barr, 140 S. Ct. 1442, 1453 (2020) ("[R]edundancies are common in statutory drafting—sometimes in a congressional effort to be doubly sure, sometimes because of congressional inadvertence or lack of foresight, or sometimes simply because of the shortcomings of human communication.").

[71]*See* United States Telecom Ass'n v. Fed. Commc'ns Comm'n, 855 F.3d 381, 422 (D.C. Cir. 2017) (Kavanaugh, J., dissenting).

change approaches to rules like the consultation of legislative history.[72] Courts on the Second, Fourth and Fifth Circuits have likewise started to consider this work.[73]

Looking ahead, one might expect, for instance, to see courts thinking about whether it actually makes sense to apply the rule against superfluities to statutes that are long and cobbled together by different committees, or other presumptions of perfection already discussed—such as presumptions of consistency, legislative omniscience, and precise drafting—to omnibus and emergency laws. In the increasingly common statutes that aggregate several single subject bills, *lesser* presumptions of coherence and against redundancy might make the most sense.

In the reconciliation statutes that were once unorthodox but are now commonly used to legislate, consistency cannot even be presumed within individual statutory provisions.[74] To comply with the Byrd rule, which is applied on a provision-by-provision basis, drafters will often cram unrelated rules into a single provision, a practice that renders questionable, in that context, courts' penchant for attributing special consistency to language within a single section. Thus, when interpreting reconciliation bills, courts should not construe statutes to clearly violate the Byrd Rule, and should keep in mind the budgetary windows and year-end fiscal rules that such bills are often contorted to fit.[75]

Finally, the increasingly overlapping jurisdictions of congressional committees and the language-slicing employed so that bills will be referred to certain committees can have implications for interpretation. For example, as suggested in the Gluck/Bressman study, statutory ambiguities could be resolved to retain jurisdiction with the drafting committee.[76] Jurisdictional referrals could also be considered by courts as direct evidence of statutory meaning.[77]

---

[72]*See, e.g.*, Council for Urological Interests v. Burwell, 790 F.3d 212, 233 (D.C. Cir. 2015) (Henderson, J., dissenting) ("The Congress often uses legislative history, rather than the text, to restrain agencies in the exercise of their delegated authority"); *see also* United States v. Torres, 910 F.3d 1245, 1247–48 (D.C. Cir. 2018) (Williams, J., dissenting) (noting that even the Gluck/Bressman study, the leading empirical work challenging the presumption that Congress imports prior judicial interpretations when it borrows a phrase from an earlier statute, recognizes the accuracy of that presumption where the relevant statutes are closely related).

[73]United States v. Koutsostamatis, 956 F.3d 301, 307 (5th Cir. 2020); Zarda v. Altitude Express, Inc., 883 F.3d 100, 130 (2d Cir. 2018), *cert. granted sub nom.* Altitude Exp., Inc. v. Zarda, 139 S. Ct. 1599 (2019); King v. Burwell, 759 F.3d 358, 378 (4th Cir. 2014), *aff'd*, 135 S. Ct. 2480 (2015).

[74]*Ibid.*

[75]*Ibid.*

[76]Gluck and Bressman (2013), p. 781.

[77]Gluck and Cross (2020).

4.2   Legislative History

Similarly, courts might pay less attention to legislative history, or its absence, for statutes that did not go through committee or that are the product of different bills drafted at different times. Courts should expect that the legislative history accompanying omnibus statutes will be of lower quality or altogether nonexistent and should not attribute too much to this fact.

On the other hand, courts might pay *more* attention to appropriations legislative history, given its importance to legislative drafters constrained by House and Senate rules preventing them from including regulatory language in the bill itself. Understanding the special nature of appropriations legislative history might make courts think twice about old chestnut rulings like *Tennessee Valley Authority v. Hill*, where the Court relied on the placement of explanatory material in the legislative history of an appropriations statute to disregard it.[78]

4.3   Legislative Mistakes

Additionally, the Court must develop a coherent doctrine of mistakes to respond to the increases in legislative errors that will likely continue to result from diminishing opportunities to fix mistakes, including the disappearing conference committee process. Currently, the Court refuses to fix even obvious errors as long as the statute can be read in plain English, with some exceptions made for particularly high-stakes cases like the challenge to the ACA. Given that the rise of unorthodox processes has led to a higher expectation of gaps and errors, courts must do better to develop a more rational and well-considered approach to the problem.[79]

4.4   Severability

Finally, some judges have recently tried to use the very existence of unorthodox lawmaking—and especially the omnibus process—to devalue a statute's content, and to upset longstanding interpretive doctrines. The most salient example, again from the ACA, concerns the rules governing when an unconstitutional portion of a statute can be severed from the rest. The dissenters in the 2012 case *NFIB v. Sebelius*, the first constitutional challenge to the ACA, argued "

> "When confronted with such an omnibus bill, "a so-called 'Christmas tree,' a law to which many nongermane ornaments have been attached . . . the proper rule must be that when the

---

[78]Gluck and Bressman (2013), p. 981.

[79]Gluck and Cross (2020).

tree no longer exists the ornaments are superfluous. We have no reliable basis for knowing which pieces of the Act would have passed on their own."[80]

In the view of the dissenters, the unconstitutionality of a major provision "require [d] the invalidation of the Affordable Care Act's other provisions."[81] While admirable in its attempt to think about different kinds of statutes as different from one another, the dissent's proposed rule is untethered to Congress in a different way; namely, it is a stark departure from the longtanding presumption, incorporated into Congress's own drafting manuals, that statutes are presumed severable unless Congress expresses a clear intent otherwise.[82] In most cases, it is unlikely Congress would want an entire statute struck down, especially an omnibus statute's bundle of deals.

Relatedly, in *California v. Texas*, the most recent challenge to the ACA, the district court opined that a provision of the ACA amended through the 2017 tax bill was of less importance than earlier provisions of the ACA because the amendment was part of an omnibus reconciliation bill.[83] Federal courts have never before given some legislation less legal weight merely because of the vehicle through which it was passed—making this an interesting, though likely misguided, application of a realist eye toward Congress.

4.5 Broader Implications

Of course, courts could dispense with any pretense of reflecting Congress's actual practices at all. Courts could instead embrace formalism and simply conceive of interpretive doctrine as a set of shared but fictitious conventions that facilitate interbranch communication. And it may be the case that an upshot of recognizing the widespread phenomenon of unorthodox lawmaking is precisely that: perhaps a more formalist, coordinating role for doctrine is the best that courts can do in a messy lawmaking environment. Harvard Law School Dean and noted textualist John Manning takes this position.[84]

Nevertheless, the idea that interpretive doctrine serves, or could serve, as a coordinating mechanism is an empirical claim that has little support. The Gluck/ Bressman staffers did not know many of the most common canons of construction and, even with respect to those they did know, often resisted them as conventions

---

[80]Nat'l Fed'n of Indep. Bus. v. Sebelius, 567 U.S. 519, 705 (2012) (Scalia, Kennedy, Thomas & Alito, JJ., dissenting).

[81]*Id.* at 706 (Scalia, Kennedy, Thomas & Alito, JJ., dissenting).

[82]*See* Alaska Airlines, Inc. v. Brock, 480 U.S. 678, 685 (1987) ("The more relevant inquiry in evaluating severability is whether the statute will function in a manner consistent with the intent of Congress.").

[83]Texas v. United States, 340 F. Supp. 3d 579, 616–17 (N.D. Tex. 2018).

[84]Manning (2015).

that Congress could or would ever adopt.[85] The canons cannot serve as a common language across branches if Congress does not know or follow them. The Gluck/Bressman staffers emphasized institutional obstacles to coordinated drafting—particularly time pressures, the omnibus process and the lack of communication across committees—that make many judicial presumptions unrealistic.

And as importantly, American courts have never been consistent enough in their own application of statutory interpretation doctrine for those doctrines to truly perform a coordinating function, even if Congress were game. The formalist project—typified by but not limited to Justice Antonin Scalia's brand of textualism—has been largely a failure in statutory interpretation because even its staunchest judicial supporters have been unwilling to carry it out. Formalism only works as a second-best interpretive regime that sacrifices accurate approximation of congressional practice in favor of efficient, and objective, system-coordinating rules if the rules deployed are clear, sufficiently limited in number to be predictable, and adopted by all involved as shared coordinating conventions.

None of this holds for even strict-textualist statutory interpretation today in the United States. When it comes to system coordinating, or the lack thereof, it is not just that empirical work reveals that Congress and the courts are not on the same page with respect to interpretive conventions. Even the courts, acting alone, are not faithfully formalist in their interpretive approach. I make this argument at length in other work.[86] Here, in brief: The rules that judges employ are too numerous to be predictably chosen; there is no ranking among them; and they are not treated as black-letter, precedential law. That is, the same interpretive rules and methodology do not apply to the same questions from case to case, even where the same statute is being construed—as a formalist approach should logically require. Our current rules thus can find little justification in their potential to advance a formalist, rule-of-law vision.

For these reasons, Judge Frank Easterbrook, one of the most highly regarded, and textualist, jurists on the bench, likewise has called the modern American approach an "absence of method."[87] He too implies that pure formalism in statutory interpretation does not exist and might be impossible.[88]

What then does justify the approach that we have—an approach nonetheless very heavily influenced by the textualist-formalists and their canons of construction? One set of possible justifications disconnected from Congress is that textualism might vindicate public-regarding values like notice or constitutional-level values like federalism, even if it does not approximate the legislative process as it actually is. But American courts have never been willing to embrace such an activist view of their own work when it comes to statutes. Instead, they continue to claim they are

---

[85] Gluck and Bressman (2013), pp. 926–947.

[86] Gluck (2015).

[87] Easterbrook (2017).

[88] *Ibid.*

mere mirrors reflecting actual congressional practice, and so the legitimacy of our current approach still turns, in large part, on understanding how Congress works.

And as for due process of lawmaking, we are not close there either. I was intrigued to learn from Ittai Bar-Siman-Tov's characteristically excellent work about a recent Israeli Supreme Court decision that invalidated an omnibus law based on a deficient process.[89] While American courts will invalidate *administrative* rules based on lack of process, ever since the Supreme Court's 1892 holding in *Field v. Clark*, the courts have largely refused to enter the sausage factory when it comes to *congressional* legislation.[90] They have expressly refused to consider whether Congress engages in "due process of lawmaking"—for example, whether Congress was sufficiently deliberate, transparent, or coherent in the enactment of a piece of legislation—in evaluating a statute's legitimacy or even its meaning. Notably, courts do scrutinize Congress's reasons in other contexts, especially when it comes to checking Congress' exercise of its constitutional authority—for instance, in deciding whether legislation is rational under the Fourteenth Amendment or sufficiently affects the interstate economy pursuant the Commerce Clause. In a sense, these kinds of evaluations bear some similarity to considerations of due process in lawmaking. But regard for legislative due process is limited to those contexts, never discussed in those terms, and fails to inform the bread and butter of judicial statutory interpretation.

And yet, and despite its public stance to the contrary, the Court does in fact attempt to influence the legislative process in subtle ways. Many of the Court's interpretive rules aim to improve how Congress drafts. Indeed, textualists have long argued that one salutary effect of a text-centric approach is that it teaches Congress to draft better the next time. Take one very popular type of interpretive presumption—the Court's "clear statement" rules requiring Congress to make its intention known with unmistakable clarity on particularly salient matters, such as federalism. Such rules are designed to make legislative drafters put their colleagues in Congress on notice, rather than bury contentious moves in ambiguous statutory language. Justice Kennedy in *Boumediene v. Bush* described these rules as helping "Congress ... make an informed legislative choice."[91]

My empirical work calls into question whether these rules are actually doing what courts want them to—if Congress notices or cares. But even still, the Court's interest in them—along with the small steps some jurists have already taken to engage with the new empirics—reveal that courts are capable of, and sometimes even interested in, engaging more with the lawmaking process.

---

[89]See Bar-Siman-Tov (2015, 2019, 2021).
[90]Marshall Field & Co. v. Clark, 143 U.S. 649, 672 (1892).
[91]Boumediene v. Bush, 553 U.S. 723, 738 (2008).

5 Conclusion

I do not suggest that the questions this chapter raises are easily answered. Even if courts were to try to understand and reflect Congress in their work, Congress—as the empirics show—changes over time, and no two statutes will ever be the same even if they pass through similar processes. Unorthodox lawmaking, including omnibus lawmaking, is not an unmitigated negative; rather, it is an adaptation to the changing complexities of the American political system and the expectations facing today's Congress. And it enables Congress to get the work of government done under these circumstances.

The rise of unorthodox lawmaking is also a symptom that things are coming to a tipping point, and congressional procedure in the United States may well be heading in a new direction. It has been 50 years since the last congressional reorganization and reconfiguration of professional staff, and it is not unrealistic to think that another revolution may be coming. The American public does not like to hear that statutes are being pushed through Congress in the dead of night. It does not seem likely that the current situation can hold. But the courts are not prepared for change—or at least seem determined to ignore it. Federal courts are extremely reluctant to engage with the dirty details of the legislative process, to consistently adhere to formalist rules that would bind them in future cases, or even to talk openly about the nature of the judicial power and role with respect to the legislative process. Given such reluctance, even a forthcoming congressional-process revolution might not change the practice of statutory interpretation. Without a fundamental shift in our approach, Blackstone's way is likely to continue to rule, even for generations who have long forgotten who he was.

References

Bar-Siman-Tov I (2015) The role of courts in improving the legislative process. Theory Pract Legis 3:295–313

Bar-Siman-Tov I (2019) Quantinsky v. the Knesset in the matter of the third apartment tax: a necessary decision or an unjustified "Major Deviation" from the case law? Bar-Ilan U Law Rev 32:877–906

Bar-Siman-Tov I (2021) An introduction to the comparative and multidisciplinary study of omnibus legislation. In: Bar-Siman-Tov I (ed) Comparative multidisciplinary perspectives on omnibus legislation. Springer, Cham. (in this volume)

Binder A (2015) The dysfunctional congress. Ann Rev Political Sci 18:85–101

Easterbrook F (2017) The absence of method in statutory interpretation. Univ Chicago Law Rev 84:81–97

Elis N (2020) CBO projects CARES Act will cost $1.76 trillion, not $2.2 trillion. The Hill. Available via The Hill. https://thehill.com/policy/finance/economy/493218-cbo-projects-cares-act-will-cost-176-trillion-not-22-trillion. Accessed 23 June 2020

Fisk C, Chemerinsky E (1997) The filibuster. Standford Law Rev 49:181–254

Gluck A (2015) Imperfect statutes, imperfect courts: understanding congress's plan in the era of unorthodox lawmaking. Harv Law Rev 129:62–111

Gluck A, Bressman L (2013) Statutory interpretation from the inside—an empirical study of congressional drafting, delegation, and the canons: part I. Standford Law Rev 65:901–1026

Gluck A, Bressman L (2014) Statutory interpretation from the inside—an empirical study of congressional drafting, delegation, and the canons: part II. Standford Law Rev 66:725–802

Gluck A, Cross J (2020) The congressional Bureaucracy. Univ Pa Law Rev. 168 (forthcomin)g

Gluck A, O'Connell A, Po R (2015) Unorthodox lawmaking, unorthodox rulemaking. Columb Law Rev 115:1789–1866

Koger G (2010) Filibustering: a political history of obstruction in the house and senate, 1st edn. University of Chicago Press, Chicago

Linde H (1976) Due process of lawmaking. Neb Law Rev 55:197–255

Manning J (2015) Inside congress's mind. Columb Law Rev 115:1911–1952

O'Connell J et al (2020) Following messy start, enormous Paycheck Protection Program shows signs of buttressing economy. Wash. Post. Available via Wash. Post. https://www. washingtonpost.com/business/2020/06/09/how-effective-is-ppp-small-business. Accessed 23 June 2020

Reynolds M et al (2019) Legislative productivity in congress and congressional workload. In: Vital Statistics On Congress. Brookings Institution. Available via Brookings Institution. https://www. brookings.edu/wp-content/uploads/2019/03/Chpt-6.pdf. Accessed 26 June 2020

Scalia A (1997) Common law courts in a civil law system: the role of United States Federal Courts in interpreting the constitution and laws. In: Gutmann A (ed) A matter of interpretation: federal courts and the law. Princeton University Press, Princeton, pp 3–47

Sinclair B (2017) Unorthodox lawmaking: new legislative processes in the U.S. Congress, 5th edn. CQ Press, Washington

Smith S, Flathman M (1989) Managing the senate floor: complex unanimous consent agreements since the 1950s. Legis Stud Q 14:349–374

Stack K (2010) The statutory fiction of judicial review of administrative action in the United States. In: Forsyth C et al (eds) Effective judicial review: a cornerstone of good governance. Oxford University Press, Oxford, pp 317–325

Wolfensberger D (2020) Procedural politics: what just happened with the coronavirus bill?. The Hill. Available via the Hill. https://thehill.com/blogs/congress-blog/politics/490106-procedural-politics-what-just-happened-with-the-coronavirus-bill. Accessed 23 June 2020

Abbe R. Gluck is a Professor of Law and the founding Faculty Director of the Solomon Center for Health Law and Policy at Yale Law School. She is an expert on Congress and the political process, federalism, civil procedure, and health law, and is the chair emerita of Section on Legislation and the Law of the Political Process for the Association of American Law Schools. Gluck has extensive experience working as a lawyer in all levels of government. She earned her B.A. from Yale University, summa cum laude, and her J.D. from Yale Law School and clerked for U.S. Supreme Court Justice Ruth Bader Ginsburg. Gluck's scholarship has been published in the Yale Law Journal, the Harvard Law Review, the Stanford Law Review, the Columbia Law Review, and many other journals. Among her most recent work are the most extensive empirical studies ever conducted about the realities of the congressional law-making process. She is co-author of a leading Legislation casebook, and is a member of the leadership body of the American Law Institute. Gluck extends special thanks to Natasha Khan and Shlomo Klapper for outstanding research assistance.

Omnibus Legislation in Spain: Between Political Expediency, Doctrinal Condemnation, and Judicial Indulgence

A. Daniel Oliver-Lalana

Abstract The proposal and passage of multiple subject bills containing unrelated measures has always been condemned as a legislative perversion. This practice, however, seems to be fairly resistant to criticism in a number of countries, where political expediency prevails over arguments of legislative method and due process of lawmaking, and where courts—in absence of explicit constitutional restrictions—are reluctant to set limits on omnibus laws. Spain is a case in point: as the Constitutional Court has recalled, the Spanish Constitution poses "no obstacle precluding or limiting the inclusion of a host of heterogeneous normative measures into a single legislative text"—a doctrine which also applies to decree-laws issued by the Cabinet. This chapter reviews the background, justification and implications of this judicial approach, and discusses to what extent it is actually defensible. After some preliminary remarks on the single subject dogma, I begin with a brief survey of the recent Spanish experience in this area (starting from the abuse of budget laws as a multipurpose regulatory tool in the 1980s). Thereafter I concentrate on the latest constitutional case law dealing with the problem of disparate legislative contents. Two distinct, albeit interwoven issues will be considered: on the one hand, the legal feasibility of multiple subject statutes, which the Constitutional Court has repeatedly affirmed when reviewing budget accompanying laws and government's urgency legislation; on the other, the somewhat loose ban the Court has established on "unconnected amendments" or riders. In the final sections I try to draw a couple of lessons from the Spanish experience, and offer a conjecture which deviates from the usual scholarly plea for adding constraints on multiple subject bills to the parliamentary standing orders: perhaps the vicious circle of omnibus lawmaking in Spain—political expediency, doctrinal condemnation, judicial indulgence—might be escaped through semi-substantive constitutional review standards that focus on the process of legislative justification.

A. D. Oliver-Lalana (✉)
Facultad de Derecho, Universidad de Zaragoza, Zaragoza, Spain
e-mail: oliver@unizar.es

© The Author(s), under exclusive license to Springer Nature Switzerland AG 2021
I. Bar-Siman-Tov (ed.), *Comparative Multidisciplinary Perspectives on Omnibus Legislation*, Legisprudence Library 8, https://doi.org/10.1007/978-3-030-72748-2_10

Keywords Single subject rule · Omnibus laws · Riders (unconnected amendments) · Due legislative process · Constitutional review

1 Introduction

At least since the ancient *rogationes per saturam*, the proposal and passage of multiple subject bills containing unrelated measures has always been condemned as a legislative perversion. This practice, however, seems to be fairly resistant to criticism in a number of countries, where political expediency prevails over arguments of legislative method and due process of lawmaking, and where courts—in absence of explicit constitutional restrictions—are reluctant to set limits on omnibus laws. Spain is a case in point: as the Constitutional Court has recalled in a landmark ruling (Judgment 136/2011), even conceding that such laws are technically flawed, the Spanish Constitution poses "no obstacle precluding or limiting the inclusion of a host of heterogeneous normative measures into a single legislative text"—a doctrine which also applies to omnibus decree-laws issued by the Cabinet (Judgment 199/2015). This chapter reviews the background, justification and implications of this judicial approach, and discusses to what extent it is actually defensible. After some preliminary remarks on the single subject dogma (Sect. 2), I begin with a brief survey of the recent Spanish experience in this area (starting from the abuse of budget laws as a multipurpose regulatory tool in the 1980s) (Sect. 3). Thereafter I concentrate on the latest constitutional case law dealing with the problem of disparate legislative contents. Two distinct, albeit interwoven issues will be considered: on the one hand, the feasibility of multiple subject statutes, which the Constitutional Court has repeatedly affirmed when reviewing both budget accompanying laws (Sect. 4) and government's urgency legislation (Sect. 5); and, on the other, the somewhat loose ban the Court has established on inserting unconnected amendments into bills during the parliamentary proceedings (Sect. 6). Despite the limited scope of the present study, in the final sections I try to draw a couple of lessons from the Spanish experience (Sect. 7), and offer a conjecture which deviates a little from the usual scholarly plea for adding constraints on multiple subject bills to the parliamentary standing orders: perhaps the vicious circle of omnibus lawmaking in Spain—political expediency, doctrinal condemnation, judicial indulgence—might be escaped through semi-substantive constitutional review standards that focus on the process of legislative justification (Sect. 8).

2 One (Puzzling) Subject

That laws should deal with one single subject is a venerable dogma whose seemingly plain formulation conceals a great deal of complexity. Four major, interrelated difficulties are worth highlighting for present purposes: how to define the unity of legislative subjects *(conceptual problem)*; what the duty or norm conveyed by this dogma exactly consists in *(normative problem)*; why it is valuable *(justificatory problem)*; and—even assuming a consensus on the latter, it remains to be seen—how the underlying values or the considerations justifying the dogma operate when it comes to applying it *(adjudicative problem)*.

The first intricacy stems from the openness of predicates like "single" or "homogenous" as referred to the "subject" of a law—the same goes for "multiple", "heterogeneous" and the like. Since such predicates are at the core of the semantic field of omnibus legislation, it becomes difficult to agree on the extension of this concept and hence on when the dogma is, or is not, honoured. As has been recurrently observed, the delimitation of a law's subject and of its necessary, contingent or impossible connections with other subjects always turns on the way these subjects and connections are construed.[1] Accordingly, any attempt to stipulate the subject of a law in its title or in a specific clause or provision within its text will always suffer from some degree of linguistic indeterminacy; and interpretation problems intensify when the subject has to be inferred from preambles, statements of reasons, or first reading debates in a legislature.[2] This irreducible difficulty should not be overstated, though. "Single subject" is just one of the many concepts that can hardly be grasped positively, and are better dealt with in the negative: in our case, by arguing on what (and why) is *not* covered by, or *not* related to, a given subject. Moreover, there are quite obvious instances of omnibus laws which are easily recognizable as such, for they are often deliberately designed to deal with plural matters or to modify a miscellany of pre-existing legislation, with a salient example of such compounds of disparate measures being the so-called arrangements laws.

A second complication concerns the "ought-part" of the dogma, and how it is converted into law. While a single subject demand can be (treated as) a merely legistic recommendation with no proper legal implications, I am primarily interested in the binding dimension to it. Like other classic legisprudential tenets, this dogma has long been embedded in many legal systems. Yet, the extent of its incorporation does vary across jurisdictions. Let us consider, for instance, the following five options. First, a single subject norm, as applied to parliamentary legislation, can be *explicit* or *implicit,* i.e. it can be formulated in legal texts such as constitutions or standing orders, or be derived from these texts through interpretation. Second, the norm can be *general* or *special*, i.e. it can cover any legislation, or only legislation in certain areas (budget), or under certain auspices (citizens' initiatives). Third, the norm can be reconstructed *as a rule* containing an intendedly indeterminate clause such as "unity" or "relevant connection"; or *as a principle* that commands keeping laws confined to one subject as much as possible. In both reconstructions, the application of the norm always involves a wide margin of discretion. Fourth, in

---

[1]See e.g. Gilbert (2006, p. 824); or Cooter and Gilbert (2010, p. 710).

[2]The problem of how the subject of a bill should be identified precedes the problem of whether the subject qualifies as single or multiple, and of whether a given provision (or amendment) is, or is not, linked to this subject.

legal-theoretical terms, a single subject requirement may be understood as a *regulative norm* (conceivable as a rule or as a principle) imposing conditions on the exercise of lawmaking powers, or as a *constitutive rule* determining how to validly produce a given institutional result—an amendment to a bill, for example.[3] Fifth, whether or not a bill meets the norm can be verified *within the legislature* or, after enactment, *by an external controller* (a constitutional or supreme court). In the latter case, a norm infringement may eventually lead to unconstitutionality, with or without annulment of the affected provisions or of the whole law; and the infringement may play as a *conclusive reason* (purely formal or purely procedural review) or simply as a *supportive reason* within a broader constitutional scrutiny of legislative contents (semi-substantive review). As this quick sample of distinctions illustrates, our old legisprudential dogma can acquire legal relevance in many ways.

If there are binding norms or conventions on the unity of legislative subjects, it must be because multiplicity is constitutionally wrong. The question is why. Answers may differ in each legal system, and depend on the type and scope of the limitations. However, on a general level, the two major lines of justification for single subject norms revolve around democracy and formal legality, with the first rationale focusing on the *process* and the second on the *product* of legislation—other pertinent values in this context can possibly be associated with this pair.[4] In some countries emphasis is placed on democracy, in others on formal legality, but both lines of justification fit in with any modern legal system—and can also be traced back to the surge of single subject demands in the Antiquity.[5] Seen from a process perspective, what single subject norms aim to protect is *due legislative deliberation (in parliament)*. This value goes hand in hand with a thick notion of democratic lawmaking which—in contrast with simple majoritarian accounts—calls for an open, pluralistic and inclusive debate of laws, as well as for decisional transparency and authenticity (as opposed to legislative capture) on the part of lawmakers. There are certainly functional requirements on the task of legislating, not necessarily tied to democracy, which are likewise protected by single subject norms: parliamentary specialization and effective committee work, time allocation to properly discussing bills, adequate fact-finding and hearing processes, etc. Still, such requirements of process rationality and legislative care may also be said to belong to a democratic conception of due parliamentary deliberation. Turning to legislation as a result or product, what justifies single subject norms is the ideal of *formal legality* (rule of law, legal security), which stands at the heart of the classic liberal understanding of

---

[3]On constitutive and regulative norms, see e.g. Atienza and Ruiz Manero (2000, p. 69 ff. and p. 107 n. 4).

[4]For example, the functionality or effectiveness of the parliamentary processing of bills is usually invoked to justify single subject requirements on citizens' initiatives.

[5]See e.g. Abelenda (2012) or Sanguinetti (2017); cf. also Luce (1922, pp. 548–549). On the rationale underlying single subject rules in the U.S., see Gilbert (2006, p. 813 ff.), or Cooter and Gilbert (2010, p. 687 ff.); cf. also Giménez (2008, pp. 543–544), highlighting the different justification of limitations on appropriation riders in the U.S. and Europe; for the French case, see e.g. Chamussy (2013) or Déchaux (2008), as well as Olivier Rozenberg's piece in this volume.

laws. In this regard, omnibus statutes are mainly reproached *(i)* for damaging legal certainty and publicity, as they make it harder for citizens or companies to know their rights and duties, particularly those related to economic and administrative matters; *(ii)* for ruining the systematicity of law by spreading antinomies and incoherencies across the legal order; *(iii)* for causing regulatory instability through periodical, unexpected changes which disrupt citizens' legitimate trust in the legal framework; or—in situations where omnibus bills include case-specific, ad hoc measures—*(iv)* for ignoring the requisite generality of laws or privileging special and even sinister interests. All in all, omnibus legislation would increase regulatory confusion, rendering the operation of law unpredictable.

Finally, it is not obvious how this twofold justification must be handled when it comes to applying the norm. For a start, one should distinguish between an actual and a potential impact on the above values: that multiple subject bills normally impinge on the principles of democracy and formal legality does not mean that any such bills always affect them in a relevant way, or do so to the same extent—affections can be more or less severe. In this respect, the application of a single subject *rule* can be either transparent or opaque to the reasons underlying it, i.e. it can be applied formalistically or blindly, regardless of any actual impingement on democracy or legal certainty,[6] or in a "principled" way, in which case the question is not only whether a law's subject is multiple (or a provision has no link to the core subject of a law), but whether this interferes, *and to what extent*, with the principles behind the rule. On the latter account, two things must be shown: that there is actually a relevant affection of formal legality or democracy (or both); and, more importantly, that no competing constitutional arguments are strong enough to override these values. The outcome of this balancing scenario largely depends on the tolerance of each legal culture to interferences with democracy (viz. due legislative deliberation) and formal legality.[7]

The conceptual, normative, justificatory and adjudicative difficulties posed by the single subject dogma may be lessened—though not totally wiped off—by regulating omnibus legislation and entrusting courts to enforce this regulation: some problems will subsist, but this surely helps to dispel others. Yet, it is the absence of explicit binding regulation what really complicates the issue. Spain may serve as an example, for neither the 1978 Constitution nor the parliamentary standing orders of the Congress and the Senate set any specific constraint on the processing or enactment of multiple subject bills. It is true that the official legistic guidelines, adopted by the Spanish Government in 2005, state that "*as far as possible*, legislative acts shall regulate one single subject, all aspects of the subject and, if necessary, those aspects which are directly related to it" (Ministerio de la Presidencia 2011, § I.3, my italics). But the guidelines are widely assumed to be non-enforceable, aspirational recommendations. Although some regional legislatures have established limits on the

---

[6]On the under- and over-inclusiveness of the single subject rule in the light of its underlying purposes, see Gilbert (2006, pp. 829–830).

[7]Cf. below Sect. 6 and Sect. 7.

subject of bills or amendment motions,[8] on the national level the only explicit regulation concerns the so-called citizens' or popular initiatives, which the Bureau of the Congress may reject, among many other reasons, if the proposed bills address "manifestly diverse" and "heterogeneous" matters.[9] Thus, when it comes to regular bills submitted by the Government or by the parliamentary parties, there is no barrier in sight. And besides this lack of specific norms—which leaves an unclear part for the Constitutional Court to play—, the "circumstances" of Spanish legislation in the last decades have fuelled the recourse to multiple subject laws, making them the focus of both political and legal controversies.

3 Playing Cat and Mouse

In a manner, the recent Spanish experience with omnibus and omnibudget legislation is a cat and mouse story about constitutional judges—the cats—who have no claws but on certain occasions use their fangs to bite, and cabinets and their supporting parliamentary majorities—the mice—which always find how to get their way.[10]

The story starts in the 1980s, shortly after the approval of the Constitution (hereinafter, CE), when budget laws became an annual regulatory tool to implement a wide range of policies. Timidly at first and blatantly from 1984 onwards, these laws were seized on to reform virtually any sector of the legal order (see e.g. Moreno 2004, p. 174 ff.). The budgetary proceedings made it easier for the parliamentary majority supporting the Cabinet to approve a variety of budget-unrelated, often politically disputed measures, but opposition parties and regional governments soon questioned the viability of this strategy before the Constitutional Court (TC). Although in early rulings the Court set no limits or, at most, quite elusive conditions on the content of budget legislation, in 1992 it finally decided to curb this practice. It did so in response to a request lodged by a trial judge against an article of the budget law for 1988 that concerned the judicial writs authorizing the entry into tax debtor's homes—this already announced that, along the omnibus spectrum, some lines cannot be crossed. Besides pointing to the interference with basic rights, the requesting judge had challenged the inclusion of such a measure in the budget law. The TC voided the article, holding that the constitutional function of this law—which must cover all revenues and expenditures of the State—*implies*

---

[8]See e.g. Art. 101.1 and Art. 107.1 of the Standing Orders of the Catalonian Parliament.

[9]Art. 5.2(c) of the Popular Legislative Initiative Act *(Ley Orgánica 3/1984)*.

[10]In what follows, I confine myself to national legislation. On the constitutional review of regional omnibus laws, see e.g. Delgado (2016, p. 248 ff.), Martínez Lago (2016, pp. 32–33), Nogueira (2018, p. 1088 ff.), or Ripollés (2020, p. 379 ff.). Neither shall I consider the recent series of rulings the Constitutional Court has delivered on the procedural flaws incurred by the (bare separatist majority in the) Catalonian Parliament when passing pro-independentism legislation.

restrictions as to its permissible scope.[11] The Court conceded that the content of budget laws cannot be categorically confined to budgetary issues proper. Such issues only make up the "necessary content" of budget laws *(núcleo mínimo, necesario e indisponible)*; these laws nevertheless may also have additional, "eventual contents" on two conditions: non budgetary measures must have a "direct" link to public revenues and expenditures, "and"—which became an "or" in some later rulings— must be an indispensable "complement" in order to improve the "comprehension" and enable a "better and more efficacious execution" of the budget and of "the Government's economic policy".[12] Though very broadly phrased, this doctrine was supposed to stop the abuse of budget laws as an all-purpose regulatory instrument.[13] Only few months later, however, lawmakers discovered a more convenient platform for omnibus legislation.

Inspired by comparable, albeit different practices in other countries, Spanish lawmakers opted for transferring the measures the TC had banned from budget legislation to the so-called budget accompanying laws, whose official titles clearly revealed the heterogeneity of their subject—Act "on fiscal measures, reform of the public service and protection of the unemployed" (1993), or Act "on fiscal, administrative and social measures" (1994–2003). For a decade, these yearly laws were processed and approved in parallel to budget laws, thereby benefiting from the special budgetary proceedings in parliament.[14] While originally conceived as a reaction to the 1992 ruling of the TC, they ended up being used to enact the "leftovers" of the annual or sessional legislation and to regulate almost everything, modifying, on average, eighty statutes each year.[15] To name but one example, the 2003 law amended 113 statutes including the Telecommunications Act, the Nuclear Energy Act, the Private Television Act, the Data Protection Act, or the Medicines Act.

Of course, accompanying laws also prompted constitutional appeals, but it took long until these were solved—as it often happens when the TC has to settle politically sensitive issues. In the meantime, the Supreme Court nevertheless paved the way for the yet-to-come constitutional rulings. A decree on the management of the healthcare system, based on a provision of the 1998 accompanying law allowing the establishment of public healthcare foundations, was brought before the administrative chamber of the Supreme Court. Leaning on the principle of legal

---

[11] According to the CE, the State budget "shall include the entire expenditure and income of the State public sector" and indicate "the amount corresponding to fiscal benefits" that relate to State taxes (Art. 134.2); the budget law "may not establish new taxes", and may modify them only if a previous tax law provides for such a possibility (Art. 134.7).

[12] Judgment 76/1992 (Ground 4.a); cf. also Judgments 195/1994 (Ground 2) or 206/2013 (Ground 2. b).

[13] For a critical analysis of the previous and subsequent case law, see Moreno (2004, p. 178 ff.; and 2005, p. 12 ff. and p. 32 ff., focusing on Judgment 34/2005).

[14] Which impaired parliamentary deliberation on both budgetary and non-budgetary issues (Giménez 2008, p. 563).

[15] For a chronology and a classification of such laws, see Giménez (2008); cf. also Moreno (2004).

security, the appellants claimed that this provision should be voided pursuant to the constitutional doctrine on budget legislation. But the Court, besides pointing out that this doctrine does not hold for accompanying laws, found no constitutional flaw, and refused to remand the case to the TC.[16] Curiously, this ruling came at the end of the golden period of omnibus lawmaking. Two sessions in the opposition had led the socialist party to repudiate its own creature: upon winning the 2003 elections, the new socialist cabinet quitted using accompanying laws. The preamble of the Act 2/2004 approving the State budget for 2005 proudly stated that such laws, from then on, would be replaced with normal legislative reforms adopted through regular parliamentary procedures. Unfortunately, good purposes alone cannot tame certain legislative interties.

Two major developments followed the nominal abandonment of accompanying laws. On the one hand, we witnessed a more or less covert return to budget legislation as a multipurpose regulatory tool (see e.g. García-Escudero 2016, pp. 124–125; Moreno 2005, p. 42 ff.). Lawmakers exploited the vagueness of the conditions the TC had set on the permissibility of "eventual", non-budgetary contents of budget laws, and filled these up with additional provisions modifying legislation in many areas. This should possibly have led the TC to intervene, but the Court was rather lenient at enforcing its own doctrine—which is said to be persistently transgressed until our days (Enériz 2014).[17] On the other hand, another wave of multiple subject laws emerged as a means to "update" and "improve" the legal framework for the sake of boosting economic growth and competitiveness, particularly as the 2008 crisis broke out. In an attempt to cope with the crisis—or on this pretext—, an increasing number of omnibus statutes and "decree-laws" (i.e. legislation issued by the Government to address urgent social needs) have since been passed which come close to the former accompanying laws: the 2011 Act on sustainable economy, for instance, modified as many statutes as the last Act on fiscal, administrative and social measures—precisely in that year the TC started delivering its long expected rulings on budget accompanying laws: as explained in the next section, it pronounced them constitutional. It is thus not surprising that multiple subject legislation plagues the current landscape of Spanish law.[18] Pervasive doctrinal attacks on it have been, at last, to little avail. One is even tempted to think that, beyond political expediency, there may be some hidden advantage in this way of lawmaking. But I am not aware of any study in the Spanish literature which vindicates the virtues or the social import of omnibus legislation *as such*.[19] All we can find are objections: criticism has been levelled at every kind of miscellaneous

---

[16]Supreme Court, Judgment 411/2003. Yet, as noted below (Sect. 7), the Supreme Court provided some insightful criteria to assess the constitutionality of accompanying laws. See further Martínez Lago (2016, pp. 36–37 and p. 47).

[17]See also Martínez Lago (2016, p. 25 ff.); cf. recently the TC judgements 122/2018 and STC 99/2018.

[18]For a painteresque variety of legislative absurdities in this context, see Zarraluqui (2012).

[19]As to the advantages from the point of view of the executive, cf. e.g. Massicotte (2013, pp. 15–16; and 2021); cf. also Ramallo (2003, pp. 16-17), pointing at the "anti-filibuster" role of omnibus financial laws.

laws,[20] with reproaches coming from all sides, including the Council of State,[21] the MPs themselves (when speaking from the opposition benches),[22] and the legal scholarship *en bloc*—even transversal superstatutes on e.g. gender equality, whose spirit is yet applauded, have also been criticized for regulating too wide a number of issues.[23] As there is no room here for an exhaustive discussion, let us concentrate on the main charges of unconstitutionality against accompanying laws (Sect. 3) omnibus decree-laws (Sect. 4), and riders (Sect. 5).

4 Omnibus Parliamentary Laws

The TC has ratified the validity of multiple subject or "heterogeneous content" legislation in a series of rulings resolving appeals against budget accompanying laws, starting with the Judgment 136/2011 (on the Act 50/1998 on fiscal, administrative and social measures).[24] The most recurrent allegation in those appeals was about the "constitutional impossibility" of enacting annual laws whose contents are unpredictable and impact on the entire legal order, thereby undermining the system of legal sources enshrined in the CE. Moreover, appellants claimed that such laws were, functionally considered, a form of budgetary legislation which did not respect the constitutional limits discussed in the previous section.[25] The Court has

---

[20]Including e.g. the so-called financial laws *(leyes financieras)*: these were presented as an "adequate instrument" to "meet the needs of the financial system" (Méndez and García Andrés 2002, p. 14 ff.), but their poor legistic quality has often been criticized (see e.g. Pérez 2003, p. 146 ff.).

[21]See Rubio Llorente (2006).

[22]See e.g. Cazorla (1997, p. 109 ff.; and 1998) or Moreno (2004, pp. 263–264).

[23]For an overview, see e.g. Mercader (2007 and 2014). In Spain, the Act on effective equality between men and women *(Ley Orgánica 3/2007)* and the Act on measures for a comprehensive protection against gender violence *(Ley Orgánica 1/2004)* affect most areas of social life and include a host of measures operating throughout the whole legal order. While their underlying purpose was largely welcome, the objection that these laws encroach upon the principle of legal security has been widespread. Both laws may be seen as "super-statutes"—Eskridge and Ferejohn (2001, p. 1216) characterise a super-statute as "a law or series of laws that (1) seeks to establish a new normative or institutional framework for state policy and (2) over time does "stick" in the public culture such that (3) the super-statute and its institutional or normative principles have a broad effect on the law – including an effect beyond the four corners of the statute".

[24]The "omnibus series" includes, among others, the Judgments 176/2011, 120/2012, 209/2012, 36/2013, 132/2013, 120/2014, or 59/2015. Unless otherwise indicated, all quotations in this section are taken from the Judgment 136/2011.

[25]Given that accompanying laws were intendedly—and openly—utilized to evade the 1992 ruling on the permissible content of budget laws, some scholars maintained that legislators had incurred a "constitutional fraud" in the sense of the classic "fraud in law" doctrine, and that, given that accompanying laws were functionally connected to budget laws, the same constraints imposed on the latter should be imposed on the former. Yet, budgetary provisions in the CE do not mention accompanying laws and far less ascribe any function to them, so that such a construction could not succeed as a constitutional argument. While not entirely abandoned, the fraud argument was soon

repeatedly counter-argued, say, in three steps. It has first replied with an unsophisticated *a contrario* argument based on the wording of the Constitution—where "no explicit restriction" on omnibus legislation can be found—, and then it has embarked on two additional lines of reasoning to dismiss implicit constraints based on *legal security* or on *democracy* grounds.

As noted, neither in the CE nor in the parliamentary standing orders there are single subject provisions. And the TC begun by clarifying that this silence cannot be taken to mean—as the appellants claimed—a prohibition of omnibus legislation. The interpretation must be quite the opposite: since the CE grants a general lawmaking power to the Parliament and prescribes no particular legistic structuration or method, omnibus accompanying laws are permitted by default. The absence of a specific ban implies *a contrario sensu* that the Parliament is constitutionally allowed to enact them. The sole fact that they are "complex" or their content is multifarious does not alter their being "ordinary laws", and, as such, they must be treated like any other laws added to the legal order. The lawmaking power, that is, can only be restrained on the basis of explicit constitutional limits, as the ones provided for in the case of budget legislation. But limits on budget laws do not apply to their escorting ones, for these are not ascribed any function by the budgetary provisions of the CE. Given that those limits impinge on the parliament's legislative competence, they must be rigidly construed—analogical or extensive readings are thus excluded. For the TC, the conclusion was straightforward: there is no visible obstacle "precluding or limiting the inclusion of a host of heterogeneous normative measures into a single legislative text, to be processed jointly in one only procedure".[26] But the Court still had to discard any eventual breach of the principles of legal security and democracy—as *implicitly* requiring some homogeneity in legislative processes or products.

Appellants complained that accompanying laws violated the *legal security* mandate of Art. 9.3 CE because they had "no predetermined subject", so their content was "indefinite" and could not be foreseen by the intended recipients.[27] Incongruent with this constitutional mandate—it was claimed—were also the massive, unmanageable amount of modifications, cross-references and repeals, and the poor, if not wholly absent systematicity, along with the countless list of legistic imperfections of the accompanying laws: faced with such a legislative mess, norm addressees could hardly make a reliable prediction of the legal consequences of their actions. Again, the TC's reply was rather simple: although the content of accompanying laws is certainly "heterogeneous", it is nevertheless not "indefinite": it was "perfectly delimited" *(sic)* when the Cabinet submitted the respective bills to the Parliament and the publication of the bills in the congressional journal made it

---

pushed to the background. See extensively Moreno (2004, p. 473 ff.), as well as Martínez Lago (2015).

[26] Judgment 136/2011 (Ground 3); see also Judgment 176/2011 (Ground 2.a).

[27] Art. 9.3 CE states: "the Constitution guarantees the legality principle, (. . .) the publicity of norms, the certainty of law *(seguridad jurídica)*, (. . .) the accountability of public authorities and the ban on their arbitrariness".

possible for any interested person or MP to access them; and the same goes for the laws as finally approved, for they were published in the official gazette upon enactment.[28] For the Court, that is, it was overly exaggerated to say that the addressees of these laws could not know their content or were misled by the alleged legislative confusion: the provisions of the 1998 accompanying law were "clear" and did not pose "special comprehension difficulties". Furthermore, the appellants failed to individualise which provisions provoked an insurmountable confusion (and why), so their "generic imputations" about a legal security breach were insufficient to weaken the "presumption of constitutionality" that parliamentary laws are endowed with. According to the TC, that statutes shall embrace but one subject may surely be a commendable tenet; however, even admitting that accompanying laws are techni-cally defective in this regard—all rulings in the omnibus series dwelled on this point—, it is not for the Court to evaluate legistic mistakes but to enforce constitu-tional law, and there is nothing in Spanish constitutional law that prevents law-makers from enacting statutes dealing with disparate topics.

Likewise unsuccessful were *democracy*-based, procedural arguments against accompanying laws. These arguments challenged the unusual parliamentary processing of the government bills—as explained below, a special focus was set on the attachment of senatorial riders. In Spain, procedural issues are tied to the democratic principle through the MP's right to political representation *(ius in officium)* which, in turn, is intertwined with the citizens' fundamental right to political participation (Art. 23 CE);[29] and this link is also strengthened through basic values defining the constitutional understanding of democracy, especially those of political pluralism, participation of minorities and separation of powers.[30] In that connection, a varied and copious set of allegations was made about proce-dural irregularities that impaired the constitutional tasks of MPs. Anomalies ranged from the lack of background reports or the impossibility to discuss the bills in standing, specialized parliamentary committees (discussions were confined to the public finances committee), to the joint debate of refusal motions against accompa-nying laws and budget laws or the unjustified use of urgency proceedings.[31] Such

---

[28]For a critique of this equation of publicity with publication, see García-Escudero (2013, p. 229 ff.; 2016, p. 141 ff.).

[29]According to Art. 23 of the Constitution, citizens are granted the right "to participate in public affairs, directly or through freely elected representatives" and the right to equal eligibility for public office. The TC has persistently affirmed that there exists a direct connection between the citizens' and the MPs' rights recognised in this article, for "it is primordially the political representatives who effectively realize the citizens' right to participate in public affairs"; both rights "would be deprived from substance" and "rendered ineffective" if MPs could not adequately exercise their constitu-tional functions (thus e.g. Judgments 202/2014, Ground 3; 1/2015, Ground 3; or 94/2018, Ground 4). See further Arruego (2005, p. 193 ff.) or García-Escudero (2011, p. 214 ff.).

[30]See already Judgment 99/1987 (Ground 1.a), where lawmaking procedures and rules are deemed "instrumental" in realising political pluralism as one of the highest values of the legal order (Art. 1 CE); see also Judgment 103/2008 (Ground 5) and Justice Aragón's dissenting opinion to the Judgment 136/2011 (paragraph 3).

[31]See further Martínez Lago (2016, p. 59 ff.)

irregularities—so the appellants' claim—effected an intolerable damage to the lawmaking functions the CE assigns to the Parliament and its members. The TC disagreed in all cases, and offered two major counterarguments: the first rested on a purely majoritarian notion of democracy, and the second drew on its habitual approach to the "vices" of the lawmaking process. For the Court, what the principle of democracy requires is that the Parliament's political will be formed "through the procedure" prescribed in the CE, and this procedure is governed by the majority rule as the best way to deal not only with competing policy interests but also with rival views on the organization of the legislative work. Therefore, it is up to the parliamentary internal organs to determine, *by voting*, whether a given procedural option is permissible or not.[32] An unconstitutional harm occurs—here comes the second reply—if, and only if, the anomalous or unusual procedural decisions have, in fact, "substantially" or "essentially" altered the political will-formation of the chambers.[33] In the Court's opinion, such a critical affection did not exist, mainly, because of two reasons: either there had been, during the processing of the bills, no formal complaints against the procedural defects that were denounced in the constitutional appeal,[34] or the MPs who filed it did not specify how—severely—the alleged irregularities had impaired their constitutional role: they made too "generic" contentions or sheer "political assessments" which cannot "render a norm unconstitutional".[35]

Omnibus laws were thus upheld, for they did not contravene any explicit or implicit limit which might be derived from the Constitution. Not everyone in the Court supported this position, though. In a very hard dissenting vote to the Judgment 136/2011, Justice M. Aragón deplored accompanying laws as a "legislative perversion" undermining legal security and as a "vicious" practice conceived to escape the boundaries of the permissible scope of budget laws; and he further claimed that the Court had visibly forsaken its duty to protect the constitutional model of norm

---

[32]See Judgment 136/2011 (Ground 5), as well as Judgments 176/2011 (Ground 2.c) and 209/2012 (Ground 2).

[33]Judgment 136/2011 (Ground 10): "only the most egregious vices or flaws" which "essentially impair" the formation of the MPs' will are capable of provoking such "a democratic deficit in the norm-making process" that "might lead to a pronouncement of unconstitutionality". Cf. also Judgment 176/2011 (Ground 4) and, in general, Judgment 99/1987 (Ground 1). See further Fernández-Fontecha (2013, p. 106 ff.).

[34]Judgment 136/2011 (Ground 10, as well as Facts 11–12, with both the Congress and the State lawyers submitting that not even the simplest breach of the standing orders could be identified). See also 176/2011 (Ground 2.f).

[35]See Judgment 136/2011 (Grounds 9, 10 and 3), stressing that "the political assessment" of legislative decisions has no bearing on the evaluation of their unconstitutionality, which only responds to "strictly legal criteria" derived from explicit or *implicit* constitutional norms; although urgently-passed omnibus bills might "somehow" affect the right to political participation, the "eventual existence of such an affection" has not proven to be "substantial" nor diminished the democratic legitimacy of the enacted law—a law, the Court added, that may possibly be questionable from a legistic viewpoint, but is by no means objectionable from a constitutional perspective (Ground 3).

production, thereby "validating the degradation" of parliamentary lawmaking.[36] While the dissenter was not certain about whether the damage to legal security was *weighty enough* to strike down the impugned 1998 accompanying law, he was nevertheless convinced that this law should have been pronounced unconstitutional, for it had *severely* infringed upon the democratic principle underlying the process of legislation "as an expression of popular sovereignty"—with the Court's equation of this principle with the rule of majority being a plainly unsustainable "conceptual mistake".[37]

5 Omnibus Urgency Legislation (Decree-Laws)

Not long afterwards the TC Judgment 199/2015—another momentous and contested ruling—extended the above doctrine on budget accompanying laws to the pieces of urgency legislation issued by the Cabinet (decree-laws).[38] This exceptional legislative competence of the government has always been a constitutional battlefield, but the number of decree-laws and that of subsequent appeals before the TC dramatically increased following the outbreak of the 2008 crisis. The enactment of urgency legislation intensified particularly during the 2011–2015 term, with the rate peaking in 2012 at 29 decree-laws vs. 25 parliamentary laws.[39]

Decree-laws are obviously exempted from regular pre-parliamentary steps in the legislative process, and present an advantageous strategy to pass a varied collection of (often contentious) measures in one batch, for they must be ratified or rejected as a whole in a single congressional sitting within thirty days after their adoption by the Cabinet. The only requirement set by Art. 86 CE is that decree-laws be adopted in case of an "extraordinary and urgent need"—and do not affect basic State institutions, fundamental rights and liberties, electoral law, or the regional system. It was on this very rationale that the conservative government issued the Decree-Law 8/2014 approving urgent measures on economic growth, competitiveness and efficiency: a patent specimen of omnibus legislation amending 28 statutes on such disparate matters as e.g. mining industry, commercial timetables, armed forces, or civil register.

---

[36]Cf. also Justice Aragón's dissenting opinion to the Judgment 132/2013, as well as Aragón (2016, pp. 102–103) and García-Escudero (2016, p. 135 ff.).

[37]While not denying the significance of the majority rule, Justice Aragón reproached the Court for failing to distinguish between the adoption of decisions by majoritarian voting and the democratic exigencies on the previous deliberative process. Cf. also Martínez Lago (2016, pp. 53–54).

[38]As García-Escudero (2016, p. 128 n. 68; and 2013, p. 221 n. 62) notes, the TC had previously accepted that decree-laws "habitually" have a "heterogeneous content", and that this poses no legal security problems in view of the "current means available to find out" official legal information (Judgment 332/2005, Ground 17). Cf. Aragón (2016, p. 101 ff.).

[39]See further Aragón (2016, p. 35 ff.), Moreno Fernández (2016, p. 81 ff.), and García Majado (2017, p. 226 ff.).

Deputies of several opposition parties immediately lodged a constitutional appeal. On the one hand, they complained that there could not exist *one single* emergency situation justifying the regulation of so many different and unrelated issues, and that there actually was no pressing need to legislate on many of them. On the other, the appellants submitted that omnibus decree-laws like this one imply a "particularly intense" interference with the constitutional rights to political representation and participation, for they utterly limit the Parliament's analysis, debate and amendment faculties. Neither argument persuaded the Court. In its view, since the only relevant constitutional yardstick against which decree-laws may be assessed is the condition set in Art. 86 CE ("extraordinary and urgent need"), any other restriction must be excluded. After recapping the doctrine already settled for accompanying laws, the TC literally translated it to the case at hand. According to the Court, even though "this decree-law reveals a deficient normative technique", it is constitutionally harmless; just as omnibus laws may encompass "a variety of economic policy measures", also transversal decree-laws containing "a variety of *urgent* economic policy measures" are allowed—provided that they keep within the boundaries of Art. 86 CE.[40] These boundaries, moreover, could not be construed as the appellants did: the requirement of an "extraordinary and urgent need", the TC argued, does not refer to the entire decree-law but to each of its provisions, so that this form of legislation may well be utilised to cope with a diversity of urgent needs, however disparate they are. The Cabinet's only constitutional duty boils down to offering a justification about the various urgencies, i.e. to give reasons that are or can be related to the respective measures addressing each of the urgencies—a "vague, generic justification" is not enough.[41] In this respect, the Court routinely checks for the existence (not for the soundness) of explanatory remarks on the situation of emergency in the decree-laws' preambles, in their accompanying memoranda, or in the ministerial speeches held during the validation debate in Congress; and then it contrasts such remarks with the measures that have been enacted, looking to whether there is some "justificatory connection" between explanations and measures. This was the approach the TC followed when reviewing the Decree-Law 8/2014: it found that a number of provisions were not linked at all to the urgent problems the Cabinet had adduced by way of justification, and voided them. But governmental omnibus legislation as such remained constitutionally unobjectionable.[42]

---

[40]Judgment 199/2015 (Ground 3, italics added). The Court did not find "any obstacle whatsoever" to apply its doctrine on omnibus parliamentary laws to omnibus decree-laws: again, it was insisted that, although such decree-laws may reveal "a deficient normative technique", the Court must only be concerned with their constitutionality, not with their "technical quality"; and that "nothing in the constitutional text" prohibits decree-laws containing "heterogeneous normative measures"—as long as these do not affect those matters excluded by Art. 86 of the CE.

[41]Judgment 199/2015 (Ground 5).

[42]Judgment 199/2015 (Grounds 5, 9 and 10). See also Judgment 211/2015 (Ground 7), as well as García-Escudero (2016, p. 151), stressing that the Court, while recognizing that the MPs' *ius in officium* stretches to the validation debate in Congress, does not take this right to cover the claim to a

Once again, the Court was split. Along the lines advanced in a series of urgent legislation cases decided in previous years,[43] in this one the dissenting judges heavily criticized both the Cabinet's ever-increasing use of decree-laws and the Court's permissive review of them.[44] But this time the dissenters went further, and pleaded for a general constitutional re-evaluation of the government's legislative powers: in their opinion, the "notoriously disproportionate, deceptive and abusive" use of these powers causes "a serious unbalance in the constitutional architecture" and calls "the very notion of parliamentary democracy" into question.[45] As concerns lawmaking—they sustained—, the Cabinet cannot be put on a level with the Parliament: the power to issue decree-laws which is granted to the former has an exceptional nature and hence must be construed strictly. It was under this perspective—the opinion went on—that the Decree-Law 8/2014 had to be inspected, which should have led to require at least some "common thread" justifying the measures taken; yet, "any attempt to find" such a common thread was doomed to fail, "for the simple reason that there was none". For the sake of argument, the dissenters admitted that there might be unexpected, highly critical scenarios where the issuing of an omnibus decree-law can be constitutionally accepted (if properly justified).[46] But this was not the case: the justifications offered were "rhetorical, empty, disputable, or simply non-existent". On the top of that—the dissent concluded—, an economic crisis that "spans over two parliamentary sessions has little of extraordinary at the present moment" and cannot legitimize a decree-law including "measures of all kind, many of which do not even bear any relation to the crisis". Still today, that the Court discounted all this and ratified such a misuse of omnibus lawmaking by the Cabinet seems hard to grasp from a constitutional perspective.

---

thorough debate of the decree-law (such a claim would only be justified if, after its validation, the decree-law is eventually processed as a regular government bill).

[43]See, for instance, Judgments 170/2012 (dissenting opinion of F. Valdés Dal-Ré); 12/2015 (dissenting opinions of F. Valdés Dal-Ré and L.I. Ortega); 48/2015 (dissenting opinion of F. Valdés Dal-Ré); or 139/2016 (joint dissenting opinion of F. Valdés Dal-Ré and A. Asúa; and dissenting opinion of J.A. Xiol); cf. also, more recently, Judgment 61/2018 (joint dissenting opinion of F. Valdés Dal-Ré, C. Conde-Pumpido and M.L. Balaguer).

[44]Cf. Aragón (2016, p. 135 ff.). As has been observed, the Court inclines to accept as extraordinary and urgent whatever the Cabinet considers to be extraordinary and urgent (García Majado 2017, p. 235, offering examples of blatantly non-extraordinary and non-urgent issues that have been regulated by decree-laws over the last years). Cf. however e.g. Judgment 211/2015 (Ground 7).

[45]Judgment 199/2015 (dissenting opinion of A. Asúa, F. Valdés Dal-Ré and J.A. Xiol Ríos).

[46]Writing in personal capacity, former TC Justice Aragón (2016, p. 111 ff.) entirely adhered to the dissenting opinion, except for this point: in his view, a multiple situation of emergency should be addressed, rather, by separated, single-subject decree-laws, not by an omnibus one.

6 Unconnected Amendments (Riders)

As noted at the outset, omnibus legislation can easily be associated with the problem of riders or *cavaliers* (unconnected amendments). Besides having no relevant link to the core subject of a law, such "intruder provisions" are often—and more or less trickily—inserted into bills during their parliamentary processing. In many countries this practice is constrained by convention or by regulation, but in Spain, abstracting from a few marginal exceptions on the national and regional level,[47] there are no explicit restrictions on it. Backed by the right to political representation (Art. 23 CE), the MPs' "right to amendment" therefore has been nearly unlimited. As the TC already ruled in 1987, "there is no norm in the Constitution or the standing orders of either chamber" requiring any "material link" between bills and amendments, so that no limit may be set on the parliamentarian's faculty of submitting amendment motions, "neither as for their subject nor as for their content".[48] Cabinets supported by broad senatorial majorities have greatly profited from this blanket endorsement, because the amended bills the Senate returns to the Congress of Deputies must be either accepted or rejected as a whole. This gives government's parliamentary parties or coalitions a useful *in extremis* chance to pass what they failed or forgot to include in the bill along the congressional proceedings—and almost whatever they like to add to it. Of course, opposition parties always protested that this malpractice violates their political representation rights. But the TC clung to its blank cheque doctrine for many years, even when it came to reviewing last minute riders approved by the Senate: as insisted in 2000, neither the CE nor the standing orders establish "any constraint on the scope of senatorial amendments" to the text of the bills received from the Congress.[49]

This lenient case law, however, was accompanied by a handful of discordant rulings, mostly concerning regional parliaments, and by the end of 2003 the Court was confronted with a perfect opportunity to clarify its stance: an incredible amendment to a bill on arbitration whereby the government party in the Senate inserted three new offences into the Criminal Code—punishing unlawful calls for elections or referenda and the use of public funds to support illegalised political parties (these new offences were grounded upon the need to better protect the electoral process).[50] The Bureau of the Senate uncritically accepted the amendment motion in question—

---

[47]See e.g. Art. 84 (amendments affecting a previous legislative delegation) or Art 134.6 (amendments impacting on the State budget) of the Spanish Constitution, as well as Art. 107 of the Standing Orders of the Catalonian Parliament.

[48]Judgment 99/1987 (Ground 1). See further Santaolalla (2011, pp. 143–144), as well as Moreno Fernández (2016, p. 90 ff.).

[49]See Judgment 194/2000 (Ground 3), where the Court nevertheless pointed out the secondary constitutional position of the Senate vis-à-vis the Congress, and conceded that "reasons of technical correction and good governance of the legislative procedure" make it advisable for senators not to sponsor "important innovations" in the bills.

[50]The original, one-article bill had been submitted by the Cabinet as a supplement to the 2003 Arbitration Act.

along with another one about the commencement of the upcoming Act—and, drawing on the aforementioned doctrine of the TC, twice refused opposition parties' requests to block the motion. Upon being returned to the Congress the amended bill was finally enacted.[51]

Sixty two senators filed an appeal of constitutional protection before the TC, alleging a breach of their political representation rights. Though it took long to be solved, the appeal was successful: the Judgment 119/2011 declared a violation of the appellants' *ius in officium* (Art. 23 CE),[52] and annulled the Bureau of the Senate's decision that had accepted the amendment motion for voting.[53] It is true—the Court acknowledged—that "the standing orders keep silence" about the possibility for the Bureau to "control the homogeneity" between the bill proposed by the Congress and the amendment motions presented by the senators. But in this case the TC considered that a "joint reading of the constitutional provisions on the lawmaking process" nevertheless obligated the Bureau to require at least some "minimal connection". For one thing, this requirement would now follow from the inherently ancillary or "subsidiary" function of amendments "with respect to the amended text": a motion inserting unrelated contents into a bill pretends to amend a previous proposal but entails, in fact, "a legislative initiative on its own", thus "perverting the nature of the right to amendment". For another thing, a minimal connection requirement must be inferred from the very "logic underlying the processing of legislation"; this logic would be disrupted by adding novel contents to a bill that has already gone through the first reading and has been accepted for examination, since this precludes any option for MPs to reject the bill on the whole afterwards.[54] In the Court's view, the conclusion that the CE does "implicitly" impose "certain material limits on the legislative activity" should come, in the last analysis, as no surprise, for such a conclusion "had been drawn before" on several occasions, e.g. with regard to budget laws.[55] An instructive remark indeed.

Yet, the TC wanted to underline that its new doctrine cannot be taken to curtail the parliament's procedural autonomy, and stressed that the internal organs of the chambers enjoy a "wide margin of assessment" and "appreciation" of the "material connection between the amendment and the [legislative] initiative".[56] In this regard—the Court observed—, undue interferences with the MPs' right to

---

[51]Debate minutes are available at: www.congreso.es (Congress Journal, VII Session, no. 307, Plenum, 18 December 2003, p. 16231 ff.). All parties in the Congress, apart from the one supporting the conservative government, abstained from even taking part in the voting (see further García-Escudero 2016, p. 101 ff.; 2010, pp. 72–73).

[52]Except for five senators who had not formally objected to the amendment motion when it was admitted by the Bureau.

[53]All three offences had already been derogated by the Criminal Code Modification Act of 2005 (in 2004 a socialist government succeeded the conservative one, which sponsored the amendment).

[54]Judgment 119/2011 (Grounds 6 and 7). See further Santaolalla (2011, pp. 147–148; cf. also pp. 140–142 and pp. 153–154).

[55]Judgment 119/2011 (Ground 6). See further Judgments 27/1981 (Ground 2) and 274/2000 (Ground 4).

[56]Judgment 119/2011 (Ground 7).

amendment must be avoided at any rate; and that is why only those amendment motions that "evidently" and "manifestly" lack any "minimal connection" with the bill may be rejected (with the burden of justification being placed on the parliamentary bureaus, which are bound to state the reasons for the motion's refusal). While this doctrine applies in general to both chambers, the TC stressed that the Congress of Deputies and the Senate "are not exactly in the same position within the legislative process", and contribute to this process neither "in the same moment nor with the same faculties". So, as concerns the admissibility of amendment motions, senatorial ones deserve a somewhat closer scrutiny to make sure that they do not unwarrantedly impinge on the constitutional function of deputies as the main legislative representatives of the people.[57]

The new review approach to riders has been confirmed in subsequent cases—yet with slight variations.[58] And it holds as well for unconnected amendments inserted into multiple subject bills: as the Court has recalled, a "correct exercise of the right to amendment" must be preserved even when a piece of legislation regulates different matters.[59] Actually, this doctrine was immediately applied to amendments to budget accompanying laws (the Judgment 136/2011 was delivered two months after the Judgement 119/2011). Lacking connection claims recurred in the constitutional appeals lodged against these laws, and all appeals were solved once the Judgement 119/2011 had given shape to the *implicit* constitutional limits on riders. But the Court was rather reluctant to make much out of such limits.[60] Consider, for example, the Judgment 136/2011—the first in the omnibus series. The appellants complained that a number of amendments bearing no relation to the original bill had been added to it along the parliamentary proceedings, especially in the Senate—where the government party had an absolute majority of seats. The Court, leaning on its freshly stated doctrine, reaffirmed that amendments must have "a minimal connection of homogeneity" with the bill; otherwise a procedural vice is incurred which may be unconstitutional if it is proven "to have altered the political will formation in an essential or substantial way". However, the TC did not even search for any such vice. Since the appellants had not identified the tainted articles nor listed the allegedly

---

[57]Judgment 119/2011 (Ground 6); cf. above note 48. In fact, only the Bureau of the Senate took this ruling seriously, whereas the Bureau of the Congress largely ignored it (García-Escudero 2013, p. 200 ff.; 2016, p. 109 ff.).

[58]See e.g. Judgments 209/2012, 324/2014, 59/2015, 216/2015 or 155/2017, and, for a recap of the TC case law, Judgment 4/2018 (Grounds 3, 4 and 5). After the Bureau of the Senate started checking for a minimal substantial link between amendments and bills, the TC has established a (defeasible) "presumption of coherence or homogeneity" in favor of any amendment motion admitted by the Bureau (Judgment 59/2015, Ground 6.a). Cf. Escuin (2018, p. 206 ff.), noting the relaxation of the latest constitutional case law on unconnected amendments. On the review of the so-called "transactional amendments", see García-Escudero (2013, p. 209 ff.; 2016, p. 107 ff.).

[59]Judgment 59/2015 (Ground 5).

[60]On the undeclared, albeit easily identifiable reluctance of the TC to void provisions resulting from riders, see recently Escuin (2018, p. 110 ff.). As for the general problem of what legal consequences should be attributed to the neglect of single-subject requirements, see Santaolalla (2011, p. 139); cf. also Gilbert (2006, p. 828 ff.).

unconstitutional amendments but "solely alluded to two examples", the Court's majority found beyond its duties to inspect the issue any further—a precarious argument on the face of it, but conveniently time-sparing: besides the 34 laws modified by the original bill, other 55 laws were reformed as a result of amendment motions.[61] In later rulings of the omnibus series the Court has certainly reviewed a number of dubious amendments; still, it has made a quite generous interpretation of its own doctrine on riders, lowering the minimal connection threshold nearly to zero.[62] Perhaps this is only normal, though, for omnibus laws (and especially budget accompanying laws) often deal with so many issues that almost any amendment can eventually be claimed to be related to them. In this respect, the Court seems trapped by its own incoherence in imposing a—loose—ban on unconnected amendments while, at the same time, giving a blank cheque for omnibus legislation. When they meet, these two doctrines are not easy to reconcile.

7 A Matter of Argumentation

Underlying the experience with omnibus legislation in Spain stands the old problem of how to deal with the silence of legal texts. The problem intensifies in formalistic legal cultures like the Spanish one: as single subject phrases are nowhere to be read in the CE or the parliamentary standing orders, our constitutional judges do not feel entitled to intervene. They were divided even when it came to reviewing the 1992 omnibudget law—with a dissenter censuring the majority for inventing restrictions which could not be anchored in any constitutional provision.[63] A similar mantra was told in omnibus legislation and (early) unconnected amendment cases. But however obstinate, formalism always ends at some critical point—in our story, a budget law

---

[61]In his dissenting opinion to the Judgment 136/2011, Justice Aragón heavily criticised this (see especially paragraph 4). Cf. also Martínez Lago (2016, pp. 55–57), as well as Santaolalla (2011, p. 159), noting that the search for homogeneity in an extremely chaotic statute is as pointless as checking for connections between its subject and its amendments.

[62]Thus, e.g., Judgment 209/2012 (Ground 4.b), stating that the requisite link between the amendment and the omnibus bill must be "flexibly" understood and "relativized" depending on the importance of the amendment—this criterion has also served to uphold unrelated measures in budget laws (Moreno 2005, p. 33, commenting on the Judgment 34/2005).

[63]Judgment 76/1992 (dissenting opinion of L. López Guerra). In that case, Justice López Guerra challenged the Court's doctrine on the non-permissible contents of budget laws for effecting an "unjustified", "constitutionally unwarranted" limitation on the Parliament's general legislative power; provided that the CE has granted this power in "universal and unlimited" terms, "any restriction on its exercise must" be based on an explicit constitutional provision or "directly and unambiguously derived from the constitutional text". Compare this position with Justice Aragón's dissenting opinion to the Judgment 136/2011, where budget accompanying laws are deemed unconstitutional for contravening implicit "structural principles" which are "deductible" from the Spanish "democratic and parliamentary system" (Judgment 136/2011, dissenting opinion of M. Aragón, paragraph 3).

bearing on the writs of entry into tax debtors' homes, or a senatorial rider creating criminal offences out of the blue; and then the time arrives for "joint readings" and "implicit limits".[64] Quite a familiar thing, I guess. Whether the situation would really change if specific prohibitions on multiple subject statutes were adopted is debatable, insofar as the inescapable semantic indeterminacy of the prohibition clauses will always open up a leeway for unexpressed norms and interpretative imagination. Anyway, it is the absence of regulation that calls for particularly cogent arguments. My difficulties with the Spanish approach to omnibus legislation have to do, precisely, with constitutional argumentation.

The first difficulty is about a classic fallacy: the false opposition or dilemma. Roughly, this fallacy consists in presenting two complementary options as if they were mutually incompatible, i.e. as an excluding disjunction, so that one has to choose either the one or the other. That is what Spanish judges do by stressing the contradistinction between constitutional law and legistics (or legisprudence), just before recalling that is not for the TC to question the legislative technique or method used by legislators.[65] That the values behind legistic or legisprudential tenets do belong as well to constitutional law is mysteriously overlooked. The judges seem to frame their reasoning this way to discard any convergence between both spheres. Yet, if there exists such a clear-cut border, why does the TC bother to underline that multiple subject legislation is technically flawed? As critically observed in a concurring vote to the Judgment 136/2011, the Court should have spared any such considerations, for they are ultimately self-contradictory.[66] Worse still: in clinging to a net contradistinction between the technical and the constitutional evaluation of omnibus laws, the Court neglects that both belong to a *continuum*—which counsels for some kind of synechism.[67] Instead of stressing the binary argument that legistics

---

[64] As discussed above in Sect. 3, until today the Court has not applied any "implicit" constitutional restriction on omnibus legislation—nevertheless, it has at least mentioned this possibility (see e.g. Judgment 136/2011, Ground 3).

[65] As quoted in Judgment 136/2011 (Grounds 3 and 9), "the assessment of constitutionality is not one of legislative technique" (Judgment 109/1987, Ground 3; Judgment 195/1996, Ground 4): taking stance "on the technical perfection" or quality of laws is beyond the TC's competences, given that "the constitutional control of legislation has nothing to do with its technical depuration" (Judgment 226/199, Ground 4); the "democratic legislator", in sum, can produce technically flawed laws, and the poor technical quality of legislation has "no relevancy" in "strictly" constitutional terms. Along the omnibus series, the Court often wonders whether the appellants had submitted a proper "allegation of unconstitutionality" or "just made a critique of the inadequate legislative technique" (thus e.g. Judgment 120/2012, Ground 3). Cf. Supreme Court Judgment 411/2003 (Grounds 3 and 6), noting that the TC often recalls how important a good legistic technique is to promote legal security and certainty, but does it "on the level of principles", whereas, "when it comes to resolving concrete cases", the TC inclines to consider "legistic problems" as "alien to the law".

[66] In that they imply what the Court denies—namely, that legislative technique is constitutionally relevant (Judgment 136/2011, concurring opinion of L. Ortega).

[67] See Gascón (2006, p. 49): legistic flaws are "gradual" and may trigger "more or less severe" responses, ranging from a purely censorial to a properly legal "disqualification" or invalidation of the affected provision.

is no constitutional law, the TC would thus do well to concentrate on the variable extent and intensity to which democracy and formal legality are actually compromised in the cases at hand—with the former value arguably being more sensitive than the latter. Had the Court followed this idea, for example, government's omnibus decree-laws would have not resisted constitutional scrutiny. But the Judgment 199/2015 deliberately ignored that the interference with the democratic principle was much more important than it was in accompanying laws cases. The chief reasons for upholding these laws were, on the one hand, that the majoritarian rule—to which democracy was reduced in that ruling—had healed the procedural abnormalities occurred during their *parliamentary* processing; and, on the other hand, that the Parliament's legislative power, being a *general* one, may only be limited on the basis of explicit constitutional provisions. But none of this holds for the *exceptional* legislative competences of the *Cabinet*. By operating a wholesale translation of its doctrine on parliamentary omnibus legislation to decree-laws, the Court did not only shut its eyes to the weightier affection of the democratic principle but also incurred another classical fallacy: that of false analogy.

Democracy and formal legality—along with human rights—must be at the centre of any serious legislative philosophy: both the democratic lawmaking *process* and the legistic quality of its *outcomes* matter. Yet, when it comes to constitutionalizing unwritten limits on multiple subject bills, placing the accent on the second perspective is possibly not a good tactic, at least in Spain. That accompanying (or similarly extreme omnibus) laws must be banned as statutory "products" contravening the legal security warranty (Art. 9 CE) proves too difficult a claim, for various reasons. As a whole, these laws are certainly harder to handle than others, but this makes almost no difference from the viewpoint of citizens, for whom the opaqueness of official legislative texts remains constant.[68] And, with regard to the amendments and repeals of pre-existing legislation, omnibus laws do not threaten legal security much more than single subject ones—moreover, the official gazette website regularly publishes updated or "consolidated" versions of all statutes, and offers search and retrieval options which make them (more or less) easily accessible. Neither does the claim work very well if referred to single provisions within an omnibus law: rather than their location in a multiple subject statute, it is their indeterminacy, unintelligibility, retroactivity, or instability that can really endanger legal security. As has been aptly observed, it would be odd to strike down a precise and clear provision that may even happen to be socially beneficial only because of its being "juxtaposed" to other provisions on different subjects (Santaolalla 2011, pp. 167–168).[69]

Despite this complication, the breach of legal security has been the key charge against omnibus laws in the Spanish legal scholarship. It is true that some authors

---

[68]Cf. Xanthaki (2019), Moreu (2020) or Oliver-Lalana (2011).

[69]Yet, such a juxtaposition often hampers the parliamentary examination of the law, which might arguably weaken its presumed constitutional legitimacy and hence the deference owed to it as the result of a democratic lawmaking process.

have prioritized democratic objections,[70] but most critics pervasively insist that "the reason for subject homogeneity lies with the principle of legal security", or that the case for the unconstitutionality of omnibus laws must be made by arguing "the violation of the principle of legal security" that is effected by "the inclusion of heterogeneous elements into one law" (García-Escudero 2016, pp. 94 and 104; García-Escudero 2013, p. 207). In a sense, this sort of fixation on the formal rationality and systematicity of legislative products has pushed the procedural and democratic side of the problem to the background.

Legistic formalism, however, can only very limitedly be transformed into proper constitutional exigencies. As the Senate's lawyer firmly contended in his reply to an appeal against the 1998 accompanying law,[71] no supposedly "canonical model of laws" that has been defined by "wise" academics who "invoke the principle of legal security" from the heights of their "ivory tower" can ever outweigh the presumption of constitutionality which must be ascribed to the laws enacted by a democratic assembly. Such a presumption—he went on—is due to the fact that parliamentary policy decisions are "much more likely to be correct" than judicial ones, with legislative technique having "nothing to do with the democratic principle". Incidentally, his reply omitted that it is this very principle that offers—to borrow from an earlier Supreme Court's ruling dealing with the same accompanying law—"the most solid" constitutional foundation for multiple subject restrictions.[72] Well, if this is so, then the strength of the presumption vindicated by the Senate's lawyer should somehow be linked to the quality of legislative deliberation, especially within the parliament. In other words, the actual (democratic) virtues or imperfections of a given lawmaking process must have some influence on the weight accorded to democracy when resolving omnibus legislation appeals. Just as deliberative quality can be greater or lesser, judicial deference on democratic grounds, too, can be modulated in view of the singularities of each legislative case (cf. Oliver-Lalana 2019, p. 219 ff.). Yet, shifting the focus from the formal quality of legislative products to the procedural quality of its making raises another difficulty.

As far as I can see, the TC follows a pure two-track approach to the review of legislation: it focuses first on the regularity of the legislative process, and then on the compatibility of legislative contents or results with constitutional norms—leaving no room for intersections between both tests. When it comes to controlling the process, the baseline doctrine of the Court is not stringent. It checks for deviations from the legislative proceedings as regulated in the CE or the standing orders of both chambers. But simple deviations are not enough: to gain constitutional relevance, the "vices" or flaws of the lawmaking process must have impacted on the political

---

[70]In this vein e.g. Martínez Lago (2015); see also Justice Aragón's dissenting vote to the Judgment 136/2011.

[71]See Judgment 136/2011 (Fact 9, Senate lawyer's submission).

[72]See Supreme Court Judgment 411/2003 (Ground 3); cf. above notes 16 and 64, and Sect. 7 below. Notwithstanding, the Senate's lawyer delved quite extensively into the constitutional notion of law *(ley)* in the light of the democratic principle—as he did shortly afterwards in Fernández-Fontecha (2013, p. 94 ff.). Cf. also Dodek (2016, p. 31 ff.), and Moreno Fernández (2016, p. 80 ff.)

will-formation in a "substantial or essential" way.[73] This qualification is commonly explained in Spain as a form of prudent self-restraint, a precaution not to impinge on Parliament's privileges.[74] Interestingly, as a consequence of this doctrine what may be called a *principled* language (i.e. a terminology that evokes the notion of legal principles as norms with a dimension of weight) always permeates the TC's discourse on omnibus legislation.[75] In all accompanying laws rulings it is recalled that too "severe" or "intense" affections or democracy may lead to unconstitutionality, but in the cases upon scrutiny these affections had not been proved to be "important enough".[76] In this respect, as discussed in Sect. 3, the Court always looks to whether there was any breach of the "parliamentary legality" and to whether formal complaints were, or were not, raised before the chamber bureaus; but the rulings are not very informative as to how the intensities of the affections of the democratic principle are determined. The TC often begs the question, or, rather apodictically, declares that there has been no "essential" affection because this cannot be derived from the "too generic" allegations of the appellants. The Court, in sum, implies that there actually was some affection, but does not argue too much about how light or severe the affection was, and why.[77] Once the procedural test is passed, the TC turns to examining the content of the challenged statute and does not consider process-related issues any more. Regardless of *how* the individual legislative measures and decisions were arrived at, they all enjoy the same presumption of constitutionality. Again, the Court argues in binary terms: either there has been an overly serious interference with democracy (or with legal security), or the alleged defects are constitutionally irrelevant and must be ignored. However, this is a misguided method, since the quality of the lawmaking process in general, and of parliamentary deliberation in particular, can also be pertinent to the constitutional analysis of heterogeneous legislative contents.

---

[73]See e.g. Judgments 99/1987 (Ground 1) or 103/2008 (Ground 5).

[74]On the TC's approach to the *interna corporis acta*, see further Fernández-Fontecha (2013, p. 83 ff. and p. 106 ff.).

[75]Cf. also Giménez (2008, p. 561), leaning on the TC Judgment 76/1990 (Ground 8) to suggest that, even if gross legistic flaws need not necessarily result in the invalidation of legislation, they should certainly be considered as an "aggravating element", i.e. a factor that counts against upholding it.

[76]In the Judgment 136/2011, both the majority (Ground 11) and the dissenter agreed, *in the abstract*, that "substantial" affections lead to unconstitutionality, but they disagreed on the intensity of the affection *in the concrete case*—only the dissenter argued about it. Nonetheless, in the Judgment 119/2011 (Ground 9) the Court, when assessing the interference with representation rights (Art. 23 CE), considered that the last minute senatorial rider appending criminal offences to a bill on arbitration was not "idle" *(inane),* and effected a substantial impairment of the MPs' legislative faculties.

[77]As the aforementioned Supreme Court's Judgment 411/2003 (Ground 3) noted, yet with regard to the legal security principle, "it is upon *a specific examination of the content and the circumstances* of the challenged regulation that we have to resolve the (...) doubts of unconstitutionality" it may pose (my italics).

8 An Alternative Path

In the aftermath of the TC rulings on both omnibus and budget laws, the Spanish legal scholarship is marked by an air of resignation: after all, "we will have to learn to live with a bad legislative technique" (Martínez Lago 2016, p. 41) and endure the problem of multipurpose legislation, for any attempt to curb it turns out "to be at odds with the reality of facts" (Giménez 2008, p. 561). Some still plea for explicit restrictions in the Constitution, others would content themselves with "symbolic" pronouncements of unconstitutionality, or with a simple reform of the standing orders, and yet others suggest keeping the whole issue off the judges' hands and placing more confidence in parliamentary self-control.[78] But this does not exhaust all options. Given that constitutional appeals involving riders or affecting provisions included in multiple subject statutes continue, the Court itself might eventually reconsider its own stance. In view of the strong dissents delivered along the omnibus series, one cannot exclude changes in the indulgent approach followed so far, which would perhaps rise an opportunity for some improvement or innovation. Particularly, the TC could further refine its reasoning about the intensities of the interferences with legal security and democratic deliberation as formal or institutional principles, and even start controlling the content of dubious provisions in the light of the quality of the process whereby they are justified and enacted (semi-substantive review).

To explore this conjecture a bit further, the Supreme Court's Judgment 411/2003 offers a good starting point. In that case, as noted earlier, one provision in an accompanying law had been challenged for legal security reasons. While the judge who wrote for the Court—now sitting in the TC—focused on the intensity of the alleged affection of legal security, he relied on criteria that might be adapted to the democratic and deliberative quality of legislation. For instance, the interference with legal security was deemed light because the disputed article did not modify any "principal" statute; because it was "studied along the parliamentary proceedings"; and because there existed a number of parliamentary, governmental and academic "background reports and documents" which supported it—with all this "lowering" the degree of the alleged interference.[79] In order to better determine how severely the institutional principle of due democratic deliberation has been affected in omnibus legislation or riders cases, the TC could resort to factors like these. Or it could also draw on the variety of due legislative process or deliberation criteria utilized by other

---

[78]See e.g. Santaolalla (2011, pp. 158, 162, 166 ss. and 170); cf. also García-Escudero (2016, pp. 139–140; 2013, p. 228).

[79]Supreme Court Judgment 411/2003 (Grounds 8–9), noting as well that the scrutiny "cannot be equally intensive for all norms", because the extent to which legal security is compromised depends on the specific features of the norms at stake, on the surrounding social realities, or on the impact on citizens' lives. Cf. also Giménez (2008, pp. 559–560), stressing the sensitiveness of tax norms in this connection; and Sánchez (2019, pp. 398 ff. and 405 ff.).

constitutional or international courts that perform procedural rationality review.[80] This inter-judicial dialogue would probably contribute to a better argumentation about the intensity of the interferences with the political will-formation in parliament.

Suppose now that, after carefully arguing on this point, the Court reaches the conclusion that an affection was not "essential", i.e. that it was not severe enough to void the measure on process-related grounds. Since even a non-essential interference with democracy remains, by definition, an interference, there must be some constitutionally important argument justifying it.[81] In the absence of such an argument, the interference could be ascribed some weight in the constitutional assessment of the content of the provision. A moderate but unjustified affection of democratic deliberation could weaken the presumption of legitimacy accorded to parliamentary legislation and hence the deference the Court owes to it. To do this, the two-track approach to the scrutiny of omnibus statutes would need to be replaced with some hybrid, semi-substantive kind of review. As we have seen, it is difficult to persuade the Court to annul disparate provisions because of procedural flaws alone. But these flaws may be an additional factor within the judicial reasoning about suspect measures which are claimed to be unconstitutional on other counts: think e.g. of alleged violations of fundamental rights, of the regional legislative competences, or even of the constitutional ban on arbitrariness enshrined in Art. 9.3 CE. When the TC examines whether the content of a legislative provision is compatible with these norms, it often has to deal with empirical and normative questions for which there is no straightforward answer. So to speak, the judges often find themselves in a twilight epistemic zone—to be sure, they can deliberately create it, but this is of no concern now. Up to now, the TC's default attitude in such situations tends to be that of blindly deferring to lawmakers. There nonetheless exists an alternative path. Since substantive constitutional uncertainties are a matter of degree, the Court could adjust its deference to the Parliament by relying on the previous procedural assessment of omnibus bills and riders. On this account, the quality of the underlying lawmaking process would be a modulating factor within a content-oriented constitutional standard (for example, a proportionality test).

It goes without saying that this is a grossly simplified depiction of semi-substantive review—delving into how institutional or formal principles can or should behave within the constitutional adjudication and balancing of substantive principles would take us too far.[82] For present purposes, suffice it to notice that such an hybrid strand of review, as applied to omnibus lawmaking, would involve searching for legislative reasons about both results and processes, i.e. reasons

---

[80]See recently e.g. Huijbers (2019) and, on the potential of constitutional review to counterbalance legislative capture, Meßerschmidt (2019, p. 258 ff.); as to this latter aspect, cf. also Judgment 176/2011 (Fact 1, appellants' submission).

[81]Cf. the dissenting vote to the TC Judgment 136/2011, where Justice Aragón denied that reasons of "efficacy" can justify the "constitutionally fraudulent practice" of inserting totally unconnected amendments into bills.

[82]For an overview, see e.g. Portocarrero (2016).

justifying not only the content of the contested measure but also the non-essential affection of the democratic principle. So lawmakers—even if only in their own interest—should provide these justifications somewhere, e.g. in preambles, in background documents submitted along with the bills, in plenary and committee debates, or, most especially as concerns riders, in the statements of reasons MPs attach to amendment motions.[83]

Unfortunately, the snag is that my conjecture hinges on a culture of legislative justification which is alien to the Spanish constitutional tradition. As discussed above, not even the Cabinet is required to duly justify the issuing of omnibus decree-laws. Accordingly, it seems improbable that the TC, in the short run, will critically strengthen the control of the actual justification of parliamentary omnibus legislation—or of legislation in general. In spite of the fact that the CE explicitly establishes a comprehensive ban on legal arbitrariness covering all state authorities' decisions without exception, constitutional judges have always been reluctant to enforce it against the Parliament. As a renowned legal scholar once lamented (Fernández 1998, p. 160), the Court "strives not to demand reasons from the legislator", thereby "complicating" the review of laws with hypotheses about the arguments that can possibly be conceived to pronounce them (un)constitutional; this approach—Fernández recalled—always casts doubts on the legitimacy of unelected judges to supervise what a democratic assembly has enacted. Such complications would decrease, however, "if it were naturally accepted" that "the legislator has long ceased to be sovereign and, like any other state authority, is constitutionally bound to give reasons for his decisions"; the justification lawmakers "actually put on the table" should therefore be the main focus of the Court's constitutional scrutiny.

9 Conclusion

Although this chapter leaves great many issues untouched, it hopefully gives an insight into the recent evolution and the constitutional repercussions of omnibus lawmaking in Spain. If now I were to suggest a single subject title for our cat and mouse story, it would definitely not be "caution: legal security hazard" or "the lost respect for formal legistics" but, rather, "the little importance of legislative deliberation in parliament". In a manner, I have pinned the hope of reverting this insignificance on a more refined constitutional argumentation, conjecturing that, in absence of explicit prohibitions, a shift towards semi-substantive review might eventually help to escape the vicious circle of Spanish omnibus legislation—political expediency, doctrinal condemnation and judicial indulgence. Still, for the moment, one cannot be too optimistic in this regard, inasmuch as the Court has always refrained

---

[83]Cf. also García-Escudero (2016, pp. 144 and 146), pleading for a better legislative justification in the light of both the principle of legal security and the constitutional ban on arbitrariness.

from pushing for a due process of legislative justification. Whether it ever changes its mind, only time will tell.

Acknowledgements I very much thank Suzie Navot for her insightful comments on a preliminary version of this essay, as well as the rest of participants in the *International Conference on Omnibus Legislation* (Bar-Ilan University, January 2019) for constructive discussions about this and other topics—a special mention goes for Ittai Bar-Siman-Tov and his excellent team. The preparation of this chapter was supported by the Spanish Ministry of Science Project RTI2018-095843-B-I00 (MCIU/AEI/FEDER, UE), the Ramón y Cajal Research Fund, and the University of Zaragoza's Legal Sociology Lab (Research Group Strategy of the Government of Aragon, 2017/2019).

References

Abelenda V (2012) Rogatio y aprobación de *leges per saturam*. In: Falchi GL, Iaccarino A (eds) Legittimazione e limiti degli ordinamenti giuridici. Pontificia Università Lateranense, Città del Vaticano, pp 85–97

Aragón M (2016) Uso y abuso del decreto-ley. Iustel, Madrid

Arruego G (2005) Representación política y derecho fundamental. CEPC, Madrid

Atienza M, Ruiz Manero J (2000) Las piezas del derecho, 2nd edn. Ariel, Barcelona. [A theory of legal sentences. Kluwer, Dordrecht/Boston/London, 1998]

Cazorla LM (1997) Características de las llamadas leyes de acompañamiento presupuestario desde el punto de vista del ejercicio de la función legislativa de las Cortes Generales. Corts (Anuario de Derecho Parlamentario) 4:107–125

Cazorla LM (1998) Las llamadas leyes de acompañamiento presupuestario. Marcial Pons, Madrid

Chamussy D (2013) La procédure parlementaire et le Conseil constitutionnel. Nouveaux Cahiers du Conseil Constitutionnel 38:1–20

Cooter RD, Gilbert MD (2010) A theory of direct democracy and the single subject rule. Columbia Law Rev 110:687–730

Déchaux R (2008) L'évolution de la jurisprudence constitutionnelle en matière de "cavaliers" entre 1996 et 2006, retrieved from www.conseil-constitutionnel.fr

Delgado D (2016) Crisis económica y técnica legislativa. Revista de las Cortes Generales 99:239–258

Dodek AM (2016) Omnibus bills: constitutional constraints and legislative liberations. Revue de Droit d'Ottawa – Ottawa Law Rev 48(1):1–42

Enériz FJ (2014) La persistencia del legislador en no respetar los límites materiales de las Leyes Generales de Presupuestos de Estado. Revista Aranzadi Doctrinal 1:1–22

Escuin C (2018) El juego entre la mayoría y las minorías parlamentarias en la elaboración de las leyes. Corts – Anuario de Derecho Parlamentario 31:197–212

Eskridge W, Ferejohn J (2001) Super-statutes. Duke Law Journal 50:1215–1276

Fernández TR (1998) De la arbitrariedad del legislador. Civitas, Madrid

Fernández-Fontecha M (2013) Teoría y jurisprudencia parlamentaria. Cortes Generales, Madrid

García Majado P (2017) Del uso al abuso: el decreto-ley en la España democrática. Diálogos jurídicos 2:217–244

García-Escudero P (2010) Seguridad jurídica y técnica legislativa. Thomson-Aranzadi, Cizur Menor

García-Escudero P (2011) El parlamentario individual en un parlamento de grupos: la participación en la función legislativa. Teoría y realidad constitucional 28:205–242

García-Escudero P (2013) De enmiendas homogéneas, leyes heterogéneas y preceptos intrusos. Teoría y realidad constitucional 31:199–236

García-Escudero P (2016) Homogeneidad de enmiendas e iniciativas legislativas. In: La última jurisprudencia relativa al parlamento. Eusko Legebiltzarra, Vitoria/Gasteiz, pp 93–154

Gascón M (2006) Calidad de las normas y técnica normativa. Revista Española de la Función Consultiva 6:41–95

Gilbert MD (2006) Single subject rules and the legislative process. Univ Pittsburgh Law Rev 67:803–870

Giménez IM (2008) Leyes de acompañamiento y el problema de las "leyes ómnibus". Teoría y realidad constitucional 22:525–565

Huijbers L (2019) Process-based fundamental rights review: practice, concept, and theory. Intersentia, Cambridge

Luce R (1922) Legislative procedure. Houghton Mifflin Company, Boston/New York

Martínez Lago MA (2015) Los presupuestos para 2016 aprobados en el tiempo de descuento de la X legislatura: ¿un fraude a la constitución? Revista Española de Derecho Financiero 168:15–51

Martínez Lago MA (2016) Los límites de la justicia constitucional: la interpretación constitucional y la técnica jurídica en las "leyes de contenido heterogéneo". Revista Española de Derecho Constitucional 106:17–71

Massicotte L (2013) Omnibus bills in theory and practice. Can Parliam Rev 36(1):13–17

Massicotte L (2021) Canada: if controversial, omnibus legislation is here to stay. In: Bar-Siman-Tov I (ed) Comparative multidisciplinary perspectives on omnibus legislation. Springer, Cham (in this volume)

Méndez JM, García Andrés G (2002) La ley financiera: un nuevo hito en la reforma del sistema financiero español. Sistema financiero: novedades y tendencias 801:13–24

Mercader J (2007) Técnica legislativa y legislación transversal. In: Mercader J (ed) Comentarios laborales de la ley de igualdad entre mujeres y hombres. Tirant lo Blanch, Valencia, pp 15–50

Mercader J (2014) Transformaciones y deformaciones de la función legislativa en materia laboral. Información laboral 2:1–30

Meßerschmidt K (2019) Special interest legislation and legislative capture. In: Oliver-Lalana AD (ed) Conceptions and misconceptions of legislation. Springer, Cham, pp 243–272

Ministerio de la Presidencia (2011) Directrices de técnica normativa. Catálogo de las publicaciones de la Administración General del Estado, Madrid (Resolución de 28 de julio de 2005, de la Subsecretaría, por la que se da publicidad al Acuerdo del Consejo de Ministros, de 22 de julio de 2005, por el que se aprueban las Directrices de técnica normativa)

Moreno S (2004) Constitución y leyes de acompañamiento presupuestario. Thomson-Aranzadi, Cizur Menor

Moreno S (2005) De nuevo sobre el contenido constitucionalmente admisible de la Ley de Presupuestos Generales del Estado. Revista de Información Fiscal 6:11–52

Moreno Fernández JI (2016) De la garantía de la ley al abandono del principio democrático como legitimación del ejercicio del poder. Diálogos jurídicos 1:77–100

Moreu E (2020) Nuestro lenguaje: el giro lingüístico del derecho. Revista de Derecho Público 1:313–362

Nogueira A (2018) Galicia: las leyes "ómnibus" se ponen de moda. In: López Ramón F (ed) Observatorio de políticas ambientales. CIEMAT, Madrid, pp 1087–1101

Oliver-Lalana AD (2011) Legitimidad a través de la comunicación. Comares, Granada

Oliver-Lalana AD (2019) Legislative deliberation and judicial review: between respect and disrespect for elected lawmakers. In: Oliver-Lalana AD (ed) Conceptions and misconceptions of legislation. Springer, Cham, pp 207–241

Pérez (2003) Las medidas de reforma de la ley financiera. Anuario de la Facultad de Derecho de la Universidad de Alcalá de Henares 2003:141–211

Portocarrero J (ed) (2016) Ponderación y discrecionalidad. Un debate en torno al concepto y sentido de los principios formales en la interpretación constitucional. Universidad Externado, Bogotá

Ramallo J (2003) El bloque presupuestario en España. Revista Jurídica de les Illes Balears 1:11–40

Rubio Llorente F (2006) El papel del Consejo de Estado en el control de la calidad técnica de las normas. Revista española de la función consultiva 6:27–40

Sánchez JA (2019) La producción normativa en materia tributaria y la seguridad jurídica. In: Martín J, Pérez B (eds) Seguridad jurídica y derecho tributario. Thomson-Aranzadi, Cizur Menor, pp 387–410

Sanguinetti A (2017) Le *rogationes per saturam* prima della *lex Caecilia Didia*. Ius Online (Rivista di scienze giuridiche) 3:10–49

Santaolalla F (2011) ¿Es la homogeneidad material condición indispensable de las iniciativas legislativas? Revista de las Cortes Generales 83:135–176

Xanthaki H (2019) Misconceptions in legislative quality. In: Oliver-Lalana AD (ed) Conceptions and misconceptions of legislation. Springer, Cham, pp 23–50

Zarraluqui L (2012) El bosque legislativo. Available at www.zarraluqui.net/articulos

A. Daniel Oliver-Lalana Dr. iur., LL.M. (Genova), is professor of legal theory at the University of Zaragoza. His publications include the books *Legitimidad a través de la comunicación* (2011) and *Derecho y cultura de protección de datos* (2012), as well as the edition of the contributed volumes *Conceptions and misconceptions of legislation* (2019), *La legislación en serio* (2019), *Rational lawmaking under review* (2016, with K. Meßerschmidt), and *The rationality and justification of legislation* (2013, with L. Wintgens).

Canada: If Controversial, Omnibus Legislation Is Here to Stay

Louis Massicotte

Abstract In recent decades, omnibus legislation has been on the rise in the Canadian Parliament, generating much concern within opposition parties and among the media. In reaction to the perceived abuses of this legislative technique under Conservative Prime Minister Harper, all major opposition parties promised to curb this practice during the 2015 election campaign. Actually, the new Liberal government did not abandon the practice of omnibus legislation, but granted the Speaker of the House the power to divide an omnibus bill into distinct parts for the purposes of voting, and to do the same for the portions of budget implementation bills that had not been announced in the budget speech. This power has been used numerous times since then. However, one of the measures included in an omnibus bill later landed the government into serious trouble, contributing to the electoral setback of 2019, when the Liberals were reduced to a minority position.

Keywords Omnibus · Bills · Canada · Parliament · House of Commons · Senate · Trudeau (Justin) · Harper (Stephen) · Budget implementation · Budget speech · Liberal Party of Canada · Conservative Party · Standing Order 69.1 · Speaker

The Canadian parliamentary system is based on the Westminster model, with a stable and dominant executive. While private law is regulated by a civil code in the mostly French-speaking province of Québec, common law prevails in all other provinces, and Canadian public law follows the British pattern, which warrants inclusion of this chapter among common law jurisdictions.

Revised and updated version of a paper presented at the International Workshop "Rearranging the Arrangements Law: Comparative, Multidisciplinary, Empirical and Normative Perspectives on Omnibus Legislation" Faculty of Law, Bar-Ilan University, Tel Aviv, Israel, January 1–3, 2019.

L. Massicotte (✉)
Department of Political Science, Université Laval, Québec, QC, Canada
e-mail: Louis.massicotte.3@ulaval.ca

This chapter deals with omnibus legislation in the Canadian federal arena since Justin Trudeau's Liberals came to office in 2015. We provide background on the nature of omnibus bills, their emergence as an issue in Canadian politics under Conservative rule, the objections they raised within Parliament and outside, and the promises included in the platforms of the opposition parties during the 2015 campaign. We then detail how the Liberal government has been dealing with the issue since the election, and try to explain why the government chose to curb the worst excesses associated with this practice instead of abolishing it. Finally, we expand on one measure dissimulated in an omnibus bill that later threw the government into turmoil.

1 Background

In the authoritative compendium of the procedure of the Canadian House of Commons, Bosc and Gagnon (2017), p. 730 state that "an omnibus bill seeks to amend, repeal or enact several Acts, and is characterized by the fact that it is made up of a number of related but separate initiatives". Previous Speakers have ruled that such a bill should have "one basic principle or purpose which ties together all the proposed enactments". Prior to the 2017 amendments to the Standing Orders (see Sect. 4.2 below), there was no agreed upon definition of an omnibus bill, though the previous edition of the same compendium by O'Brien and Bosc (2009), pp. 724–727 offered some clues. Apart from budget implementation bills, which are clearly identifiable, Massicotte (2013), p. 13 found that there are no authoritative statistics showing how many omnibus bills were introduced in, and passed by, the Canadian Parliament. To this author's knowledge, no measure has ever stated explicitly that it was an omnibus bill.

It is not known with certainty when omnibus bills appeared, but Bosc and Gagnon (2017), pp. 730–734 mention an 1888 private bill that confirmed two separate railway agreements. The earliest objection in the House to this legislative technique was recorded in 1953. In December 1967, Pierre Elliott Trudeau, then Minister of Justice, introduced his landmark *Criminal Law Amendment Bill,* which dealt with issues as varied as homosexuality, abortion, contraception, lotteries, gun ownership, drinking-and-driving penalties, harassing phone calls, regulated misleading advertising and even cruelty to animals.[1] The measure was soon nicknamed "Trudeau's omnibus bill", and so a legislative technique, while not exactly reaching household words status, became known to a wider public.

An omnibus bill of more dubious fame was Bill C-94, *The Energy Security Act 1982,* which raised the ire of the Progressive Conservative opposition due to its omnibus nature. In keeping with precedents, Speaker Sauvé did not accept to divide

---

[1]On this omnibus bill, passed in 1969 as the *Criminal Law Amendment Act 1968-69* (SC 1968-69 c 38), see Dummitt and Sethna (2020) and Gunther (2012).

the bill. In retaliation, the Conservatives refused to allow their whip to join the Liberal whip after bells started ringing for a division, with the result that the sitting of March 2, 1982 lasted two full weeks during which the bells rang continuously.[2] In the end, the government agreed to split the measure into eight separate pieces of legislation. In 1988, Bill C-130, implementing the Canada-US Free Trade Agreement, raised concerns as well.

The underlying "basic principle or purpose" cited in earlier Speakers' decisions can be anything, ranging from the most innocuous to the most controversial. As an example of hardly objectionable purpose, one can cite the British practice of passing at times, from the 1860s onwards, a *Statute Law Revision Act*, that repealed spent legislative enactments. Some Commonwealth countries, like Canada and Australia, have emulated this practice. Hundreds of different statutes could be altered on one stroke by such measures, the basic purpose of which was to expunge from the statute book provisions that were either obsolete or spent.[3] However, the underlying logic of omnibus bills can easily degenerate. As Speaker Lamoureux noted in 1971, "Where do we stop? (. . .) We might reach the point where we would have only one bill, a bill at the start of the session for the improvement of the quality of life in Canada which would include every single proposed piece of legislation for the session (. . .) Would it be acceptable legislation?".[4] While warning the House about such possible abuse, Speaker Lamoureux and his successors consistently refused to accept requests from the opposition to split omnibus bills in the absence of a rule that would empower them to do so.

From the point of view of the executive, omnibus bills have the advantage of reducing the time spent in the House for debating government measures, because a single debate will take place at both second and third reading instead of dozens of debates of that nature on as many shorter bills. Another consideration is that by lumping together measures that the opposition parties agree with, and measures they strenuously object too, the government can generate embarrassment among them. In minority government contexts, when it is more difficult to cut off debate on controversial measures, omnibus bills may become a much-needed substitute for closure and time allocation orders. Critics retort that Parliament will have less time to scrutinize such measures appropriately, especially at the committee stage because they include topics that would be studied more closely by different committees.

The 2004 election inaugurated a succession of indecisive elections and minority governments, during which omnibus bills became an issue in Canadian legislative politics, and so remained after a return to single-party majorities in 2011. Prime Minister Harper did not invent omnibus bills or budget implementation bills. Yet, he will be remembered for having given them a bad name because under his leadership,

---

[2]On this episode, see Franks (1987), pp. 33–34.

[3]Ireland once passed a statute of that nature that repealed no less than 3225 statutes, arguably a world record. See the *Statute Law Revision Act 2007*, Acts of the Oireachtas No. 28 of 2007. http://www.irishstatutebook.ie/eli/2007/act/28/enacted/en/pdf.

[4]Cited by Dodek (2017), pp. 15–16.

the logic behind omnibus bills was pushed to extremes never seen before. The main technique used by the Conservatives was the budget implementation bill, dubbed the "omnibudget", a measure that purportedly enacted the various policies announced in the budget speech, but that came to include matters that had not been announced in the budget, or indeed that had no real connection with it.

According to Wherry (2012), budget implementation bills under Liberal administrations between 1994 and 2005, averaged 73.6 pages, while under Harper, from 2006 to 2015 they averaged 298.1 pages—four times longer. The increase is even sharper than it looks. While during the first period a single budget implementation bill was presented each year (there were none in 2002 and two in 2004), bills of that nature have since then been presented twice a year except in 2008, when there was a single one because an election took place during the fall. The yearly average of budget implementation legislation in recent years is therefore closer to 550 pages— this is seven times longer! Another contrast is that during the first period, budget implementation bills tended to be slimmed down markedly between first reading and Royal Assent, while in recent years they kept their initial size throughout.[5]

Figures are also available on the amount of time consumed in the House and in committee by budget implementation bills for the years 2002 to 2013.[6] The number of minutes spent on each page of each budget implementation bill varied from 4 in 2011 to 19 in 2005, with an average of 11.

Worse, omnibus budget bills at times degenerated into a kitchen sink in which the government buried controversial measures that hardly related to the implementation of the budget. One of the most egregious examples occurred in October 2013, in relation to the appointment of Justice Nadon to the Supreme Court of Canada. Whether the nominee was legally qualified to sit in the Supreme Court was an issue that had just provoked a court challenge. The government tried to solve the problem by inserting at the very end of its 322-page budget implementation bill (C-4) two clauses that amended the *Supreme Court Act* so that the wording of the sections describing the qualifications of a judge reflected its own reading of the Act. This attempt was ultimately futile. The government decided at the same time to refer the issue to the Supreme Court of Canada with the hope of getting a favourable judicial decision sooner. In March 2014, an almost unanimous Court decided that the nominated judge was not legally qualified. Further, one of the two amendments to the Act found in the budget implementation bill was declared *ultra vires*, and the other one, while constitutional, was declared redundant.[7]

---

[5]See Table 1 in appendix on budget implementation bills 2001 to 2019.

[6]See Cockram (2014), pp. 37–39 and 42–43.

[7]*Re Supreme Court Act, ss 5 and 6*, [2014] SCC 21.

2 Concerns of Opposition MPs Formally Expressed in Motions and Bills

Omnibus bills became vilified by the opposition parties, in the media, by parliamentary scholars like Franks (2010) and Dodek (2017) or former bureaucrats like Clark and DeVries (2015) as authoritarian devices purporting to avoid proper scrutiny of government measures, that exemplified the ruling Conservatives' contempt of Parliament, though former Harper aide Wilson (2016) qualified these views. Apart from multiplying amendments to the controversial measures, opposition members had few weapons at their disposal to prevent them from becoming law.[8] However, they could debate the issue in general terms, and propose solutions, which they did.

On October 16, 2012, Liberal MP and former astronaut Marc Garneau's motion on omnibus bills was debated in the House on a day reserved for opposition motions.[9] The tone of the motion was somewhat sarcastic: "That the House agree with the comments of the Right Honourable Member for Calgary Southwest [*then Prime Minister Stephen Harper*] on March 25, 1994, when he criticized omnibus legislation, suggesting that the subject matter of such bills is so diverse that a single vote on the content would put Members in conflict with their own principles and dividing the bill into several components would allow Members to represent views of their constituents on each of the different components in the bill; and that the House instruct the Standing Committee on Procedure and House Affairs to study what reasonable limits should be placed on the consideration of omnibus legislation and that the Committee report back its findings, including specific recommendations for legislative measures or changes to the Standing Orders, no later than December 10, 2012".[10] Predictably, all three opposition parties supported the motion. No less predictably, it was voted down by the Conservative majority.

A private member motion (M-561) was placed on notice by NDP MP Jean-François Larose in February 2015. It read: "That, in the opinion of the House: (*a*) the introduction of omnibus budget implementation bills is undemocratic, does not give Parliament enough time for review, and prevents Members from fulfilling their parliamentary responsibility to their constituents; (*b*) any omnibus budget implementation bill that proposes substantial amendments should be divided among the appropriate committees; and (*c*) omnibus budget implementation bills should be studied exclusively by the Standing Committee on Finance only if the proposed

---

[8]On the use of such weapons, see Saint-Pierre et al. (2015).

[9]In Canadian parliamentary jargon, these are known as "supply day motions". Twenty-two days in each year are "allotted", i.e. set aside within government business for debating a motion selected by one of the opposition parties. A distinctive feature is that the motion debated must be put and voted on, in contrast with private members' motions, which are routinely talked out after one hour. See Standing Order (SO) 81 para. (10) to (22).

[10]*Debates of the House of Commons*, October 16, 1012, pp. 11012–11072. https://www.ourcommons.ca/Content/House/411/Debates/162/HAN162-E.PDF#page=6.

amendments are minor, technical or corrective".[11] The motion was never debated and died on the order paper when a new general election was called.

How Parliament deals with omnibus bills could also be regulated by law, which would have greater force than a House rule because the consent of the Senate is needed for its repeal. On February 19, 2015, NDP Member Peter Stoffer introduced Bill C-654. The measure provided that neither the Senate nor the House of Commons could adopt a bill that proposed to amend, enact or repeal more than one Act or that proposed a combination of those actions, unless the bill related to a single subject-matter or to subject-matters that had a clearly demonstrable interrelationship and might reasonably be regarded as implementing a single broad policy. This prohibition did not apply to Miscellaneous Statute Law Amendment bills, or budget implementation bills, "if all of the substantive provisions of the bill have a purpose that is primarily financial in nature".[12] The presentation of the bill was echoed in the media by Desjardins (2015) and Janus (2015), which is very rare indeed, because of the wide and well-founded expectation that public bills sponsored by private MPs will not proceed further and will not even be debated, a common fate this bill indeed did not escape.

3 Omnibus Bills During the 2015 Campaign

As could be expected for a topic that usually attracts little attention beyond MPs and professional Parliament-watchers, omnibus bills were not a major issue throughout the longest—78 days—election campaign in modern Canadian history. Yet, this campaign became the first one where three opposition parties inserted in their respective platforms commitments related to what had hitherto been dismissed as an arcane topic of little public interest. All castigated omnibus legislation, and promised to curb or abolish this practice. While they had the longest platform, the ruling Conservatives, unsurprisingly, ignored the issue.

Tom Mulcair's left-wing New Democratic Party, then the official opposition and the leading party in the opinion polls at the start of the campaign, proposed to empower the Speaker to break up omnibus bills "like the ones that Stephen Harper used to ram changes through Parliament in order to avoid scrutiny".[13] Justin Trudeau's Liberals (center-left), who started the campaign running third, were even more categorical: "Stephen Harper has also used omnibus bills to prevent Parliament from properly reviewing and debating his proposals. We will change

---

[11]http://www.ourcommons.ca/Parliamentarians/en/members/Jean-Francois-Larose(71503)/ Motions.

[12]Bill C-654, *An Act to amend the Parliament of Canada Act (omnibus bills)*, First reading, February 19, 2015, http://www.parl.ca/Content/Bills/412/Private/C-654/C-654_1/C-654_1.PDF.

[13]See New Democratic Party of Canada (2015), p. 55. The party is commonly known as the NDP.

the House of Commons Standing Orders to bring an end to this undemocratic practice".[14]

Omnibus bills received comparatively more attention in the Green Party's platform, probably because they had been used for bringing legislation pertaining to the environment, a key issue for the Greens. Under the heading "REVERSE HARPER'S LEGACY TO PUT OUR GOVERNMENT BACK ON TRACK", the document stated: "The Harper Conservatives' invented (sic) the use of omnibus budget bills – bills that cover dozens of diverse and unrelated changes to law and policy. Such bills have been rammed through Parliament time and time again since 2011, without proper study (. . .) Omnibus budget bills have severely damaged our democracy. The Harper administration has used omnibus bills to devastate centuries-old environmental legislation, curb free speech, and cut billions in funding from health care. A single omnibus bill in spring 2012 (C-38) changed 70 laws, which even former Conservative ministers said undermined our fisheries and environment".[15] The Greens promised to work to end "the illegitimate use" of omnibus bills and declared that such sweeping bills had no place in our democracy. In addition, they promised to restore all the environmental protections eliminated over the past ten years.

4 Omnibus Bills Under Justin Trudeau

On October 19, 2015, against the expectations of most observers, the Liberals won a majority in the House of Commons with 184 seats out of 338, based on 39.5% of the vote.[16] A gender-parity Cabinet was appointed on November 4, while Justin Trudeau embarked on a prolonged honeymoon with Canadians that lasted for about two years and a half.

The Throne Speech, read on December 4, had something on democratic reform. The new government repeated its major commitments like introducing a new electoral system and reforming appointments to the Senate. It also delivered, *in fine*, a pointed rebuke to the former administration: "Also notable are the things the Government will not do: it will not use government ads for partisan purposes; it will not interfere with the work of parliamentary officers; and it will not resort to devices like prorogation and omnibus bills to avoid scrutiny".[17]

---

[14]See Liberal Party of Canada (2015), p. 30.

[15]See Green Party of Canada (2015).

[16]Canadian elections are held under the First-Past-the-Post system, which explains the discrepancy between the popular vote and the seats won by each party. Ironically, Justin Trudeau's brave promise, that the 2015 election would be the last one held under that system, fell by the wayside in less than 15 months.

[17]*Debates of the Senate*, Dec. 4, 2015, p. 5. The Throne Speech is read in the Senate chamber.

4.1   The First Budget Implementation Bills 2016–2017

It soon became clear that in the eyes of the new government, budget implementation bills were *not* omnibus bills, provided they were connected to the budget. The new government's first budget was tabled on March 22, 2016, by Finance Minister Bill Morneau, and was followed four weeks later by a budget implementation bill.[18] The Minister denied the contention, made by NDP members, that the measure was an omnibus bill, arguing that "our budget implementation act is absolutely not an omnibus bill. Every measure in the budget implementation act is related to our budget, unlike previous omnibus bills from the members opposite".[19] Drawing such a line came as a surprise to many, as earlier budget implementation bills had been labeled omnibus, yet with the benefit of hindsight, this statement heralded what became a key feature of the new approach of the government with regards to omnibus legislation. The entire clause-by-clause study of the bill in the House took place in the Standing Committee on Finance, as before.

A second bill of the same nature was presented during the fall.[20] A Conservative MP was the only one to refer to its omnibus nature: "It is necessary, sometimes, to move a budget into law that impacts lots of different pieces of legislation. The Liberals called it omnibus. I just call it good governance and how a budget is actually put into action".[21] It was passed without arousing too much controversy.

That the Liberals intended to continue the use of omnibus bills with regards to budget implementation (while still denying they were omnibus bills) became clearer than ever on April 11, 2017, when the Budget Speech of March 22 was followed by the tabling of a 300-page budget implementation bill.[22] This time, much was made, by the opposition parties and the media, notably by Wyld (2017), of the fact that this measure was an omnibus bill that enacted new rules governing the Parliamentary Budget Officer, and created a Canadian Infrastructure Bank. The scenario of the previous year unfolded again, with the House entrusting the clause-by-clause consideration of the Bill to a single committee. This measure happened to be the last budget implementation bill adopted before the rules of the game were altered by the adoption of SO 69.1.

---

[18]Bill C-15, *Budget Implementation Act, 2016, No. 1*, S.C. 2016 c. 7. http://www.parl.ca/Content/Bills/421/Government/C-15/C-15_4/C-15_4.PDF.

[19]*Debates of the House of Commons*, April 21, 2016, p. 2544.

[20]Bill C-29, *Budget Implementation Act, 2016, No. 2*, SC 2016 c. 12, http://www.parl.ca/Content/Bills/421/Government/C-29/C-29_4/C-29_4.PDF.

[21]*Debates of the House of Commons*, October 28, 2016, p. 6297.

[22]Bill C-44, *Budget Implementation Act, 2017, No. 1*. S.C. 2017, c. 20. http://www.parl.ca/Content/Bills/421/Government/C-44/C-44_4/C-44_4.PDF.

4.2   A New Standing Order on Omnibus Bills, June 2017

On March 10, 2017, the Liberal government released a wide-ranging discussion paper on the reform of the procedure of the House, which *inter alia* dealt with omnibus bills (Leader of the Government in the House of Commons 2017). The document was poorly received by the opposition parties, to the point of provoking an 80-hour filibuster in committee. In the end, while most of the contents of the document were dropped, the parts pertaining to omnibus bills, which were less controversial, survived the purge.[23] They were passed by the House as an amendment to the Standing Orders on June 20, 2017, and came into force on September 18. The motion adopting the rule changes was carried on division, with all opposition parties voting against.[24] The NDP sponsored an amendment which would have allowed the Speaker to divide omnibus bills *into distinct bills*, instead of merely imposing distinct votes on groups of clauses at some stages. This was rejected by the Liberal majority.[25]

The new Standing Order (69.1) is as follows:

(1) **Omnibus Bills**. In the case where a government bill seeks to repeal, amend or enact more than one act, and where there is not a common element connecting the various provisions or where unrelated matters are linked, the Speaker shall have the power to divide the questions, for the purposes of voting, on the motion for second reading and reference to a committee and the motion for third reading and passage of the bill. The Speaker shall have the power to combine clauses of the bill thematically and to put the aforementioned questions on each of these groups of clauses separately, provided that there will be a single debate at each stage.

(2) **Budget implementation bills**. The present Standing Order shall not apply if the bill has as its main purpose the implementation of a budget and contains only provisions that were announced in the budget presentation or in the documents tabled during the budget presentation.[26]

In a nutshell, as the sponsor of the new rule put it, SO 69.1 gives the Speaker the authority to divide bills for the purpose of voting for second reading, third reading, and passage of a bill. The Speaker is also authorized to group a bill thematically for

---

[23]For an account of the process, see Wherry (2017a, b) and Bryden (2017).

[24]The Conservative House Leader suggested during the debate that the negative attitude of the Conservative Members had less to do with the substance of the new Standing Orders than with the way the government had handled the issue in recent weeks. See *Debates of the House of Commons,* pp. 12903–12905.

[25]*Debates of the House of Commons,* June 19, 2017, pp. 12899–12915, https://www.ourcommons.ca/Content/House/421/Debates/197/HAN197-E.PDF; *Idem,* June 20, 2017, pp. 12976–13005, https://www.ourcommons.ca/Content/House/421/Debates/198/HAN198-E.PDF.

[26]*Journals of the House of Commons,* June 20, 2017, pp. 2010–2016. For the text of the rejected NDP amendment on omnibus bills, see pp. 2004–2005. https://www.ourcommons.ca/Content/House/421/Journals/198/Journal198.PDF.

that purpose. There will be a single debate at each stage, and members will then be able to vote on parts of a bill separately.[27]

The new rule provides an authoritative definition of what an omnibus bill is: a bill that seeks to repeal, amend or enact more than one act, *and* where there is not a common element connecting the various provisions *or* where unrelated matters are linked. This definition is not based on the length of the piece, even if in common parlance the sheer size of the measure is often cited, indeed lamented. This is appropriate. With respectively 3220 and 1287 pages, the *Income Tax Act* and the *Criminal Code*,[28] are apparently the longest federal statutes now in force.[29] Yet, if either was introduced tomorrow as a brand new bill, it would not be considered an omnibus bill. On the other hand, much shorter measures were deemed to be omnibus in the past because of their heterogeneous nature.

An omnibus bill as defined by the new rule has two distinctive features. First, *the number of statutes* (simply put: more than one) that it purports to repeal, amend or enact. If the definition stopped here, nearly every bill today would likely be considered omnibus, because consequential amendments included in bills usually cover a fairly wide range of existing legislation. This is why a second, and decisive, criterion is added: *there is not a common element connecting the various provisions,* or *unrelated matters are linked.* The heterogeneous nature of the piece is key.

The new rules obviously fall short of the categorical promise made in the Liberal platform, that omnibus bills would be brought to an end. No power is given to the Speaker to split them up into distinct bills. All the Speaker can do, upon a request made by an MP raising a point of order, is to *divide the questions, for the purposes of voting,* on the motion for second reading and reference to a committee, and later on the motion for third reading and passage of the bill. Upon having found that the measure includes matters that are unrelated, the Speaker has the power to "combine clauses of the bill thematically" into separate groups of clauses, all of which will be *voted on separately.* However, there will be no distinct debate on each group, as the rule provides there will be *a single debate at each stage.* If a specific group of clauses is rejected at second or third reading, these clauses are removed from the bill. The rule does not impose either that the measure be split up among various standing committees for the purpose of clause-by-clause consideration. From the government's point of view, the chief inconvenience of the new rule is that there may be more than one vote at second and third reading.

Budget implementation bills are commonly viewed as omnibus bills, yet under SO 69.1(2) they are exempted from the ambit of SO 69.1(1), in keeping with the incumbent Minister of Finance's view, quoted above, that they are not omnibus bills.

---

[27]Hon. Bardish Chagger, *Debates of the House of Commons*, June 19, 2017, p. 12901.

[28]Canada, Department of Justice, *Income Tax Act*, R.S.C., 1985, c.1 (5th Suppl.); *Criminal Code*, R.S.C., 1985, c. C-46. The most recent consolidations of both statutes can be found at https://laws-lois.justice.gc.ca/PDF/I-3.3.pdf, and https://laws-lois.justice.gc.ca/PDF/C-46.pdf.

[29]Duhaime.org, "Canadian Legal History: 1892 Canada's Criminal Code". http://www.duhaime.org/LawMuseum/CanadianLegalHistory/LawArticle-94/1892-Canadas-Criminal-Code.aspx.

They become "omnibus bills", and then can be divided for the purposes of voting, *only* if they include provisions that had not been announced in the budget presentation or in the documents tabled during the budget presentation. It is up to the government, then, to make sure that there exists an obvious link between each provision of the budget implementation bill and the budget statement.

4.3   Speaker's Rulings Based on Standing Order (SO) 61.1.

It is probably too soon to assess the full impact of the new Standing Order, which has been in force for a mere 16 months. So far, the effectiveness of SO 61.1 has been tested in relation to eight bills. Four were non-budgetary omnibus bills, while the others were budget implementation bills.

4.3.1   Omnibus Bills Unrelated to the Budget

As of March 2021, four bills of that nature raised requests for division due to their alleged omnibus nature, one of them (Bill C-59) at two distinct stages. The first test came in relation to the relatively short (16 pages) Bill C-56, *an Act to amend the Corrections and Conditional Release Act and the Abolition of Early Parole Act* (no short title).[30] On October 31, 2017, Conservative House Leader Candice Bergen rose on a point of order requesting that the Speaker apply SO 69.1 to this measure. She argued that the bill contained one part that amended the Corrections and Conditional Release Act to address issues relating to the use of administrative segregation, and a second part that aimed to amend the Abolition of Early Parole Act in relation to accelerated parole for certain offenders, and that these two matters were unrelated.[31] On November 7, 2017, Speaker Reagan stated that since the subject matter of the bill dealt with the treatment of inmates, it was his view that the two parts were related and that the question on Bill C-56 should not be divided.[32]

A second issue arose in relation to Bill C-59, the *National Security Act, 2017*, an omnibus bill with three parts, each enacting a distinct statute, and that ran 160 pages.[33] On November 20, 2017, NDP MP Matthew Dubé raised a point of order requesting that, pursuant to SO 69.1, the Speaker divide the question for the purpose of voting on the motion for the referral to Committee *before second reading* of the bill. The same day, Speaker Regan ruled that SO 69.1 could not apply to a

---

[30]Text of Bill C-56 in http://www.parl.ca/Content/Bills/421/Government/C-56/C-56_1/C-56_1. PDF. This Bill died on the order paper.

[31]*Debates of the House of Commons*, October 31, 2017, pp. 14747–14748.

[32]*Idem*, November 7, 2017, pp. 15116–15117.

[33]Text of Bill C-59 in http://www.parl.ca/Content/Bills/421/Government/C-59/C-59_3/C-59_3. PDF.

motion to refer a bill to committee before second reading, and he invited members to raise the issue again prior to third reading of the bill, if necessary.[34]

Accordingly, on June 11, 2018, Mr. Dubé once again rose on a point of order requesting that SO 69.1 be applied to Bill C-59 at third reading. On June 18, Deputy Speaker Stanton ruled that the Chair would agree to split the bill for the purpose of voting. He acknowledged that Bill C-59 did clearly contain several different initiatives, and that "while the Chair has no trouble agreeing that all of the measures contained in Bill C-59 relate to national security, it is the Chair's view that there are distinct initiatives that are sufficiently unrelated as to warrant dividing the question. Therefore, the Chair is prepared to divide the question on the motion for third reading of the bill".[35]

Another test came with Bill C-69 (no short title), which purported to undo another omnibus bill passed during the Harper era.[36] On February 27, 2018, NDP House Leader Ruth Ellen Brosseau rose on a point of order and requested that the Speaker apply SO 69.1 to Bill C-69. She argued that the bill contained several different initiatives that should be voted on separately, noting that this bill would delete two existing acts, would enact new ones, and would amend over 30 other acts.[37] On March 1, 2018, Speaker Regan delivered his ruling, stating: "Bill C-69 does clearly contain several different initiatives. It establishes two new agencies (. . .), and makes a series of amendments to the Navigation Protection Act. One could make the case, as did the parliamentary secretary, that there is indeed a common thread connecting these various initiatives, in that they are all related to environmental protection. However, the question the Chair must ask itself is whether the purpose of the standing order was to deal only with matters that were obviously unrelated or whether it was to provide members with the opportunity to pronounce themselves on specific initiatives when a bill contains a variety of different measures. [. . .] In this particular instance, I have no trouble agreeing that all of the measures contained in Bill C-69 relate to environmental protection. However, I believe there are distinct initiatives that are sufficiently unrelated that they warrant multiple votes. Therefore, I am prepared to allow more than one vote on the motion for second reading of the

---

[34]*Debates of the House of Commons*, November 20, 2017, pp. 15333–15335 (point of order raised) and p. 15344 (Speaker's ruling).

[35]*Debates of the House of Commons*, June 11, 2018 (point of order raised), p. 20664; *Idem*, June 12, 2018 (government reply to the point of order), p. 20775; *Idem*, June 18, 2018 (Deputy Speaker's decision), pp. 21198–21200. No such request had been made at second reading.

[36]Bill C-69, *An Act to enact the Impact Assessment Act and the Canadian Energy Regulator Act, to amend the Navigation Protection Act and to make consequential amendments to other Acts,* now SC 2019 c. 28.

[37]*Debates of the House of Commons*, February 27, 2018, pp. 17430–17431.

bill".[38] Later, the same procedure was applied for the vote on third reading of the measure.[39]

The most recent ruling occurred on September 29, 2020 in relation to Bill C-4, the COVID-19 Response Measures Act. Following an objection raised the day before by a Conservative MP, Speaker Rota ruled that all of the measures contained in Bill C-4 related to the COVID-19 pandemic, and this constituted a common element linking them together. Therefore, the objection was rejected.[40] Not all omnibus bills were brought to the Speaker's attention. Bill C-49, a 67-page measure on transport modernization,[41] was described in November 2017 by an NDP MP as "a poorly and hastily crafted omnibus bill that would undermine worker's fundamental rights to privacy and protect the rights of investors". In her speech, she suggested severing the two initiatives her party agreed with from what she called "the pointless and ineffective remainder" of Bill C-49, so they could be studied at committee and passed into law.[42] However, no point of order was raised under SO 69.1 in relation to the measure, which was passed.

4.3.2   Budget Implementation Bills

In October 2017, the government introduced a 328-page budget implementation bill (C-63) which related to the budget speech of March 22.[43] A point of order was raised during the second reading debate by the Hon. Pierre Poilievre (Conservative), arguing that this bill included measures that were not in the budget speech, and asking the Speaker to divide the question on the motions for second and third reading.[44] Speaker Regan ruled on the issue five days later.[45] While conceding that the link between the budget and the measures included in the implementation bill was not always obvious, he agreed that many measures in Bill C-63 were not related to the budget speech and that, therefore, he would divide the question at second and, if necessary, at third reading. Specifically, four parts of the bill would be

---

[38]*Debates of the House of Commons*, March 1, 2018, pp. 17574–17576. The Speaker decided to divide the Bill in the following way: part 3 and clauses 85, 186, 187 and 195 of clause 4 were voted together; the remainder of part 4, as well as parts 1 & 2 were voted together.

[39]*Debates of the House of Commons*, June 20, 2018, pp. 21379–21381.

[40]Debates of the House of Commons, Sept. 29, 2020, pp. 269–270.

[41]Bill C-49, *Transportation Modernization Act*, SC 2018 c. 10. http://www.parl.ca/Content/Bills/421/Government/C-49/C-49_4/C-49_4.PDF.

[42]http://irenemathyssen.ndp.ca/in-debate-bill-c-49-transportation-modernization-act.

[43]Bill C-63, *Budget Implementation Act, 2017, No. 2*, SC 2017, c. 33, http://www.parl.ca/Content/Bills/421/Government/C-63/C-63_4/C-63_4.PDF.

[44]*Debates of the House of Commons*, November 3, 2017, pp. 14969–14971. See also *Debates*, November 7, 2017, pp. 15070–15081, where the other opposition parties agreed with the point of order raised and the government stated its case against it.

[45]*Idem*, November 8, 2017, pp. 15165–15167. A short notice can be found in *Canadian Parliamentary Review*, 41 (1), Spring 2018, p. 48.

put to separate votes. They dealt with agricultural and fisheries co-operatives, the sales tax rebate for public service bodies and the discharge of debt and amendments to the Excise Act in relation to beer made from concentrate. A few hours later, five distinct votes took place on the second reading of Bill C-63, four on the non-budget portions and one on the budget elements.[46] At third reading, the vote was conducted in a similar way.[47]

This was the only ruling from the Chair under SO 69.1 that found echo in the media. As an observer put it with a touch of irony, "The Liberals came to office with a commitment to do something about the issue [of omnibus bills]. And, after an acrimonious process that itself resulted in opposition protest and filibuster, the Liberals put forward a new rule this spring as part of a small set of parliamentary reforms. The Liberals have at least now succeeded in proving the effectiveness of that rule".[48]

Politicians are learning animals, and the Minister of Finance was much more careful the next year in order to avoid this kind of embarrassment. The budget speech of February 27, 2018, was duly followed four weeks later by the introduction of a budget implementation bill (C-74).[49] If only because of its size (559 pages), the measure met with the usual criticisms from the opposition, while the Minister of Finance again strenuously denied it was an omnibus bill.[50] On April 23, on a point of order raised by the NDP, Speaker Regan ruled that there was a "direct link" between what was announced in the budget and what was contained in the implementation bill, thereby rejecting the point of order.[51] The bill included amendments to the Criminal Code that led some members to request that these provisions be split from the bill and studied by the Justice committee, but the office of the Minister of Finance countered that this provision was mentioned in the budget speech.[52] These amendments remained in the bill. Few people noticed at that time the provision creating deferred prosecution agreements (DPAs) which later threw the government in turmoil (see Sect. 7 below).

The government was less fortunate during the fall with the second budget implementation bill of the year, which happened to be, at 884 pages, the second-longest bill of that nature ever presented.[53] On October 31, NDP MP and finance critic Peter Julian raised a point of order and asked the Speaker to divide the question on the bill pursuant to SO 69.1. He argued that specific measures in the bill, namely the clauses dealing with protections for workers, and the clauses dealing with the

---

[46]*Debates of the House of Commons*, November 8, 2017, pp. 15182–15189.

[47]*Idem*, December 1, 2017, pp. 15905–15907.

[48]Wherry (2017c).

[49]Bill C-74, *Budget Implementation Act, 2018, No. 1*, SC 2018 c. 12. http://www.parl.ca/Content/Bills/421/Government/C-74/C-74_4/C-74_4.PDF.

[50]See Aiello (2018).

[51]*Debates of the House of Commons*, April 23, 2018, pp. 18610–18611 (point of order) and 186555–186556 (ruling).

[52]Blatchford (2018).

[53]Bill C-86, *Budget Implementation Act, 2018, No. 2*, SC 2018 c. 27. http://www.parl.ca/Content/Bills/421/Government/C-86/C-86_2/C-86_2.PDF.

head of compliance and enforcement, did not appear to arise out of measures announced in the budget, and should be separated out for a distinct vote.[54] The Parliamentary Secretary to the government's House Leader contended that the government had signalled its intention to amend and modernize the Canada Labour Code *in last year's budget* and that these provisions were in response to that commitment.[55]

Speaker Regan ruled on the point of order on November 6. He stated that the intention of the Standing Order was not to exempt provisions from *previous* budgets. Some commitments implemented by the bill had been expressed in the 2017 budget and had not been repeated this year, while the bill's title claimed to implement "the budget tabled in Parliament on February 27, 2018". For this reason, he allowed a separate vote on all provisions of the bill relating to the head of compliance and enforcement in the Canada Labour Code (clauses 535 to 625), while the next vote would deal with all remaining provisions of the bill.[56] The same procedure was followed for the vote on the third reading of the bill.[57]

An election was scheduled for the Fall of 2019, so for practical purposes the proceedings of Parliament were over by June. The Budget Speech was delivered on March 19, and the 400-page budget implementation bill (C-97) came three weeks later.[58] On April 10, NDP MP Jenny Kwan argued that the bill included measures that were not mentioned in the budget speech, but Speaker Regan came to the opposite conclusion and rejected her point of order.[59]

Parliament was dissolved on September 11 and an election was held on October 21, 2019. The new Parliament first met on December 5. The Budget speech was announced for March 30, 2020, but had to be postponed, as the House was adjourned on March 13 due to the COVID-19 pandemic.

Summing up, successive rulings so far have established that SO 69.1 is not applicable to the vote on the motion referring an omnibus bill to a committee *before* second reading. Requests that non budgetary omnibus bills be divided for the purpose of voting have been made in relation to four bills, and failed twice. Rulings have determined that the provisions of a budget implementation bill must be connected with the specific budget speech referenced in the bill, and may not implement an item referred to in a *previous* budget speech. Points of order were raised in relation to each of the four bills of that nature introduced since the coming into force of SO 69.1(2), and were successful twice. Requests for dividing an omnibus bill for voting purposes have made their way into the weaponry of the opposition parties.

---

[54]*Debates of the House of Commons*, October 31, 2018, pp. 23119–23120.

[55]*Idem*, November 5, 2018, pp. 23310–23311.

[56]*Idem*, November 6, 2018 pp. 23378–23379.

[57]*Idem*, December 3, 2018, pp. 24390–24392.

[58]Bill C-97, *Budget Implementation Act, 2019, No.1*. SC 2019 c. 29. https://www.parl.ca/Content/Bills/421/Government/C-97/C-97_4/C-97_4.PDF.

[59]*Debates of the House of Commons*, April 10, 2019, pp. 26942–26944 and April 12, 2019, pp. 27035–27036 (point of order), and April 29, 2019, pp. 27122–27123 (ruling).

5   Omnibus Bills in the Senate

The Parliament of Canada includes an appointed upper house known as the Senate. This body is co-equal with the House of Commons for the passage of bills, except that money bills must originate in the House. Because of its appointive nature and the partisanship displayed by its members, the Senate had little prestige, and most of the time passed bills sent from the Commons without amendments, except when the Senate was dominated by the opposition parties, in which case senators became quite active, some would say activist.

Following the change of government in 2015, the Senate underwent a gradual transformation towards becoming a less partisan and more active body.[60] The main change was the appointment, based on merit instead of party affiliation, of so-called "Independent" senators, now numbering 42 in a house of 105.[61] In order to fulfill its role as a chamber offering "sober second thought" in the legislative process, the "new Senate" has tried to find the right balance between blind endorsement of government measures and legislative stalemate. As a result, throughout the 42nd Parliament (2015–2019), no less than 29 (34.5%) of the 84 government bills passed by the House have been amended by the upper house. Senate amendments were accepted by the House in relation to 7 bills, led to a compromise with the House on 18 bills, and were not insisted upon on 4 bills.[62] This record stands as a huge contrast with the previous 35 years, when the percentage of bills amended by the Senate during each Parliament was about 7%, and exceeded 10% only once.[63] It is worth pointing that none of these amendments led to a genuine confrontation between both houses, leading a Thomas (2018) to speak of "judicious combativeness" from the upper house. Whether the new Senate will grow more aggressive in the future remains of course matter for speculation.

With regards to budget implementation bills, the Senate is constrained by the fact that they must be first introduced in the House. Amending such bills in the Senate is extremely difficult, as both houses disagree on the right for the Senate to amend money bills. An alternative is to "pre-study" the bill *while it is still under consideration in the House*. This practice allows the upper house to consider a bill in detail, and eventually to suggest possible amendments thereto, *before* the bill is adopted by the House and formally transmitted to the Senate. In Canada, no bill can be considered simultaneously by both houses, which in practice obliges the Senate to deal with bills only when the House has made up its mind. In order to overcome this

---

[60]On this reform, which the Conservatives still challenge, see Massicotte (2018), Thomas (2018), McCoy (2017) and Pratte (2020).

[61]Critics of the reform, however, point out that so-called "Independent" senators voted with the government 95% of the time, compared with 78% of Senate Liberals. The full set of figures can be found in O'Brien et al. (2017).

[62]Author's computations. Only government bills whose consideration in the Senate had been completed (i.e given third reading) are included in these figures.

[63]Massicotte (2016).

hurdle, the Senate refers to one of its committees not the bill itself, but the "subject-matter" thereof. This allows Senate committees to suggest amendments to a bill sooner in the legislative process, hoping that the House will incorporate them into its own bill.[64]

In practice, the treatment of budget implementation bills in the Senate has been uneven. Up to 2005 inclusive, no budget implementation bill was pre-studied in the Senate. A new attitude was adopted in 2006 with the change of government, when the Liberal majority in the Senate was facing a Conservative minority government. From then onwards, such bills were pre-studied by the Senate Standing Committee on National Finance, except in 2009–2010, when no pre-study took place (meanwhile, the Conservatives had obtained control of the Senate). From May 2012 onwards, the Senate developed a new practice. Instead of the budget bill being pre-studied in its entirety by the Senate Standing Committee on National Finance, as had been done intermittently in the past, the bill was split up into pieces, each being pre-studied by five of six standing committees in addition to the National Finance committee. This amounted to an acknowledgement of the heterogeneous nature of the measure that was not emulated by the House. The practice has been followed ever since except once.[65] When the first Liberal budget implementation bill was tabled in the House in 2016, the Representative of the Government in the Senate[66] initially proposed to refer the measure to the Standing Committee on National Finance, but ultimately proposed, following consultations, to split the bill for the purposes of pre-study, and to refer parts thereof to four Senate committees.[67]

During the fall of 2016, the Senate again apportioned the pre-study of the budget implementation bill among three committees.[68] The measure hit a snag in the Senate with regards to a provision that would have removed some of the protection already enjoyed by consumers in the province of Québec. Following intense lobbying by the Québec government, unrelated to its omnibus nature, the bill was amended by the Senate and the House, after some reluctance, concurred with the amendment (Pratte 2020, pp. 149–156). On May 8, 2017, the Senate decided to apportion the study of the subject-matter of the budget implementation bill among six different

---

[64]On the pre-study of bills, see Senate of Canada (2015), pp. 151–152, 187–188, and Senate of Canada (2013), p. 243. This long-standing practice was formalized in the *Rules of the Senate* only in 1991, as Rules 10–11.

[65]*Debates of the Senate*, May 3, 2012, p. 1753; *Idem*, October 30, 2012, p. 2707; *Idem*, November 5, 2013, pp. 398–399; *Idem*, April 9, 2014, pp. 1354–1356; *Idem*, October 30, 2014, pp. 2347–2351; *Idem*, May 14, 2015, p. 3384. The only exception was Bill C-60, which was again pre-studied exclusively by the National Finance committee (*Debates of the Senate*, May 2, 2013, p. 3844). No explanation was given for that change, which proved temporary.

[66]Since 2016, under the Senate reform package adopted by the present administration, the Senator responsible for introducing and piloting government legislation in the Senate is now styled the "Representative of the Government in the Senate", stands as a "non affiliated", and does not sit in Cabinet. Hitherto, this role was fulfilled by the Leader of the Government in the Senate, who most of the time had the status of a cabinet minister.

[67]*Debates of the Senate*, May 3, 2016, p. 566.

[68]*Journals of the Senate*, November 22, 2016, p. 980.

committees.[69] In dealing with the spring 2018 budget implementation bill, the Senate stuck to its habit of having such bills pre-studied by various committees, as many as seven this time.[70] In the Fall of 2018 and the Spring of 2019, the Senate found the budget implementation bill so massive and multifaceted that pre-study was shared among eight committees.[71]

Not all Liberal Senators agreed with the new government's continuance of budget implementation bills.[72] In May 2018, Senate Liberal Leader Joseph Day expressed his disappointment, that "with this budget bill, the government has apparently abandoned its election promise to end the practice of introducing omnibus bills".[73] He noted that in addition to the normal and traditional budget bill amendments, such as the Income Tax Act, Bill C-44 would amend the Immigration and Refugee Protection Act, the Canada Labour Code, the Proceeds of Crime (Money Laundering) and Terrorist Financing Act and the Parliament of Canada Act. In addition, the bill would enact three entirely new stand-alone pieces of legislation that could easily have been introduced as distinct measures: the Canada Infrastructure Bank Act, the "Invest in Canada Act," and the Service Fees Act. Contrasting this bill with the more prudent measure to the same effect introduced the previous year, the Senator concluded: "What a change a year makes".[74]

Senator Day was even more incisive in his intervention during the second reading debate of the measure on June 14, when he compared Bill C-44 to a set of Ukrainian dolls: "You open up the first doll and there is another doll inside it, and you open up the second doll and there is another doll, and you keep going and peeling off the onion skins. But while that may be fun in a doll, it is absolutely no way to present legislation for proper study".[75] He pointed out an escalator clause that would automatically increase taxes on alcoholic beverages each year based on the Consumer Price Index, and complained that the bill reinforced Cabinet control over borrowing authority, a field that had already been removed from parliamentary prerogatives by another omnibus bill in 2007. "The bill contains provisions that quietly — one might say stealthily — remove Parliament's oversight of government

---

[69]*Journals of the Senate*, May 8, 2018, pp. 1870–1871.

[70]*Debates of the Senate*, April 24, 2018, p. 5270.

[71]*Debates of the Senate*, November 7, 2018, pp. 6749–6750; May 2, 2019, pp. 7969–7970.

[72]Liberal Senators were expelled from the Liberal caucus by Justin Trudeau in 2014, and can no longer be counted as reliable supporters of the present Liberal administration. Since 2015, no one has been added to the dwindling group of "Liberal Senators". In November 2019, the nine remaining Liberals chose to call themselves the "Progressive Senators Group". This group quickly lost official party status following two retirements and one defection. For the first time since Confederation, a house formerly nicknamed the "Grit Heaven" includes no Liberals.

[73]*Debates of the Senate*, May 8, 2017, p. 2987.

[74]*Idem.*

[75]*Debates of the Senate*, June 14, 2017, p. 3414.

finances and increase the power of the executive — of the cabinet".[76] Speeches made in the Senate rarely find echo in the media, but this one did.[77]

6   How the Liberals' Thinking on Omnibus Bills Evolved

Parties' electoral platforms are not famous for over-emphasizing nuances or qualifiers, and the Liberal 2015 document, echoing years of criticism from the opposition benches, was quite blunt on omnibus legislation: "bring an end to this undemocratic practice". A newly-elected government's first Throne speech may be less sharp, reflecting the prudence that comes with the assumption of power, yet the Liberals' was equally straightforward: "not [to] resort to devices like (. . .) omnibus bills".

Contrasted with such bold statements, the Trudeau government's attitude on omnibus legislation was decidedly mild. Budget implementation bills are still introduced at the rate of two per year, and their size, which at the outset already exceeded those of the pre-Harper years, has continued to grow. They now simply have to relate unambiguously to the budget speech. The new Standing Order neither prohibits omnibus bills in general, nor empowers the Speaker to split them up, except for the purposes of voting at two crucial stages whenever the Speaker sees it fit. Should we conclude with melancholy that *"Plus ça change, plus c'est pareil"*? This would be unfair. The new rule (SO 69.1) has been successfully invoked against the government too many times so far for being dismissed as a mere decorative ornament, a fig leaf covering a broken promise. What happened is simply that the Liberals were less deeply opposed to omnibus bills than their rhetoric in opposition suggested. This should come as no surprise, as the Liberals had been in office for a long time and had themselves been skilled practitioners of omnibus legislation. Like many Canadians, they may have been outraged by the excesses of the Harper era, when the Conservatives pushed the practice of omnibus bills to heights never reached before. The advantages of omnibus legislation for any government, they never lost sight of.

There is indeed evidence that within the government side, the advantages of omnibus legislation are now candidly and publicly acknowledged. In April 2018, the Representative of the Government in the Senate, Peter Harder,[78] issued a discussion

---

[76]*Idem* p. 3419.

[77]See Platt (2017).

[78]Senator Harder's background as a consummate government insider deserves mention. His distinguished career in the federal public service included 16 years as Deputy Minister, heading the Departments of Foreign Affairs and International Trade, Solicitor General, Public Security, and the Treasury Board Secretariat. Harder was the head of Trudeau's transition team in 2015, eliciting the following comment from the upper reaches of the bureaucracy: "his experience sends the message that the Liberals understand how government works". See Anonymous (2015). He was appointed to the Senate the next year and was a key figure in the new Senate envisaged by Prime Minister Justin Trudeau.

paper on the role of the Senate. Included is a substantial passage on omnibus legislation that offers a good perspective on how the government's thinking on this topic evolved with years. The author started by saying that "a caveat must apply to *abusive* omnibus bills" (emphasis added) and cited some of the most egregious examples of such abuses under Stephen Harper.[79] Yet, as he pointed out, "this caveat has a caveat", and he went on with an impassioned defence of this legislative technique that deserves full quotation:

> There is nothing inherently ominous about an omnibus bill (...) [they] have been a feature of our parliamentary life for some time, and not all are abusive. In this day and age, with a modern and complex economy, it would be practically impossible for a federal government not to bring forward omnibus budget legislation. BIAs [Budget Implementation Acts] are necessarily and naturally wide-ranging because they implement the yearly budget of a G-7 country, and more broadly enact the Government of Canada's ongoing economic plan. Omnibus budget bills are reflective of the complex and multifaceted nature of Canada's economy, and of the related budgetary and fiscal policy of its federal Government. Budget bills are now definitionally omnibus bills. (...) To present all the separate budgetary, economic and fiscal policies of the Government in separate bills would be cumbersome in the extreme and the wheels of government would grind to a halt (...) The Senate would face hundreds of separate bills.[80]

Whether the splitting up of budget implementation bills would have the effect of grinding the wheels of the government to a halt, is at least debatable. But omnibus legislation undoubtedly has the effect of preventing the number of sitting days necessary to deal with government legislation from rising up and up again, with the resulting multiplication of question periods (one per sitting), the portion of parliamentary proceedings the Canadian public and the media pay most attention to.

7   The Pitfalls of Omnibus Legislation: The SNC-LAVALIN Affair

One of the measures passed through omnibus legislation later created a major problem for the Trudeau government, and contributed mightily to the outcome of the ensuing general election.

---

[79]*Idem*, pp. 33–34. The examples listed are worth quoting: "Measures affecting the right to strike for some federal employees and, notoriously, amendments to the Supreme Court Act in response to the controversy surrounding the appointment of a new Justice. Bill C-9, the BIA of 2010, was a 880-page document that notably authorized the Government to sell off the Atomic Energy of Canada's business activities; reduced the scope of the Environmental Protection Act and the number of projects requiring environmental assessments; and eliminated the monopoly of Canada Post over some kinds of mail. And not one of these items was included in the budget. In 2007, Bill C-10 contained 21 lines in a 568 page document effectively imposing censorship on the Canadian film industry".

[80]Harder (2018), pp. 34–35.

The budget implementation bill passed in June 2018 (C-74) provided for the introduction of so-called deferred prosecution arrangements for dealing with corporate crimes. In a nutshell, a new type of sentencing agreement was added to the Canadian Criminal Code, to be negotiated between federal prosecutors and a corporation charged with an offence in the context of fraud and corruption. Few paid any attention to its provisions, which had been drafted by the Department of Finance.

It was later revealed that a major Canadian engineering company, SNC-Lavalin, had lobbied the government for the introduction of this new mechanism. However, once the procedure became available, the Director of Public Prosecutions in the Department of Justice refused to conclude a similar agreement with SNV-Lavalin. As she was under the authority of the Attorney General, her decision could have been reversed by the Minister of Justice and Attorney General, Jody Wilson-Raybould. The latter complained that she was repeatedly pressured by the Prime Minister, the Clerk of the Privy Council and the Prime Minister's Principal Secretary, to reverse the decision. She sternly refused, which probably led to her demotion to a lesser department in January, followed by her resignation from the Cabinet 29 days later. The issue then reached crisis proportions, leading ultimately to the resignation of another Cabinet minister, in support of her colleague, and of the two officials who had been accused of pressuring the Attorney General. Wilson-Raybould was expelled from the Liberal caucus in April.[81] Ultimately, in August 2019, Parliament's Ethics Commissioner concluded that the Prime Minister had contravened section 9 of the *Conflict of Interest Act* by improperly pressuring the Attorney General (Conflicts of Interests and Ethics Commissioner 2019). The episode threw the government in turmoil, tarnished its image in the wider public, and most likely had a major impact in reducing the Trudeau government to a minority at the October election. It is profoundly ironical that the very government that tried to curb the excesses associated with omnibus bills is also the only one that was thrown into serious crisis due to one of them.

8   Conclusion

That omnibus legislation is liable to abuse can hardly be doubted. This chapter found ample evidence of discomfort with that legislative technique, within Parliament and outside of it, though not necessarily among the wider public. Yet the short story remains that after having echoed such concerns while they were in opposition, and after having promised to abolish that practice, the Liberals settled on a more moderate course once they reached office. Budget implementation bills are here to stay, and many other omnibus bills are still being introduced and passed. An abusive procedure that smacked contempt of Parliament came in the end to be seen as an appropriate legislative instrument for a G-7 country. Like closure and time allocation orders, omnibus bills are seemingly bound to be vilified by one side of the House,

---

[81]She ran as an Independent in her riding in the October general election, and was re-elected.

but gleefully used once those members find themselves on the other side. Some healthy dose of cynicism, hopefully blended with a touch of humour, may be helpful for those whose duty it is to observe closely the antics of politicians.

Yet, for the first time in Canadian parliamentary history, the Speaker has been empowered to throw a pinch of sand in the carefully oiled government legislative machine that ensures the passing of omnibus legislation. The rules now allow for distinct votes on unrelated parts of omnibus bills, and the provisions of budget implementation bills that are unrelated to the budget speech will also be subject to a separate vote. This allowed the opposition to win numerous points of order, and arguably obliged the government to curb the worst abuses associated with omnibus bills. One last detail is worth pointing out. During the 2019 campaign, *no* major party's platform had a word to say about omnibus bills.

Appendix

Table 1 Budget implementation bills 2001–2019

Parliament	Session	Years	Bill No.	Short title	Statutes of Canada	Number of pages[a]
37th 2000–04	1st	2001–2002	C-49	Budget Implementation Act, 2001	2002 c 9	124
	2nd	2002–2003	C-28	Budget Implementation Act, 2003	2003 c 15	144
	3rd	2004	C-30	Budget Implementation Act, 2004	2004 c 22	64
38th 2004–05	1st	2004–2005	C-33	Budget Implementation Act, 2004, No. 2	2005 c 19	82
			C-43	Budget Implementation Act, 2005	2005 c 30	120
39th 2006–08	1st	2006–2007	C-13	Budget Implementation Act, 2006	2006 c 4	198
			C-28	Budget Implementation Act, 2006, No. 2	2007 c 2	140
			C-52	Budget Implementation Act, 2007	2007 c 29	146
	2nd	2007–2008	C-28	Budget and Economic Statement Implementation Act, 2007	2007 c 35	378
			C-50	Budget Implementation Act, 2008	2008 c 28	152
40th 2008–11	1st	2008		None		
	2nd	2009–2010	C-10	Budget Implementation Act, 2009	2009 c 2	552

(continued)

Table 1 (continued)

Parliament	Session	Years	Bill No.	Short title	Statutes of Canada	Number of pages[a]
			C-51	Economic Recovery Act (Stimulus)	2009 c 31	60
	3rd	2010–2011	C-9	Jobs and Economic Growth Act	2010 c 12	904
			C-47	Sustaining Canada's Economic Recovery Act	2010 c 25	152
41st 2011–15	1st	2011–2013	C-3	Supporting Vulnerable Seniors and Strengthening Canada's Economy Act	2011 c 15	58
			C-13	Keeping Canada's Economy and Jobs Growing Act	2011 c 24	658
			C-38	Jobs, Growth and Long-term Prosperity Act	2012 c 19	452
			C-45	Jobs and Growth Act, 2012	2012 c 31	36
			C-60	Economic Action Plan 2013 Act, No. 1	2013 c 33	128
	2nd	2013–2015	C-4	Economic Action Plan 2013 Act No. 2	2013 c 40	322
			C-31	Economic Action Plan 2014 Act, No. 1	2014 c 20	380
			C-43	Economic Action Plan 2014 Act, No. 2	2014 c 39	478
			C-59	Economic Action Plan 2014 Act, No. 2	2015 c 36	172
42nd 2015–19	1st (only)	2015–2019	C-15	Budget Implementation Act, 2016, No. 1	2016 c 7	190
			C-29	Budget Implementation Act, 2016, No. 2	2016 c 12	194
			C-44	Budget Implementation Act 2017, No. 1	2017 c 20	308
			C-63	Budget Implementation Act, 2017, No. 2	2017 c 33	328
			C-74	Budget Implementation Act, 2018, No. 1	2018 c 12	584
			C-86	Budget Implementation Act, 2018, No. 2	2018 c 27	884
			C-97	Budget Implementation Act, 2019, No. 1	2019 c 29	399

[a]Number of pages in PDF bilingual version of final document, as enacted, including table of contents. May differ from media counts

References

Aiello R (2018) Morneau's office doesn't consider 556-page budget bill omnibus. CTV News, March 28, https://www.ctvnews.ca/politics/morneau-s-office-doesn-t-consider-556-page-bud get-bill-omnibus-1.3862652

Anonymous (2015) Former Bureaucrats praise Justin Trudeau's decision to appoint Peter Harder to his transition team. The National Post, October 22. https://nationalpost.com/news/politics/ former-bureaucrats-praise-justin-trudeaus-decision-to-appoint-peter-harder-to-his-transition-team

Blatchford A (2018) Federal budget bill quietly proposes tool to ease penalties for corporate crime. The Canadian Press, May 15 https://www.cbc.ca/news/politics/federal-budget-corporate-wrongdoing-1.4664490

Bosc M, Gagnon A (2017) House of Commons procedure and practice, 3rd edn. Thomson Reuters and Éditions Yvon Blais, Montreal

Bryden J (2017) Liberals shelve House of Commons reform plans after opposition criticism. Global News, April 30. https://globalnews.ca/news/3415895/house-of-commons-rules-reform-dropped/

Clark S, DeVries P (2015) Ominous, odius, omnibus: Big bills with big problems", iPOLITICS, May 19. https://ipolitics.ca/2015/05/19/ominous-odious-omnibus-big-bills-with-big-problems/

Cockram L (2014) "Grievance before Supply": Omnibus Budget Implementation Legislation as a Case when Party Discipline Damages Parliamentary Democracy. MA dissertation, Department of Political Science, Dalhousie University. https://dalspace.library.dal.ca/bitstream/handle/ 10222/49097/Cockram-Louise-MA-POLI-March%202014.pdf; jsessionid=7FBAA68ADAB5F6B77F3F40F736D84523?sequence=1

Conflicts of Interests and Ethics Commissioner (2019) Trudeau II Report. August 14. https://ciec-ccie.parl.gc.ca/en/investigations-enquetes/Pages/TrudeauIIReport-RapportTrudeauII.aspx

Desjardins L (2015) Omnibus bills are 'unconscionable', says MP. CBC News, February 19. http:// www.rcinet.ca/en/2015/02/19/omnibus-bills-are-unconscionable-says-mp/

Dodek A (2017) Omnibus Bills: constitutional constraints and legislative deliberations. Ottawa Law Rev 48:1–42

Dummitt C, Sethna C (eds) (2020) No place for the state: the origins and legacies of the 1969 Omnibus Bill. UBC Press, Vancouver

Franks CES (1987) The Parliament of Canada. University of Toronto Press, Toronto

Franks CES (2010) Omnibus bills subvert our legislative process. The Globe and Mail, July 14. https://www.theglobeandmail.com/opinion/omnibus-bills-subvert-our-legislative-process/ article1387088/

Green Party of Canada (2015) Building a Canada that Works. Together. September 9. http://s3. documentcloud.org/documents/2454432/green-party-platform.pdf

Gunther L (2012) Omnibus bills in Hill history. The Toronto Sun, June 18. https://torontosun.com/ 2012/06/18/omnibus-bills-in-hill-history/wcm/5b85232b-b8b4-4c9b-b5b7-9480b9821292

Harder P (2018) Complementarity : The Constitutional Role of the Senate of Canada. April 12. https://senate-gro.ca/wp-content/uploads/2018/04/Complementarity-The-Senates-Constitu tional-Role-2018-04-12-Final_E.pdf

Janus A (2015) NDP MP introduces legislation to stop omnibus bills. CTV News, February 19. https://www.ctvnews.ca/politics/ndp-mp-introduces-legislation-to-stop-omnibus-bills-1. 2243719

Leader of the Government in the House of Commons (2017) Reforming the Standing Orders of the House of Commons. March 10. https://www.canada.ca/en/leader-government-house-commons/ services/reform-standing-orders-house-commons/2017/march.html

Liberal Party of Canada (2015) Real Change. A New Plan for a Strong Middle Class. October 9. https://www.liberal.ca/wp-content/uploads/2015/10/New-plan-for-a-strong-middle-class.pdf

Massicotte L (2013) Omnibus bills in theory and practice. Can Parliam Rev 36:13–17. http://www. revparl.ca/36/1/36n1_13e_Massicotte.pdf

Massicotte L (2016) Has the Senate changed since the 1980s? Some quantitative indicators. Can Parliam Rev 39:14–18. http://www.revparl.ca/39/1/39n1e_16_Massicotte.pdf

Massicotte L (2018) Le Sénat et son rôle dans la fonction législative. In: Michaud N (ed) Secrets d'États? Les principes qui guident l'administration publique et ses enjeux contemporains, 2nd edn. Presses de l'Université du Québec, Québec, pp 226–260

McCoy E (2017) Why a more independent Senate is working better for Canadians. Macleans Magazine, August 21. https://www.macleans.ca/opinion/why-a-more-independent-senate-is-working-better-for-canadians/

New Democratic Party of Canada (2015) Building the Country of our Dreams. Tom Mulcair's Plan to Bring Change to Ottawa. October 9. http://s3.documentcloud.org/documents/2454378/2015-ndp-platform-en.pdf

O'Brien A, Bosc M (2009) House of Commons procedure and practice, 2nd edn. Thomson Reuters, Montreal

O'Brien L, Mohyeddin S, Nelson K (2017) How independent is the Senate under Trudeau's rule? CBC, June 26. https://www.cbc.ca/radio/thecurrent/the-current-for-june-26-2017-1.4175376/how-independent-is-the-senate-under-justin-trudeau-s-rule-1.4175401

Platt B (2017) 'Profoundly disappointed'. Senate Liberal leader tears into Trudeau over omnibus budget bill. The National Post, June 14. https://nationalpost.com/news/politics/profoundly-disappointed-senate-liberal-leader-tears-into-trudeau-over-omnibus-budget-bill

Pratte A (2020) Sénateur, moi? Les Éditions La Presse, Montréal

Saint-Pierre E, Lapointe A, Maher C (2015) Législation : Entre rationalité institutionnelle et parlementarisme. J Parliam Polit Law 9:363–386

Senate of Canada (2013) Companion to the Rules of the Senate, 2nd edn. https://sencanada.ca/media/106242/companion-rules-senate-2nd-nov13-e.pdf

Senate of Canada (2015) Senate Procedure in Practice. https://sencanada.ca/media/93509/spip-psep-full-complet-e.pdf

Thomas PG (2018) The 'new' improved Senate. Policy Options, February 26. http://policyoptions. irpp.org/magazines/january-2018/the-new-improved-senate/

Wherry A (2012) A rough guide to Bill C-38. Maclean's Magazine, June 6. https://www.macleans. ca/politics/ottawa/a-rough-guide-to-bill-c-38/

Wherry A (2017a) Liberals propose changes to how House of Commons works. CBC News, March 10. https://www.cbc.ca/news/politics/liberals-parliament-reform-discussion-paper-1.4019904

Wherry A (2017b) Liberals ready to make changes to House rules on omnibus bills and prorogation. CBC News, June 15. https://www.cbc.ca/news/politics/liberals-house-reform-rules-1.4162329

Wherry A (2017c) Speaker splits up Liberal omnibus budget bill, thanks to new Liberal rule. CBC News, November 8. https://www.cbc.ca/news/politics/omnibus-liberals-speaker-analysis-wherry-1.4393690

Wilson P (2016) Harper and the House of Commons: an evidence-based assessment. In: Ditchburn J, Fox G (eds) The Harper Factor. Assessing a Prime Minister's Policy Legacy. McGill-Queen's Press, Montreal & Kingston, pp 27–43

Wyld A (2017) Opposition MPs cry foul over Liberals' tabling of 300-page bill. The Globe and Mail, April 11

The Practice of Omnibus Laws in Belgium: An Empirical Test

Patricia Popelier

Abstract It is a common practice for legislators all over the world to assemble a bulk of unrelated rules in one law to modify a whole range of existing statutes. Omnibus laws are often criticized, but the persistence with which they are used suggests substantial advantages. Procedural guarantees may secure these advantages while addressing the objections. This paper examines whether the procedural guarantees that were adopted in Belgium—one of the first countries to adopt omnibus laws—have proved effective safeguards for the democratic and legal quality of the law, both in fact and in the perception of advisors to and members of Parliament. To this end, the paper subdivides omnibus laws in different categories and develops indicators to find whether the use of omnibus laws in each category is still problematic. Subsequently, the paper examines whether possible problematic use is also identified by the advisors to and members of Parliament. The paper points out which measures have indeed led to improvement, and concludes that especially arrangement laws—i.e. omnibus laws with a budgetary purpose—remain most problematic and vulnerable for abuse. In the end, it takes a serious shift in political culture to make safeguards effective.

Keywords Omnibus laws · Procedural guarantees · Legal quality · Democratic quality · Indicators

P. Popelier (✉)
Faculty of Law, University of Antwerp, Antwerpen, Belgium
e-mail: patricia.popelier@uantwerpen.be

1   Introduction

It is a common practice for legislators all over the world to assemble a bulk of unrelated rules in one law to modify a whole range of existing statutes.[1] They are called 'omnibus laws' or 'mosaic laws'[2] or, if they serve a budgetary purpose, 'arrangement laws' or 'program laws'. For this paper we use 'omnibus laws' as the overall term, 'arrangement laws' if they have a budgetary purpose.

Omnibus laws are often criticized, but the persistence with which they are used suggests substantial advantages. Procedural guarantees, then, might secure these advantages while addressing the objections. Belgium, which was probably one of the first to adopt arrangements law,[3] introduced several procedural requirements to optimize the use of omnibus laws. This makes Belgium eligible as a showcase for the discussion of omnibus laws world-wide. The question is whether the procedural interventions have legitimized the use of omnibus laws. This research question is broken down into two sub-questions. The first one looks for indications of a problematic use of omnibus laws in Belgian parliamentary practice. The second one is whether these problems are identified by the advisors to and members of Parliament. This is a relevant question, because problematic usage will only be remedied if it is perceived as such by the actors involved in the process.

The paper is structured as follows. Section 2 provides the theoretical framework. The pros and cons of the legislative technique are summarized,[4] followed by an overview of the rules of procedure in Belgium with regard to omnibus laws in general and arrangement laws in particular. The next section presents the research design. Here, the theoretical framework is operationalized. In Sect. 4, the practice of federal omnibus laws in Belgium is tested against this framework to enable, in the final section, a conclusion that answers the research question.

2   The Theoretical Framework

2.1   Why Omnibus Laws Are Put to Practice

Roughly, omnibus laws have five advantages. First, omnibus laws facilitate minor or technical corrections to existing laws which, in themselves, may not have enough

---

[1]For an overview of European countries, see the report 'Note du service juridique à l'attention de la Commission spéciale du règlement' published in the parliamentary proceedings of the Belgian House of Representatives, *Parl.Doc.* House of Representatives 2004–2005, 51-51/3, annexe. The proceedings can be found on the House's website: www.dekamer.be.

[2]Savignac and Salon (1986), pp. 3–9.

[3]In 1974—see Parisis (1981), p. 95; Van Nieuwenhove (2006a), p. 75.

[4]The overview is an elaborated version of Popelier (2006), pp. 48–53.

substance for the initiation of an entire parliamentary procedure. Hence, they secure the quality of laws that are already in place.[5]

In doing so, they secure the purity of budget laws. Before omnibus laws came into practice, budget laws were sometimes contaminated with 'budgetary riders': substantive provisions that were inserted in the budget proposal.[6] This was an alternative way to redress minor defects without having to start a new parliamentary procedure. This way, however, consultation requirements and parliamentary debates on the substance of the law were circumvented. By assembling these types of minor amendments in an omnibus law, the budget law can remain free of budgetary riders.

Moreover, they ensure an efficient use of parliamentary procedures.[7] It is far more efficient to have one debate for a series of minor and technical modifications than to start a procedure for each of them. This saves time for parliamentary debate on more substantial laws.[8]

There is also a more political interpretation of this argument. Omnibus laws enable package deals which allow the passing of controversial provisions in exchange for concessions.[9] This applies in particular to presidential systems, where Presidential bills may face Congressional opposition. Empirical studies in the US give evidence that controversial laws are indeed more often inserted in omnibus laws and that the use of omnibus laws improves the productivity of Parliament.[10] Here, efficiency is conceived as the avoidance of heated parliamentary debate, vetoes, transparency and filibustering. By contrast, in parliamentary systems, the government is supported by the majority in Parliament, and in proportional systems, package deals are concluded in an earlier phase, between coalition partners.

Fourthly, arrangement laws ensure the transparency of government. They enable the authorities to implement their social and financial policy with respect of the budget and to avoid over-expenditure owing to unforeseen circumstances and legislative defects. By concentrating this in one arrangement law, the public can check which domains are specifically affected, which gives it some insight in the overall policy to moderate over-expenditure.[11]

Finally, omnibus laws help to overcome fragmentation and facilitate the implementation of more integrated programs that require amendments of a series of laws in a broader policy field.[12] This is the case if the implementation of a new transversal

---

[5]Van Nieuwenhove (2006b), p. 304.

[6]The French Council of State warned against this practice in its report on Legal Certainty: Council of State (1991), pp. 35–36.

[7]Popelier (2006), p. 49; Van Nieuwenhove (2006a) and the Belgian House of Representatives Commission Report, *Parl.Doc.* 2004–2005, 51-51/3, 4.

[8]Which is used as the main rationale for mosaic laws: Savignac and Salon (1986), p. 6 and Belgian House of Representatives Commission Report, *Parl.Doc.* 2004–2005, 51-51/3, 4.

[9]Garrett (2002), p. 2.

[10]Krutz (2000), pp. 533–549.

[11]Parisis (1981), p. 95.

[12]Garrett (2002), p. 5.

policy or the transposition of an EU Directive affects different laws. The use of an omnibus law for these amendments ensures the public insight in the implications of the new policy, or facilitates a check on whether the Directive is completely transposed.[13]

All this implies that omnibus laws that are not budget related consist, either, of only minor and technical provisions or of provisions that are situated within a broader policy field and share a common purpose or *rationale*.

2.2 Why Omnibus Laws Are Under Attack

In 2018, the widespread use of omnibus laws drove the usually reserved Belgian Council of State to a long complaint. It warned that the hastiness to implement reforms and new legislation through these type of laws makes for errors and incorrect policy assessments, necessitating repair laws within a short period of time. It jeopardizes legal certainty and the legality principle, important especially in the field of tax laws which are often the subject of omnibus laws, to the point that nowadays, as the Council noticed, personal tax provisions are rarely adopted in autonomous laws. The Council stated that persons are no longer able to foresee the legal and fiscal consequences of their actions. On top of that, in the present case, the government submitted the bill, fully aware that it was not complete, and making it impossible for the Council to give thorough advice.[14]

This was the culmination of critique that, over time, has been frequently uttered in doctrine. Criticism of omnibus laws comes down to the following objections, which can be ranked in three categories: problems of democratic quality, legal and substantive quality, and legal certainty.

A first objection is that omnibus laws undermine the democratic quality of legislation. Usually, urgency procedures are invoked. This puts Parliament under time limits that are too constrained to enable the careful scrutiny of the many provisions.[15] Moreover, time for hearings and parliamentary debate are often cut and studies and opinions that normally inform the parliamentary debate, are lacking or submitted with delays. Finally, the complexity and length that characterize omnibus laws, make it difficult for members of parliament to grasp the scope and impact of the provisions they approve. Controversial provisions, then, are inserted in omnibus laws to make it difficult for the opposition and the public to scrutinize the bill. It gets even more complicated when new amendments are proposed in the course of the parliamentary proceedings, short-cutting the parliamentary

---

[13]Van Nieuwenhove (2006b), p. 304.

[14]Council of State, advisory opinion of 5 February 2018, *Parl.Doc.* House of Representatives 2017–2018, No 3147/1, pp. 53–55.

[15]Van Nieuwenhove (2006a), p. 79.

proceedings even more.[16] For these reasons, these laws are sometimes called 'a democracy bypassing statute'.[17]

Next, the procedures that affect the democratic quality of the law, also affect its substantive or legal quality. Studies, opinions and parliamentary debate do not only make the law more legitimate, they also make sure that the law is well reasoned and balanced. Obligatory advisory councils, if not circumvented, are put under time pressure, making it difficult for them to give thorough advice.[18] This way, the practice of omnibus laws shows the Executive's disdain for those actors that perform the role of watchdogs of legislative quality. Sometimes, important reforms are hidden in omnibus laws with the purpose of circumventing time-consuming advisory procedures and parliamentary debate. Technical errors are easily made if in the course of the proceedings new amendments are adopted and articles are renumbered.[19] A recent study showed that in Turkey, the larger the number of laws changed by an omnibus law, the more likely provisions are annulled by the Constitutional Court, which shows that large omnibus laws are more likely to incur legal deficiencies.[20]

A third set of objections concerns legal certainty. The Councils of State in both France and Belgium have criticized omnibus laws for encroaching upon the principle of legal certainty, because they are difficult to access.[21] Citizens are able to learn the content of the law once the law is codified, but the fact that laws have been changed and the purpose behind these modifications reach citizens with some delay and difficulty: the omnibus law consists of a large number of provisions, often of a technical nature, that affect a broad range of laws, whereas its inscription does not make clear which laws are affected.[22] As Zieske remarked: "Considering the sheer number of such amendments, affecting so many already complex federal statutes with numerous cross references, it requires a long sabbatical of intensive study to learn the Act's full legal impact".[23] Omnibus laws may even be plainly misleading where they suggest that they consist of minor or technical amendments, but actually hide more substantial provisions or even an autonomous law.

Next, omnibus laws, with their low threshold for legislative action, facilitate hasty modifications of existing laws.[24] This makes it difficult to retrieve which version of a

---

[16]Hazama and Iba (2017), p. 314.

[17]Arrangements laws have been labeled this way in Israel: Ziv (2004) fn. 21.

[18]See Van Nieuwenhove (2006a), p. 82.

[19]Savignac and Salon (1986), p. 8; Van Nieuwenhove (2006b), p. 305. For two examples in Belgian omnibus laws, where cross-references were erroneous and two different provisions were numbered identically, see Popelier (2006), p. 53.

[20]Hazama and Iba (2017), p. 328.

[21]Council of State (France) *supra* fn 6; Council of State (Belgium), *Annual Report 1994-1995* at pp. 200–201 and *Annual Report 1995-1996* at pp. 230–231.

[22]Popelier (2006), p. 50; Van Nieuwenhove (2006b), p. 305.

[23]Zieske (2004), p. 82.

[24]Van Nieuwenhove (2006b), p. 306.

contested provision applied at the point of time relevant for the solution of a concrete case.[25] Moreover, the frequency of omnibus laws entice legislators to interfere without necessity, or to introduce partial modifications instead of more general reforms.[26] Hence, modifications are adopted that either would not have deemed necessary if a separate trail had to be entered, or would have been initiated and discussed as stand-alone acts.

In sum, omnibus laws are vulnerable to carelessness—leading to complexity, hastiness, errors and instability—or, at worst, abuse, if autonomous laws are inserted or substantial government amendments are introduced in the course of the proceedings and if watchdogs and substantial parliamentary debate are circumvented.

2.3   How to Arm Omnibus Laws Against Its Weaknesses

Tools and procedures may help to make sure that omnibus laws serve their purposes while protecting them against sloppiness and abuse. In what follows, the Belgian toolbox is presented: procedural requirements, mostly flowing from the House's Rules of Procedures and the Council of State's guidelines on legislative drafting, that address the conditions and risks enumerated above.

2.3.1   Check on the Content of Omnibus Laws

In Belgium, the House of Representatives' Rules of Procedures allow for the splitting of a bill into different separate bills.[27] This may be used to ensure the coherence of the law. However, it can only be done if the provisions resort to different ministerial departments. In the case of arrangement laws, the Rules of Procedure explicitly prohibit provisions that are not clearly related to the budget. Any political party fraction can send the bill to a special commission[28] to decide whether these provisions should be lifted from the bill and inserted in a separate bill.[29] Further, the Council of State in its drafting guidelines discourages the use of stand-alone provisions in omnibus laws, unless they are limited in time.[30] The

---

[25]Lavilla Rubira (2001), p. 599.

[26]Savignac and Salon (1986), p. 7.

[27]Art. 72.1 House of Representatives Rules of Procedures.

[28]The 'Conference of Chairs', including the present and former chairs and the vice-chairs of the House, as well as the chair and another member of each political party fraction.

[29]Art. 72.4 House of Representatives Rules of Procedure. If no consensus is found, the plenary will decide.

[30]Council of State, *Principes de techniques législatives. Guide de redaction des textes législatifs et règlementaires* (further: Drafting Guidelines), Brussels 2008, at p. 65, No 85. See also the 'bad practice' at p. 52.

drafting guidelines prescribe the inclusion of transposition tables in the legislative file.[31]

2.3.2 Improving the Accessibility of the Law

For the sake of clarity, the Rules of Procedure require the inclusion of a coordination table for any bill, and they require that the tenor of the bill is summarized.[32]

2.3.3 Reducing the Risk of Hidden Controversies

The Rules of Procedure require that impact assessments and advisory opinions are included in the legislative file.[33] There is a legal obligation to perform impact analyses, unless exceptions apply, or in the case of urgency.[34] In urgency procedures, the Council of State still has to be consulted, but the time frame for rendering an opinion may be reduced to five days.[35] The Council of State will verify whether sound reasons are given for the urgency procedure. If there is no urgency, the request is not admissible. However, the obligations to conduct impact analyses and request advisory opinions do not apply to government amendments.[36]

2.3.4 Avoiding Hasty Work

According to the Rules of Procedure, a time lapse of 48 h is in place if new amendments are adopted, to allow for the drafting of a text in which all amendments are included and to enable technical corrections, before the voting of the entire bill. This, however, does not apply in the case of urgency.[37]

---

[31] Drafting Guidelines, at p. 118, Nos 191–194.

[32] Art. 74 Rules of Procedure.

[33] Art. 74 Rules of Procedure.

[34] Art. 6 and 8, § 2, 2° Law 15 December 2013 holding diverse provisions related to administrative simplification.

[35] Art 84, § 1, 3° coordinated laws on the Council of State.

[36] It is still possible but not required to ask the Council of State for advice, except if a specific number of MPs demand the consult of the Council of State, Art. 2 coordinated laws on the Council of State.

[37] Art. 82 Rules of Procedure.

2.3.5   Securing the Parliamentary Debate

The Rules of Procedure give each MP in the parliamentary commission the right to demand a second reading, which takes place after a time lapse of ten days. In urgency procedures, the time limit is reduced to five days.[38]

3   Research Design

3.1   *Research Questions and Indicators*

To find whether there are any indications of a problematic use of omnibus laws (sub-question 1), the characteristics of all federal omnibus laws adopted in a 5 year reference period were coded. To find whether these problems were identified by the actors in the parliamentary procedure (sub-question 2), I analyzed the opinions of the Council of State as well as the commission reports to identify concerns and objections that directly relate to the practice of omnibus laws.

   The following indicators for a problematic use were selected on the basis of the general framework:

3.1.1   Coherency Within Types of Omnibus Laws

The theoretical framework concluded that for omnibus laws to achieve their purpose, they should only consist of budget related provisions (arrangement laws), minor or technical provisions, or of provisions that are situated within a broader policy field and share a common purpose. For each law, it is coded whether the law is an arrangement law or not, whether it is limited to one policy field (or related policy fields), or whether its main purpose is to transpose EU Directives within one policy field. Omnibus laws that are no arrangement laws but contain amendments of a variety of unrelated laws, are seen as problematic. The same goes for omnibus laws that include autonomous provisions which are not of a temporary nature but should have been adopted as a separate law.

3.1.2   Complexity

As omnibus laws grow larger and the number of amended laws grows, it gets more difficult to access the law and have insight in the new legal regime. Complexity (c) is

---

[38] Art. 83.1 Rules of Procedure. Each MP may also demand a second reading in the plenary, but Art. 94 of the Rules of Procedure does not mention a time frame.

put in the following formula as the relation between the number of articles (α) and the number of amended laws (λ):

$$c = \sqrt{\alpha.\lambda}$$

The complexity of omnibus laws is assessed against the average complexity of a reference set of regular laws (see further). Omnibus laws are considered problematic if c has a value of three times the average value of regular laws. The absence of (publicly available) consolidation tables and, where applicable, transposition tables, strengthens the indication that access to the law is problematic.

3.1.3 Stability

It is difficult to establish that omnibus laws encourage modifications that otherwise would not have been introduced or obstruct more general reforms. Instead, as an indication of frequent modification as a result of hastiness, I coded the number of times the omnibus law was amended by subsequent laws according to the Chrono database. This includes provisions that directly amend the omnibus laws—for example temporary provisions or stray autonomous provisions—as well as provisions that refer to the basic law 'as amended' by the omnibus law. Again, stability is assessed against a sample of regular laws.

3.1.4 Parliamentary Debate

Several indicators were used to identify procedures that obstructed the parliamentary debate: the use of urgency procedures, the length of the parliamentary procedure in days and the length of the parliamentary commission reports in relation to the number of provisions, and the introduction of government amendments after the introduction of the bill. If the latter lead to a considerable increase in the size of the law, this is an indication, according to Hazama and Iba, that the government's purpose is to prevent opposition challenges rather than efficiency gains.[39] Government amendments, however, are sometimes hidden. Sometimes, the Council of State notices that an amendment to the bill was in fact a government initiative, but submitted by members of Parliament to avoid formal requirements that secure the quality of the law.[40] These hidden government amendments are not included in the codebook.

To calculate the intensity of the parliamentary debate (i), the formula

---

[39]Hazama and Iba (2017), pp. 323–324.
[40]Council of State, advisory opinion of 10 July 2013, *Parl.Doc.* House of Representatives, N° 53-2891/9, at p. 5.

$$i = \sqrt{\frac{p.r}{\alpha}}$$

was used, with p being the length of the parliamentary procedure, r the length of the combined commission reports and α the number of articles in the law. The intensity of the omnibus law debates was assessed against the average intensity of regular laws.

These are only rough data, overestimating rather than underestimating the parliamentary work: summer holidays are not included, and reports from several commissions concerning the same omnibus law—within the House, and in both the House and the Senate—are combined, which implies a multiplication of introductory pages that do not report on the actual debate. A distinction must be made between two periods, before and after the sixth state reform, when the bicameral system was turned into a quasi-unicameral system. By cutting the Senate's involvement, the parliamentary procedure was shortened, which means that the intensity of the parliamentary debate must be assessed separately for these two periods.

3.1.5 Legal Quality

Finally, for ach omnibus law it is examined (1) whether the Council of State was given ample time for legal advice and (2) whether the law was challenged before the Constitutional Court and if so, what the outcome of the judicial dispute was. If the law was (partly) invalidated, I (3) examined whether the problem had been noticed by the Council of State and/or the members of the parliamentary commission.

The government is obliged to ask the Council of State for legal advice before submitting the bill before Parliament or before adopting a government decree with a general normative scope. The terms for an opinion vary, upon the government's request, from no term, to 60 calendar days (extendible to 75 days, e.g. if the opinion is delivered by two chambers), 30 calendar days (extendible to 45 days) or 5 workdays (extendible to 8 days).[41] In the latter case, the government must demonstrate urgency, and the Council's opinion is limited to questions of competence, procedural requirements, and legality tests, leaving out questions of drafting technique and coherence; in the case of 30 days it is the Council's discretion to restrict the opinion to these three questions. In the case of urgent decrees, it is not required to consult the Council of State, Legislation Section, but the Council's Administrative Litigation Section may annul the decree if no urgency is demonstrated. Considering the workload of the Council of State, with over 2000 opinion requests per year[42] for

---

[41] Art. 84 coordinated laws on the Council of State.

[42] Based on the Council of State's last activity report, an average of 2.101 opinion requests per year were submitted over the period 2012–2017. See Council of State, Activity Report 2016–2017, at p. 55.

14 Councilors of State and 6 assessors (assisted by 24 auditors for a first draft), the term of five days leaves only little space for a thorough examination of the bill, especially if the bill is rather complex.

The Constitutional Court reviews the constitutionality of (federal and subnational) acts of Parliament. Governments as well as each person with an interest may petition the annulment of the act within six months of its publication in the Official Gazette. Courts may—and sometimes must—refer a preliminary question to the Constitutional Court if the constitutionality of an act of Parliament is questioned and the act is determinant for the outcome of the concrete case before the court.

The reference period is 2012–2016. I did not include laws adopted after 2016 because petitions before the Constitutional Court challenging these laws may still be pending. Court decisions are included in the study, since vulnerability of omnibus laws for invalidations by the Constitutional Court was identified as one of the weaknesses of this legislative technique. Annulment requests can be brought before the Court within 6 months after publication in the Official Gazette and it usually takes a little more than one year for the Court to decide.

3.2 Population and Coding

For my study, I used the Council of State's Chrono database, which, for each law, provides several data as well as links to the published version of the law, the parliamentary documents and the Constitutional Court database. To identify omnibus laws, I searched for laws that contain the words 'diverse provisions' or 'arrangement law' in its title. In this list, I selected those laws that hold amendments of at least three other laws. In some cases—before the reform of the Senate in 2014—one omnibus law was split into two laws, because some provisions had to go through a fully bicameral procedure while most did not. To avoid misrepresentation, I did not include the separated act. The result was a population of 91 acts.

For this set, I coded:

- characteristics of the act: the date of enactment and publication, subject matters, the type of omnibus law, the size of the law (i.e. the number of provisions of the law), the original bill size in those cases where government amendments were introduced, the number of amended laws, the number of autonomous provisions. As to type of omnibus law, I distinguish arrangement laws; other omnibus laws within the domain of one specific policy field; other omnibus laws within the domain of several policy fields; omnibus laws with the purpose of transposing EU Directives.
- characteristics of the proceedings: the use of urgency procedures, the introduction of government amendments, the inclusion of coordination tables and the length of the parliamentary proceedings;

- objections and concerns found in the (mostly mandatory) opinions of the Council of State as well as the parliamentary commission's report that were made regarding the use of this type of legislative technique;
- characteristics of the proceedings before and decision of the Constitutional Court if the act was challenged before this Court: type of procedure, bench, number and type of petitioners in annulment proceedings, outcome and, if a violation was found, whether the objection had already been captured by the Council of State or in the parliamentary proceedings.

A reference sample of regular laws was assembled by selecting (1) the first federal act of parliament (2) with normative content[43] (3) that was no omnibus law or could not qualify as such, and (4) was published in the official gazette of the 11th of each month in the reference period, or the first available or relevant gazette after resp. before that date within this month. As no relevant federal parliamentary law was published in the months of September and October 2014, January 2015 and October 2016, the reference sample consists of 56 acts.

Throughout this selection process; several laws popped up that were not formally identified as omnibus laws, but also amended at least three other laws. Distinguishing (informal) omnibus laws and regular laws required further criteria. Laws that amended at least three other laws were nonetheless qualified as regular laws if (a) they did not consist entirely or mainly of amendment provisions, or (b) if only one law was amended and other laws were simply abolished, or (c) if the amendment of various laws served the purpose of introducing one specific new regulation. The first type consisted of autonomous laws accompanied by smaller amendments that followed from the new regulation. The second type of laws came up in codification processes.[44] The last type of laws differs from omnibus laws in that the law does not consist of various new regulations within one domain, but is focused on one particular innovation that requires the amendment of different laws.[45] In the end, 3 laws remained that were to be qualified as omnibus laws but had escaped the Chrono's search engine. They were left aside.

---

[43]Excluding, for example, naturalization laws, budget laws and laws holding approval of international treaties.

[44]For example the Law of 15 December 2012, Official Gazette of 14 January 2013, to include Book XII in the Code of Economic Law, and thereby abolishing 3 laws which are now codified.

[45]For example the Law of 18 December 2014, Official Gazette of 23 December 2014, amending 5 different laws in view of creating gender equality with regards to passing their surnames to children.

4   Results: The Practice of Omnibus Law by the Belgian Federal Government

4.1   A Problematic Use of Omnibus Laws?

4.1.1   Coherency Within Types of Omnibus Laws

In the 5-year reference period, 91 omnibus laws were adopted, which points to a high frequency of, on average, 18 omnibus laws each year. The largest group consists of regular omnibus laws within one policy field (58). The second largest group contains omnibus laws with the specific purpose of transposing EU Directives (17),[46] followed by arrangement laws (11). The smallest group consists of omnibus laws that address several policy fields (5).

The high number of laws within the first groups gives an indication that efforts have been done to ensure the coherence of the law: reforms that are not related to the budget are excluded from the arrangement bill and a separate bill is introduced for each reform. This explains the high number of omnibus laws. Most of these laws are situated in the field of social security and labor law (13) and financial, fiscal and economic law (13), followed by justice (10), health (8), internal affairs (7) and others (agriculture and environment, energy, penal law, animal welfare, mobility, defense). Omnibus laws specifically dedicated to the transposition of EU Directives are mainly situated in the field of financial law (8) and energy (4), followed by other policy fields (communication, animal welfare, administrative procedures, labor law). In the other categories, a range of policy fields are addressed. Transposition tables to control whether the Directive is fully transposed, are frequently included, but not yet as a rule.

The government used the omnibus law to hook up autonomous laws in 9 cases. This took place in omnibus laws within 1 policy field (5), arrangement laws (3) and omnibus laws spanning different policy fields (1). This means that the government does not frequently use omnibus laws to rush an autonomous bill through parliament, but omnibus laws are still vulnerable for this practice.

4.1.2   Complexity

The number of articles in an omnibus law and the number of amended laws varies considerably in the reference period: from 6 to 352 articles, and from 3 to 55 amended laws. The average complexity is 31.7. This is high above the average complexity of regular laws, which is 6 in the reference sample, and high above the threshold of 18 (three times the average complexity of regular laws) that marks the complexity of laws as problematic. To make this concrete: a law with 84 articles

---

[46]Some other laws also include transposition provisions, amongst other amendments with other purposes.

Table 1 Complexity level and coordination tables

Category	Type	Complexity level	Coordination table
1	1 policy field	28.3	56.5%
2	+ policy fields	30.1	40%
3	Arrangement law	58.8	0%
4	Transposition law	26	82.3%
Total		31.7	59.3%

amending 12 different laws has a complexity value of 31.7. On the other hand, in 40 cases the value is less than 18, which means that omnibus laws are not by definition very complex laws that are difficult to access. Moreover, in the majority (54 cases) a coordination table was provided. in 1 case an alternative version, without the consolidated text, was included.

If we compare categories, visualized in Table 1, it is clear that the transposition laws (average complexity = 26) are the least, and the arrangement laws (average complexity = 58.8) are the most problematic type of omnibus laws. Only 5 out of 17 transposition laws surpassed the threshold of 18, but this was compensated by a coordination table. By contrast, the majority of arrangement laws is difficult to access. Here, only 1 out of 11 remained below the threshold of 18,[47] whereas all the others surpassed twice the complexity threshold (+36). Notably, none of the arrangement laws was accompanied by a coordination table.

The other two categories show a more differentiated picture. Within the category of omnibus laws within 1 policy field (average complexity = 28.3), the size of laws varies from 6 to 352 articles. The number of amended laws also varies, ranging from 3 to 44. Almost half of the laws (25 out of 58) remain below the complexity threshold of 18. Nevertheless, even in this category there is still a substantial number of omnibus laws that are difficult to access, with 16 cases even exceeding twice the threshold (+36). In most of these cases, however, a coordination table enhances the accessibility of the law. Only 3 laws have a complexity value of at least 36, and no coordination table. Within the category of 5 omnibus laws that stretched over several policy domains (average complexity = 30.1), two remained below the complexity threshold, while the other three surpassed the complexity value of 36. One of these problematic laws did not provide a coordination table.

4.1.3 Stability

After the adoption of the omnibus law, provisions of that law were amended in 34 cases, which comes down to 37.3% of the cases. This is above the average of 17.8% in the reference sample of regular laws. This gives an indication that omnibus laws are indeed less stable than regular laws.

---

[47] Arrangement law of 3 August 2016, Official Gazette 16 August 2016.

Again, the transposition laws are the least problematic, with only one case with subsequent amendments. In absolute numbers, most subsequent amendments are situated in the category of omnibus laws within one policy field (24), but in terms of percentage, arrangement laws are most vulnerable for subsequent amendments (8 out of 11). Omnibus laws within several policy fields were subsequently amended in 2 cases out of 5.

4.1.4 Parliamentary Debates

Not all omnibus laws are adopted under urgency procedures. Overall, urgency was invoked in 50 cases out of 91. Again, the type of omnibus law matters. Urgency was invoked for all arrangement laws and for all other omnibus laws that cover several policy fields. For omnibus laws within one policy field and for transposition laws, urgency procedure were only followed in somewhat less than half of the cases (26 out of 58 cases resp. 7 out of 15 cases). Importantly, urgency is usually invoked for the most complex omnibus laws (value 36 or more). Only in seven such cases, all concerning omnibus laws within one policy field, there was no urgency procedure.

Urgency procedures limit the time for preparation and discussion. This is especially the case if on top of that, the government does not submit the entire bill, but adds additional amendments in the course of the parliamentary procedure. This is not a common practices: it occurred in 13 out of 91 cases—although with the reminder that hidden government amendments, introduced via members of parliament, are not included. The practice is spread quite evenly over the different types of omnibus laws (5 for omnibus laws within 1 policy field, 5 for arrangement laws, 1 for other omnibus laws in different policy fields, 2 for transposition laws). However, taking into account the relative weight, arrangement laws seem more vulnerable for this, as in this category, it was used in almost half of the cases. Moreover, here, a sixth case (out of 11) in the form of a hidden government-initiated amendment was noticed by the Council of State.[48] What's more, this practice is used for highly complex bills: 11 out of 13 were used for laws with a complexity rate of 36 or more. The other two cases concerned transposition laws with a complexity rate below the threshold of 18. As Table 2 shows, the size of the law increased with 20% or more compared to the original bill in 6 cases. This is an indication that the government's purpose was containing opposition rather than procedural efficiency. 4 of these concerned omnibus laws within one policy field, the other two were arrangement laws. In one of these, the size increased with 158%.

To have an indication of whether urgency procedures actually obstruct the parliamentary debate, the intensity rate of the parliamentary debates was calculated and presented in Table 3. In the reference sample of regular laws, the average intensity rate is 21.5. For omnibus laws, this drops to 7. This shows that omnibus

---

[48] As mentioned above, in Sect. 3.1.(4). See Council of State, advisory opinion of 10 July 2013, *Parl.Doc.* House of Representatives, N° 53-2891/9, at p. 5.

Table 2 Last-minute amendments

Category		Size original bill	Size law	Difference	Difference %
1	1 policy field	51	82	+31	+60.8%
		146	232	+86	+58.9%
		38	54	+16	+42.1%
		97	113	+16	+16.5%
		145	182	+37	+25.5%
2	+ policy fields	70	73	+3	+4.3%
3	Arrangement laws	123	130	+7	+5.7%
		45	116	+71	+157.8%
		185	215	+30	+16.2%
		96	115	+19	+19.8%
		131	129	−2	−1.5%
4	Transposition laws	32	34	+2	+6.25%
		95	97	+2	+2.1%

Table 3 Intensity rate parliamentary debate

Category	Type	Before reform Senate	After reform Senate	All	Commission debate: complexity (after reform)
1	1 policy field	10.2	5.2	**7.9**	
2	+ policy fields	6	2.4	**5.28**	
3	Arrangement laws	6	5	**5.6**	2.1
4	Transposition laws	5.3	7	**5.5**	
1–4	**All**	**8.4**	**5.3**	**7**	
Reference set	Regular laws	25.6	15.2	**21.5**	5.5

laws indeed considerably reduce the intensity of the parliamentary debates conceived as the combination of length of the parliamentary procedure and length of the commission debate.

A distinction must be made between laws adopted before the sixth state reform and laws adopted after that date, as the abolishment—in most cases—of the bicameral procedure obviously reduces the length of the parliamentary procedure and therefore the intensity rate. For regular laws, the average rate is 25.6 before the state reform, and 15.2 after. For omnibus laws, this is respectively 8.4 and 5.3. Remarkably, for arrangement laws and transposition laws, the abandonment of the Senate's involvement has no impact on the intensity of the parliamentary debate. On the contrary, the intensity rates increases from 6 to 6.4 for arrangement laws and from 5.3 to 5.7 for transposition laws.

When we zoom further in to arrangement laws, however, we find that urgency procedures explain the drop in debate intensity, but at first sight, the reduced time for

Table 4 Invalidation rate

Category	Type	Challenged	Invalidation	Invalidation %
1	1 policy field	22	10	17.2%
2	+ policy fields	2	1	20%
3	Arrangement laws	10	3	27%
4	Transposition laws	6	4	23.5%
All	Omnibus laws	40	18	19.8%
Reference set	Regular laws	15	4	7.1%%

reflection does not seem to impact upon the intensity of the commission debates. When we take the length of commission reports alone, the average number of pages after the reform of the senate is 15.6 for regular laws versus 115.4 for arrangement laws. However, if we take into account the complexity of the laws, the average value is 5.5 for regular laws versus 2.1 for arrangement laws. The difference between the two sets of laws is much smaller, but still noteworthy. The conclusion is that urgency procedures, while not entirely silencing MP's, do hamper the intensity of the commission debates.

4.1.5 Legal Quality

There is no direct correlation between urgency procedures that are invoked before the Council of State on the one hand and urgency procedures invoked in Parliament on the other. In all, the Council of State's term for delivering an opinion was restricted to 5 days (once extended to 8 days) in 20 cases.[49] With 23%, this considerably exceeds the average of 8.1% of cases in which the Council of State is required to give an opinion within a term of 5 days.[50] Again, arrangement laws stand out as most problematic (100%) and the transposition laws as least problematic (0%). While in other categories the 5 days' term is mostly reserved for less complex laws (6 out of 9 cases have a complexity rate of 18% or less), this is different for arrangement laws, where only one law had a low complexity rate (12.7), one other law had a high complexity rate (22) and the other nine were extremely complex (36 or more). The conclusion is that arrangement laws in particular are vulnerable for legal errors, as the term for a legal opinion is severely reduced while the complexity rate is extremely high.

Whether this affects the legal quality in fact is measured by the number of invalidations before the Constitutional Court, as presented in Table 4. 40 out of 91 omnibus laws were challenged before the Constitutional Court, leading to 76 judgments. This is considerable more than the reference set of regular laws

---

[49]Taking into account the first opinion only.

[50]Based on the Council's Activity Reports 2012–2013, 2013–3014, 2014–2015, 2015–2016 and 2016–2017.

(43.9% versus 26,726.7%%). In two cases, a final decision is still pending.[51] The Constitutional Court found at least one violation, leading to an invalidation, with regards to 18 different omnibus laws, which is more than twice the percentage in the reference set of regular laws (19.8% vs 7.1%). In addition, the Constitutional Court found in another case that the law was unconstitutional when interpreted in one way, but constitutional when interpreted in another.[52] Overall, the laws which were found to violate the Constitution, were more complex than the average omnibus law (43.9 vs 31.7) and parliamentary debate was slightly less intense than usual for omnibus laws (43.9 vs 31.7). The urgency procedure for the advisory opinion of the Council of State does not seem to matter: only in four cases was the time for an opinion restricted to 5 days.

The unconstitutionalities in these 18 laws, established in 19 different judgments, were identified by the Council of State and/or discussed in Parliament in 8 cases. On average, these cases were slightly more debated than the cases where the legal problem had not been identified during the parliamentary process (7.6 vs 5.5). Remarkably, in the first category, the average complexity of the laws at stake was considerably higher than in the latter case (56.4 vs 34.9). This means that the complexity of the law does not seem to impact the vigilance of the Council of State and the MP's—or, at least, not once a certain threshold is passed.

As Table 4 shows, in absolute numbers, most violations were found in the category of omnibus laws within one policy field. However, in terms of percentages, the omnibus laws are, once more, most vulnerable for invalidation by the Constitutional Court (27%), followed by transposition laws (23.5%), omnibus laws within several policy fields (20%) and omnibus laws within one policy field (17.2%). This means that omnibus laws, and arrangement laws in particular, are more vulnerable for legal errors as well as invalidations by the Constitutional Court.

Unlike what was observed in Turkey,[53] the practice of government amendments after the initiation of the bill, does not lead to more invalidations. Laws that resulted from this practice were challenged more often (9 out of 13 cases), but only in one case did the Constitutional Court find a violation.

4.1.6 Interim Conclusion

The overview of findings in Table 5 shows that all omnibus laws are problematic in terms of legal certainty and democratic quality, but that arrangement laws are the most problematic category. It has the worst score for every indicator; only for the intensity of the parliamentary debate, other categories do worse, but only slightly.

Indicators to measure legal certainty in terms of accessibility and stability are (i) the complexity rate, (ii) the use of coordination tables and (iii) the stability of the

---

[51] See Const.Court No 82/2017, with a preliminary reference to the ECJ, and Case No 6728.

[52] Const. Court No 92/2017.

[53] Hazama and Iba (2017), pp. 323–324.

Table 5 Overview

Category	Type	Nr	Aut. law	Complex. level	Coord. table	(In)stability	Urgency CoS	Urgency Parl	GovAm	Intensity	Invalidations
1	1 policy field	58	*8.6%*	*28.3*	*56.5%*	*41.3%*	*10.3%*	*44.8%*	*8.6%*	*7.9*	*17.2%*
2	+ policy fields	5	20%	30.1	40%	40%	60%	100%	20%	**5.3**	20%
3	Arr. laws	11	**27.3%**	**58.8**	**0%**	**72.7%**	**100%**	**100%**	**45.4%**	5.6	**27%**
4	Transp. laws	17	0%	26	82.3%	5.9%	0%	46.7%	11.8%	5.5	23.5%
Total	Omnibus laws	91	9.9%	31.7	59.3%	37.3%	22%	53.8%	14.3%	7	19.8%
Ref. set	Regular laws	56	na	6		17.8%	8.1%			21.5	7.1%

In bold: the most problematic laws. In italic: the least problematic omnibus laws law. Arrangement laws are, by far, the most complex and most unstable laws, and never include coordination tables.

Indicators that the government uses omnibus laws to push a law through the parliamentary process in a fast-track procedure by hiding it in an omnibus law, hoping to avoid democratic debate, are (i) the insertion of autonomous laws, (ii) the introduction of amendments by the government after submitting the bill, (iii) the use of urgency procedures and (iv) the intensity of the parliamentary debate. The first indicator does not occur very often, but omnibus laws nevertheless remain vulnerable for this practice. In relative terms, arrangement laws have the worst score for the first three indicators and almost the worst score for intensity of the parliamentary debate.

Indicators for legal quality are (i) the time granted to the Council of State to deliver a legal opinion and (ii) the invalidation rate before the Constitutional Court. Again, arrangement laws have the worst scores.

Summarizing, arrangement laws are the most complex laws, and yet this is the category where the Council of State and Parliament are most curtailed, and no coordination table is provided to improve accessibility and to facilitate parliamentary debate. As a consequence, these are the least stable laws, and the laws that are most likely to be invalidated by the Constitutional Court. Omnibus laws within several policy fields have a bad score for most indicators. While all omnibus laws are problematic in terms of legal certainty, democratic quality and legal quality compared to regular laws, omnibus laws within one policy field and omnibus laws with the purpose to transpose EU law are the least problematic types. The first have the best scores for democratic and legal quality, whereas the latter score better for legal certainty.

4.2 The Perspective of the Actors in the Parliamentary Procedure

The next question is whether the actors in the parliamentary procedure actually care about the deficiencies that go with the use of omnibus laws. To this end, the Council of State opinions and the parliamentary commission reports were scrutinized for comments concerning the drafting technique and its consequences for the quality of the law. They ware categorized as concerns for democratic quality, legislative quality and legal certainty. The latter two are closely linked: legal certainty is a legal principle and thus part of legislative quality; and bad legislative quality affects the accessibility and stability of the law. Concerns of legal quality, however, explicitly take the perspective of individuals that are affected by the law.

The Council of State made comments on the general practice of omnibus laws in 20 out of 91 occasions. Most of them (8) concerned arrangement laws, followed by laws within one policy field (6), transposition laws (4) and laws within several policy fields. This indicates that the Council of State generally accepts the use of omnibus laws, but regards arrangement laws as most problematic. The Council's intuition aligns with the quantitative finding in the previous section. As mostly arrangements laws are addressed, it is no surprise that the complexity rate of the laws under fire is higher than the average rate for omnibus laws (45 vs 31.7) and the intensity rate of the parliamentary debate is lower (6 vs 7). In line with its task as legal watchdog, the Council of State is merely concerned about legal aspects: the legal quality—in particular the space assigned to it for giving thorough advice—and the legal certainty for individuals. By contrast, concerns with regard to the democratic quality of the law are not very outspoken.

Members of Parliament have been somewhat more critical of the technique of omnibus laws: comments were given in 29 out of 91 cases. Again, in absolute numbers, most critique is aimed at omnibus laws within one policy field, but in terms of percentage, arrangement laws are most frequently addressed (72.7%) and transposition laws are least likely to get criticized (17.6%). MP's will more easily complain about the technique when the parliamentary debate is curtailed: the average intensity rate of the laws subjected to criticism on the legislative method, is below the average intensity rate of omnibus laws (5.9 vs 7). These laws are also more complex than the average omnibus law (41.3 vs 31.7). Comments invariably come from opposition members.

Majority MPs, in support of the coalition, generally resign themselves to the drawbacks of the legislative method. For example, when MP's requested the organization of hearings concerning the proposed regulation on diamond taxes, which was quite controversial at that moment and caused the Council of State to voice concerns about its conformity with the equality principle while the government refused to make public the Financial Auditor's advice and a preparatory study, the members of majority parties still voted against this request.[54] Also, the majority did not support the request to ask the Council of State for an advisory opinion on those provisions for which the urgency request was deemed inadmissible by the Council of State in the absence of real urgency.[55] These provisions were kept in the bill and submitted by the government without an advisory opinion, contrary to the House's Regulations. Another telling example is the report that gives an account of how the session is adjourned an hour and a half to allow the photocopying and reading of amendments, and how the majority votes against the request to discuss these amendments only after the Council of State has delivered an advisory opinion as requested by the Minister.[56] In another session as well, the majority did not support the request to give more time to study a complex bill and to examine old case law to which the memorandum referred and which was difficult to find.[57]

On some occasions, however, the opposition's protest is met by the majority. For example, after criticism on the fact that some provisions in an omnibus laws were not

---

[54]Report, *Parl.Doc.* House of Representatives, 2014–2015, N° 54-1125/9, at pp. 4, 31, 37.

[55]Report, *Parl.Doc.* House of Representatives 2012–2013, N° 53-2853/11, at p. 3.

[56]Report, *Parl.Doc.* House of Representatives 2014–2015, N° 54-672/13, at p. 3.

[57]Report, *Parl.Doc.* House of Representatives 2014–2015, N° 54-1161/4, at p. 4.

of a mere technical nature and that the Council of State had been bypassed by submitting the bill as a Parliamentary proposal, the majority agreed to lift these provisions out from the bill.[58] On another occasion, the parliamentary commission agreed to consult stakeholders, which the government had neglected to do.[59]

4.2.1 Democratic Quality

When the Council is asked for an advisory opinion, it has no insight in how the parliamentary procedure will develop. The use of autonomous provisions and the submission of government amendments after the initiation of the bill, may nevertheless indicate that the government is trying to hide provisions to avoid thorough democratic debate. The Council of State treats this mainly as a problem of legal certainty and legal quality. Yet, in one case, the Council of State criticized that an important complex of autonomous provision was inserted, which deserved a thorough examination, considering its social and legal import.[60] While the critique was mostly phrased from the angle of legal quality, the need for democratic debate also shined through this formulation: the Council regretted that this way, it cannot feed the democratic debate with a thorough opinion.[61]

The fact that omnibus laws curtail the parliamentary debate, is, as can be expected, a particular concern of MPs.[62] This is especially the case if the law contains a revision that is deemed fundamental or has considerable impact on society or fundamental rights, and therefore in need of a separate discussion.[63] The reply that the technical nature of arrangements laws justify the reduction of parliamentary debate, is contradicted with the argument that clear political and ideological choices underpin the provisions.[64]

The curtailing of parliamentary debate is felt (i) in the absence of social dialogue, hearings or consultations with stakeholders of important or controversial pieces of legislation[65] (ii) by the lack of time for study and debate, when bills, advisory

---

[58]Report, *Parl.Doc.* House of Representatives 2014–2015, N° 54-683/4, at p. 10.

[59]Report, *Parl.Doc.* House of Representatives 2011–2012, N° 53-2429/6 at p. 13.

[60]Council of State, Legislation Section, Advisory Opinion of 5 May 2015, *Parl.Doc.* House of Representatives 2014–2015, N° 54-1125/1, at p. 160.

[61]*Ibid.*

[62]E.g. Report, *Parl.Doc.* House of Representatives, 2015–2016, N° 54-1889/3, at p. 12.

[63]Report, *Parl.Doc.* House of Representatives, 2012–2013, N° 53-2872/4, at pp. 33 and 35; Report, *Parl.Doc.* House of Representatives, 2013–2014, N° 53-3149/5, at pp. 7, 21, 23 and 41; Report, *Parl.Doc.* Senate, 2013–2014, N° 5-2443/3, at pp. 7 and 15; Report, *Parl.Doc.* House of Representatives, 2015–2016, 54-1951/3, at pp. 10–11.

[64]Report, *Parl.Doc.* House of Representatives, 2014–2015, N° 54-672/9, at p. 11; Report, *Parl. Doc.* House of Representatives, 2015–2016, 54-1951/3, at pp. 8 and 9.

[65]Report, *Parl.Doc.* House of Representatives, 2012–2013, N° 53-2561/8, at p. 15; Report, *Parl. Doc.* House of Representatives, 2012–2013, N° 53-2872/4, at p. 35; Report, *Parl.Doc.* House of Representatives, 2011–2012, N° 53-2198/16 at pp. 6 and 16; Report, *Parl.Doc.* House of

opinions or amendments are submitted at a very late stage,[66] and (iii) in the urgency invoked for the discussion of the bill, while more time is needed to examine a complex bill.[67] In this respect, the government is blamed for poor planning. One sign of poor planning is the practice to hold back a regulation until the very last moment and then inserting it in an arrangement law or a regular omnibus law for a hasty passage through parliament.[68] Another is the negligence in transposing an EU Directive until the very last moment, when judicial action is initiated against the Belgian State.[69] At other times, MPs doubt whether there is any urgency at all.[70]

Also, MP's find fault with the practice of initiating government amendments when parliamentary debate of the bill has already started.[71] This is especially the case when amendments for which the Council of State has not been consulted add important pieces of legislation, that bear no relation with the original bill[72] and should have been submitted as a separate bill[73]—which, in some cases, the Council of State has advised to do.[74]

Representatives, 2014–2015, N° 54-1125/9, at pp. 30–31, 37; Report, *Parl.Doc.* House of Representatives, 2014–2015, N° 54-6721/4, at pp. 16–17; Report, *Parl.Doc.* House of Representatives, 2015–2016, 54-1951/3, at pp. 10 and 15; Report, *Parl.Doc.* House of Representatives, 2015–2016, 54-14791/2 at p. 4; Report, *Parl.Doc.* House of Representatives, 2015–2016, 54-1644/3, at p. 5.

[66]Report, *Parl.Doc.* Senate 2012–2013, N° 5-1904/3 at pp. 2–3; Report, *Parl.Doc.* House of Representatives, 2012–2013, N* 53/2561/6 at pp. 19 and 31–32 and N° 53-2561/8, at p. 14; Report, *Parl.Doc.* House of Representatives, 2012–2013, N° 53-2572/3, at p. 8; Report, *Parl.Doc.* House of Representatives 2012–2013, N° 53-2891/7, at p. 3; Report, *Parl.Doc.* House of Representatives 2012–2013, N° 3236/3, at p. 5; Report, *Parl.Doc.* House of Representatives 2012–2013, N° 53-254/6, at pp. 7, 19 and 23; Report, *Parl.Doc.* Senate 2013–2014, N° 5-2434/3, at p. 4; Report, *Parl.Doc.* House of Representatives, 2015–2016, 54-1479/13, at p. 4; Report, *Parl.Doc.* House of Representatives, 2015–2016, N° 54-1459/5, at pp. 6 and 12; Report, *Parl.Doc.* House of Representatives, 2015–2016, N° 54-1479/9, at p. 9 and 54-1479/13 at p. 8; Report, *Parl.Doc.* House of Representatives, 2015–2016, N° 54-1951/3, at pp. 5, 10, 14 and 15; Report, *Parl.Doc.* House of Representatives, 2016–2017, N° 54-2154/5 at p. 17 and N° 2154/8 at p. 3.

[67]Report, *Parl.Doc.* House of Representatives, 2012–2013, 53-2512/3 at p. 5; Report, *Parl.Doc.* Senate 2012–2013, 5-2169/5 at p. 16; Report, *Parl.Doc.* House of Representatives 2014–2015, N° 54-1161/4, at p. 4; Report, *Parl.Doc.* House of Representatives, 2015–2016, N° 54-1505/3, at p. 12.

[68]Report, *Parl.Doc.* House of Representatives, 2015–2016, 54-1479/13, at p. 6; Report, *Parl.Doc.* House of Representatives, 2015–2016, 54-1951/3, at p. 8.

[69]Report, *Parl.Doc.* Senate 2012–2013, N° 5-1904/3 at pp. 2–3.

[70]Report, *Parl.Doc.* House of Representatives, 2011–2012, N° 53-2198/16 at p. 6.

[71]Report, *Parl.Doc.* Senate 2012–2013, N° 53-2853/17 at pp. 29 and 36; Report, *Parl.Doc.* Senate 2012–2013, N° 5-2169/5 at p. 16; Report, *Parl.Doc.* House of Representatives 2012–2013, N° 53-2891/7, at p. 3; Report, *Parl.Doc.* House of Representatives, 2013–2014, N° 53-3473/4, at p. 7; Report, *Parl.Doc.* House of Representatives, 2015–2016, 54-1459/5, at p. 7; Report, *Parl.Doc.* House of Representatives, 2015–2016, N° 54-1505/3, at p. 12.

[72]Report, *Parl.Doc.* House of Representatives, 2013–2014, N° 53-3473/4, at p. 7.

[73]Report, *Parl.Doc.* House of Representatives, 2012–2013, 53-2853/17, at p. 36; Report, *Parl.Doc.* House of Representatives, 2015–2016, 54-1459/5, at p. 7.

[74]Report, *Parl.Doc.* House of Representatives, 2015–2016, 54-1459/5, at p. 7.

Democratic quality is also at stake when the government takes advantage of the speedy procedure for arrangement laws to insert non-budget related provisions in the bill, contrary to the House's Regulations. MPs criticize the fact that when the Council of State finds a request inadmissible for this reason, the bill is submitted to Parliament anyway without an advisory opinion for these provisions.[75] Majority members reply that the government is not at fault in these cases, as it has requested an advisory opinion,[76] thereby denying their own Regulations.

4.2.2 Legal Quality

Most comments uttered by the Council of State express the concern for the quality and thoroughness of its legal advice, and the respect for procedural guarantees for proper law-making. This is why it criticizes parliamentary amendments that in fact originate from the Government.[77] It is also the reason why the high complexity of a bill is criticized, especially when combined with a 5 days' term for an advisory opinion. The Council of State notes that this makes it impossible to fulfil its task of legal advisor to the parliament and government in a satisfactory way.[78] Such remarks are made more regularly in a more subtle way, when the Council notes that, considering the complexity of the text and the short term provided for a legal opinion, it had to remain concise and warns that for this reason, its advisory opinion is not exhaustive and the absence of comments cannot be interpreted as an approval.[79] Therefore, if urgency is invoked to reduce the term for an advisory opinion to 5 working days, the Council of State will examine whether the urgency is real, and, in arrangement laws where the urgency is linked with the budget control, whether each provision is indeed implementing the current budget. If this is not the case, the Council considers the request for these provisions inadmissible.[80] This way, the Council of State respects the Chamber Regulations, which demand that

---

[75]Report, *Parl.Doc.* House of Representatives 2012–2013, N° 53-2853/11, at p. 3.

[76]Report, *Parl.Doc.* House of Representatives 2012–2013, N° 53-2853/11, at p. 3.

[77]Council of State, Legislation Section, Advisory Opinion of 10 July 2013, *Parl.Doc.* House of Representatives 2012–2013, N° 53-2891/9, at p. 5.

[78]Council of State, Legislation Section, Advisory Opinion of 5 May 2015, *Parl.Doc.* House of Representatives 2014–2015, N° 54-1125/1, at p. 160.

[79]For a few examples, see Council of State, Legislation Section, Advisory Opinion of 31 January and 2 February 2012, *Parl.Doc.* House of Representatives 2011–2012, N° 53-2081/1, at p. 213; Advisory Opinion of 10 July 2013, *Parl.Doc.* House of Representatives 2012–2013, N° 53-2891/9 at p. 4; Advisory Opinion of 22 August 2016, *Parl.Doc.* House of Representatives 2015–2016, N° 54-2058/1, at pp. 177–178.

[80]For a few examples, see Council of State, Legislation Section, Advisory Opinion of 31 January and 2 February 2012, *Parl.Doc.* House of Representatives 2011–2012, N° 53-2081/1, at p. 213; Advisory Opinion of 17 November 2014, *Parl.Doc.* House of Representatives 2014–2015, N° 54-672/1, at p. 176; Advisory Opinion of 6 June 2016, *Parl.Doc.* House of Representatives 2015–2016, N° 54-1941/1, at p. 49.

provisions that are not linked with the budget, are lifted from the arrangement law.[81] This, however, does not always happen: at times the bill is nevertheless submitted with the non-budgetary provisions included.

The Council of State reminds the Government very frequently of procedural requirements that must be fulfilled, such as impact assessments where obligatory. This is the same for regular laws. However, characteristic of omnibus laws is that these requirements are evaded through the submission of government amendments by members of parliament. The Council of State has criticized this practice, because these formal requirements secure the quality of regulation.[82] In this respect, it has in particular in view the arrangement laws, for which urgency is always invoked. An exception to the legal obligation to draft an impact assessment is in place when urgency is invoked before the Council of State. As a result, all arrangement laws pass by definition without having to fulfill procedural requirements that secure the quality of the law.[83] With regard to regular omnibus laws, the Council of State requests that the bill is ordered in such a way that it is easy to follow up whether the different procedural requirements for different types of regulations have been fulfilled.[84]

Finally, the Council of State is concerned about the coherence of legislation. Where innovations impact upon the basic principles behind the legislation, the Council of State asks the Parliament to reflect on whether these provisions should be inserted by way of an omnibus law, or should rather be part of a global reform.[85]

MPs regularly show their concern for the quality of the law, which they consider threatened by several practices that characterize many omnibus laws: the short deadline for the Council of State, the lateness of bills as well as government amendments submitted to Parliament, and the absence of consultations. They also deplore the lack of coherency.

MPs make their wish known to have a timely and thorough advice.[86] The government is accused of consciously bypassing the Council of State by abusing the urgency procedure[87] or by submitting a bill in the form of a parliamentary proposal.[88]

MPs also caution that bills that are submitted at a late stage and then speedily rush it through Parliament, are harmful for the quality of the law and often lead to new

---

[81] Art. 72.4 Rules of Procedure, as discussed above.

[82] Council of State, Legislation Section, Advisory Opinion of 10 July 2013, *Parl.Doc.* House of Representatives 2012–2013, N° 53-2891/9 at p. 5.

[83] For example, Council of State, Legislation Section, Advisory Opinion of 5 December 2012, *Parl. Doc.* House of Representatives, N° 53-2561/001, 138–139.

[84] For example, Council of State, Legislation Section, Advisory Opinion of 6 January 2014, *Parl. Doc.* House of Representatives, N° 53-3359/1, at p. 53.

[85] Council of State, Legislation Section, Advisory Opinion of 23 September 2015, *Parl.Doc.* House of Representatives, N° 54-1418/1, at p. 264.

[86] Report, *Parl.Doc.* Senate 2012–2013, N° 5-1904/3 at p. 3; Report, *Parl.Doc.* House of Representatives, 2015–2016, 54-1479/13, at p. 4.

[87] Report, *Parl.Doc.* Senate 2012–2013, N° 5-1904/3 at p. 3.

[88] Report, *Parl.Doc.* House of Representatives 2014–2015, N° 54-683/4, at p. 3.

legislation to correct previous errors and malfunctions.[89] The same goes for late
government amendments: especially if they are voluminous and submitted at the
session in which they are discussed, the lack of time for careful study and consideration is criticized.[90]

Finally, MPs sometimes describe the bill as a hotchpot of ideas that lacks a
univocal view on the matter, even if the bill remains within one policy domain.[91] In
one case, where an autonomous law was inserted in the omnibus law instead of
submitted as a separate bill, the opposition, envisaging problems when the law is
applied, succeeded in inserting an evaluation clause.[92]

4.2.3 Legal Certainty

On a few occasions, the Council of State made specific comments about the legal
uncertainty generated by the technique of omnibus law.

On some occasions, the Council of State criticizes the inaccessibility of the
omnibus law. The first comment concerned an arrangement law. The Council of
State criticized the government for creating an impenetrable jumble, threatening
legal certainty for individuals who cannot foresee the consequences of their actions.
It also noted that the amended provisions were the subject of frequent amendments;
considering the speediness of the procedure to make repairs, the Council of State
warned for new errors leading to instability.[93] The other concerned an omnibus law
within several policy fields, where the Council criticized the frequent revisions and
the opaque way in which they were presented, leading to legal uncertainty for
individuals.[94] In both cases, the Council's comments addressed the fiscal provisions
in particular. Also, both laws have a problematic score for the indicators of legal
certainty. The first law[95] has a complexity rate of 50.8 and was subsequently revised.
The other[96] has a complexity rate of 39.9 and was subsequently revised by 5 different

[89]Report, *Parl.Doc.* House of Representatives 2012–2013, N° 53-2891/7, at pp. 4 and 60; Report, *Parl.Doc.* House of Representatives 2012–2013, N° 3236/3, at p. 8.

[90]Report, *Parl.Doc.* House of Representatives, 2012–2013, N° 53-2891/7, at pp. 4 and 60; Report, *Parl.Doc.* House of Representatives, 2015–2016, N° 54-1479/9, at p. 9 and 54-1479/13 at p. 8.

[91]Report, *Parl.Doc.* House of Representatives, 2011–2012, N° 53-2429/6 at pp. 13 and 14; Report, *Parl.Doc.* House of Representatives, 2015–2016, 54-1418/5, at pp. 31 and 40–41; Report, *Parl. Doc.* House of Representatives, 2015–2016, 54-1644/3, at p. 5; Report, *Parl.Doc.* House of Representatives, 2015–2016, 54-1889/3, at p. 13; Report, *Parl.Doc.* House of Representatives, 2015–2016, 54-1951/3, at p. 8.

[92]Report, *Parl.Doc.* House of Representatives 2012–2013, N° 53-1864/3.

[93]Council of State, Legislation Section, Advisory Opinion of 5 December 2012, *Parl.Doc* House of Representatives 2012–2013, N° 53-2561/1, at pp. 155–156.

[94]Council of State, Legislation Section, Advisory Opinion of 10 July 2013, *Parl.Doc.* House of Representatives, N° 53-2891/9, at p. 5.

[95]Arrangement law of 27 December 2012, *Official Gazette* 31 December 2012.

[96]Law of 30 July 2013 holding diverse provisions, *Offical Gazette* 1 August 2013.

laws. Yet, other laws with a high complexity rate and an instability rate passed without any comment, including the most complex law with a complexity rate of 101. Remarkably, the Council of State requested a coordination table in none of the cases before it. It did ask for transposition tables on five different occasions.

In addition, the Council of State criticized the insertion of autonomous provisions for the sake of accessibility of the law, in two cases.[97] On one of these occasions, this perspective led to a merely formal follow up, not by removing it from the omnibus law and introducing it as a separate law, but by changing the inscription of the law to point out that the law (also) includes an autonomous regulation on crowdfunding.[98]

The Council of State also comments on the instability of the law in those cases where the technique of the omnibus law and the speediness that goes with it, was used to amend laws which already had been subjected to several amendments in the past years.[99]

MPs also show concern for the stability of the law. On one occasion, it was noticed that amendments were made to provisions that only recently were adopted in previous arrangement laws. The hastiness of the legislative work was assigned blame for the instability of omnibus laws.[100] In other cases, MPs caution that new legislation will be needed to repair deficiencies that come with the sloppiness with which the current legislation is adopted, which is found to undermine legal certainty.[101]

The fragmentation resulting from the technique of omnibus laws is also deplored as harmful to legal certainty. It is criticized that yearly contributions are inserted in arrangement laws instead of providing for a structural and legislative framework.[102] Also, it is feared that the technique will lead to incoherencies and instability, to the detriment of individuals.[103]

The complexity of omnibus laws is also addressed on some occasions, with the request to ensure that individuals are swiftly and correctly informed.[104] Noticeably, MPs only rarely complain if complex omnibus laws are not accompanied by a coordination table, to facilitate access to the law.[105]

---

[97]Council of State, Advisory Opinion of 31 January and 2 February 2012, *Parl.Doc.* House of Representatives 2011–2012, N° 53-2081/1, at p. 228; Council of State, Advisory Opinion of 26 June 2016, *Parl.Doc.* House of Representatives, N° 54-2072/1, at p. 228.

[98]Commission Report, *Parl.Doc.* House of Representatives, N° 54-2072/9, p. 11.

[99]Council of State, Advisory Opinion of 5 December 2012, *Parl.Doc* House of Representatives 2012–2013, N° 53-2561/1, at p. 156; Advisory opinion of 10 July 2013, *Parl.Doc.* House of Representatives, N° 53-2891/9, at p. 5.

[100]Report, *Parl.Doc.* House of Representatives 2011–2012, N* 53-2198/12, at pp. 3 and 12.

[101]Report, *Parl.Doc.* House of Representatives 2012–2013, N° 53-2891/7, at pp. 4 and 60.

[102]Report, *Parl.Doc.* House of Representatives 2014–2015, N° 672/13, at p. 10.

[103]Report, *Parl.Doc.* House of Representatives, 2015–2016, N° 54-1418/5, at p. 42.

[104]Report, *Parl.Doc.* House of Representatives, 2012–2013, N° 53-2405/4, at p. 8.

[105]Report, *Parl.Doc.* Senate, 2012–2013, N° 5-1864/3, at p. 8.

4.3   Interim Conclusion

Council of State and MPs are aware of the problems that come with omnibus laws. The Council of State's sharpest outburst came in 2018, outside the scope of the empirical study, but referred to in Sect. 2 of this paper. Mostly, however, it remains restrained, and interferes mainly when it feels that not adequate time is given for a thorough examination. MPs criticize more broadly the technique of omnibus laws and government practices that come with it. However, criticism is an opposition tool, whereas majority MPs support the government. This renders the tools to control omnibus laws rather ineffective.

5   Conclusions and Recommendations

5.1   Conclusions

The purpose of this paper was to examine whether the procedural requirements that were adopted in Belgium to optimize the use of omnibus laws, have proved effective safeguards for the democratic and legal quality of the law, both in fact and in the perception of advisors to and members of Parliament. Three conclusions can be made by way of lessons for other jurisdictions.

The first conclusion is that the requirement to lift provisions that are unrelated to the budget from the arrangement laws and the practice to use omnibus laws by preference for amendments within one policy field or for the transposition of EU Directives, have alleviated the complexity rate. Also, complexity is often compensated by the inclusion of a coordination table.

The second conclusion, however, is that, once introduced, omnibus laws are there to stay; and that arrangement laws are the most problematic of all. In Belgium, omnibus laws have become a common practice, and are introduced with a high frequency, yet remain vulnerable for abuse: at times, the advisory opinion of the Council of State is consciously circumvented, omnibus laws are used to rush separate laws through Parliament, sometimes in the form of government amendments. Also, the parliamentary discussions seem to confirm that the frequency with which omnibus law bills are introduced, leads to fragmentation instead of more encompassing and thorough revisions. All in all, arrangements prove by far the most problematic form of law in terms of legal quality and legal certainty as well as democratic quality and vulnerability for abuse. Notably, these laws, with the highest complexity rate, do not conform with the requirement to include coordination tables.

The third conclusion is that the actors in the parliamentary process, even if they have objections, rarely stand in the way. In the Belgium context, these actors are an advisory judicial body and the Members of Parliament. They are aware of the problems, but protest remains relatively limited. The Council of State vents very occasionally. Its main concern is the lack of time to give thorough advice. It does verify whether, in conformity with the House's Rules of Procedure, all provisions in an arrangement law are related to the budget. In turn, MPs from the opposition raise objections on all aspects, but the majority very easily close the ranks. Apparently, it needs a serious shift in political culture to make safeguards effective.

5.2   Recommendations

Finally, some recommendations can be made to partly overcome the weaknesses of omnibus laws. First, omnibus laws should be based on coherent starting points. In Belgium, the requirement to lift non-budget related provisions from the arrangement law is generally observed. The Council of State acts as a watchdog and finds such provisions non-admissible. For other omnibus laws, the possibility to split bills, seems to work: most omnibus laws are situated within one policy field. The Guidelines discourage the insertion of autonomous regulations in omnibus laws. Again, this is generally, but not always observed. The same goes for the insertion of transposition tables.

Secondly, coordination tables should be attached to all bills, including in the case of omnibus laws. In Belgium, the requirement to insert coordination tables is only observed in 60% of the cases, mostly in transposition laws, but never in the case of arrangement laws. Again, bills that do not comply, should be held inadmissible from the start. In the Netherlands, it has been argued by the government that such requirement should not apply to omnibus laws, because the workload would be disproportional.[106] Yet, coordination tables are vital precisely in these cases, to ensure accurate work by the drafters and to enable the Parliament to assess the content of the bill.

Third, observance of admissibility requirements should be made enforceable in one way or the other. As, in Belgium, the President of the House is to decide whether bills can be forwarded,[107] it is his or her task to check whether the bill is accompanied by all required documents. If this examination by the President, in principle being a majority member, does not suffice, it could be considered to introduce judicial review. In France, an Institutional Act determines which documents should accompany a bill.[108] According to Art. 39 § 4 of the Constitution, government bills may not be put on the agenda if the Conference of Presidents of the first House declares that the rules determined by the Institutional Act have been ignored. In the case of disagreement between the Conference and the Government of whether the rules of the Institutional Act have been ignored, the matter may be referred to the Constitutional Council.[109] In a parliamentary system as Belgium, where majority

---

[106]Borman (2004), pp. 37–38.

[107]Art. 74.2 Rules of Procedure.

[108]Loi Organique n° 2009-403.

[109]Art. 39 § 4 of the French Constitution.

and government are closely linked, any MP should have the right to discuss the observance of admissibility requirements, under judicial supervision.

Fourth, to reduce the risk that controversial provisions are hidden in an omnibus law, a procedural rule might be introduced to limit the practice of government amendments. Hence, the government might be prohibited to introduce amendments to its own bill, unless they answer to the comments made in the parliamentary debate on the bill before them. In Belgium, this might require a constitutional revision, as the right to amend is considered the extension of the right of initiative, secured by the Constitution.[110]

Fifth, to reduce the risk that omnibus laws invite the government to produce hasty work and to avoid urgency procedures, the government may be required to plan its legislative work through legislative programs and roadmaps.[111] If legislation is well planned, the need for urgency procedures will lessen. Also, even in urgency cases the government should not be allowed to introduce bills without the impact assessments and consultation reports that are normally required. Careful preparation is, in all circumstances, paramount to the good quality of a law. This requirement might even force the government to better plan its legislative work. Also, the Rules of Procedure should allow a time laps to study new amendments also in cases of urgency, or at least on the request of a number of MPs.

References

Borman TC (2004) Verzamelwetgeving. RegelMaat 19:28–38

Council of State (1991) De la sécurité juridique. Etudes & Documents 43:35–36

Delpérée F (2000) Le droit constitutionnel de la Belgique. Brussels, Bruylant

Garrett E (2002) Attention to context in statutory interpretation: applying the lessons of dynamic statutory interpretation to omnibus legislation. Issues Legal Scholarship 2: art1. https://doi.org/10.2202/1539-8323.1020

Hazama Y, Iba S (2017) Legislative agenda setting by a delegative democracy: omnibus bills in the Turkish parliamentary system. Turk Stud 18:313–333

Krutz GS (2000) Getting around gridlock: the effect of omnibus utilization on legislative productivity. Legis Stud Q 25:533–549

Lavilla Rubira JJ (2001) Some trends in administrative law in the 21st century. Texas Int Law J 36:599–604

Parisis A (1981) Les lois-programmes en Belgique: tendances et contenu. Rev Int Sc Adm 47:95–104

Popelier P (2006) Mosaics of legal provisions. Eur J Law Reform 7:48–53

Savignac J-C, Salon S (1986) Des mosaïques legislatives? L'Actualité juridique – Droit administrative:3–9

---

[110]Art. 75 of the Belgian Constitution. See Delpérée (2000), p. 792.

[111]See also Popelier (2006), p. 57.

Van Nieuwenhove J (2006a) Programmawetten : voor verbetering vatbaar? In: Popelier P, Van Nieuwenhove J (eds) Wie maakt de wet? die Keure, Bruges, pp 73–90
Van Nieuwenhove J (2006b) Verzamelwetgeving in België. Tijdschrift voor Wetgeving 7:153–166
Zieske WF (2004) Demystifying the USA Patriot Act. Illinois Bar J 7:92–111
Ziv N (2004) Lawyers talking rights and clients breaking rules: between legal positivism and distributive justice in Israeli poverty lawyering. Clin Law Rev 11:209–239

(Absence of) Omnibus Legislation in Sweden: When Legislative Drafting Affects the Political Discourse

Mauro Zamboni

Abstract Unlike many other Western European countries, Sweden has had an astoundingly low rate of omnibus legislation in its legislative history, in particular if looking at the "deep" omnibus legislation, *i.e.* the model of legislation which regulates different topics, but where their regulation lacks a unifying underlying function, at least from a legal perspective. The purpose of this chapter is not only to present this peculiarity and investigate the specific reasons behind it (reasons that relate to the particular Swedish legal and political environment). The goal is also to attempt to draw some general conclusions (*i.e.* ones possibly valid outside the borders of the Scandinavian country), in particular as to the role of legal actors and legislative drafters on structuring the agenda for the discourses taking place in the political arena.

Keywords Omnibus legislation · Legislative drafters · Political arena · Sweden · Rule of law

1   Introduction

It is certainly striking that, unlike many other Western European countries, Sweden has had an astoundingly low rate of omnibus legislation in its legislative history. The purpose of this short work is not only to present this peculiarity and investigate the

I would like to thank Jane Reichel, Peter Melz, Pernilla Leviner, Peter Wahlgren, and Jori Munukka for their extremely valuable inputs. I would also like to thank the *Law Faculty's Trust Fund for Publications*, Stockholm University, *Cassel Foundation*, Stockholm University, and the *Foundation for Jurisprudential Research* for financial support during this study. The usual disclaimer applies.

M. Zamboni (✉)
Faculty of Law, Stockholm University, Stockholm, Sweden
e-mail: mauro.zamboni@juridicum.su.se

specific reasons behind it (reasons that are connected with the particular Swedish legal and political environment). The goal is also to attempt to draw some general conclusions (*i.e.,* ones possibly valid outside the borders of the Scandinavian country), in particular as to the role of legal actors and legislative drafters on the political arena.

Before starting, it is necessary to give some clarifications as to the term "omnibus legislation," at least as it is used in this work. As it is well known, omnibus legislation is a term commonly used to indicate bills or statutes which cover a number of diverse topics.[1] Within the scope of this term, however, are also included those bills or statutes regulating diverse *and* unrelated topics, *i.e.,* a type of legislation covering not only different topics, but also topics whose regulations do not fall within a unifying functional framework.[2]

In this respect, one should then distinguish between two ideal-types of omnibus legislation. The first ideal type can be defined as *superficial* omnibus legislation: it is the type of legislation which covers very different topics, but where there is a functional link unifying the various parts which are regulated.[3] A classic example of superficial omnibus legislation is the budget bill: it is true that budget bill belongs to the omnibus legislation category, since it usually regulates various aspects of a legal system. However, as can easily be understood, there is a unifying function behind the variegated targets of the bill, namely the regulation of the state budget for the upcoming financial year.[4]

The second ideal type of omnibus legislation can be defined as *deep*: it is the model of legislation which regulates different topics, but where their regulation lacks

---

[1]See Krutz (2001a), p. 1 ("Omnibus legislating is the practice of combining numerous measures from disparate policy areas in one massive bill"); and Gluck et al. (2015), p. 1804. See also Kardasheva (2009), p. 55 (where omnibus legislation is defined as the case where "two issues y and w can be joined in a single proposal and be voted on as a package").

[2]See Sinclair (2000), p. 71 ("Legislation that addresses numerous and not necessarily related subjects, issues, and programs, and therefore is usually highly complex and long"). See also Krutz (2001a), pp. 3–5.

[3]See, e.g., Schwartz (2013), pp. 1973–1974 (as to the flourishing at the national level of omnibus legislations in the area of data protection law as a consequence of the European Commission's 1995 Data Protection Directive); the Canadian House of Commons (2011), p. 38 (where an *omnibus bill is defined as* "[a] bill consisting of a number of related but separate parts that seeks to amend and/or repeal one or several existing Acts and/or to enact one or several new Acts."); or the same House of Commons (1988), p. 15880 (where Herb Gray, then Opposition House Leader, stated that an omnibus bill has "one basic principle or purpose which ties together all the proposed enactments and thereby renders the Bill intelligible for parliamentary purposes"). It is worth mentioning that sometimes, in the English-speaking parliamentary discussion, a distinction is made between a "proper omnibus bill" (mirroring the superficial omnibus legislation used in this work) and a "not proper omnibus bill" (similar to the deep omnibus legislation). See, e.g., the Canadian House of Commons (2012), p. 1205. This terminology is avoided in this work, due to the qualitative evaluation embedded in it.

[4]See, e.g., Schick (1987), p. 48. See also, as another and more recent example of superficial omnibus legislation, the Irish Withdrawal of the United Kingdom from the European Union (2019), where the legislative bodies prepared the country in case of a disorderly Brexit.

a unifying underlying function, at least from a legal perspective.[5] An example is an hypothetical bill or a statute that increases the budget for the police force and, in the same text, authorizes Sunday opening of food stores. Uniting these regulations, despite their very different functions (increasing security vs. stimulating commerce), makes sense only if one considers the piece of legislation from a political perspective. From a political discourse standpoint, such deep omnibus legislation, or "logrolling" as it is sometimes defined, has a unifying (and rather clear) function, namely the fulfillment of electoral promises through compromises between different political parties.[6]

In this paper, due to space constraints, attention will be devoted exclusively to the presence (or absence) of "deep omnibus legislation" within the Swedish legislative discourse, *i.e.*, legislation with variegated contents whose only unifying feature is being within the same piece of legislation. This choice is made mainly because, as will hopefully be shown in the paper, it is in this very type of omnibus legislation that one can most clearly observe the conflicting logics of the legal and political discourses, and the role that legislative drafters may play in relation thereto.

2 The Reality

Moving our attention to the position of deep omnibus legislation within the Swedish legislative discourse, the reality is rather simple and uncontroversial: this type of omnibus legislation (where a bill or statute regulates different and unrelated topics) is practically absent on both the legal practitioners' and legal scholars' horizon.[7]

---

[5]See van Beek (1995), p. 6; and Gluck (2015), p. 97 ("omnibus bills. . . tend to bundle together bills drafted by different committees at different times, or by multiple drafters (often not even internal to Congress) that are not in communication with one another"). See also Gluck et al. (2015), p. 1805 ("Omnibus vehicles also sometimes mask transparency for certain objectives. The 2008 [financial] bailout, for instance, had a variety of individual goodies attached to it, ranging from subsidies for wooden arrow makers to those for racetrack owners"). See, e.g., Galnoor (2011), p. 90 (as to the use of omnibus legislation, or "arrangements law" as it is termed in Israel, to encompass many unrelated legislative issues); or McKay and Johnson (2010), p. 445.

[6]See Garrett (2002), p. 2; Ferejohn (1986), pp. 223–253; Krutz (2001b), p. 211; and Ruud (1958), p. 391. See also Krutz (2001a), pp. 30–43 (pointing out the various institutional political reasons, both of a micro and macro nature, behind the increasing use of omnibus legislation in a Western democracy like the U.S.A.); and Denning and Smith (1999), p. 974 ("omnibus bills often provide ideal political cover for members' sops to influential constituencies").

[7]The terms "omnibus legislation (or bill)" used in its deep meaning (or its Swedish translation, *sammanläggning lagstiftning* or *proposition*), does not appear in any relevant legislative documents or work of legal scholarship in the last 70 years. But see Wahlgren (2014), p. 69 (pointing out the increasing "lack of identity" when it comes to the contemporary Swedish legislative production, in particular due to its internationalization).

Actually, since World War II no one single case of a deep omnibus document (either as an act or simply as a bill) is recorded in the Swedish legislative history.[8]

It is worth mentioning that, being as this type of legislation is so unfamiliar in the Swedish legislative discourse, legal actors sometime use "omnibus legislation" as a synonym for "superficial omnibus legislation" (*i.e.,* legislation touching differentiated topics, but with a unifying functional goal). For instance, the Swedish Social Services Act (2001) is often described as a typical case of omnibus legislation because it contains rules governing varied topics such as elderly care and adoptions.[9] As can be easily understood, the various regulations in the act are unified by its underlying structure, *i.e.,* the promotion by the same public agency of the economic and social security of individuals and equality in living conditions.[10]

The absence of examples of deep omnibus legislation from the Swedish reality is quite surprising at a closer glance, due to the presence of several factors and conditions (which are strongly interconnected) which should, at least in theory, promote or facilitate such statutes. Firstly, like in any other country, political actors working with legislation, at least in their intentions, have a predisposition towards omnibus legislation (or there is nothing, in principle, that would stop them from using it). This type of legislation is considered a sort of "aberration" by most of the Swedish legal actors—the legislative practitioners and scholars in particular.[11] However, for the political actors it is (or at least it appears to be) a rather efficient way to "satisfy" particular and/or corporativist interests, *i.e.,* to allow the political actors to set a legitimacy rope between themselves and specific sectors of their electoral body. This efficiency is at hand as the method does not require the writing and promulgation of a new specific act for each interest that the political actors aim at satisfying. Instead, deep omnibus legislation makes it possible, by inserting just a few paragraphs in an upcoming legislative act, to achieve diversified and myriad results with a single piece of legislation.[12] In other words, it can come as no surprise

---

[8]Compare, e.g., Sinclair (2000), p. 72 (stating that "[o]mnibus measures have made up about 11 percent of major legislation in recent [USA] Congresses").

[9]See, e.g., Leviner (2011), pp. 28–31, where the idea of superficial omnibus legislation overlaps, to a certain extent, with the Swedish concept of "framework legislation," in Swedish *ramlagstiftning.* Cf. deZafra (1978), p. 276 ("these [omnibus] laws say what to do rather than how to do it; i.e. they set forth general principles rather than prescriptive requirements").

[10]See Socialtjänstlag (2001), Chapter 1, art. 1. See, e.g., Alexandersson (2018), p. 115 (where the author points out the Swedish legislator's goal of unifying the regulation of various social areas in order to implement certain fundamental ethical values).

[11]See Hellner (1990), pp. 137–139 (stressing that the strive for internal coherence in each legislative act is the same for both drafters and legislative scholars). See, e.g., Wahlgren (2014), pp. 54–56 (pointing at the fact that the rules within the legislative document should be related in an unambiguous and systematic way, as a necessary criterion for the very legitimacy of the act); or Hellner (1990), pp. 199–216.

[12]See Krutz (2001a), p. 2; and Frantzich and Berube (2010), p. 256 ("*Omnibus legislation that covers a wide range of topics* provides the opportunity to buy the support of a wide range of members, who, while not agreeing with all the components, judge that the overall package provides more benefits than detriments"). See also Krutz (2002), p. 213. See, e.g., Miller (2009), p. 23.

that political actors, even in Sweden, should not reject deep omnibus legislation *a priori,* since also in this Scandinavian country statutes are considered by politicians as simple vessels capable of transporting their different and most heterogeneous political merchandise.[13]

There is a second factor, connected with the previous one, pushing for a wider use of omnibus legislation in Sweden, a factor that is particular to the constitutional culture of this Scandinavian country. Unlike in most of the countries belonging to the so-called Western-style democracies, one of the major pillars in the Swedish constitutional architecture is a refusal of the principle of division of power, and instead an endorsement of the separation of functions.[14] Legal actors have traditionally taken a rather strict interpretative stand when it comes to the first paragraph of one of the Swedish constitutional documents (Instrument of Government, 1974, article 1: *"All public power in Sweden proceeds from the people. Swedish democracy... is realized through a representative and parliamentary form of government and through local self-government"*).[15] As a result, the Parliament (*i.e.* the primary legislative lawmaking agency) is regarded as the true and only power (being the only one representing "the people"), which, in its turn, delegates the other two functions to the judicial bodies and the public agencies.[16] Being that this is the situation, the environment should be favorable for deep omnibus legislation: considered as the "people's voice," the political actors sitting in the legislative bodies are perceived as the only and supreme lawmaking power (from a constitutional architecture perspective), and their logics should always prevail over all the other logics (*in primis,* those of legislative drafting).

As to the last condition which should, at least in theory, promote or facilitate a wider use of deep omnibus legislation in Sweden, one should mention the Swedish or social-democratic model of the welfare state.[17] In a society organized in accordance with this model, the law and its systems constitute a necessary but "soft" component. They are necessary, because the Swedish concept of the welfare state is dependent on values being implemented by means of regulatory instruments, primarily of legislative character (*e.g.,* via taxation law).[18] However, in order for the law to be used to implement the values of the economic and political model of the

---

[13]See Petersson (2015a), p. 98 ("Swedish political culture has been described as involving a pragmatic approach to decision-making and as stressing utilitarian considerations rather than rights-based principles... Among other things, this means that negotiations and compromise are preferred rather than overt conflicts and legal battles").

[14]See Nyman (1988), p. 57; Reichel (2011), p. 246; Wind et al. (2009), p. 63; and Nergelius (1996), p. 133.

[15]See The Instrument of Government (1974); and Algotsson (2001), pp. 52–54.

[16]See Strömberg and Lundell (2014), p. 95; and Nergelius (2015), p. 15.

[17]See Esping-Andersen (1990), p. 27; Bergh (2004), pp. 749–754; and Forslund (1997), pp. 124–138 (as to the cardinal socio-economic points of the Swedish model of welfare state). See also *Pierson* and *Leimgruber* (2010), p. 40.

[18]See Aubert (1986), pp. 32–39; Habermas (1998), pp. 405–407; and Dean (1997), pp. 3–27. See, e.g., Norrman and McLure Jr. (1997), p. 110.

welfare state (*e.g.,* economic justice), the legal instruments and the legal culture must be "soft:" the legal discourse and the legal actors must be prepared and willing to abandon their fundamental principles and dogmas in cases where such legal paradigms end up conflicting with political and economic values.[19] For example, in tax law, legal actors must be prepared to sacrifice their dogma of foreseeability in taxation in favor of the political and social value of reallocation by means of taxation.[20]

In this context, the use of omnibus legislation should not be a problem, even in its deep form. The basic assumption of the Swedish model of the welfare state is the dominance of the logics of the political discourse over the legal ones, with a flexible idea and use of the law and its "dogmas," as long as they help to fulfill the goals set by the political actors. However, alongside the conditions that should facilitate (or at least not discourage) the use of a deep omnibus legislation, profounder and stronger reasons coexist, that have made such legislation absent from the Swedish legislative panorama.

3   The Reasons

Despite several institutional and structural conditions being favorable for having a more widespread use of deep omnibus legislation, the Swedish reality shows the opposite. As stated above, the idea of deep omnibus legislation, *i.e.,* a legislation where a bill regulate various *and* unrelated topics within the same legislative text, is foreign to both the legislators and the legal scholarship in general. In the Swedish legislative history this type of omnibus legislation has been very rarely used (and not one single time since 1945) and the term does not appear in the legal literature (unless when referring to what has here been defined as "superficial omnibus legislation," *i.e.,* a legislative text that regulates various topics, but with a single purpose).[21] Therefore, it is necessary to examine which forces have stopped such legislation from appearing in the Swedish legislative landscape. In particular, one can identify three basic factors, with a cumulative character (*i.e.,* adding to one another): the high status of the preparatory works in the Swedish legal system, the searching for the largest consensus possible already while drafting the bills, and the rather "unpolitical" positioning of the legislative drafters in the Swedish legislative law-making. These three factors all originate from some of the characterizing aspects of the Swedish legal discourse, its constitutional architecture, and the role and

---

[19]See Peczenik (1995), pp. 46–47; Bjerstedt (2009), pp. 40–42; and Sundberg (1978), pp. 223–224.

[20]See, e.g., Fast Lappalainen (2019), pp. 178–198; or Sundberg (2000).

[21]See Hellner (1990), p. 192 (as to the Swedish general "minimalist" tradition when it comes to the formation of the bills and acts, i.e. "not to include more explicit rules in an act than it is required by the factual circumstances").

position in it of the legislative drafters. Together, they create a legislative process that tends to reject deep omnibus legislation.

First, one should consider the very high status that preparatory works have in the Swedish legal discourse. For several historical and institutional reasons (which will not be touched upon in this presentation, due to lack of space), the preparatory works to an act are considered a source of law, hierarchically just below the act itself.[22] Both for the doctrine and, even more importantly, for the judicial actors and the public agencies, the preparatory works are the first place to look in case of uncertainty regarding a legislative text (since they enable one to understand "the true meaning" of a certain act).[23] Even more importantly, preparatory works are openly and widely used by both judges and public agencies in order to legally argue for (or "justify") a certain decision or course of actions.[24] Thus, it should not come as a surprise that the legislators (and in particular the legislative drafters) invest quite a lot of time and efforts in bringing to life such preparatory works. These legislative documents are usually the results of long and very detailed processes, which also involve a quite complicated and extended system of consultation with external actors (*e.g.,* interest associations and universities) as to the feasibility and general legal quality of the text proposed.[25]

Due to this high status and the consequent complex and articulated procedure behind the works leading to the legislative bill (in order to ensure its quality), it becomes quite difficult to push through the system a legislative text that has the quality of being deep omnibus, *i.e.,* that regulates in a rather random fashion (at least from a legal perspective) the most variegated and unrelated topics. The legislative drafters and the external actors are often legal actors, *i.e.,* actors specifically educated in law and working professionally with law.[26] This makes it quite difficult for political actors, during the long and rather rigidly regulated process, to insert into the draft any articles that are not connected with the original proposal, and which may jeopardize the systematic nature of either the bill or the legal system in which the bill will most likely operate. In short, being that the preparatory works are so

---

[22]See Sundberg (1978), pp. 232–237. See also Petersson (2015b), p. 650 ("Swedish system stands out because of its strong emphasis on the preparatory stages. Considerable time and effort is spent on investigations and discussions before a policy proposal becomes a government bill"); Tala (2005), p. 101 and pp. 112–113; and Wahlgren (2014), p. 88 (pointing out some of the negative effects of such system).

[23]See Strömholm (1996), pp. 453–455; and Peczenik (1999), pp. 12–17.

[24]See Petersson (2015b), p. 650 ("When adjudicating a case, a Swedish judge does not primarily refer to legal precedents set by the courts of law. More important are the 'travaux préparatoires' of the policy process, which consist of a chain of legal sources such as legislative acts, parliamentary committee proposals, government bills, and, importantly, reports from the commissions of inquiry and results from the referral process"). See, e.g., Lind (1993), pp. 301–318; or Nergelius (1997), pp. 432–434.

[25]See Zamboni (2019), pp. 8–16.

[26]See Petersson (2015b), p. 658. See, e.g., Lind (1996), pp. 359–360 (1996); or von Sydow (2007), pp. 49–50. See also Popelier and Verlinden (2009), pp. 31–33 (as to the central role of legal actors in the legislative processes of many Western-based legal systems).

highly regarded and with such a high degree of legal legitimacy within the Swedish legal discourse, they are thoroughly regulated by constitutional praxis. This makes it difficult for the political actors to insert "ad hoc" provisions, which are unrelated and do not logically fit into the contents of the bill under discussion (at least from a legal perspective).[27]

This factor alone (*i.e.* the high legitimacy and therefore rigid regulation of the bill drafting) could not guarantee the absence of omnibus legislation. In other countries (and one could think here for instance of the United States of America), the legislative text often acquires its omnibus character outside the ordinary drafting phase, since political "leaders assemble the bills themselves and bring them to the floor with little or no committee considerations."[28] However, and this is the second factor which prevents the Swedish legislative system from being open to deep omnibus legislation, it is well-established constitutional praxis in Sweden to aim, already in the drafting committee, at reaching the largest consensus possible as to the bill to be sent to the legislators.[29] This striving for consensus has several reasons historically (*e.g.,* a Swedish culture of avoiding conflicts in so far as possible).[30] Among those reasons, one should for instance point out the fact that the vast majority of the Swedish governments after World War II have been minority governments.[31] This political feature has meant that the political party in charge (though having a relative majority) has always needed the (either active or passive) support of other parties in order to pass its bills. This is often achieved in the drafting committees, where a process of extended negotiations and balancing various interests takes place among the representatives of the parties.[32] As a result, when a final text is produced and sent to the Parliament for discussion and approval into an act, a rather strict cross-party discipline prevents the jeopardizing of the text of the bill, so precariously drawn up during the drafting, by allowing the insertion at the last stage (or outside the drafting phase) of "interest paragraphs" in the proposal to be voted into law.[33]

---

[27]See Strömholm (1988), p. 36; and Wahlgren (2014), pp. 47–48. See, e.g., Sterzel (2015), p. 79.

[28]Nightingale (2016), p. 1686 (2016). See also Sinclair (1998), pp. 176–178; Krutz (2001a), pp. 3–4; and Odishaw (1988), p. 228 ("Omnibus legislation, termed by some a 'Christmas tree,' often passes at the end of a congressional session").

[29]See Petersson (2015b), p. 660 ("A frequent gesture used in political discourse by politicians from the government as well as the opposition is to stretch out a hand as invitation to the opponent to negotiate a broad agreement on a specific issue"); *OECD (2007), p.* 35; and *OECD* (2010), p. 109.

[30]See Petersson (2015b), p. 654. See also Anton (1969), pp. 88–102. But see Svensson et al. (2012), pp. 64–85 (questioning the very idea of the Swedish welfare state as based on a consensus around common values). Cf. Petersson (2015b), p. 658.

[31]See Bäck and Bergman (2015), pp. 210–211.

[32]See Mattson (2015), p. 680 (though, as pointed out by the author, "[t]he committees are still grounds for working out compromises between the main political parties, but less so now than before," 688). See also Sannerstedt (1996), pp. 17–58.

[33]See Jensen (2000), pp. 210–236; and Mattson (2015), p. 679 ("Party discipline in voting is very strong which means that it is the parties and party leaderships that control the Members of Parliament"). See also Möller (2020), chapter 4. As pointed out by Christopher J. Kam, the Swedish legislative system is characterized by a rather strong autonomy of the members of the parliament

As a third factor contributing to a climate hostile to the idea of having omnibus legislation, one should mention the specific institutional position of legislative drafters in the Swedish lawmaking process. Unlike in other countries, the legislative drafters in Sweden tend not to be connected to the political parties; instead, they are public servants, either as legal counsel in a Department (often the Department of Justice, though several exceptions exist, *e.g.,* when dealing with tax issues) or as a former or current judge with previous working experience in the public administration.[34] In the few cases they do not belong to the public apparatus, they are law professors. As is usually the case, the work of the Swedish legislative drafters is caught between the world of politics and the world of law; however, their institutional positioning within the public administration (or the academia) has meant that the drafters are considered (and consider themselves) to be professional (and rather independent) legal bureaucrats (or legal scholars), rather than connected to any specific political party.[35] For instance, while it is very common to change the political experts within each department when a new government comes into place, legal experts (and *in primis* legislative drafters) tend to remain over the years and follow a career within the department, independent of the change in the political climate.

As an effect of their institutional positioning (and their traditional legal education), legislative drafters tend to be more loyal to the dogmas of the legal discourse than the ones of the political world.[36] In drafting a bill, this loyalty means that the legislative drafters have a legal systematic approach to the topics to be regulated rather than a political one. In its turn, this embracing of the "legal systematic loyalty" means that the legislative drafters have the procedural criterion of constructing a bill with a legally coordinated content (both internally, between the bill's different parts,

---

when sitting in the drafting committees; however, at the same time, political parties maintain a strong hold on their fellows as soon as the work moves into the general assembly. See Kam (2009), p. 210.

[34]See Petersson (2015b), p. 658 ("Today around 75 percent of the commissions consists of one single person and in most cases a judge or a senior civil servant"). See also Axberger (1995), pp. 140–142 (where the author strongly criticizes this overlapping of role within the legislative law-making, in particular when the judges are involved as drafters).

[35]As pointed out previously, the drafter is usually picked from within the public apparatus (either from the public administration *stricto sensu* or among the judges with previous experience in the public administration). In Sweden, public servants are trained in an environment which tends to be strongly independent of the Government, from both an institutional perspective and a legal perspective. See Reichel (2007), pp. 104–105 (as to the Swedish dualist model, where there is a division in both organization and accountability between the government and the administration). See, e.g., Rosén (2011), pp. 796–798. See also Jones (1990), p. 153. But see Modéer (2011), pp. 745–747 and Öberg (2011), p. 770 (where both authors point out a recent shift towards a more political nature of the work made by the drafting committee).

[36]See Håstad (2011), pp. 775–776. See, e.g., Rosén (2011), pp. 798–799. See also Wahlgren (2014), pp. 46–47; and Matz (2011), p. 726 (pointing out how, from a legal perspective, "social issues receive an objective and comprehensive treatment within the framework of the committee system").

and externally, between the bill and the legal system at large).[37] The political systematic nature of the bill instead becomes a secondary (even non-existent) guiding light in their work: the legislative drafters are insensible to the fact that with omnibus legislation the bill may have a variegated and unrelated content, but serves to fulfill a political goal, namely the satisfaction of as many, and therefore equally variegated, potential voters as possible.

To conclude this section, one can easily see how these forces preventing the deep omnibus legislation from entering into the Swedish legislative discourse, all tend (directly or indirectly) towards a specific nature. They are all constitutive elements of the legal institutional environment in which the Swedish legislative process occurs: the preparatory works being a highly legitimized source of law (the *what*), the consensus-based *modus operandi* within the legislative process (the *how*), and the positioning of legislative drafters within the system as public officials (the *who*).[38] In other words, the general (and therefore mostly crude) assumption that legislation operates simply as a rather passive extension of the political will, may not always be true. The Swedish example instead highlights how the legal discourse, its culture, and its institutions (in particular the legislative ones) can have a say not only in shaping the form of the law, but also in determining the content of the legislation (*e.g.,* as in the case of Sweden, in a non-omnibus direction).

---

[37] See Hellner (1990), p. 138 and pp. 194–198. See, e.g., Heckscher (2011), p. 845. As pointed out by Kaarlo Tuori, "efforts in this direction [of politicizing the legislative drafting] constitute a constant source of disappointment for politicians and bureaucrats, who often enough see their political goals sacrificed on the altar of the internal rationality of the law." Tuori (2002), p. 138.

[38] Among the institutional forces pushing the Swedish law-maker away from the omnibus legislation model, in theory one could also count the presence of the Council on Legislation (in Swedish, *Lagrådet*). This Council is a body composed of judges, who have previously served on one of the Supreme Courts, with the specific duty of evaluating bills sent to them by the competent departments and concerning central areas of law. According to Chapter 8, Article 22, section 2, of the *Instrument of Government*, among the other duties the Council has the one of controlling "the manner in which the various provisions of the draft law relate to one another." See Hellner (1990), p. 137. However, the presence of such a legal institutional force should not be overestimated, at least when it comes to its capacity to block bills with an omnibus shape. First, the opinion expressed by this high evaluative body is a mere recommendation to the legislator, with no binding formal and (as praxis has shown) practical character. *See* Nergelius (2019), p. 336. See, e.g., Borg (2006), pp. 5–9. Second, since the qualitative evaluation by the Council on Legislation is taking place exclusively on the bill, this intermediary step could not stop hypothetical omnibus features to be attached to it later on, i.e. when the bill is transformed into an act after a discussion in front (and by decision) of the Parliament.

4 The Significance

The importance of the legal discourse in shaping the political discourse is certainly not new.[39] However, the Swedish case of omnibus legislation shows the relevant role that the legislative drafters may play in affecting how the political will can be transformed (or not, as in this case) into law. In order to be carried via the legislative process into society, the values expressed in the political arena need to go through a more or less radical process of transformation into legal categories and concepts.[40] The necessity of this step is particularly evident in general contemporary Western culture, in which the ideology of legality dominates and heavily affects the lawmaking process. As an Italian political scientist stated:

> [T]he modern state's specific form of legitimacy is its appeal that its commands be recognized as binding because *legal*, that is because issued in conformity with properly enacted, general rules.[41]

The process of transformation is usually carried out by specific actors devoted thereto (*e.g.*, the legislative drafters). These actors are usually persons formally educated in legal matters, an education that is based on a specific way of thinking (legal rationality) and which (to a greater or lesser extent) gives birth to a specific legal arena.[42] This can be defined as the ideal place in which the political goal of having values implemented into society (with value-based reasoning) is taken over by the goal of transforming (with a legal rationality-based reasoning) the values into legal categories and concepts, inserting them into the existing legal order.[43] Hypothetically, if the political actors (*e.g.*, members of a legislature) would themselves do the work of transforming their values into a draft for a bill, they would still be forced to make use of legal language and, moreover, to take into consideration the structure of the legal system (at least at a constitutional level) into which their proposal for a statute is going to be inserted.

This central role played by the legislative drafters may be ascribed to a broader tendency of increasing *legalization* of legislative processes, *i.e.,* processes aimed at

---

[39]See, e.g., Weber (1991), p. 95; Bourdieu (1987), p. 830; or Tuori (2002), p. 162.

[40]See Teubner (1989), p. 745 (1989); Cotterrell (1995), pp. 240–248; MacCormick (2008), pp. 11–12; and Zamboni (2007), pp. 130–131. See, e.g. Friedman (1986), pp. 27–28. "Radicalism" is the degree of change into legal language that the value expressed inside the political arena, i.e., in a political language, has to go through in order to be accepted into the legal order. This depends, among other things, on the national legal order under consideration, on the branch of law, and also on the dominant legal culture among the different legal actors. See Summers (2000b), p. 50; and Teubner (1996), p. 165. See also Luhmann (2004), pp. 366–367.

[41]Poggi (1989), p. 132. See also Weber (1978), p. 34.

[42]See Abbot (1988), pp. 52–57; and Cotterrell (1995), pp. 108–110. See, e.g., Xanthaki (2014), pp. 354–365; or Uhlmann and Höfler (2016).

[43]See McLeod (2009), p. 1 ("In the simplest of terms, the drafter's task is to convert policies into provisions which comply with the relevant formal conventions and are capable of being applied effectively in practice"); Xanthaki (2013), p. 142; and Tuori (2002), p. 161.

transforming values into law in the shape of statutory provisions.[44] The legalization of legislative processes denotes the phenomenon that the process of transformation of values into law, and its results, can better be understood by taking into account the perspective that legislative drafters have as to the issue of transforming values into a category or concept which is directly relevant for the legal order.[45] The reasons for such a transference of many aspects of the legislative process inside the legal arena (and its logics) or, in other words, for the growing importance of the views of legislative drafters as to how and why politics are transformed into law, are mainly two in Sweden (though they may be valid for other Western legal systems as well).

The first is that Sweden, like practically all Western legal and political orders, has adopted the rule of law (or, in Europe, the *Rechtsstaat*) as one of the models according to which the regulations of the relations between public authorities (and the legislators, such as the parliament *in primis*) and the private individual are sculpted. The rule of law and the *Rechtsstaat* provide a model focusing attention on the respect that public authorities must accord the law (and, in the case of the rule of law, certain basic rights), and therefore shift the lawmaking process towards the law and the legal system.[46] The values espoused by the political actors have to fit into the latter and, therefore, both the legal forms (legal categories and concepts) taken by the values and the views of that transformation that the legal actors (in particular legislative drafters) have, become of primary importance.[47] Actually, one of the functions that the rule of law plays in the Western legal systems is to allow the law (and in the Swedish case, the legislative drafters) to occupy some spaces which were previously the monopoly of politics.[48]

The other factor that encourages a shifting of the legislative process deeper into the legal arena and its logics is connected to the specific features that the legal phenomenon has acquired in contemporary legal history in Sweden (as in other Western legal systems). One of the constitutive elements of the lawmaking process is the fact that, in the end, such a process must externalize itself in the form of specific

---

[44]See Abbott et al. (2000), pp. 401–402 (2000) (as to the main components upon which the legalization of an institution, as the legislative law-making institutions in this case, may be measured). See Loughlin (2000), pp. 229–233 (as being this process a part of a more contemporary phenomenon of legalization of politics).

[45]See Habermas (1998), p. 151; and van Hoecke (2002), p. 133. See also Kennedy (1998), p. 219; Zamboni (2007), pp. 156–157; Balbus (1977), p. 582; and Cotterrell (1995), pp. 151–152. See, e.g., Zander (2004), pp. 2–3; or Lund (1993), p. 452.

[46]See Loughlin (2000), pp. 184–185.

[47]See Cormacain (2017), chapter 5; and Bellamy (2003), pp. 127–129 (as to the central role the law-making process plays in the very idea of rule of law). See also Summers (2000a), pp. 167–168; Habermas (1998), pp. 134–135; Luhmann (2004), pp. 362–363; Raz (1994), pp. 359–361; and Waldron (2000), p. 1845.

[48]See Kramer (2004), pp. 172–222; and Tamanaha (2012), pp. 236–246. See also Kelsen (1955), p. 77; Dworkin (1985), pp. 11–13; and Llewellyn (1971), pp. 130–135. But see Kairys (1998), p. 6. Cf. Taylor Hamara (2013), p. 22 (as to the difficulty in defining a political ideal, such as "the rule of law" is, where it is presupposed to have a clear idea of its essential legal component, i.e. what "law" is).

linguistic utterances, with an authoritative nature and a performative function, expressed (often in a written form) by specific actors or groups of actors (*e.g.,* the legislature).

In recent decades, it is possible to see in Sweden (as in other Western legal systems) an increasing *professionalization* of both such externalizing actors and their linguistic utterances.[49] Professionalization means that a specific training (*e.g.,* a law degree) and a specific legitimation (usually of a legal nature itself, *e.g.,* a selection according to specific legal procedures) is required of individuals in order to become institutional actors (*e.g.,* legislative drafters) in the lawmaking process. Moreover, the linguistic utterances mentioned are (or should be) translations made by qualified translators (namely legislative drafters) from the political will into a particular kind of language, the legal language.[50]

Therefore, the function played by the 'interpreters of the political will' or, in other words, by the actors having the job of transforming the values expressed in the political arena into a specific language, becomes crucial for the entire lawmaking process.[51] Even when in conflict with the values expressed on the political arena, it is usually the final product (*i.e.,* the statute) of the work of such interpreters (*i.e.,* legislative drafters) that, in the end, becomes the law in force that actually binds and shapes the behavior of the members of society.[52]

To sum up, in Sweden (and in many Western legal systems) two major factors contribute to the legalization of legislative lawmaking and therefore the marginalization of forms of legislation which, like omnibus legislation, tend to disrupt the legal logics in favor of the political ones. Firstly, the diffusion of the rule of law (or the *Rechtsstaat*) obliges the political arena to transform its values into, and according to, the categories and concepts provided by the legal order, and, in this case, by the legislative drafters. Secondly, this transformation, which requires professional skills and language, usually occurs 'under the guardianship' of the legal actors. Because of these concurring (and often interrelated) factors, the processes and the results constituting legislative lawmaking tend not only to be removed

---

[49]See Wahlgren (2014), pp. 139–146. See, e.g., Schultz (2012), pp. 211–214. See also Cotterrell (1992), pp. 180–204; and Sutton (2001), p. 223 (as to a possible connection between the professionalization of the legal arena and the establishment of the rule of law).

[50]See Daintith and Page (1999), p. 254 (where the legislator's main task consists in "translating the government's intentions into legislative form"). See also Bourdieu (1987), pp. 834–839; and Summers (1997), p. 1204.

[51]See Laws (2008), p. 20 (where the author points out how legislative drafters "are not just wordsmiths; they are also counsel, who advise the instructing department on a whole range of matters"); and Cormacain (2017), pp. 25–26. See also Howarth (2013), p. 41.

[52]See Nzerem (2008), p. 132 ("In practice... a drafter often participates in defining the meaning of policy and in translating the broad terms of policy into the law's details. Between policy and legislation, there are open spaces which the drafter may have to fill."); Laws (2013), pp. 89–93; and Seidman et al. (2001), p. 6 and pp. 23–24. See, e.g., Laws (2011), pp. 1–16 (as to the central role in the legal system of the work of legislative drafters, in particular when misinterpreting the policies laid down by the political actors). But see Stefanou (2008), pp. 321–333 (with a more critical voice as to the actual influence of the drafting moment in a legislative process upon the policy-making).

from the monopoly of the political arena (and the idea that "legislation is simply politics in legal jargon"). They also become incorporated into the activities occurring inside the legal arena (and the idea that, at least partially, "legislation is politics as legislative drafters perceive it").

5 Conclusions

To conclude where I started, the lack of omnibus legislation in the Swedish law-making should not be treated, in the way I initially did, as a shocking phenomenon. On the contrary, at least in the Swedish case, it is a sign of the central position that legislative drafters play in the legislative process. In particular, the absence of a deep type of omnibus legislation indicates that the legislative process has moved in the right direction: it signals a true rule of law state (where not even the elected politicians are above the law and its logics) and, at the same time, it allots the job of creating law to actors (like legislative drafters) who are professional trained for it and, therefore, tend to obey to the rules of the law rather than those of politics. As pointed out by Roger Cotterrell,

> [Legal actors] are of vital importance in producing in contemporary Western societies the ideological effects of law ... they tend to promote through highly developed techniques of legal argument and doctrinal reasoning the idea of law as a rational integrated system of knowledge.[53]

It is for this very reason that deep omnibus legislation is avoided at all cost in Sweden: while it creates a rational system for political discourse, it violates the basic ideas of a rational integrated legal system. At the end of the day, law in its legislative form may be a political product (and therefore should try to express the political will as best as it can), but it gains legitimacy in a rule of law system when expressed in accordance with the rules of the legislative grammar. These rules cannot easily accept a bill or statute that looks like Frankenstein's monster—or that takes the shape of deep omnibus legislation, as defined in this work.

References

Abbot A (1988) The system of professions: an essay on the division of expert labor. University of Chicago Press, Chicago

Abbott KW, Keohane RO, Moravcsik A, Slaughter A-M, Snidal D (2000) The concept of legalization. Int Organ 54:401–419

Alexandersson P (2018) Socialtjänstens värdegrunder: Etik i förarbeten och lagar om fattigvård, socialvård och socialtjänst. http://esh.diva-portal.org/smash/get/diva2:1259728/FULLTEXT02.pdf. Accessed 10 Apr 2020

---

[53]Cotterrell (1992), pp. 203–204.

Algotsson K-G (2001) From majoritarian democracy to vertical separation of powers: Sweden and the European Union. Scand Polit Stud 24:51–65

Anton TJ (1969) Policy-making and political culture in Sweden. Scand Polit Stud 4:88–102

Aubert V (1986) The rule of law and the promotional function of law. In: Teubner G (ed) Dilemmas of law in the welfare state. de Gruyter, Berlin, pp 28–39

Axberger H-G (1995) Tänka fritt är större. Juristförlaget, Uppsala

Bäck H, Bergman T (2015) The parties in government formation. In: Pierre J (ed) The Oxford handbook of Swedish politics. Oxford University Press, Oxford, pp 210–211

Balbus ID (1977) Commodity form and legal form: an essay on the "relative autonomy" of the law. Law Soc Rev 11:571–588

Bellamy R (2003) The rule of law. In: Bellamy R, Mason A (eds) Political concepts. Manchester University Press, Manchester, pp 118–130

Bergh A (2004) The universal welfare state: theory and the case of Sweden. Polit Stud 54:745–766

Bjerstedt D (2009) Tryggheten inför rättan. Lund University, Lund

Borg H (2006) Lagrådet -Rättssäkerhetsgaranti eller ren formalitet? https://timbro.se/app/uploads/2017/01/9175666235.pdf. Accessed 10 Apr 2020

Bourdieu P (1987) The force of law: toward a sociology of the juridical field. Hastings Law J 38:814–853

Cormacain R (2017) Legislative drafting and the rule of law. https://sas-space.sas.ac.uk/6693/1/Cormacain%2C%20R%20-%20IALS%20-%202018.pdf. Accessed 10 Apr 2020

Cotterrell R (1992) The sociology of law: an introduction, 2nd edn. Butterworths, London

Cotterrell R (1995) Law's community: legal theory in sociological perspective. Clarendon Press, Oxford

Daintith T, Page A (1999) The executive in the constitution: structure, autonomy and internal control. Oxford University Press, Oxford

Dean HV (1997) The juridification of welfare: strategies of discipline and resistance. In: Kjonstad A, Wilson J (eds) Law, power and poverty. CROP Publications, Bergen, pp 3–27

Denning BP, Smith BR (1999) Uneasy riders: the case for a truth-in-legislation amendment. Utah Law Rev 1999:957–1025

deZafra DE (1978) A management model for the implementation of omnibus legislation: a case study from the U. S. Public Health Service. Public Adm Rev 38:276–280

Dworkin R (1985) A matter of principle. Harvard University Press, Cambridge

Esping-Andersen G (1990) The three worlds of welfare capitalism. Princeton University Press, Princeton

Fast Lappalainen K (2019) Om skyddet mot retroaktiv beskattning -En studie i konstitutionell rätt. Stockholms universitet, Stockholm

Ferejohn J (1986) Logrolling in an institutional context: a case study of food stamp legislation. In: Wright GC Jr, Rieselbach LN, Dodd LC (eds) Congress and policy change. Agathon Press, New York, pp 223–253

Forslund A (1997) The Swedish model: past, present, and future. In: Giersch H (ed) Reforming the welfare state. Springer-Verlag, Berlin, pp 121–162

Frantzich SE, Berube C (2010) Congress: games and strategies, 4th edn. Rowman & Littlefield Publishers, Plymouth

Friedman L (1986) The limits of law: a critique and a proposal. Center for Studies on Changing Norms and Mobility, Siegen

Galnoor I (2011) Public management in Israel: development, structure, functions and reforms. Routledge, London

Garrett E (2002) Attention to context in statutory interpretation: applying the lessons of dynamic statutory interpretation to omnibus legislation. Issues Leg Sch 3:6–12

Gluck AR (2015) Imperfect statutes, imperfect courts: understanding Congress's plan in the era of unorthodox lawmaking. Harv Law Rev 129:62–111

Gluck AR, O'Connell AJ, Po R (2015) Unorthodox lawmaking, unorthodox rulemaking. Columbia Law Rev 115:1789–1866

Habermas J (1998) Between facts and norms: contributions to a discourse theory of law and democracy. The MIT Press, Cambridge

Håstad T (2011) Vad har vi rätt att vänta oss av kommittéväsendet? Svensk Juristtidning 2011:772–776

Heckscher S (2011) Reflektioner kring utredningsväsendet. Svensk Juristtidning 2011:844–847

Hellner J (1990) Lagstiftning inom förmögenhetsrätten -Praktik, teori, teknik. Juristförlaget, Stockholm

House of Commons [Dominion of Canada] (1988) Debates, 30 May 1988. Library of Parliament, Ottawa

House of Commons [Dominion of Canada] (2011) Glossary of parliamentary procedure, 7th edn. Canadian Government Publishing, Ottawa

House of Commons [Dominion of Canada] (2012) Debates, 11 June 2012. Library of Parliament, Ottawa

Howarth D (2013) Law as engineering: thinking about what lawyers do. Edward Elgar, Cheltenham

Jensen TK (2000) Party cohesion. In: Esaiasson P, Heider K (eds) Beyond Westminster and Congress: the Nordic experience. Ohio State University Press, Columbus, pp 210–236

Jones BM (1990) Sweden. In: Kingdom J (ed) The civil service in liberal democracies: an introductory survey. Routledge, Oxon, pp 143–162

Kairys D (1998) Introduction. In: Kairys D (ed) The politics of law: a progressive critique, 3rd edn. Basic Books, New York, pp 1–20

Kam CJ (2009) Party discipline and parliamentary politics. Cambridge University Press, Cambridge

Kardasheva R (2009) Legislative package deals in EU decision-making: 1999–2007. http://etheses. lse.ac.uk/33/1/Kardasheva_Package_Deals_In_EU_Decision_Making.pdf. Accessed 10 Apr 2020

Kelsen H (1955) Foundations of democracy. Ethics LXVI:1–101

Kennedy D (1998) A critique of adjudication (fin de siècle). Harvard University Press, Cambridge

Kramer MH (2004) Where law and morality meet. Oxford University Press, Oxford

Krutz GS (2001a) Hitching a ride: omnibus legislating in the U.S. Congress. Ohio State University Press, Columbus

Krutz GS (2001b) Tactical maneuvering on omnibus bills in Congress. Am J Polit Sci 45:210–223

Krutz GS (2002) Omnibus legislation: an institutional reaction to the rise of new issues. In: Baumgartner FR, Jones BD (eds) Policy dynamics. University of Chicago Press, Chicago, pp 205–229

Laws S (2008) Drawing the line. In: Stefanou C, Xanthaki H (eds) Drafting legislation: a modern approach. Ashgate, Aldershot, pp 19–34

Laws S (2011) Giving effect to policy in legislation: how to avoid missing the point. Statute Law Rev 32:1–16

Laws S (2013) Legislation and politics. In: Feldman D (ed) Law in politics, politics in law. Hart Publishing, Oxford, pp 87–104

Leviner P (2011) Rättsliga dilemman i socialtjänstens barnskyddsarbete. Jure Förlag, Stockholm

Lind J (1993) Förarbeten som rättskälla. In: Anders A (ed) Festskrift till Bertil Bengtsson. Nerenius & Santérus, Stockholm, pp 301–318

Lind J (1996) Högsta domstolen och frågan om doktrin och motiv som rättskälla. Juridisk Tidsskrift 2:352–370

Llewellyn K (1971) Jurisprudence: realism in theory and practice. University of Chicago Press, Chicago

Loughlin M (2000) Sword & scales: an examination of the relationship between law & politics. Hart Publishing, Oxford

Luhmann N (2004) Law as a social system. Oxford University Press, Oxford

Lund N (1993) Rational choice at the office of legal counsel. Cardozo Law Rev 15:437–505

MacCormick N (2008) Questioning sovereignty. Oxford University Press, Oxford

Mattson I (2015) Parliamentary committees: a ground for compromise and conflict. In: Pierre J (ed) The Oxford handbook of Swedish politics. Oxford University Press, Oxford, pp 679–690

Matz H (2011) Kommittéväsendet förr, nu och i framtiden. Svensk Juristtidning 2011:725–734

McKay W, Johnson CW (2010) Parliament and Congress: representation and scrutiny in the twenty-first century. Oxford University Press, Oxford

McLeod I (2009) Principles of legislative and regulatory drafting. Hart Publishing, Oxford

Miller N (2009) Environmental politics: stakeholders, interests, and policymaking, 2nd edn. Routledge, Oxon

Modéer KÅ (2011) Jurister på politikernas arenor. Svensk Juristtidning 2011:735–752

Möller T (2020) Political party dynamics and democracy in Sweden: developments since the 'Golden Age'. Routledge, Oxon

Nergelius J (1996) Konstitutionellt rättighetsskydd: svensk rätt i ett komparativt perspektiv. Fritze, Stockholm

Nergelius J (1997) Domstolarna, grundlagen och rättighetsskyddet –några reflektioner kring de senaste årens debatt och praxis. Svensk Juristtidning 1997:426–457

Nergelius J (2015) Constitutional law in Sweden, 2nd edn. Kluwer Law International, Alphen aan den Rhijn

Nergelius J (2019) The constitution of Sweden and European influences: the changing balance between democratic and judicial power. In: Albi A, Bardutzky S (eds) National constitutions in European and global governance: democracy, rights, the rule of law. T.M.C. Asser Press, The Hague, pp 315–358

Nightingale RL (2016) How to trim a Christmas tree: beyond severability and inseverability for omnibus statutes. Yale Law J 125:1672–1743

Norrman E, McLure CE Jr (1997) Tax policy in Sweden. In: Freeman RB, Topel RH, Swedenborg B (eds) The welfare state in transition: reforming the Swedish model. The University of Chicago Press, Chicago, pp 109–154

Nyman O (1988) Some basic features of Swedish constitutional law. In: Strömholm S (ed) An introduction to Swedish law, 2nd edn. Norstedts, Stockholm, pp 47–77

Nzerem RC (2008) The role of the legislative drafter in promoting social transformation. In: Stefanou C, Xanthaki H (eds) Drafting legislation: a modern approach. Ashgate, Aldershot, pp 131–150

Öberg SA (2011) Kunskap och politik -mellan nonchalans och teknokrati. Svensk Juristtidning 2011:764–771

Odishaw CP (1988) Curbing legislative chaos: executive choice or congressional responsibility. Iowa Law Rev 74:227–248

OECD (2007) OECD reviews of regulatory reform: Sweden 2007 -achieving results for sustained growth. OECD Publishing, Paris

OECD (2010) Better regulation in Europe: Sweden 2010. OECD Publishing, Paris

Peczenik A (1995) Vad är rätt? Om demokrati, rättssäkerhet, etik och juridisk argumentation. Norstedts Juridik, Stockholm

Peczenik A (1999) Lagstiftningen, domstolarna, rättsmedvetandet och rättsvetenskapen. In: Nergelius J, Peczenik A, Wiklund O (eds) Löser juridiken demokratins problem? -SOU 1999:58. https://www.regeringen.se/49bb77/contentassets/175b3882a0bd4ff28c67a509baa4e675/loser-juridiken-demokratins-problem. Accessed 10 Apr 2020, pp 7–54

Petersson O (2015a) Constitutional history. In: Pierre J (ed) The Oxford handbook of Swedish politics. Oxford University Press, Oxford, pp 89–102

Petersson O (2015b) Rational politics: commissions of inquiry and the referral system in Sweden. In: Pierre J (ed) The Oxford handbook of Swedish politics. Oxford University Press, Oxford, pp 650–662

Pierson C, Leimgruber M (2010) Intellectual roots. In: Castles FG, Leibfried S, Lewis J, Obinger H, Pierson C (eds) The Oxford handbook of the welfare state. Oxford University Press, Oxford, pp 32–44

Poggi G (1989) The development of modern state: a sociological introduction. Stanford University Press, Stanford

Popelier P, Verlinden V (2009) The context of the rise of ex ante evaluation. In: Verschuuren J (ed) The impact of legislation -a critical analysis of ex ante evaluation. Martinus Nijhoff Publishers, Leiden, pp 13–37

Raz J (1994) The politics of the rule of law. In: Raz J (ed) Ethics in the public domain: essays in the morality of law and politics. Clarendon Press, Oxford, pp 354–362

Reichel J (2007) Svenska myndigheter som EU-myndigheter. In: Källström K, Öberg J (eds) Juridisk Tidskrift -Jubileumshäfte. Jure, Stockholm, pp 103–112

Reichel J (2011) European legal method from a Swedish perspective -rights, compensation and the role of the courts. In: Nielsen R, Neergaard UB, Roseberry L (eds) European legal method: paradoxes and revitalisation. DJØF Publishing, Copenhagen, pp 245–278

Rosén J (2011) Arbetet i utredning -finns det framgångsrecept? Svensk Juristtidning 2011:793–800

Ruud MH (1958) No law shall embrace more than one subject. Minn Law Rev 42:389–455

Sannerstedt A (1996) Negotiations in the Riksdag. In: Stenelo L-G, Jerneck M (eds) The bargaining democracy. Lund University Press, Lund, pp 17–58

Schick A (1987) The whole and the parts: piecemeal and integrated approaches to congressional budgeting. U.S. Government Printing Office, Washington

Schultz M (2012) The impact of institutions and professions in Sweden. In: Mitchell P (ed) The impact of institutions and professions on legal development. Cambridge University Press, Cambridge, pp 198–230

Schwartz PM (2013) The EU-U.S. privacy collision: a turn to institutions and procedures. Harv Law Rev 126:1966–2009

Seidman A, Seidman RB, Abeyesekere N (2001) Legislative drafting for democratic social change: a manual for drafters. Kluwer Law International, The Hague

Sinclair B (1998) Legislators, leaders, and lawmaking: the U.S. house of representatives in the postreform era. Johns Hopkins University Press, Baltimore

Sinclair B (2000) Unorthodox lawmaking: new legislative processes in the U.S. Congress, 2nd edn. Congressional Quarterly Press, Washington

Socialtjänstlag (2001:453) [Kingdom of Sweden] (2001) https://www.riksdagen.se/sv/dokument-lagar/dokument/svensk-forfattningssamling/socialtjanstlag-2001453_sfs-2001-453. Accessed 10 Apr 2020

Stefanou C (2008) Drafters, drafting and the policy process. In: Stefanou C, Xanthaki H (eds) Drafting legislation: a modern approach. Ashgate, Aldershot, pp 321–333

Sterzel F (2015) Sverige. In: Jonsson Cornell A (ed) Komparativ konstitutionell rätt, 2nd edn. Iustus, Uppsala, pp 71–92

Strömberg H, Lundell B (2014) Allmän förvaltningsrätt, 26th edn. Liber, Malmö

Strömholm S (1988) Introduction. In: Strömholm S (ed) An introduction to Swedish law, 2nd edn. Norstedts, Stockholm, pp 21–45

Strömholm S (1996) Rätt, rättskällor och rättstillämpning: en lärobok i allmän rättslära, 5th edn. Norstedts juridik, Stockholm

Summers R (1997) How law is formal and why it matters. Cornell Law Rev 82:1165–1229

Summers R (2000a) A formal theory of the rule of law. In: Summers R (ed) Essays in legal theory. Kluwer Academic Publishers, Dordrecht, pp 165–182

Summers R (2000b) Law as a type of "machine" technology. In: Summers R (ed) Essays in legal theory. Kluwer Academic Publishers, Dordrecht, pp 43–54

Sundberg JWF (1978) Fr. Eddan t. Ekelöf: Repetitorium om rättskällor i Norden. Studentlitteratur, Malmö

Sundberg JWF (2000) High-tax imperialism, 2nd edn. Institutet för offentlig och internationell rätt, Stockholm

Sutton J (2001) Law/society: origins, interactions, and change. Pine Forge Press, Thousand Oaks

Svensson M, Urinboyev R, Åström K (2012) Welfare as a means for political stability: a law and society analysis. Eur J Soc Secur 12:64–85

Tala J (2005) Förarbeten och lagstiftningspolitik. In: Palmgren S (ed) Lagstiftningspolitik -Nordiskt Seminarium om Lagstiftningspolitik. Nordic Council of Ministers' Publishing House, Copenhagen, pp 99–116

Tamanaha BZ (2012) The history and elements of the rule of law. Singapore J Leg Stud 2012:233–247

Taylor Hamara C (2013) The concept of the rule of law. In: Flores IB, Himma KE (eds) Law, liberty, and the rule of law. Springer Science+Business Media, Dordrecht, pp 11–26

Teubner G (1989) How the law thinks: toward a constructivist epistemology of law. Law Soc Rev 23:727–757

Teubner G (1996) Altera Pars Audiatur: law in the collision of discourses. In: Rawlings R (ed) Law, society and economy: centenary essays for the London School of Economics and Political Science 1895–1995. Clarendon Press, Oxford, pp 149–176

The Instrument of Government [Kingdom of Sweden] (1974). http://www.riksdagen.se/globalassets/07.-dokument%2D%2Dlagar/the-constitution-of-sweden-160628.pdf. Accessed 10 Apr 2020

Tuori K (2002) Critical legal positivism. Ashgate, Aldershot

Uhlmann F, Höfler S (eds) (2016) Professional legislative drafters: status, roles, education. DIKE, St. Gallen

van Beek SD (1995) Post-passage politics: bicameral resolution in Congress. University of Pittsburgh, Pittsburgh

van Hoecke M (2002) Law as communication. Hart Publishing, Oxford

von Sydow H (2007) Rättsstatens rötter -reformer av domarutnämningar. http://lup.lub.lu.se/luur/download?func=downloadFile&recordOId=1562821&fileOId=1566085. Accessed 10 Apr 2020

Wahlgren P (2014) Lagstiftning -Rationalitet, Teknik, Möjligheter, 2nd edn. Jure, Stockholm

Waldron J (2000) Lex Satis Iusta. Notre Dame Law Rev 75:1829–1858

Weber M (1978) Economy and society: an outline of interpretive sociology. University of California Press, Berkeley

Weber M (1991) Politics as a vocation. In: Gert HH, Wright Mills C (eds) From Max Weber: essays in sociology. Oxford University Press, Oxford, pp 129–156

Wind M, Martinsen DS, Rotger GP (2009) The uneven legal push for Europe: questioning variation when national courts go to Europe. Eur Union Polit 10:63–88

Withdrawal of the United Kingdom from the European Union (Consequential Provisions) Bill [Republic of Ireland] (2019). https://merrionstreet.ie/en/News-Room/News/Brexit_Omnibus_Bill.pdf. Accessed 10 Apr 2020

Xanthaki H (2013) Thornton's legislative drafting, 5th edn. Bloomsbury Professional, West Sussex

Xanthaki H (2014) Drafting legislation: art and technology of rules for regulation. Hart Publishing, Oxford

Zamboni M (2007) The policy of law: a legal theoretical framework. Hart Publishing, Oxford

Zamboni M (2019) Methods of ex-ante evaluation in legislation: the Swedish model. In: Kim K-H (ed) Goals and methods of ex-ante evaluation of legislation. Korea Legislation Research Institute, Seoul, pp 3–31

Zander M (2004) The law-making process, 6th edn. Cambridge University Press, Cambridge

9 783030 727505